The
Northumbrian
Renaissance

The Northumbrian Renaissance

A Study in the Transmission of Style

Carol L. Neuman de Vegvar

Selinsgrove: Susquehanna University Press
London and Toronto: Associated University Presses

Associated University Presses
440 Forsgate Drive
Cranbury, NJ 08512

Associated University Presses
25 Sicilian Avenue
London WC1A 2QH, England

Associated University Presses
2133 Royal Windsor Drive
Unit 1
Mississauga, Ontario
Canada L5J 1K5

The paper used in this publication meets the
requirements of the American National Standard for
Permanence of Paper for Printed Materials Z39.48-1984.

*All photographs and plans are used by the permission of the holders of
copyright. Photographs without citation of permission are the work of the
author.*

Library of Congress Cataloging-in-Publication Data

Neuman de Vegvar, Carol L. 1953–
 The Northumbrian Renaissance.

 Revision of thesis (Ph.D.)—University of
Pennsylvania, 1981.
 Bibliography: p.
 Includes index.
 1. Art, Anglo-Saxon—Northumbria (Kingdom)—Themes,
motives. I. Title.
N6795.N67N48 1986   720'.9428'8   85-40507
ISBN 0-941664-11-2 (alk. paper)

Printed in the United States of America

In Memoriam

Geza E. Neuman de Vegvar

Habe nun, ach! Philosophie
Juristerei und Medizin
Und leider auch Theologie
Durchaus studiert, mit heissem Bemuhn.
Da steh' ich nun, ich armer Tor!
Und bin so klug als wie zuvor.

Goethe, *Faust*

Contents

Illustrations

Figures

Plates

Acknowledgments

THIS BOOK is a revised and updated version of my doctoral dissertation, *The Northumbrian Golden Age: The Parameters of a Renaissance,* completed in 1981 for the Department of Art History at the University of Pennsylvania.

I wish to express my gratitude to all those without whose assistance, advice, and encouragement I would never have been able to bring this work to completion.

The greatest debts of thanks are owed to David N. Wiley, Director of Susquehanna University Press, and to my adviser, Charles Minott of the Department of the History of Art at the University of Pennsylvania. Dr. Wiley gave me the opportunity to publish this work as a unit and to avoid fragmenting it into a scattered and less cohesive series of articles. He also gave me very necessary encouragement to undertake the necessary revisions, and he had the patience to answer the inquiries of a novice author. Professor Minott's encouragement was among the most essential sustaining forces of the research for the original dissertation, and his advice has continued to refine and focus my perception of the issues. I would also like to express my gratitude to the members of my dissertation committee: C. L. Striker of the Department of Art History at the University of Pennsylvania; David Robb, professor emeritus in the same department; Bernard Wailes of the Department of Anthropology at the University of Pennsylvania; and Dale Kinney of the Department of History of Art at Bryn Mawr College.

Additionally, I would like to thank the following scholars in the United States who assisted the project in various ways: Martin Biddle, during his tenure as Director of the University Museum of the University of Pennsylvania, advised me on English facilities and elucidated obscure references. In permitting me to give a paper based on the issues of the thesis at his symposium, "Early Irish Art," held at Temple University on 19 April 1979, Martin Werner

13

of Temple University gave me a first public forum for the discussion of my theories with the leading lights of the field in this country. In that context, Carl Nordenfalk asked several interesting questions that led to the rethinking of major issues.

In England, the following are owed a debt of gratitude: Rosemary Cramp of the University of Durham for her time and interest and for the most recent plans of Jarrow and Monkwearmouth; Richard N. Bailey of the University of Newcastle-upon-Tyne for new information on Wilfrid's Hexham and for permission to use his version of the Hodges plan. Furthermore, I wish to thank the directors and staffs of various research institutions in England. J. B. Trapp, Director of the Warburg Institute of the University of London, not only permitted my use of the Warburg Library but also took an interest in my work. I wish to thank John Hopkins, Director of the Library of the Society of Antiquaries in London, for his permission for use of the Library, and his resourceful staff for their assistance. Of the staff of the British Museum, I particularly wish to acknowledge my debt to Mrs. L. E. Webster, Assistant Keeper, and John Russell, Research Assistant, both of the Department of Medieval and Later Antiquities, who gave me access to and facilitated my perusal of the monumental Stone Cross Index founded by Sir T. D. Kendrick. I am grateful to B. S. Benedikz, Head of Special Collections at Birmingham University Library for allowing me firsthand access to the *Book of Saint Chad*. Roger Norris, Librarian of the Library of the Dean and Chapter at Durham Cathedral likewise provided access to manuscripts, as did Bruce Benfield, Assistant Librarian of the Bodleian Library, Oxford; R. I. Page, Librarian of Corpus Christi College, Cambridge; and Penelope Morgan, Joint Honorable Librarian of the Cathedral Library, Hereford. I wish to thank William Foster, Administrator of the Works at Ripon, for showing me the extant early stonework there, and the Right Reverend Anthony G. W. Hunter, Rector of Hexham, for access to the crypt at Hexham while the latter was under repair in 1978. An additional debt of gratitude is owed to the following for assistance with or access to the objects in their keeping: Michael Robson, Curator of the Museum, Wilton Lodge, Hawick; A. E. Truckell, Curator, the Burgh Museum, Dumfries; and Steven Kerry, Keeper of the Manor House Museum and Gallery, Ilkley. I also wish to thank Tom Bryce, Chief Conservation Officer, and Joanna Close-Brooks, Curator, National Museum of the Antiquities of Scotland, Edinburgh, for their permission of access to certain cross shafts that were under conservation when I visited the Museum. Moreover, I wish to acknowledge the permission of R. E. Steel, Manager of the Cathedral Gifts, Canterbury, to photograph the fragments of the Reculver Cross in the Cathedral Crypt Museum.

Others were most helpful in obtaining photographs: Steven Croad of the National Monuments Record (Royal Commission on Historical Monuments [England]); Graham Fairclough, Assistant Inspector of Ancient Monuments, and W. S. Fermin, Clerk of Stationery and Printing in the Department of the Environment; and W. D. Casson of the Historical Plans Room of the Royal

Commission on Historical Monuments. I wish to thank equally those who responded to my written requests for photographic material, and/or for permission to use such material here: Dottoressa A. Morandini, Directress of the Biblioteca Medicea Laurenziana, Florence; William O'Sullivan, formerly Keeper of Manuscripts, and Bernard Meehan, current Keeper of Manuscripts, and the Board of Trinity College Library, Dublin; D. J. Smith, Keeper at the Museum of Antiquities of the University and Society of Antiquarians of Newcastle-upon-Tyne; Mrs. Elizabeth Hartley, Senior Keeper of Archaeology at the Yorkshire Museum, York; Fiona Marsden, Curator of the Sussex Archaeological Society Collection in Lewes, Sussex; Alexander Fenton, Director, National Museum of the Antiquities of Scotland, Edinburgh; J. P. Murray, Director, National Museum of Ireland, Dublin; Angelo Paredi, Director, Biblioteca Ambrosiana, Milan; R. I. Page, Librarian, and the Master and Fellows of Corpus Christi College, Cambridge; Roger Norris, Librarian, Dean and Chapter Library, Durham; Ken Osborne, Publications Director, Historic Buildings and Monuments Commission for England; and the Trustees of the British Museum.

In addition, I wish to thank the individual scholars whose assistance on various questions illuminated the corners into which my own training could cast no light. David Thompson of the Warburg Institute assisted me with translations from Byzantine Greek. Diane Droste of the Pontifical Institute, Toronto, took time from her own thesis research in London to instruct me on the early history of ecclesiastical chant.

Finally, I wish to thank those colleagues and friends whose contributions were both material and spiritual. I would like to thank Professor Gino Corti for assisting me in obtaining photographs from Italy. Additionally, I owe a debt of gratitude to two friends who assisted my research in England: Kathleen E. Harman, who made arrangements for a visit to Breedon-on-the Hill under most congenial circumstances and kept me informed of developments at the Brixworth excavations; and Barbara A. Teichert, who was navigator on a photographic expedition to northern England and Scotland. Jane Macintosh redrew the ground plans of Hexham, Jarrow, and Monkwearmouth. Nancy Henderson and friends typed the original thesis; and Helen Cutner of Words Are My Business, Philadelphia, processed the revised edition for publication. Finally, this revised edition would not have been possible without the encouragement, patience, and support of Martin P. Doyle, Jr., and our friends in Stone Harbor during the long summer of 1984.

Introduction

IN THE NORTHERN English kingdom of Northumbria, roughly between A.D. 690 and 750, there occurred a sudden florescence of the visual arts remarkable in its maturity, strength, and refinement for an area so remote from the Mediterranean centers of Late Antique culture. This phenomenon has often been called the Northumbrian Renaissance. This book is a synthetic study of the art of the Northumbrian Renaissance as a whole. It provides a frame of reference in which the extremely diverse art styles of this period may be understood as part of a larger unified cultural moment.

The kingdom of Northumbria in its heyday, from the beginning of the rule of Edwin in 625 to the mid-eighth-century ascendancy of the rival kingdom of Mercia, held the largest and most powerful political hegemony in England. Under these circumstances, Northumbria provided a relatively peaceful and prosperous milieu for the development of art. It is also the best-documented area in early Anglo-Saxon England, as Bede's *Ecclesiastical History of the English People,* the most thorough historical record of the period, was written in Northumbria, at Jarrow on the Tyne, by a Northumbrian. For the other six kingdoms of Anglo-Saxon England, the documentation is more sparse. Bede gives them relatively passing notice, primarily when they come into ecclesiastical matters. Besides Bede's narrative, we have only the abbreviated notices in the *Anglo-Saxon Chronicle,* the regional regnal lists, some hagiography, and a very few surviving examples of correspondence remaining as a basis for the reconstruction of events in Kent, East Anglia, Mercia, and elsewhere. However, the other Anglo-Saxon kingdoms were not only Northumbria's political rivals, but also valuable trade connections and independent art-producing centers, as the archaeological record and the currently accepted provenances of certain manuscripts indicate. For these reasons, and because of the general scarcity of evidence for the epoch as a whole, the Northumbrian material must be considered in its broader Anglo-Saxon context as well as within its more specific regional constraints.

Another factor critically affecting the art of Northumbria is the historical climate, or more specifically the ecclesiastical politics surrounding its evolution. The Northumbrian Renaissance followed the conversion of the Northumbrians to Christianity. The conversion opened England to an almost overwhelming flood of Mediterranean art, in the form of manuscripts, painted panels, metalwork, and all the paraphernalia used in the service of the new faith. These imports were taken up by Anglo-Saxon craftsmen as models for indigenous Christian art, and stimulated an exceptionally rich variety of responses, particularly in Northumbria. That variety stemmed in part from the very nature of the conversion of Northumbria, which was carried out under the separate and often conflicting auspices of missions from two Churches, the Celtic Church of Ireland, and the Church of Rome. Consequently the dynamics of the period as a whole have been studied in terms of either the role of the Celtic Church as the conveyor of both Mediterranean models and Celtic styles and motifs, on the one hand, or the role of the Roman Church as a source of the importation and emulation of Mediterranean art, on the other. Such a segmented approach has been a hindrance to the formulation of an understanding of the Northumbrian Renaissance in its entirety, as a single moment in the development of early medieval art. The interaction among Celtic, Roman, and indigenous Anglo-Saxon elements in Northumbrian art is fundamental to the dynamics of the development of the art of the period as a whole. It is more appropriate to consider the variations in the art of the Celtic and Roman Churches in Northumbria as stylistic modes within a larger period, examining each on the basis of the cultural roots and political goals of its source. Further, the fusion of styles in the period following the Synod of Whitby of 664, which partially resolved the differences between the Churches, constitutes a third mode, based on new demands and considerations. The new imagery of Northumbrian secular art, based on a combination of Mediterranean art imported through ecclesiastical channels with the traditions and temporal symbolism of the Northumbrian royal court, is the fourth mode in the art of the Northumbrian Renaissance. The present text is an exploration of the nature and evolution of these modes and of their relative roles in the Northumbrian Renaissance.

When we consider the art of Northumbria in the conversion period and its incorporation of Mediterranean models as constituting a "renaissance," several questions spring to mind. The first group of questions concerns the means of transmission of foreign models for art and the preconditions for their reception. Were the received models entirely imported, or was there a lingering remembrance of the Roman past in Britain and of the roles of the various northern tribal nations as federates of the empire? What were the nature and results of cultural contacts via trade and travel between the Mediterranean and the inhabitants of the British Isles, both Celtic and Anglo-Saxon, before the conversion? What was the role of the Continental peoples—the Merovingian

Franks, the Lombards, and the Visigoths among others—in these contacts, and how (if at all) did they affect postconversion art in England? Was this art purely a revival of late classical antiquity, a renaissance in the classic sense, or were there links between this art and contemporary Mediterranean and Continental art?

The second group of questions concerns the variables in the response to the imported models. How and why did the reception of foreign images and styles vary from center to center and between media? Under what circumstances did Northumbrian art directly emulate imported models, and when did it integrate these models more completely with indigenous styles? What political, philosophical, or cultural factors affected or wholly conditioned each center's response to the imported models? The answers to these questions provide an outline of the parameters (in the sense of defining or limiting factors) of the Northumbrian Renaissance.

A synthetic study of this remote period and culture takes a few risks, for most of the art produced at the time has not survived. The sudden and violent end of the kingdom of Northumbria at the hands of the Vikings around the year 800 radically reduced the quantitative legacy of Northumbrian art, and many other objects and monuments have since fallen victim to the accidents of history. We must realize that in discussing Northumbrian art today, we are dealing with only a fraction of what must have been produced at the time. The problems arising from nonsurvival have been only partially alleviated by continuing archaelogical research. For art-historical purposes, we must resign ourselves to dealing with those artifacts and structures which we have on hand or for which we have descriptions of variable reliability of contemporary or later date. We may hope that we have a few of the finest products of the period, preserved through time for their intrinsic or traditional value, and that for the rest we retain a fairly random sample. On this basis we may attempt to establish an overview of the art-historical moment and to generate a set of guidelines for understanding it on the basis of its cultural context and motivations. Nonetheless, any hypotheses evolved in the process must remain flexible. Our knowledge of the art and culture of Northumbria grows with each new archaeological site and in each season of excavation, and any theoretical interpretation of the epoch and its objects must be constantly reevaluated, and validated or discarded, on the basis of the cumulative material evidence.

The
Northumbrian
Renaissance

The Development of Secular Trade Routes and the Impact of the Anglo-Saxon Invasion of England

ARCHAEOLOGICAL EXCAVATION of sites both in the Anglo-Saxon east and in the British west of England and in Ireland has produced evidence of trade with both the Continent and the Mediterranean basin in the preconversion period. The development of trade routes can be traced by distribution patterns of such consistently identifiable series as pottery types or metalwork ewers or buckles. These patterns indicate separate and distinct foreign sources and choices in imports in the Anglo-Saxon as opposed to the earlier and contemporary Celtic areas. Nonetheless, evidence is also found indicating trade between these two groups within Britain. An examination of the patterns of internal and external trade reveals the extent to which postconversion patterns of artistic importation, distribution, and assimilation follow lines previously established in secular trade.

British Trade Patterns

The Roman military occupation of Britain continued in at least a minor way into the late fourth century. It was only in 409 that Honorius informed the British chieftains that his legions would no longer be available to assist them against both northern and Continental invaders. By this time, parts of Britain as far north as Dumfries and Strathclyde had been converted to Christianity. Hence, despite their crumbling political situation, the British were not only closely linked to Rome by the bonds of empire, but were also tied to the

Continent and the south, however loosely, by the Church. These connections were so strongly embedded a way of life that trade continued, not as a rarity, but as a norm of culture in the western British area long after the departure of the legions.

For the period before the conversion of the Anglo-Saxons, trade among the western British areas, the Mediterranean, and the Continent has been well established in the archaeological record. Mediterranean pottery sequences, both late Roman B ware (a late-fifth to early-seventh-century red ware), mostly amphorae, and C ware (a fifth- and sixth-century eastern Mediterranean rough reddish brown ware), mostly jugs and pitchers, are found at western British coastal sites, such as Dinas Emrys, Dinas Powys, and Tintagel.[1] These sequences are significantly absent from sites along the Continental river-valley trade routes established in Roman times.[2] This evidence is supported by documentary sources for the period. The *Vita* of Saint John Almoner, patriarch of Alexandria, who died in 616, includes mention of a merchant ship belonging to the episcopate of Alexandria, which sailed west with a cargo of twenty thousand bushels of grain, and arrived after twenty days in Britain where a *protos,* or local chieftain, purchased half of the grain for one *nomisma* of gold per bushel and the other half for a return cargo of tin.[3] The tone of the text indicates that as a trading voyage, this voyage was by no means unprecedented.[4] Other documentary sources substantiate the story in the *Vita.* These sources emanate primarily from Spain, especially from Galicia, which served as a stopover or turnabout point on the British-Mediterranean trade route. Parallels for British finds of C ware have been found in Portugal, near the Galician ports.[5] Galicia, occupied in the fifth and sixth centuries by the Teutonic Suevi, had ancient migration-period Celtic associations, but it is probably a result of later developments through the western seaways trade that one finds there records of an ancient diocese of Britona, of which the church of Santa Maria de Bretoña, near Montenedo, is a modern survival. A list of bishops of this diocese going back to the Suevic period includes near the outset the distinctly Celtic name Mailoc.[6] Moreover, Orosius, in his early fifth-century *Historia* (1.2.27), refers to the lighthouse at La Coruña as "ad speculam Britanniae," implying that it was used by ships from Britain.[7]

There is very little archaeological evidence in western Britain of trade with the Visigothic areas of Gaul; only one shard, from Dinas Emrys, and three coins from southern English sites, have been conclusively typed as from that region.[8] Thus the coastal traders seem to have found landfall in Spain rather than in southern Gaul. Indeed, confirmation of the mutual exclusivity of trading patterns in this period is found in Isidore of Seville's *Etymologies,* where the author notes that good glass is to be found in Britain but not in Gaul or Italy.[9] In fact, glass manufacture in Britain in Isidore's day was remarkably minimal, but as A. R. Lewis has suggested, perhaps this implies that glass from the Rhineland found its way to Spain so exclusively by British ships that its production became associated with their homeland.[10]

These lanes of trade seem to break down in the late seventh century, possibly as a result of the spread of Islamic control of the Mediterranean seaways. In this period, Merovingian royal documents change over from Egyptian papyrus to locally available vellum, and most pottery imports in the Celtic littoral region are from Gaul.[11]

On the other hand, trade between the western British seaways and the Merovingian ports of the northern coasts of Gaul seems to have continued briskly from the late Roman period onward. One type of pottery, E ware, which originates in the north of France, possibly in the Paris basin, occurs in western British and Irish sites but not in Saxon England, indicating separation of trade connections to the Continent between the two predominant English cultural areas.[12] Although some types of finds occur in both settings, these probably indicate common taste rather than necessarily shared trading patterns. Other Continental materials found in western British sites include fragments of glass from the Rhineland and of Germanic metal intended for use in enamelwork, as at Dinas Powys.[13] More exotic materials, such as the Coptic beads at Dinas Powys and a Romano-Egyptian glass fragment from Tintagel, probably found their way to Britain by a hand-to-hand transcontinental trade, much as did garnets and cowrie shells from India found in contemporary and later Anglo-Saxon jewelry.[14] Fifth-century funerary inscriptions in the western coastal areas of Britain demonstrate the continuity of the sea trade between Gaul and the Celtic littoral in the post-Roman period. These inscriptions not only perpetuate Roman formulas but share a range of popular names with inscriptions in contemporary Gaul.[15]

Later documentary evidence substantiates the archaeological data concerning trade between the western seaways and the Continent. Jonas's eighth-century *Vita Columbani* (1.23) mentions Irish traders at Nantes in the sixth century.[16] Similar traders, dealing in cloth and shoes, are noted at Ile de Noirmoutier at the mouth of the Loire in the eighth-century *Vita* of Filibert, a seventh-century Gallic abbot.[17] "Naves brittanicae" are at Angoulême in *Vita Eparchii reclusi Ecolismensis,* a ninth-century life of a sixth-century hermit saint.[18] In this context, "brittainicae" probably refers to Celtic western seaways traders, as contemporary Merovingian sources refer to traders from Anglo-Saxon eastern England as "Saxones" from "ultra mare in Saxonia."[19]

The evidence, both archaeological and documentary, indicates that the British connections to the Continent and the Mediterranean, probably established during the Roman occupation, were fairly continuous up to and beyond the time of the Anglo-Saxon conversion despite the socioeconomic setbacks of the invasion period.[20] The Britons had been converted to Christianity in large numbers already in the Roman period, but it would be erroneous to give the Church the preponderant credit for the maintenance of contact with the rest of the civilized world after the departure of the legions. Indeed, British Christianity suffered a major decline of contact with the Western Church between Honorius's final recall of the legions in 409 and the arrival of Augustine in 597. Bede documents the hostile confrontations between Augustine and the British bishops because of variances in both dogma and practice generated by two centuries' lack of communication.[21] On the other hand, the British secular world had become accustomed to the availability and use of Mediterranean and Continental wine, oil, grain, and luxury goods during the Roman occupation. The continuity of economic markets was thus the foremost factor in maintaining British contact with mainland Europe and the Mediterranean.

Ireland and the Western Seaways Trade

The Irish were also included in the trade patterns established under Roman rule and were thus put in contact with Mediterranean and Continental culture. The Irish were never conquered by the legions of Rome, and their cultural experience did not include the extensive romanization evident in Romano-British life. However, the Irish were involved in the western seaways trade during and after the Roman occupation of Britain. Roman objects of the period of the occupation of England have been found in Ireland in sufficient quantity to confirm the early entry of the Irish into this trade pattern.[22] On Lambay Island off the east coast near Dublin, a first-century A.D. hoard was found, containing four Roman brooches, and a provincial, possibly British, copy of a Roman fibula. Excavations of the crannogs of Balinderry have produced Arretine, Samian, and E ware pottery. The sites at Lagore Crannog, Garryduff, Ballycateen and Garranes also contained E ware; Garranes has in addition both A and B wares. The strongest Irish concentration of E ware is, however, found in the northeast, at Langford Lodge, Armagh, Nendrum, Ballyfounder, Spittle Ballee, Downpatrick, and Lough Faughn.[23] These sites are all near the narrowest crossing point of the Irish Channel to southern Scotland, which may perhaps indicate an overland trade across England in addition to the western seaways trade. These distribution patterns demonstrate that the Irish imported wine and oil from Gaul and from the Mediterranean basin. It is known, in addition, from the Roman author Symmachus (*Epistola* 2) what the Irish exported; their wolfhounds were famous throughout the Roman Empire, albeit they more commonly exported cattle and hides as well.[24]

The trade contact continued, like that of the western British, after the departure of the legions, as the presence of the late-dated E ware demonstrates. The contact was also profound enough to leave its mark on the most fundamental Celtic ornamental motif, the spiral. In Britain and Ireland alike, it was combined loosely with the Roman *pelta* motif and became the double-spiral or trumpet motif so basic to later Celtic art.[25]

The early conversion of the Irish to Christianity also contributed to their contacts with the outside world. The earliest extant mention of Christianity in Ireland is in Prosper of Aquitaine, who in his *Chronicle* mentions that Pope Celestine, in the year 431, sent Palladius as bishop to the Irish, "who believed in Christ," implying that by that date there were already a substantial number of converts.[26] Saint Patrick, nonetheless, is usually given credit for the conversion of the Irish, albeit at this time the Irish "nation" consisted of a loose hierarchy of tribal units or kingdoms. Saint Patrick, a well-educated and thoroughly romanized Briton, was captured as a young man by Irish raiders and lived among the Irish as a slave. He escaped and later returned to Ireland in 456 to evangelize his former captors. His mission was by no means universally successful but nonetheless met comparatively little resistance. Thus Ireland was largely Christian by the end of the fifth century, earning Patrick an exclusive reputation as the apostle to the Irish.[27] Their conversion, relatively early in the northern European region, strengthened Ireland's ties to mainstream European civilization and produced a steady trickle of ideas, motifs, and models for art.

From the outset, the Irish Church was based on monastic rather than on episcopal centers. The episcopal structure elsewhere was based on the Roman subdivision of provinces into dioceses, which Ireland had not experienced. Rather, Irish practice was derived from the monastic Church of the Desert Fathers of Egypt, which explains to some extent the eastern Mediterranean sources for early Christian art in Ireland. Nonetheless, the contacts of trade and faith were never so strong a cultural tide in Ireland as was the occupation of Britain by the Romans. The civilization of Ireland thus remained resolutely independent, attached to Late Iron Age Celtic ways and styles in social and artistic patterns alike.[28] Imported motifs, both in preconversion and in Christian art, were frequently so thoroughly assimilated that it is difficult for the unpracticed eye to distinguish them from indigenous material. In some cases, as in the spiral-*pelta* combination producing the trumpet motif, this assimilation is so complete that arguments can be and have been made for parallel invention of patterns without contact or borrowing. On the other hand, it may be said that the strength of early Irish art is precisely the self-confident independence of the indigenous tradition, able to absorb selectively and thoroughly whatever imported models were available, acceptable, and appropriate to the project at hand, be it Christian manuscript or secular metalwork. Moreover, the homogeneity and universal technical excellence of early Irish art is such that in many cases it is impossible to differentiate solely on the basis of style or degree of perfection between works of the Christian era and those of an earlier period. Estimates of date, in the absence of provenance or find data, must indeed depend on the presence or absence of datable foreign inputs, the importance of which must consequently not be underestimated.

In the Celtic realms of Britain and Ireland, the links of trade that made possible the borrowing and assimilation of foreign motifs predate the introduction of Christianity. Christianity itself may well have been introduced initially through these very patterns of contact. As was the case with the British Church, the Irish Church, primarily because of the attenuation of ecclesiastical contact, evolved separately from the Church of Rome and her subsidiaries in provinces that had been closer to the heart of the old empire. Many of the same deviations from orthodox Roman practice, such as the dating of Easter, occurred both in Ireland and Britain and were later to become major issues of contention between the Celtic and Roman Churches in their eventual confrontation in Northumbria. The introduction of foreign motifs into the earliest

Irish Christian art thus indicates not so much a cosmopolitan Church as a continuity of trade with an outside world no longer imperial Roman but now in large part Christian.

Trade and the Anglo-Saxons

The departure of the legions and the subsequent decline of British political and military hegemony in England set the stage for the Anglo-Saxon settlement of southeastern England. From contemporary accounts, it appears that certain British leaders originally invited Saxon and Anglian fighters from the Frisian and Germanic littorals to assist them in resisting a series of incursions by the Picts and Scots from northern England, with the promise of arable land as payment.[29] Two British authors, Gildas and Nennius, are the most detailed sources for the events that followed.

Gildas's *De Excidio et Conquestu Britanniae* is thought on linguistic grounds to date from the sixth century. The historical section of Gildas—the first twenty-six chapters—is vague on historical detail but gives a highly emotional account of the brief period of British resistance to the spread of Saxon control.[30] The *Historia Britonum* of Nennius is a later text, probably compiled about 800 from earlier sources, including Gildas and Bede.[31] Nennius was reconciled to the Saxons, who by his day had become stalwart Christians, but he remembered the violence of earlier times. The major calendar chronicles—both the *Anglo-Saxon Chronicle* and the Welsh *Annales Cambriae*—are later compilations, relying on earlier accounts, primarily Bede and Gildas, for the invasion period.[32] All these narrate the invitation by the British chief Vortigern to the Saxon war chiefs Hengist and Horsa to assist him in repelling a Pictish invasion, and the subsequent conquest of Britain by these Continental mercenaries and their followers.

The archaeological record demonstrates that the Anglo-Saxon advance into southeast England, and their later extension of control northward along the eastern coast in the fifth and sixth centuries, were more a progressive colonization than an armed invasion. The British population in these areas was amalgamated rather than destroyed, and their royalty intermarried with Saxon nobility.[33] Open conflict occurred only when the Anglo-Saxons advanced into heavily settled British areas with strong political centers and hierarchies. These battles and their aftermath, though slight in overall territorial importance, were, however, memorable enough to produce the horror stories in Gildas, and also the Welsh elegy *Gododdin,* which narrates the disastrous resistance of the northern Welsh to Æthelfrith and the Bernician Angles in the late sixth century. The largest areas that successfully resisted the invasions were Wales and Cornwall. These remained independently British down to the period of the Norman invasions, and maintain a separate cultural identity to the present day.

The Anglo-Saxons in England traded with the Continent from the very outset, predominantly with the areas from which they themselves had migrated; Frisia, the Rhineland and the Germanic littoral, and Frankish Gaul. This trade developed slowly at first. Most imported finds date from the sixth and seventh centuries, a time when political bonds to the Continent were also being formed by Anglo-Saxon kings, possibly as a political encouragement to commercial venture.[34] The classic example is the marriage of Æthelbert of Kent to a literate Christian Merovingian princess, Bertha, who with her chaplain Liudhard paved the way for Augustine's mission to Kent.[35] Æthelbert's legal system, codified between 597 and 616, was derived in large part from the *Lex Salica* of Merovingian Gaul. Moreover, the cult of Saint Martin at Canterbury—both in the dedication of the church used by Bertha and Liudhard before Augustine's arrival and in that of the royal burial porticus at Augustine's abbey church of Saints Peter and Paul—is most probably copied from Merovingian court practice.[36] Later the marriage of Æthelbert and Bertha's daughter to Edwin of Deira, ruler of one of the twin kingdoms of the early period of Northumbrian history, opened the north to Paulinus's mission from Kent in 627. Christianity did not establish trade contacts any more in Anglo-Saxon England than in the Celtic west. On the contrary, evangelization was made possible by preexistent bonds of trade and mutual political recognition that were then strengthened in turn by the ties and needs of the new faith.

Archaeological evidence of trade across the Channel is most extensively found in the southeastern Anglo-Saxon kingdoms, those closest to the Continental ports of Quentovic and Dorestad. The number of finds increases dramatically in the sixth and into the seventh century, paralleling documentation on diplomatic contacts, although patterns of survival and find probability may affect the evidence. Merovingian coins are found widely in English sites of this period, and Anglo-Saxon *sticcas* and *sceattas* appear in Continental hoards. Morever, the debasement of the gold used in Merovingian coinage, due in large part to the economic crises of Byzantium, is reflected after only a minimum lag in Kentish coin and jewelry.[37] Jewelry, especially brooches, from Merovingian Gaul and other areas of the Continent, has been widely found in Kent in this period.[38] Further, the Kentish goldsmiths freely copied Merovingian designs, modifying them slightly to suit indigenous taste.[39] Continental objects of more practical use—pottery of the Mayen, Pingsdorf, Badorf, and Tating sequences; glass from the Rhineland; and millstones from the Eifel district—have become common finds in Saxon sites excavated in the past two decades. These allow not only determination of progressively well-stocked distribution patterns but also relative dating of English and Continental sites well into the postconversion period.[40]

Trade contact between the Mediterranean basin and Anglo-Saxon England was not so direct as had been the case in the western British seaways. Mediterranean finds at Anglo-Saxon sites tend to be less utilitarian than the B ware amphorae of Celtic sites. Rather, they appear to be the result of a specialized market in luxury exotica. The most classic example of this trade in specialty goods is a series of bronze vessels, some with engraved designs. These were produced in Coptic Egypt, where an identical series of bronze bowls, ewers,

Coptic bronze bowl, Sutton Hoo; British Museum *(photo: Trustees of the British Museum, by permission)*

Interior engraving, Sutton Hoo Coptic bowl *(Photo: Trustees of the British Museum, by permission)*

Coptic bronze ewer, Wheathampsted (Herts.); British Museum *(photo: Trustees of the British Museum, by permission)*

and vessels has been found, dating from the fourth to sixth century.[41] The English series includes four basic forms. The first is a round bowl of low profile, with base, flat rim, and round drop handles. Of these, one was found at King's Field, Faversham, Kent, and another at Sutton Hoo in Suffolk, both now in the British Museum.[42] The interior of the Sutton Hoo bowl is decorated with a procession of engraved animals, in which it resembles a vessel of the second type—a bucket with drop handles—found at Chessel Down on the Isle of Wight.[43] The third type of vessel is a shallow bowl on a high base, with square drop handles, as for example that found at Taplow, Buckinghamshire, in 1883, now in the British Museum.[44] The fourth and most bizarre shape is a small ewer on three feet with hinged lid, spout, and handle, resembling a modern Turkish coffeepot. One of these was found at Wheathamsted, Hertfordshire (British Museum), and another at Cuddeston, Oxfordshire. The transcontinental trade pattern for these bronze vessels has been established by a series of Lombard grave finds in northern Italy, and by the discovery of a three-footed ewer and a low bowl in a grave at Wonsheim in Rheinhessen, Germany. The latter are conveniently given an earliest possible date of deposit by the presence in the same find of a coin of Heraclius and Tiberius (613–641) set in a ring.[45]

Byzantine silver has also been found in Anglo-Saxon secular sites and in burials. The earliest hoard of Mediterranean silver in England is the Traprain Hoard buried at Traprain Law, Buckinghamshire, in the fifth century and now in the British Museum. This includes several antique flagons with raised vintage motifs. The Traprain silver was probably owned by wealthy Britons and hidden during the political chaos following the departure of the legions. It had most likely arrived in England about 400 through the lines of trade established by the Roman conquest.[46] The seventh-century ship burial at Sutton Hoo, Suffolk, by contrast, contained several pieces of eastern Mediterranean silver that probably arrived via Anglo-Saxon trade connections, or possibly as a direct gift, or series of gifts, to the royal house of East Anglia.

Byzantine silver salver with stamps of Anastasius I, Sutton Hoo; British Museum
(*photo: Trustees of the British Museum, by permission*)

The Sutton Hoo burial hoard includes Mediterranean silver of a variety of dates and provenances. The largest object is a circular salver, 28.5 inches in diameter, ornamented with three concentric rings of engraved geometric patterns: one at the center, one in the interior that includes four rondels of seated Tyches, and a third at the rim. The back of the salver bears the imperial stamps of Anastasius I (491–518). The elaborate, somewhat fussy ornament is conservative for that date, resembling work of around 400, as on the Concesti plate in the Hermitage. Anastasian silver is generally more simple and monumental in design. This plate is therefore believed not to have been intended for the imperial collection but to be of second quality, possibly a product of the workshops at Lampsacus, but in any case remote from centers of advanced design.[47]

Also at Sutton Hoo was found a fluted bowl with round drop handles, 15.5 inches in diameter. The shallow and rather weak fluting terminates at an interior border—a leaf design rendering faithfully the late classical cymatium motif. This band encircles a stiff and rather crude profile of a female head.[48] The bowl is unstamped. Ernst Kitzinger has suggested that the design of the bowl is a late copy, in a dry, conventional style, of earlier classical pieces, possibly executed in the eastern hinterlands of the Mediterranean basin, in the Balkans or in southern Russia.[49] The lifelessly brittle profile and hair and the sharp break in the neck indicate a distinct poverty of craftsmanship, borne out by the crudely undisguised compass mark marring the throat. The bowl is nonetheless of great intrinsic value, having been beaten from a great mass of solid silver, and must have made quite an impression on its Anglo-Saxon observers.

In addition, the Sutton Hoo find included a set of ten nested silver bowls, one completely destroyed in situ. These were decorated with bands of decorative motifs, which vary in pattern from bowl to bowl but are laid out identically in each bowl in the shape of an equal-armed cross. Similar motifs, particularly a certain star pattern, have been found on a group of seventh- or eighth-century gold vessels from Nagyszentmiklós in Hungary. Such patterns were possibly inspired by sixth-century work from the Sassanid Empire under Khosrau II (590–628), infiltrating workshops of the Byzantine hinterland by the seventh century. A possible provenance for the Sutton Hoo bowls can be postulated in the Danube basin or in Asia Minor.[50] The arrangement of the decorative bands in the cross on the interiors of these bowls can be construed to have Christian significance, which would have direct bearing on the date of the Sutton Hoo burial.[51] It is possible that the Sutton Hoo silver, particularly the nested bowls and a related pair of silver spoons, were baptismal gifts to one or more of the earliest Christian kings of East Anglia, either from eminent clergy or from earlier royal converts, whether Anglo-Saxon or Frankish. Bede mentions or describes several such gifts, sent by popes to English kings as inducements to conversion or congratulations upon conversion.[52] Nonetheless, the finds are present in an Anglo-Saxon grave, possibly royal, and hence fit into the general category of Mediterranean objects in England in secular contexts, possibly in part preconversion, and also potentially present as a result of trade, at least at some point in their histories.

Fluted silver bowl, Sutton Hoo; British Museum *(Photo: Trustees of the British Museum, by permission)*

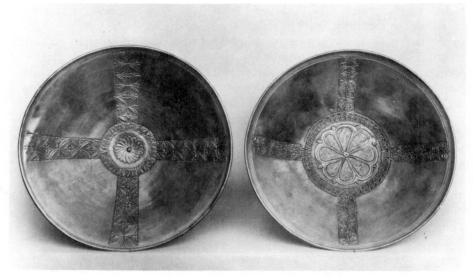

Two of a set of ten nested silver bowls, Sutton Hoo; British Museum *(Photo: Trustees of the British Museum, by permission)*

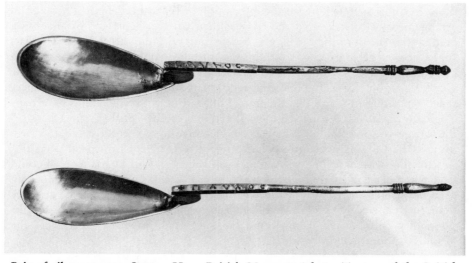

Pair of silver spoons, Sutton Hoo; British Museum *(photo: Trustees of the British Museum, by permission)*

The ship burial also contained a pair of silver spoons. These follow in general shape late classical spoons found throughout early medieval Europe. They are about ten inches in length, consisting of an egg-shaped bowl joined by a vertically set disc to a slender handle terminated by a beaded finial. At the juncture of bowl and handle, the stem of each flattens and thickens into a rectangular prism, which bears an inscription in Greek letters. One spoon reads "ΠΑΥΛΟΣ" (Paulos), the other apparently "ΣΑΥΛΟΣ" (Saulos). Early writers believed that the two spoons were made as a set, particularly appropriate as a conversion gift because of its reference to the conversion of Saint Paul (Acts 13:9). Also, the Greek inscriptions were considered to indicate an eastern Mediterranean provenance for both spoons.[53] However, in 1967, R. E. Kaske noted that there are significant differences between the two spoons, particularly in the inscriptions.[54] He noted that the letters of "Paulos" are well formed, symmetrical, and evenly spaced, consistent in size and style, and have even uprights and terminal knobs in correct proportion. By contrast, the "Saulos" inscription is relatively crude, assymmetrical, and inconsistent in design, with overly prominent end knobs and uneven spacing relative both to the margins and to the other letters. The letters lean to the left and diminish in size to the right. The Greek alphabet is frequently misinterpreted—the alpha is V-shaped, the lines of the upsilon do not meet, and the omicron is not round but triangular. The writer of "Saulos" is thus not nearly so comfortable with or accurate in the Greek alphabet as the writer of "Paulos." Kaske has therefore suggested that the "Saulos" spoon is not an import but a domestic copy. In addition, the slant of the letters of "Saulos" suggested to Kaske that "Saulos" is actually a miscopying of the inscription "Paulos," the sigma replacing pi when the copyist erroneously began the inscription in vertical rather than horizontal arrangement, a mistake that the copyist then tried to "correct" by making a gradual transition to the horizontal by slanting his letters to the left. This last suggestion is debatable, as so clumsy a mistake would probably have been noticeable even to an otherwise illiterate East Anglian chieftain. Although the "Saulos" spoon may certainly be of a different and perhaps local provenance, there is nothing to prove that the model did not in fact read "Saulos." Perhaps originally there was a pair of imported spoons reading "Saulos" and "Paulos," the former was irreparably damaged, and a native copy was substituted. Moreover, as R. L. S. Bruce-Mitford has pointed out, there is no proof that this substitution was made in East Anglia, or in England, for that matter.[55] It could have taken place in Merovingian France, where Greek was no more commonly used in this period. However, the possibility remains that this may be an early example of the copying of a Mediterranean model in an English context. This possibility is enhanced if, as Kaske has suggested, we have its model—the "Paulos" spoon—found beside it.

Early copies of Mediterranean art are very rare in pagan Saxon sites and cemeteries. The only known example of native Saxon silverwork taking Mediterranean work for its model is a buckle-tab plaque of local manufacture found in the cemetery site at Alfriston, Sussex, and now in the Lewes Museum.[56] This tiny plaque shows a rudimentary version of the perennial Late Antique acanthus vine, a motif that was certainly not part of the vernacular Saxon

Silver buckle tab with acanthus scroll, from grave 24, Alfriston (Sussex); Sussex Archaeological Society, Barbican House, Lewes *(by the permission of the Curator)*

decorative vocabulary. Elsewhere, imported work, especially bronze and silver as at Sutton Hoo, was highly valued but usually not copied. If the "Saulos" spoon is a local copy, the motivation for replication is peculiar to the situation.

One may well question the inclusion of the Sutton Hoo material in the discussion of preconversion trade patterns, particularly as some of the objects (the spoons and possibly the nested bowls) have Christian symbolic content and possibly even liturgical usage. Debate concerning the identity of the person commemorated by the ship burial has centered on these very objects. The presence of such a wealth of ornaments—both imported and domestic—the inclusion of items that may be part of royal or ceremonial regalia, and the geographic proximity of Sutton Hoo to Rendlesham (one of the foremost East Anglian royal sites) indicate that the site is a royal burial, probably of an East Anglian king.[57] Contemporary burial finds equal in value and complexity are extremely rare. Only two other northern grave sites include Byzantine silver: one at Ittenheim, Bavaria, held a set of *phalerae*, or horse trappings, and a prince's grave at Krefeld held a spoon with a Chi-Rho monogram.[58] The tombs of Merovingian kings opened in the nineteenth century contained even greater amounts of goldwork, often inlaid with garnets, but no comparable collection of foreign luxury items.[59] Other finds of wealth in the British Isles, such as at the Saint Ninian's Isle treasure found in the Shetlands, are generally hoards of locally manufactured valuables, buried for protection in time of strife, with the intention of eventual recovery.[60]

The earliest possible date for the Sutton Hoo burial, as derived from the dates of the thirty-seven Merovingian coins included in the treasure, is about 623.[61] This is the only dating evidence from the site accurate to within a decade.

At the original excavation of Sutton Hoo, no skeleton was found, hence the burial was originally postulated to have been a cenotaph. Bruce-Mitford suggested that the burial was a commemoration of a king who had converted to Christianity and whose treasure contained Christian artifacts, but whose loyal but still-pagan followers decided to raise the traditional burial mound, regardless of the fact that the body would be buried elsewhere in sanctified ground. The Merovingian coins included in the burial hoard were considered to be evidence of the extent of postconversion contact with Gaul.[62] Cenotaphs are not lacking in the British Isles at an even earlier date; the Benty Grange mound site is a British Celtic cenotaph.[63]

Bruce-Mitford has recently revoked his cenotaph hypothesis for Sutton Hoo on the basis of spectrographic analysis of certain remains in tomb.[64] The soil at Sutton Hoo is sufficiently acidic and the conditions consistently damp enough to dissolve human remains completely. All that remains under such circumstances is usually a solution of phosphoric salts derived from bones that eventually binds itself chemically to any available metal. Analysis indicates an unusually high phosphorous content in the deposits on the sword found along the keel line, where by the arrangement of personal ornaments the body would logically have been placed. However, other materials, such as a bone chess set, could produce similar results.

Especially confusing to issues of date and identity at Sutton Hoo and in goods burials elsewhere are the excavations of Anglo-Saxon cemeteries in southern England by S. C. Hawkes and A. Meaney.[65] It was previously believed that burial with grave goods indicated a pre-Christian date. However, these investigations have indicated that burial with grave goods continued to some extent into the Christian era. The advent of the new faith is indicated in the cemeteries only by the sudden and consistent orientation of burial on an east-west axis. Thus the presence of grave goods per se at Sutton Hoo can no longer be considered sufficient evidence of a preconversion date. Sutton Hoo nonetheless has overtones of pagan afterlife concepts that the lesser, nonroyal graves excavated by Hawkes and Meaney seem to lack, both in the richness and in the symbolism of the grave goods.

If Sutton Hoo is pagan, the presence of the potentially Christian silver items—spoons and nested bowls—could be explained as booty from raids on Christian sites. However, there is no documentation for armed confrontation or raiding between late-pagan East Anglia and any predominantly Christian area, such as Kent. Sutton Hoo thus appears to be bizarrely syncretistic: a pagan warrior's burial, complete with military and royal paraphernalia, and including evidence of contact with, if not conversion to, Christianity.

A more simple and elegant solution to the Sutton Hoo paradox may be found in Bede. In his discussion of East Anglia, only one king draws attention in this context—Rædwald, the only East Anglian ruler to hold widespread hegemony south of the Humber, beyond the borders of East Anglia proper.[66] Rædwald, Bede tells us, accepted Christianity in Kent in the court of Æthelbert, but only as one faith among many, maintaining an altar to his old gods beside the Table of the Host in his court temple.[67] Moreover, his dates correspond with the numismatic evidence. Consequently, he is the most likely East Anglian king to have been honored by the syncretistic Sutton Hoo ship burial.[68] This would place Sutton Hoo at a relatively early date in the history of East Anglian trade, before establishment of the strong links of the church to the Continent and the Mediterranean and before the development of local coinage.[69]

It is therefore legitimate to include the Byzantine silver of Sutton Hoo—both the purely secular group (such as the Anastasius dish) and the objects of real or potential Christian meaning (the spoons and the nested bowls)—in the discussion of early preconversion trade patterns. Both groups conform to the general pattern of find situations seen in the Coptic bronze vessels, in that they are part of a specialty trade or personal exchange of luxury goods and foreign exotica not domestically available. Neither the Coptic bronzes nor the Byzantine silver found in Anglo-Saxon sites argues for a direct trade connection to the Mediterranean. The distribution of the bronzes on the Continent suggests a hand-to-hand transcontinental drift of metalwork from the eastern Mediterranean to the Frankish and Saxon Channel traders, which may also apply to some or all of the Sutton Hoo silver at some point in the histories of the various pieces. The Anglo-Saxons, unlike the romanized Britons, had no historical ties to the Mediterranean basin. Their trade reflects instead their origin in the northern

European Germanic hinterlands. It is no puzzle why their first trade in objects of Mediterranean provenance, and also their first contacts with the Christian faith, came from or via the Merovingian Franks, the strongest political unity and most pervasive cultural influence in northern Europe at that time. The Angles and Saxons must have been aware of the rise of power and prosperity in Merovingian Gaul from its inception, as originally they had been its neighbors. By contrast the Britons had a much more complex series of connections to the world outside England, for they remembered life under Roman rule. Even in the darkest years of economic impoverishment due to the advancement of the Anglo-Saxons, they still maintained a broader view of cultural and historical development. To them, wine from Spain and olive oil and grain from Byzantium were the last threads of the Roman cloak that had once covered their world. The Irish, too, were well aware of the advantages of trade with the Mediterranean from their experience as neighbors of the empire. To the Anglo-Saxons, Continental trade brought fifth-century Mediterranean exotica, some of which they buried with their heroes and princes, but there was no long-standing association with the Mediterranean basin. Their ties of trade and cultural experience would only be broadened later by their eventual inclusion in the later Roman Empire, the realm of the Western Church.

Postinvasion Insular Trade

The complete mutual independence of Saxon and British trade patterns in regard to the extrainsular world is the most significant factor in this study of preconversion trade to the later discussion of postconversion art. Despite the evidence in the archaeological record that the invasions were for the most part peaceable colonization, the two cultures remained essentially separate in identity and socioeconomic function. The emotional strength of Gildas's account of the invasions indicates that even where armed confrontation did not occur, an undercurrent of mutual hostility kept the Britons and their conquerers apart.[70]

The scarcity of evidence concerning trade within England between the two cultures in the preconversion period strengthens the probability of mutual hostility. The material evidence for such trade comes primarily from Anglo-Saxon sites and was for a long time construed as plunder taken during the invasions. It is only in recent years—since it has become popular to speak of an Anglo-Saxon settlement rather than of an invasion—that discussion of mutual trade has been considered a reasonable area for speculation. Hence only a very small amount of literature in this area has thus far been put forward. The two types of objects considered in this trade are penannular brooches and hanging bowls. David Longley's recent examination of a broad spectrum of finds indicates that both of these types moved, probably via trade, from British, Pictish, Dalriada Scottish, and Irish areas into predominantly Anglo-Saxon regions.[71]

Penannular brooches of a fifth- to sixth-century series, called type H in

Longley's typology, are widely found in the Pictish north, where they were probably made. In addition, they distribute to ports and inlets along the northeast coast of England, indicating their transport by coastal trade. The northern Angles along this coast also began to manufacture roughly similar annular brooches about the same time as type H distributed southward from Pictland. Longley has conjectured that the annular brooch is an Anglian variant on the Celtic penannular style, adapted to allow greater surface area for decoration.[72] This would, however, indicate a greater degree of contact than has been thus far suggested by the quantity of type H brooches found south of the Antonine Wall. Moreover, the derivation of forms per se remains speculative.

The hanging bowls are far more controversial both in provenance and function. A hanging bowl is usually a round metal basin, generally bronze, broad and shallow in form, with at least three rings mounted on its outer edge for suspending the bowl from a higher point. Generally, at the junctions of bowl and rings, ornamental escutcheons are applied, decorated with either metal chipwork or in more lavish circumstances with champlevé enamel and millefiori insets. Both the metalworking and enameling techniques and the designs used—trumpet spirals in particular—are Celtic in origin. Yet the bulk of the finds are from Saxon sites, primarily in the southeastern quadrant of England,

Hanging bowl, Sutton Hoo; British Museum *(photo: Trustees of the British Museum; by permission)*

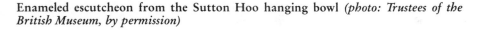

Enameled escutcheon from the Sutton Hoo hanging bowl *(photo: Trustees of the British Museum, by permission)*

where Saxon settlement was earliest and most solidly established.[73]

The function of the bowls is difficult to determine, although this issue is vital to a discussion of their peculiar distribution. In the Roman period, unornamented bowls suspended from tripods were widely used for ritual purification, for the mixing and serving of wine, for mundane hand washing in wealthy homes, and, in the early Christian period, for baptism.[74] Some of these uses must have permeated into native households in Roman Britain, for early bowls have been found at Romano-British sites at Silchester and at Barton in Cambridgeshire, as well as in the Traprain Hoard.[75] Bowls hung from tripods were part of the equipment of hospitality in Wales in the Dark Ages, although their exact function is unknown. The author of the Welsh epic, *Gwarchan Tudfwlch* compliments his patron by describing him as a host as *trybedawt rawt*, or "rich in tripods," an indication of prestige gained by entertaining in style.[76] Perhaps they were used to offer newly arrived guests the option of washing before a feast, reminiscent of the baths at Roman villas. This possibility is furthered by the frequent use of a fish motif in decorating bowls. The largest bowl from Sutton Hoo contains a small metal fish raised on a pivoting base, and the motif is quite common on escutcheons elsewhere.[77]

The presence of fish, of course, also may be an allusion to the early Christian use of the fish symbol and the anagram ΙΧΘΥΣ for Christ. Consequently, the hanging bowls may have been part of the equipment of the early Church in Britain, as portable baptismal fonts during the conversion of the Britons, or subsequently as holy water basins in early churches. However, a fish is appropriate decor for any vessel, sacred or secular, designed to hold water. The bowls were probably used in both Christian and profane circumstances, excluding such obvious cases as the Faversham bowl, where, on each escutcheon, a pair of fish flank a Greek cross.[78] It has also been conjectured that the bowls were used as oil lamps with floating wicks, suspended above the altars of British churches, but this is unlikely because the bowls are too large and deep to have been used effectively in this way.[79] Certainly any Christian usage of the bowls would be deleted at their removal to their predominantly pagan Saxon find contexts.

The Roman use of the bowls in the serving of wine and other alcoholic beverages may have carried over to British use, for in Anglo-Saxon sites the bowls have been found with objects of similar function: with ladles at Whitby, with drinking bowls at Sutton Hoo, and with drink-horn mounts at Loveden Hill.[80] However, this use may have been exclusive to Saxon practice without transmission of Roman usage by the Britons, for there is no confirmation of this tradition in British sites.

Other uses of the bowls among the Britons in the period before their conversion probably stem from trade with Roman dealers who did not tell their customers the traditional functions of the vessels. Thus hanging bowls are found that were used to contain early cremation burials, or to hold thoroughly pagan food offerings to the dead, such as the onions and crab apples at Forddown.[81] These practices had probably been discontinued by the time of contact with the Anglo-Saxons, when the Britons were for the most part Christian.

As has been seen, the general form and possibly several functions of the bowls in the British Isles stem from the occupation of England by the Romans. However, most evidence of the metalworking and enameling practices used in the escutcheons of the bowls has been found at settlement sites in Ireland.[82] Françoise Henry has suggested that the practice of making the bowls spread from Roman Britain to Ireland at a very early date, and that the techniques used in their ornamentation evolved in Ireland, but as Ireland was Christian from a comparatively early date, fifth- and sixth-century grave goods are more rarely found there than in pagan Anglo-Saxon sites in England, and archaeological evidence is consequently scarce.[83] Moreover, excavation of early sites in Ireland began later and has proceeded more slowly than in England, and it is generally believed by both Irish and foreign archaeologists that much of the archae-ological record there is still in the ground. Other early metalwork from Ireland demonstrates the availability of both the techniques and the skill required for the bowls.[84] However, there is also evidence for sophisticated enamelwork and metalcraft at British Celtic settlements in Wales, as at Dinas Powys, and in the north, as at the Mote of Mark.[85]

Other areas in the British Isles may well also have produced some of the bowls. The bowl from Lullingstone (British Museum) is covered with small applied plaques in the form of animals and great double-headed axes. The animals include stags that show the characteristic spirals at the joints seen in some of the earliest Pictish symbol-stone animals, such as the incised Burghead Bull. Beyond this striking stylistic parallel, recent finds indicate that some of the bowls may have been produced in Pictland and traded southward. A series of fifth-century openwork escutcheons, which Longley has typed group 1, distributed southward from eastern Scotland. Several were found along with a collection of type H penannular brooches in the Tummel Bridge hoard on the Border Marches, and the two series have almost identical distribution patterns. A mold for this type of escutcheon was found at Craig Phadrig, near Inverness, indicating that Pictland was not only trading in these bowls but also producing them. The hanging bowls are thus probably not endemic to any particular section of the British Isles but seem to have been produced throughout the Pictish and Celtic regions, with a variety of intended uses.[86]

The discovery of the bowls primarily at Saxon sites is not surprising in that the Saxons, unlike their Celtic neighbors, were pagans in the fifth and sixth

Hanging bowl with applied metal escutcheons, Lullingstone (Kent); British Museum *(photo: Trustees of the British Museum, by permission)*

Burghead Bull, Burghead, Moray *(photo: National Museum of Antiquities of Scotland, by permission of the Director)*

centuries and practiced inhumation with grave goods. The distribution of Longley's group 1 hanging bowls parallel to that of type H penannular brooches southward from Pictish areas into the northern Anglian littoral indicates the possibility that some of the bowls, too, were present in the south not as the booty of invasion but as traded goods.[87] This may indicate that the Anglo-Saxons were not so isolated from the rest of the population as was suggested by patterns of external trade. However, the pattern may have a different significance. Saxon trade to the Continent for Mediterranean goods consisted primarily of a taste for luxury exotica, later used as grave goods in burials of nobility or the wealthy. The hanging bowls may have fulfilled the same function, as they appear largely in otherwise rich burials. Their association with drinking vessels at Saxon sites but not in the Celtic literary or archaeological record might indicate that the Saxons purchased the bowls from traders without contact with their manufacturers, who may well have intended them for a different use. Hence the presence of the bowls and brooches in Saxon graves does not necessarily indicate intimate contact between the heartlands of the Celtic and Saxon cultures.

The study of trade patterns in the period before the Anglo-Saxon conversion to Christianity indicates that the Anglo-Saxons and the Celts in England had relatively little internal trade contact between them and that their trade patterns toward the Continent and the Mediterranean basin were largely mutually exclusive. Moreover, the British and Irish attitude toward mainstream Europe, stressing their inclusion in the continuity of the Roman past, however fragmentary, was completely different from the viewpoint of the Anglo-Saxons, who considered themselves outsiders, new arrivals, to whom all things Mediterranean were relatively remote. These factors conditioned the relative receptivity of these two cultures to the rapid influx of foreign, and especially Mediterranean, art immediately after conversion.

[2]

Historical Circumstances of the Northumbrian Renaissance

THE NORTHUMBRIANS were converted to Christianity relatively early in their history. Due to the dynastic struggles involved in the establishment of a unified Northumbria, the conversion was brought about by the missions of two distinctly different Churches, that of Ireland and that of Rome. The confrontation of these two Churches and their inherent cultures is one of the major factors determining the course of the Northumbrian Renaissance.

The region known later as the kingdom of Northumbria was subdivided in the early Anglo-Saxon period into two smaller kingdoms, both controlled by a northern group of Angles. Deira, the more southerly of the two, encompassed the area of northeastern England north of the Humber and south of the Tyne, and extended as far west as the Pennine Ridge. Bernicia, at its greatest extent, extended north from the Tyne to the Firth of Forth, although the northern border was frequently disputed with the Picts of Lothian.[1] To the west a frontier was maintained by several ancient British kingdoms, of which the strongest was Rheged, or Strathclyde, with its capital at Dumbarton on the Clyde. To the northwest was the kingdom of Dalriada, ruled by the descendants of fifth-century invaders from Ireland, who like the Irish themselves were referred to by the Angles as "Scotti," or Scots. To the southwest was Mercia, the Kingdom of the Middle Angles, against which the Northumbrians waged continual territorial warfare. In the eighth century, Mercia was to succeed Northumbria as the premier kingdom of the Anglo-Saxon heptarchy.[2]

At the beginning of the Anglian occupation, Northumbria was populated predominantly by Celtic Britons. Saxon mercenaries in Roman or British pay had settled as early as the fourth or early fifth century in the area around York and the coastal East Riding of Yorkshire.[3] They had control of the area by the second half of the sixth century, when the Deiran regnal lists begin with Ælle.[4] Bernicia, on the other hand, was initially settled by a group of Anglian raiders from further south, who found the rocky coastal islands, Bamburgh and the Farnes, ideally suitable as fortifiable bases. Their first recorded king, Ida, ruled at Bamburgh from 547.[5] Unlike the lands of the settled mercenaries in Yorkshire, however, the mainland in the north has yielded less evidence of Anglian cemeteries, and very little distinctively Germanic settlement material. Thus the resident Anglian population must have been considerably smaller in the north, probably geared throughout the early period to raiding, followed by casual overlordship rather than intensive settlement.[6] The excavation of the Anglian center at Yeavering has indicated a remarkable continuity of Celtic-British usage patterns at the site despite the superimposition of an Anglian royal center with its own needs and purposes.[7] This implies that Anglian cultural hegemony pertained only to the coastal area, and political control alone was extended to the interior by Ida and his successors. On the other hand, early peaceful cultural interaction between Angles and Celts at a few shared sites such as Yeavering provides a pre-Christian basis for the subsequent artistic synthesis of multiple cultures—Celtic, Anglian, and Mediterranean Christian—in religious and secular art in the same region.

The Northumbrians first appear in Bede's historical narrative in 603 when Æthelfrith of Bernicia (592–616) secured his borders against the Scots at a battle at Degsastan, possibly in Liddesdale. He then turned southward and drove out the ruling dynasty of Deira, of which the surviving heir, Edwin, was forced into exile. Finally, he reduced the threat of a British uprising to the west by conquering their predominantly Welsh army near Chester shortly before 615. Bede characterizes Æthelfrith as a fierce pagan warrior and applies to him the description by the patriarch Jacob of his son Benjamin (Genesis 49:27): "a ravenous wolf; in the morning he shall devour the prey and in the evening shall divide the spoil."[8] Nonetheless, Æthelfrith was the first descendant of the pirates of Bamburgh to unify Deira and Bernicia under one crown, however impermanently.

Edwin, meanwhile, traveled extensively for at least ten years from one court to the next, always escaping the plots of Æthelfrith to end both his life and his line.[9] Tradition has it that he spent part of this time in Wales, for he is one of the "three chief pests of Anglesey nurtured by itself," in the Welsh triads.[10] He may have spent time in Mercia as well, for he had children by a Mercian princess named Coenburg. It is known from Bede that he also passed some years at the court of Rædwald of East Anglia.[11] Rædwald, high king of the heptarchy, worshiped both Christ and the ancient gods of his people, in what Bede considers scandalous apostasy, but which Rædwald must have considered a shrewd hedging of bets.[12] It was in Rædwald's syncretistic court that Edwin first encountered the Christian faith and where, in gratitude for miraculous aid in escaping yet another conspiracy against him, he may have first contemplated the possibility of conversion.[13]

The Christian mission that reached Rædwald's court was an offshoot of the Roman mission to the English based at Canterbury. The seat of the royal court of Kent, a kingdom long in contact with the Continent through trade and political alliance, Canterbury was also the seat of the Roman Church in England, established by Augustine in 597.[14] Augustine had been sent by Gregory the Great, and the Canterbury mission was in all things a Roman foundation. In its earliest years, relying primarily on its foreign roots, the mission imported most of the necessary paraphernalia of the Christian Church, both for its own rites and for the service of its converts. The Church thereby opened the floodgates of mainstream European, and specifically romanized art and culture, onto the Anglo-Saxons, particularly in Kent.[15] Hitherto relatively secluded by their resolute paganism, the Saxons of Kent were now brought precipitously into the northern European ecclesiastical and cultural world. Trade contacts established earlier through the availability of markets were now confirmed, strengthened, and extended through the advance of the Church and broadened northward and westward with the extension of Christianity through gradual conversion. This process of cultural infiltration began to reach Northumbria along with the Roman Church.

In due course, Edwin succeeded to the throne of Northumbria by overwhelming Æthelfrith in battle, relying in part on troops put at his disposal by Rædwald of East Anglia.[16] Edwin's proposal of marriage in 625 to Æthelburh, sister of King Eadbald of Kent and daughter of that King Æthelbert who had converted on the arrival of Augustine, brought the missionary bishop Paulinus from Canterbury to the Northumbrian court as chaplain to the Christian princess and her entourage. By 627 Paulinus had convinced Edwin and his court that conversion was to their benefit. The decision was signaled by the sensational moment, famous in Bede's otherwise staid narrative, when Coifi, pagan high priest of the court, cursed his own altars and broke his vows of priesthood by riding a horse up to the temple gates and casting a spear through them.[17] The king and his court were baptized at York on Easter Day, 12 April 627, in the church of Saint Peter the Apostle, "which [the king] had hastily built of wood while he was a catechumen and under instruction before he received baptism."[18]

Edwin's reign was seventeen years long and relatively prosperous. Edwin was high king of the heptarchy as had been the formidable Rædwald, and was the first Northumbrian to claim that honor. Bede tells us that in Edwin's day the realm was so secure that a woman could travel alone and unmolested across the breadth of northern England, and that brass dippers, hung at springs for the use of thirsty travelers, were left unstolen.[19] However, in 638 a Welsh chieftain, Caedwalla, formed an alliance with Penda of Mercia against the spreading political hegemony of the Northumbrians, met Edwin in battle at Hatfield near Doncaster, killed him and one of his sons, and routed their army. Edwin's peace was shattered as Penda and Caedwalla slew and pillaged their way across the land. Paulinus fled with the queen to Kent and was subsequently appointed bishop of Rochester; meanwhile, only a deacon, James, was left in charge of the converts of the Roman Church in the north. Secular rule passed to the claimants of the two rival Northumbrian dynasties: Osric, Edwin's nephew, reigned in Deira, and Eadfrith, Æthelfrith's son, regained Bernicia for his house. These kings immediately renounced Christianity and reverted to ancient Anglian forms of paganism. Both were eradicated by Caedwalla within a year of assuming their separate thrones, an event that Bede construes as divine justice.[20] There followed a brief interregnum during which Caedwalla dominated the area by force and plundered the land repeatedly. Finally Eadfrith's brother Oswald, a devout Christian, succeeded in defeating Caedwalla at Heavenfield in 634.

Oswald, the second Northumbrian high king, wished that the realm as a whole might once again become Christian. However, rather than sending to Canterbury for a bishop and a staffed mission, Oswald chose instead to send to the outpost of the Irish Church at Iona, for as Bede tells us, he had himself become a Christian through his contact with the faith during his exile among the Dalriada Scots, who were under the spiritual tutelage of Iona.[21] This monastery had been founded on an island off the west coast of Scotland in 565 by Saint Columba, both as part of his system of monastic centers in Ireland and as a base of missionary activity primarily among the Picts.[22]

The Irish Church was fundamentally different from the Roman Church in several important matters of structure and practice. Most significantly, it was primarily monastic in organization, whereas the Roman Church was episcopal. This proclivity for monasticism dated from the foundation of the Irish Church. Ireland was converted largely by clergy from Lérins and other communities in southern Gaul and the Mediterranean littoral where the rule of monastic life was derived from the ascetic houses of Christian Egypt.[23] The Irish were aware of the ultimately Coptic origins of their monastic Christianity, as is evident from a quatrain in the poem on the rule of Bangor, copied into the *Antiphonary of Bangor* (Milan, Ambrosian Library, MS C.5 inf.):

> Domus deliciis plena,
> Super petram constructa;
> Necnon vinea vera
> Ex Aegypto transducta.[24]

Saint Patrick, traditionally considered responsible for the conversion of the Irish, was not the source for this particular bent of the Irish Church.[25] Patrick was probably trained in Gaul, and his church in Ireland was at first diocesan, in imitation of the Gallic Church.[26] Moreover, his writings are wholly Roman in style; the *Confession* and the *Letter to Coroticus* are written with all the literary conceits of the Late Antique world rather than in the stark style of the Egyptian Fathers.[27] His successors in the evangelization of Ireland, however, were adherents of the ascetic monastic practices of Lérins and similar houses. These strongholds of Egyptian monasticism were developing in fifth-century Gaul in the period of missionary activity in Ireland, and their patterns of practice took hold in Ireland as well.

How or exactly when this turnabout in the focus of the Irish Church took place remains unknown. Ireland lacked the established secular system of diocesan organization, available in areas formerly part of the Roman Empire, as a foundation for ecclesiastic structure and geographic subdivision. Secular rule was based on ancient tribal and clan groupings, controlled by a hierarchy of kings with varying degrees of political power and control. Perhaps the *paruchia*, a hierarchic and interlocking system of monastic houses, was preferred over the Roman diocese because of its similarities to the secular power structure. It has been suggested that the Church imitated a secular system of interlocking clans and tribal groups, so that an individual leaving the temporal world for the service of the Church would find his new environment comfortingly similar in structure to his former society, on which he abandoned all claims of kinship, loyalty, and legal and social support.[28] Moreover, as churchmen evangelized individual small kingdoms, it was most logical to establish separate monastic centers in each, with land grants from the local monarch. Eventually monastic systems involving several houses would spread over considerable areas, providing an ecclesiastical system of authority and support functionally similar to the diocesan system in use elsewhere.

In spite of the partial continuity of trade in the post-Roman period, Ireland was sufficiently isolated that organizational conformity to the established Roman system was not inevitable. Bishops were ordained in Ireland to supervise the clergy ministering to the laity, but they were either identical or subservient to the abbot of the leading monastic establishment in their region.[29] When the Irish and the Roman Churches encountered one another in seventh-century Northumbria, this difference of structure generated problems of precedence of authority. In an area with both a bishop appointed by the Roman Church and an abbot of the Irish Church in charge of a substantial monastic *paruchia*, it was debatable who should have final say in issues of policy and church practice and represent the authority of the Christian faith to the secular ruler and his people.[30]

Despite the confrontation inherent in their structural differences, overt conflict in Northumbria between the monastic Irish Church and the episcopal Roman Church evolved primarily around issues of practice. Due to its relative isolation, the Irish Church used a different method of calculating the date of Easter than was used by contemporary Rome and her affiliated Churches. Bede tells us that this particular "Irish heresy" was shared by the British bishops who confronted Saint Augustine at Bangor-is Coed in 603, and was practiced in Wales in Bede's own time.[31]

Bede errs consistently in referring to the Celtic heresy concerning the date of Easter as Quartodeciman. The Quartodeciman heresy flourished in Asia Minor in the second century and was condemned by the Council of Nicaea. The Quartodecimans held that Easter should be celebrated on the fourteenth day of the Hebrew month of Nisan, regardless of the day of the week, to coincide with Passover, in accordance with the Gospel of Saint John (13:1). The Celtic dating of Easter was based on a different heterodox logic. The Celtic Church insisted, like the Church of Rome, that Easter begin on the Sabbath eve. However, the appropriate Sabbath for the Celtic Church was that falling between the fourteenth and the twentieth day of Nisan, in accordance with the calculations of the pre-Nicaean chronologer Anatolius of Laodicea. The Roman Church, on the other hand, had severed its connections with Judaism in accordance with the decisions of Nicaea, and celebrated Easter beginning on the Sabbath evening that fell between 15 and 21 Nisan, basing this computation on Victorinus of Aquitaine.[32] As a result of this difference in practice, it was possible that Easter in Northumbria might be celebrated on two consecutive Sundays, each vehemently preferred by the adherents of one Church or the other. This division became conspicuous in the secular court of Northumbria about 650, where King Oswy, Oswald's brother and successor, adhered to the Irish Easter through the authority of Lindisfarne, the missionary outpost established from Iona at Oswald's request.[33] Oswy's queen, Eadfled, on the other hand, was the daughter of Edwin and had been brought up under the tutelage of Paulinus and later of the clergy of Canterbury. She was thus accustomed to the practices of Rome, and continued these usages under the direction of her aptly named chaplain, Romanus.[34] Bede explicitly tells us that much confusion resulted at court when Easter was kept twice, under which circumstances the king would be feasting in celebration of the Resurrection while the queen would still be observing the Lenten fasts on what she considered Palm Sunday.[35] The difference between the two Churches concerning the calculation of the date of Easter became the *cause de guerre* over which the deeper issue of precedence in authority was finally fought out in 664 at the Synod of Whitby.

An additional difference between the Celtic and the Roman Church was the manner of the clerical tonsure. The Roman tonsure involved the shaving of a round area at the crown of the head. Clerics of the Celtic Church, adhering perhaps to Egyptian precedent, shaved a frontal rectangular section of the head from ear to ear. Examples of Celtic tonsure can be seen in some Irish and Anglo-Irish manuscript illuminations.[36] This variation seems not to have inflamed the more zealous adherents of each party nearly so much as the Easter issue, as it was more a question of clerical practice rather than of dogma concerning the Church's most holy feast. Contemporary sources on the Roman side mention this difference parenthetically, usually in conjunction with the Easter question, to emphasize by its addition the distance of the Irish Church from orthodoxy.[37] The letter from Ceolfrith, abbot of Jarrow, to King Nechtan of the Picts refers to the Celtic tonsure as that of Simon Magus, cast down from his prideful perch by the Roman Saint Peter, who is the source of the Roman tonsure, resembling his martyr's crown. This may be a purely symbolic association, as there is no description of the tonsure of Simon Magus in Scripture or hagiography.[38] Leslie Hardinge has suggested that the Irish clerical tonsure is derived from that of Celtic druids; hence the association with the Magi of Persia as pagan priests, and Ceolfrith's reference to Simon Magus.[39]

The Irish Church may not have conformed to Roman orthodox usage in several other aspects of practice, possibly lingering elements of Egyptian or

Antonian usage in the Celtic Church. One possible Egyptian element in the *Antiphonary of Bangor*, written between 680 and 691, is a reference to a vigil on Saturday nights before Sunday services.[40] This source was written, however, after Bangor had conformed to Roman usage, and a direct reference to Coptic practice is difficult to prove. It may also be that the practice was isolated at Bangor and not part of general Celtic ritual. It would also be very odd—were the Celtic Church widely practicing nonconforming Egyptian rites or celebrating the Mass irregularly—that the major writers for the Roman cause—Bede, Aldhelm of Malmesbury, and Archbishop Theodore of Canterbury—never mention or attempt to confute this lack of orthodoxy along with the Easter and tonsure issues.[41]

Certain other variations of practice persisted in Ireland as in other remote Christian areas, but these did not draw the hostile attention of Rome. For example, the rite of pedilavium, the washing of the feet of the catechumens before baptism by the officiating bishop and his staff, continued in this period in Ireland, although it had long faded from Roman use. Outlawed by the Synod of Elvira in 306, pedilavium had nonetheless persisted in major Christian centers to the end of the fourth century. Saint Ambrose of Milan discarded it only because the large numbers of catechumens made the rite unwieldy.[42] Pedilavium was only one of several variances in church practice historically preserved or maintained in Ireland. Some Celtic centers celebrated the Sabbath on Saturday rather than on Sunday, or excluded Sundays from the Lenten fast. Similarly, differences in the ordo of the Mass developed in Ireland as they had earlier elsewhere due to eclecticism in date and orthodoxy of available sources.[43] These variations were perhaps tolerated because similar variations in practice had been common in the orthodox Church in earlier times and in remote places. Certainly they were not brought under the same scrutiny as the issue of the date of Easter, which as the single most significant feast of Christianity became a focal point of Christian unity and continuity, and the tonsure, which as an issue may have been construed to be symbolic of the separation of and formal difference in power structure between the Roman and Celtic Churches.

To some Irish clergy, maintenance of the unusual usages of the Irish Church had become a matter of pride, and differences with Rome the mutual testing of equals. Columbanus, the early missionary to the Continent in the late sixth and early seventh century, twice wrote to Rome concerning the Easter issue. His first letter, to Gregory the Great, noted that Saint Jerome himself had approved of the Anatoline *computatio,* and audaciously inquired whether the pope opposed himself to a saint and Church Father in condemning the Irish dating of Easter on doctrinal grounds. Later, in a more conciliatory tone, he addressed Gregory's as yet unknown successor during a papal interregnum. Changing the direction of his argument, he now inquired whether the new pope would consider assisting him in opposing the Frankish bishops who wished to impose the Roman Easter on Luxeuil, since the choice in dating methods was one of custom and discipline rather than one of doctrine.[44]

Elsewhere, however, the Irish clergy was not so stubbornly set in its ways. The Irish Church had already made several attempts at reconciliation with Rome by the time of the Synod of Whitby in 664. In 629 a synod was held at Maghlene, near Tullamore in southern Ireland, in response to a letter from Pope Honorius in 628, wherein he exhorted the Irish to conform to the Roman Easter, as in their small number and remote location they were unlikely to possess a wisdom above all other churches concerning computation of the universal feast.[45] Cummian, abbot of Durrow, a leading advocate of conformity, promoted the synod. As the attending bishops and abbots could reach no consensus on the matter, it was decided to send a delegation to Rome. The delegation returned after three years, and another synod was convened at Whitefield near Carlow. Cummian and Laserian, abbot of Leighlin, were spokesmen for Rome, opposed by Fintan of Ulster, who stood for the old ways of the Celtic Church. In a letter of 633 to his superior, Seghene of Iona, Cummian explained his preferences in precisely the terms of Honorius's encyclical:

> What can be worse for Mother Church than to say: Rome is mistaken, Jerusalem is mistaken, Alexandria is mistaken, Antioch is mistaken, all the world is mistaken; the Scots and Britains alone have sound wisdom?[46]

By 636 the southern Irish had conformed. The northern Irish, however, were more adamant in their ways. A second papal letter, from John IV in 640, failed to move them. Some headway was made at the Synod of Tars in 697, but it was not until Adamnan, abbot of Iona, came into extensive contact with Roman practice at the Northumbrian court about 703 that the northern Irish were convinced by his admonishments of the necessity of conformity. However, Adamnan failed to convince his own house, and Iona did not accept Roman usage until 716 at the preaching of Egbert, an Englishman who had studied in Ireland.[47] Even at this point, however, there continued to be a sizable dissenting faction in the Celtic Church. At Iona, there were for a while two rival abbots, each leading a faction.[48]

Bede informs us that the Roman Church, concerned for orthodoxy and uniformity of practice throughout Christendom—and the concomittant primacy of Rome—pressed its suit against the dissident Celtic Church from the very outset of contact. In 603 Augustine, established in Saxon Kent for some six years, summoned a synod, the Synod of Augustine's Oak, of British clergy to attempt to convince them of the necessity for conformity. According to Bede, they were at first prepared to accept his message, if he should prove a truly humble messenger for Christ, according to the advice of Abbot Dinoot of Bangor-is-Coed. However, Augustine chose to remain seated as they approached, which they interpreted as a gesture appropriate to a superior individual receiving supplicants. One wonders, considering Augustine's haughty tone in the subsequent dialogue, whether he, too, was aware of the implications of his posture and was attempting to use it to his political advantage. Bede, however, who records this entire encounter, was a monk of romanized Jarrow and was himself a computist firmly on the Roman side in the Easter question. He treats the gesture as inadvertent, and the reluctance of the British to submit on that basis as a feeble excuse for their obstinacy in error.[49] Augustine's successor in the archepiscopacy of Canterbury was Lawrence, who attempted to convince the Irish as well as the Britons of the necessity for orthodoxy.[50] The Irish proved as intractable in 605 as did their colleagues in Wales; a visiting delegation led by Bishop Dagan refused to share meals with the clergy of Canterbury, and the Britons likewise showed no further interest in the question. In Lawrence's day, however, there was widespread apostasy among the Anglo-Saxons, and the Roman Church quickly turned to the more important matter of the reintroduction of Christianity in the royal houses of Kent and Essex.[51]

The Easter issue emerged forcibly into the light of Northumbrian politics during the reign of Oswy. Oswy, like his brother and predecessor, Oswald, was a convert of the Irish Church based at Iona. The Irish had been widely successful in evangelizing the north and particularly the royal household of Northumbria, due in large part to the saintly character and forceful personality of Aidan, founder of Lindisfarne.[52] Aidan was succeeded at Lindisfarne by the Irish-born and -trained Finan, whose adherence to the Irish viewpoint in the Easter question showed him to be as obstinate as his predecessor had been holy.[53] He rapidly found an equally zealous opponent in Ronan, an Irishman who had been trained in Gaul and Rome, and the disputes between these two brought the issue into open contention. Other champions of the Roman Easter came to the fore in this period as well, most notably James, the deacon who had been left behind at York to care for the faithful when Paulinus abandoned the north after the death of Edwin in 633.[54] The situation was further aggravated by the polarization of practice within the royal household between Oswy and his queen Eadfled. This not only generated political and domestic tension, but, more critically, might have led the recently converted lay population of the kingdom to doubt the universality of Christian truth.

In 664, during the episcopacy of Finan's successor, Colman of Lindisfarne, a direct confrontation between the Churches finally occurred. A synod was convened at Whitby on the coast of Yorkshire, then the site of a double abbey, Streanaeshalh, founded and ruled by Hilda, niece of King Edwin. The Celtic Church was represented by Oswy, Colman, Hilda, and Cedd, a Celtic monk who had been instrumental in the conversion of Mercia and Essex in 653 and founder of the abbey of Lastingham in 659. Rome had equally formidable representatives. Preeminent in ecclesiastical rank among these was Bishop Agilbert of the West Saxons, born in Gaul and trained in Rome, one of the leading prelates of his day.[55] Present as Agilbert's assistant and translator was a young cleric, Wilfrid, then a comparative unknown, but later to carve a substantial niche for himself in Northumbrian politics and history. Wilfrid had been educated in Gaul by Archbishop Dalfinus of Lyons, and had been to Rome. He was thoroughly aware not only of the ecclesiastical practice and temporal power and wealth of the Roman Church and her leading clerics, but also of the importance of the primacy of Rome as the source of spiritual and political power, knowledge that he put to good use later in his career.[56] Alchfrith, Oswy's son and underking of Deira, was present at his father's side, but represented the cause of Rome as well. Alchfrith had been instructed in Roman Christianity by Wilfrid and had subsequently taken him under his protection and had given him the monastery of Ripon, evicting the Celtic monks who had previously held it, which must have been a considerable political embarrassment for Oswy.[57] The final addition to the Roman contingent at Whitby was the elderly deacon, James, who may have represented the queen. Bede provides us with the substantive part of the discussion. Essentially, after discussion of differences in *computatio*, Wilfrid, as spokesman for Agilbert's faction, invoked the primacy of the Petrine donation and of Roman authority. Oswy acquiesced to this argument, in his own words, lest Peter, as the keeper of the keys, turn him away from the heavenly gates.[58]

Whether Oswy's turnabout was purely a matter of faith, after he had adamantly supported the Celtic Church for many years, is open to question. The initiative for the synod may have been Alchfrith's, as an attempt to further political ends. Oswy's tolerance of the diversity of practice in his own court does not hint of a desire for a final resolution of the issues. Oswy's sudden change of heart was most probably due more to a desire to preempt his son at backing the obviously more powerful faction. Alchfrith had perhaps thought to replace Colman of Lindisfarne with a bishop of his own choosing—a Roman, closer to himself than to Oswy—just as he had replaced the community at Ripon.[59] It has been speculated that Alchfrith's disappearance from Bede's *Ecclesiastical History* within two years after the synod may indicate an attempted rebellion against his father.[60]

Whatever the motivations for Oswy's decision, however, the dictates of the synod began almost immediately to transform the ecclesiastical power structure in Northumbria. Colman of Lindisfarne, with those Irish and English monks of his community who preferred Celtic practice, left Lindisfarne voluntarily rather than conform to Roman usage. He went to Ireland, where he established a community on the remote island of Inishboffin, off the coast of Mayo. He was replaced as abbot of Lindisfarne by Eata, an Englishman trained by Aidan but now scrupulously Roman in orientation. Eata, however, was elevated to the abbacy without the heretofore corollary elevation to the bishopric. Since Aidan's time, the offices of abbot of Lindisfarne and bishop of Northumbria had been held conjointly by one individual, in accordance with Celtic practice. It was now decided in light of the Whitby decision to divide the authority between two individuals. Tuda, conforming to Rome in tonsure and practice, assumed the office of bishop. His appointment was satisfactory to all concerned, but his reign was cut short by his sudden death a year later in 665. At this juncture, Alchfrith assumed the authority of appointing a bishop, although this was not strictly in keeping with his position as underking. Bede suggests that he meant only to appoint a bishop for Deira, but as the diocesan center for all Northumbria had at this point been shifted to York, the appointment was actually in Oswy's jurisdiction.[61] To what extent this act was a further power play on Alchfrith's part is difficult to determine. However, as previously mentioned, shortly after this point Alchfrith is believed to have had a serious falling-out with his father and disappears from Bede's record and presumably also from the throne of Deira.

Oswy, under whose jurisdiction the appointment properly fell, also named a bishop to the vacant see. While Alchfrith sent Wilfrid to Gaul to be consecrated by Agilbert, who had in the interim become bishop of Paris, Oswy sent to Canterbury, for the same purpose an Irish-trained priest named Chad, brother to the Cedd of Celtic sympathies at Whitby. It appears that in this case at least, Oswy had not completely abandoned the Celtic faction in Northumbria, which had conformed in large part to Roman usage since Whitby. On his arrival in Canterbury, however, Chad discovered that Archbishop Deusdedit had died and had not yet been replaced. Chad and his companions, determined not to return to Northumbria without complying with Oswy's orders, went to Wessex, where Chad was confirmed with the assistance of two nonconforming bishops, presumably from Wales or Cornwall. This was probably not a deliberate contravening of Whitby, despite the suggestion by Wilfrid's biographer Eddius Stephanus that this irregularity was the result of either deliberate ignorance or envy on the part of Oswy, who thus allowed a "Quartodeciman" plot to gain control of the situation.[62] Bede tells us, however, that at this time Wini of the West Saxons was the only canonically consecrated bishop in England.[63] It was against ordinary church practice to permit one bishop alone to consecrate another; ordinarily three or four bishops were required to be present, as Gregory the Great explains in his letter to Augustine.[64] Hence the participation of the British bishops was necessary. The unusual cooperation of the latter is nonetheless astonishing and certainly may be construed as having had political overtones from their viewpoint.

Eddius tells us that when the duplication of consecration was discovered, Wilfrid retired to his monastery at Ripon while Chad ruled at York. Eddius exaggerates drastically when he refers to Chad as "one bishop, like a thief, grabbing another's diocese," but this overstatement certainly indicates the depth of feelings involved.[65]

Wighard, the successor to Deusdedit, was meanwhile appointed by Oswy and Egbert of Kent and was sent from Canterbury to Rome for consecration as archbishop. He died in Rome, however, before the consecration could take place. In his place, Pope Vitalian chose his own successor to Deusdedit, a candidate whose authority might put an end to the divisive arguments of the English. He appointed Theodore, a native of Tarsus in Cilicia, a venerable churchman and scholar. Vitalian also appointed Hadrian, abbot of Niridano in Campania, to accompany Theodore and assist him, as Hadrian had traveled extensively in Gaul on papal missions and, unlike Theodore, was familiar with northern customs. Moreover, as Theodore was a product of the eastern Mediterranean in religious background and training, Vitalian wanted Hadrian, a confirmed servant of Rome, to prevent the introduction by Theodore of any Eastern inorthodoxies into an already volatile area of Christendom in which heresies seemed to flourish.[66] There were several long delays in Theodore's journey to England; even his initial consecration was held up by the necessity of allowing his Greek Pauline tonsure to grow out so that he might be shorn in the Roman orthodox manner. His arrival in Canterbury in the spring of 669 brought order at last to the churches of the English.

Theodore first reconsecrated Chad according to canonical rites, although he retired him temporarily to Lastingham to allow Wilfrid the see of York. Meanwhile, the see of Mercia had fallen vacant, a position to which King Wulfhere had, according to Eddius, unsuccessfully invited Wilfrid.[67] Theodore eventually appointed Chad to this vacancy, and the latter soon found himself also in the graces of Wulfhere, receiving a land grant for a substantial monastic establishment.

Bede extensively describes the modesty, faith, and piety of Chad, his willingness to resign his office at the first hint of inorthodoxy, and his personal asceticism. Bede also commends Chad on the orthodox regularity of his house at At-Barwe.[68] This is scarcely the profile of a man who would plot with alleged Quartodecimans, or "grab" a crust of bread, let alone a diocese, from anyone. The ill feelings seem to have originated in Wilfrid's circle of friends and supporters, and to have been documented in hard words by his biographer Eddius alone.[69] Wilfrid's subsequent political struggles within the ecclesiastical hierarchy, and his later journeys to Rome to obtain papal authority to retain his see against the will of his fellow English bishops, suggest that he, not Chad, was a man of contentious character, who had moreover held himself in opposition to all things and persons even vaguely Celtic since Whitby. Eddius's hostile attitude toward Chad, who, although orthodox in practice was Celtic in origin and education, may be a reflection of Wilfrid's own sentiments. Eddius himself, however, also was personally involved in the politics of the epoch. He had come to the north from Kent in 669 primarily as a choirmaster, on Wilfrid's invitation, to teach the chants of the Roman Church in Northumbria, but was probably selected because of his adamant stance on orthodoxy, as Bede puts it, "to introduce the Catholic way of life to the English churchs."[70] By the time he wrote Wilfrid's *Vita*, after the latter's death in 709, Eddius had spent a lifetime in Northumbria, probably confronting the remnants of the Celtic heresy. Moreover, Eddius was loyal to the point of fanaticism to Wilfrid. In his text, kings of Northumbria who opposed Wilfrid met their ends not in the course of nature but as divine retribution for obstructing the path of a saint.[71] Hence, both Wilfrid's opposition to the Celtic Church at Whitby and the quandry over the diocese of York gave Eddius justification to heap abuse on the relatively innocent Chad.

It may well be asked how much importance should be given to the attitude of one man and his circle of friends and followers concerning the two-Churches controversy. Elsewhere in Northumbria, toward the end of the seventh century, the relationships between centers and groups of differing orientation were certainly less acrimonious, particularly as the issue gradually became a question of origins rather than of current practice. Lindisfarne, Aidan's Celtic foundation, for example, became especially closely linked to Jarrow, the foundation of Benedict Biscop, which was from its origin completely Roman in orientation.[72] The extensive connections between these two centers is evident in the connections between their respective manuscripts.[73]

Elsewhere, however, matters were not so benignly worked out. Theodore of Tarsus, on his arrival in 669, found it necessary to use forceful measures to quell the remnants of the Celtic heresy. Despite the direct and immediate effects of Whitby on the central Celtic house at Lindisfarne, it must be remembered that the Picts and Scots, including at this point the Columban motherhouse at Iona, remained unwilling to accept Roman orthodoxy. Theodore's *Penitential* clearly announced his view on the issues.[74] He recognized neither episcopal consecration nor baptism as performed by the Celtic Church. Eddius tells us that he insisted on reconsecrating Chad, "through every episcopal grade," and demanded the rebaptism of the converts of the Celtic Church.[75] He also ordered a year's penance for anyone receiving communion from Celtic clerics. The hostility along the Welsh and Cornish borders was apparently mutual. Aldhelm of Malmesbury wrote that the Welsh bishops considered the clergy of Rome to be excommunicated until they should individually perform forty days penance, and refused to pray with them or join them at meals. The leftovers of food touched by Roman clerics were ordered thrown to swine so that Celtic Christians would not suffer spiritual contagion. Their vessels were to be purified with fire or sand, and they were to receive neither salutation nor the kiss of peace.[76] Apparently the British had not forgotten the lessons of Augustine's Oak. It was not until 768 that the southern Welsh Christians of Somerset, Devon, and Cornwall accepted the Roman Easter; and not until 777 that Elbodus, bishop of Bangor, succeeded in bringing the northern Welsh into conformity on the Easter question.[77] Other inorthodoxies lingered much later into history; in 1142 Malachy O'Morgair, abbot of Bangor and coarb of Comgal, had to enforce the Roman canonical hours on his uncooperative flock.[78]

In Rome, on the other hand, the Celtic anomalies were considered a full-fledged heresy into the seventeenth century, when Caesar Cardinal Baronius, Vatican Librarian, in describing the work of Augustine's successor Lawrence, tells how the latter, "labored with might and main for the purpose of extricating the Britons and Scots from their schism and reconciling them to the Catholic Church."[79] The durability of such ill feeling is a reflection of the harshness of the tactics of the earlier period. Certainly the forcible eviction of the Celtic Church from Scotland in 717 by the Pictish King Nechtan, at the suggestion of Ceolfrith of Jarrow, was not so gentle as Colman's voluntary self-removal from Lindisfarne.[80] Such strong-arm actions must have had their political and emotional repercussions elsewhere, even in centers now Celtic only in origin.[81]

Thus the political history of Northumbria, most particularly the dynastic struggles of Deira and Bernicia, resulted in the parallel and almost simultaneous introduction of the Irish and Roman Churches. Because of fundamental differences in ideology and practice, which prevented the successful combination of the two Churches under the aegis of one ecclesiastical power structure, confrontation became inevitable. The resultant conflict was not easily and permanently resolved by the formal process of the Synod of Whitby, which, although outwardly presenting a resolution to the Easter controversy by the determination of Oswy for the Roman Church, served rather to polarize the factions more clearly by giving one group the authority to extirpate the other. The animosity of Wilfrid's circle concerning Chad, and the ongoing resistance of Iona and of the Celtic Church in Pictland, Wales, and Cornwall to conformity, indicate the strength of the feelings involved. It was probably this intensity of emotion that drew the attention of Pope Vitalian to the crisis and indicated to him that the heresy of the Celts was of sufficient gravity to require outside intervention. His remedy was the appointment of a foreign archbishop to act as disciplinarian and anchor of authority for the Churches of the English. Plainly the issue was not minor, and might be expected to find its clear reflection in several facets of Northumbrian culture in the conversion period. To some extent, one may therefore expect to see the reflection of ecclesiastical politics in art—particularly the art of the religious centers. However, the correspondences are nowhere entirely obvious. Although newly imported Mediterranean models for art were in almost all cases correctly or otherwise identified with Rome and her Church, their use is not limited to romanized centers, and response (if any) to their political content (if any) is very subtle and difficult to trace. Nonetheless, the Easter controversy was the major political event in the history of early Northumbrian Christianity. Consequently, its effects should be evident in the development of the art of the Northumbrian Renaissance.

Art in the Early Celtic Church: The *Book of Durrow* and Its Context

THE EARLY CELTIC CHURCH in Ireland and in England provided a unique context for the development of art. Before contact was made with the Anglo-Saxons, through either trade or evangelical missions, this art had established a character of its own, a fusion of the pre-Christian secular crafts of the Celtic peoples and the Mediterranean heritage of media and imagery that was the artistic vocabulary of the Christian Church. When the Celtic Church came to Northumbria, the style and technique of its artistic products were also imported and became a major contributing factor in the development of Northumbrian art.

Celtic Monastic Plans and Architecture

By the sixth century (the probable date of the earliest substantial archaeological remains of Celtic Christian life), the Church in Ireland and Britain was profoundly monastic in structure and practice. The monasteries of the Celtic Church emulated the ascetic communities of Gaul, such as Tours and Lérins, which derived their own practices from the foundations of the Desert Fathers of Egypt. From the Celtic monasteries, the faith spread along the Irish and British coasts of the western Irish Sea, along trade routes already established in Roman and earlier times.[1] Wherever they went, the Celtic missionary monks established monastic communities as bases of evangelical operations. These monasteries basically copied the monastic centers of contemporary Ireland.

The popular image of early Celtic monasteries has generally been formed from a touristic appreciation of the more spectacular sites. It is indeed true that some sites, such as Skellig Michael, off the coast of county Kerry, or Colman's Inishboffin, off the Connaught shore, cling like stony limpets to the cliffs of the most inhospitable rocks imaginable, their simple dry-corbeled beehive huts exposed to the undeflected, constant battering of the North Atlantic winds. The archaeological and documentary evidence suggests that early Celtic monks used these extreme locations year round, not only in the milder seasons. The rigors to which these spiritual descendants of Saint Anthony and Saint Paul the Hermit subjected themselves in daily life is suggested also by the Irish penitentials, which indicate the severity of discipline in the early Irish Church.[2] These penitentials were designed as handbooks for confessors, prescribing specific penances for particular sins. In the *Penitential* of Cummian, each possible variation of every possible type of sin is discussed. Under the heading of gluttony, for example, the *Penitential* advises that a cleric who gets drunk is to fast forty days on bread and water, but a layman for a week. Moreover, one who incites another to drunkenness is also to fast for a week.[3] The penances are relatively severe, applying to laity as well as to clergy, and confirm the ascetic image of the Celtic Church in Ireland.

The Celtic Church, however, had another aspect that contributed substantially to the development of early Christian art in Ireland—royal patronage. Ireland was in this period subdivided into small and relatively autonomous kingdoms. The kings of these local units were the primary patrons of the religious establishments within their territory. This relationship between secular and religious authorities apparently descended from pre-Christian practice throughout the Celtic world. In the pagan period, the secular ruler provided for the temporal needs of the religious community, in response to which the latter provided a variety of spiritual and ritual services for the king and his people.[4] Much of this rapport was simply transferred to the Christian abbeys. It was not until the ninth century that Christian priests were relieved of the legal responsibility of accompanying their king to war, as Tacitus describes of the druids.[5] The tradition was so deeply embedded, however, that in one known case at least a Christian manuscript was consistently carried into battle as a token of divine grace. The famous *Cathach of Saint Columba* takes its name from this practice; *cathach* literally means "battler," and the codex was used for this purpose by the O'Donnell clan over several centuries.[6]

Not surprisingly, many early Celtic monastic settlements occupied former secular sites—donations of local nobility to the clergy—and followed patterns of former usage in their ground plans. Two forms dominate: the fortified farmstead (or *rath*) and the temporary fortification (or *dun*). *Duns* lack evidence of long-term settlement in premonastic usage and were probably used as shelter for folk and cattle during frequent periods of warfare and cattle raiding. The *dun* and the *rath* had the same primarily defensive plan, consisting of one enclosing circular embankment or a concentric series of them. Moreover, they were generally located on tactically defensible sites, particularly cleared hilltops or peninsulas, descendants in form and function of the great Iron Age hill forts.[7] A classic example is the fort at Cahercommaun, county Clare, although the latter is only semicircular in form, constructed with its back at the top of a steep limestone cliff. An early monastery that follows this plan is Nendrum, county Down, which was a *rath* until the seventh century, when it became a monastery. Nendrum originally maintained the form of the *rath*, a massive circular inner wall and two thinner outer concentric ring ramparts, or *cashels.* At Nendrum the inner wall was eventually demolished to give more space for monastic construction. Similar reuse is evident at Armagh, Kells, and Glendalough. In some cases, monasteries on completely new sites copied the fort plan, partly because of its familiarity, partly for defensive purposes. Some island monasteries follow this pattern as well, despite the naturally defensible nature of their sites. These include Caher Island (county Mayo), Inish Cleraun in Lough Ree, and Inishmurray (county Sligo), where the original rampart, fourteen feet thick, remains largely undisturbed. A plan for the layout of a monastery in the *Book of Mulling*, (Dublin, Trinity College Library, MS 60, A.I.15), shows a similar double ring, which may indicate two concentric ramparts or a single embankment of great thickness.[8]

Of Irish monastic foundations in England, very few survive in the archaeological record. Some sites are known from documentary sources, but the overall material is scanty. Saint Cuthbert's hermitage on Inner Farne near Lindisfarne can be reconstructed, from the description in the *Anonymous Vita,* as a truly Celtic eremitic *refugium* in the tradition of Skellig Michael's limpetlike stone huts.[9] It consisted of an enclosure with an excavated floor and walls of stone and earth so substantial as to be considered a miraculous feat for one man working alone. Within this personal fortress, the saint built an oratory and a small dwelling hut, "from which he could see nothing but the sky above." Either the windows of the hut were placed very high, or else the writer refers to the great height of the enclosure wall. Bede's *Vita* of the saint specifies that no mortar was used; hence the buildings were probably constructed by the Irish dry-corbeling method also seen at Skellig Michael and the Gallerus Oratory.[10] In other respects, however, Cuthbert built according to the traditions of the Anglo-Saxons; both buildings had sunken floors, timber-framed walls, and thatch roofs.[11] Nonetheless, this hermitage is Celtic in form and inspiration: the *rath*-like rampart and the intention of the subjugation of the flesh by spending the Northumbrian winters in such remote, exposed, and lonely circumstances—in the severe tradition of Egypto-Celtic asceticism. The plan resembles other Irish hermitages, such as Duvillaun, county Mayo, or Loher, county Kerry, all of which are designed as miniature versions of the Celtic monastic plan.[12] Other documentary sources mention similar hermitages in England among clergy of Celtic Church background, such as the "small house" Chad built for himself near Lichfield, where he lived out his last years.[13] More eremitic still was the dwelling of Saint John of Beverley near Hexham. Trained by Hilda of Whitby and hence Celtic by inclination, John was elevated to the see of Hexham about 685. Despite the responsibilities of his diocese, John lived whenever possible in an isolated house a mile and a half from the church at

Hexham, a retreat protected from the world by both a thick woods and an enclosing embankment.[14]

A few full-size monasteries in England are also known to have had the Celtic *rath* plan. At Old Melrose, where Saint Cuthbert trained, a rampart protects the neck of the promontory on which the monastery stood, flanked on the remaining three sides by the River Tweed. The choice of site made the circular embankment unnecessary, but the rampart hints at the Celtic tradition. Other Northumbrian sites have yielded little evidence of worth in this context.[15] Most Irish communities known in detail so far are not Northumbrian. Burgh Castle in Suffolk, founded in 663 by the Irishman Fursey, was constructed inside an old Roman fort, a gift from the East Anglian king, Sigbert, with a perimeter wall nine feet thick and an interior complex of wattle-and-daub beehive huts, discovered in Charles Green's 1960 excavations.[16] The continuity here of the Celtic plan is striking despite the ready availability of Roman ruins for materials and foundations and of Saxon models for secular communities. Elsewhere, the Roman fort enclosure was used unaltered, at Cedd's foundation of Saint Peter-on-the-Wall at Bradwell, Essex, and at Reculver, Kent. Abington, Oxfordshire, had a circular stone enclosure 120 feet in diameter, originally built as a perimeter wall and defense for the foundation, although data on its founders are unavailable. Other English sites have rectangular perimeters, notably Saint Benet Hulme and Barnsley, South Yorkshire, both with bank-and-ditch arrangements known from aerial observation. To what extent they derive their plans from Celtic practice is difficult to determine. They could easily be construed as a combination of the defensive *rath* plan and the quadrilateral layout of Continental monasteries. Wimbourne, Dorset, had a very substantial perimeter wall, albeit oblong in plan. Some English sites had perimeter walls of less durable materials, known only through documentary sources. Oundle, Northamptonshire, was enclosed by a circular hedge of thorn bushes.[17]

Other foundations took advantage of naturally defensible and isolated promontories or peninsulars. Selsey in Sussex, and Hartlepool, Old Melrose, and Whitby in Northumbria are typical.[18] To what extent this latter practice may be derivative of the isolation and defensibility of monasteries in Ireland, or simply a matter of defensibility regardless of origin, is difficult to ascertain. Nonetheless, Melrose was a daughterhouse of Iona, and Hartlepool and Whitby were both the foundations of religious Northumbrian noblewomen of Celtic affinities.[19] Thus it remains possible that the selection of sites in these cases may at least in part be due to affiliation or feelings of association with the Celtic Church.

Of these latter houses, Whitby is the best known—excavated and published by Sir Charles Peers and C. A. R. Radford in 1943.[20] Whitby was founded in 657 by Abbess Hilda, a truly remarkable woman related to the Northumbrian royal house, and baptized with King Edwin by Paulinus in 627. Upon entering religious life in 647, she was called by Aidan of Lindisfarne to oversee a small community on the north bank of the Wear.[21] From this charge she was transferred as abbess to Hartlepool before establishing her own foundation at Whitby.

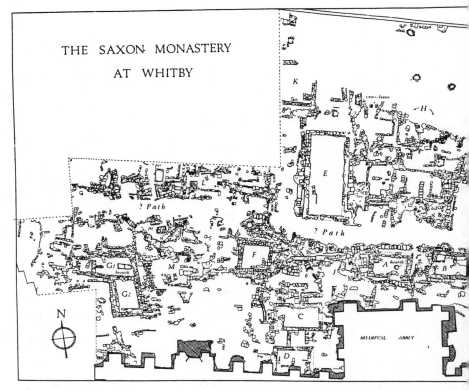

THE SAXON MONASTERY

AT WHITBY

N

Plan of Whitby Abbey *(redrawn by Philip Rahtz after Peers and Radford et al; from R. Cramp, with permission)*

Whitby was founded in accordance with the severe practices of the Celtic Church, as was the current style of Lindisfarne under the rule of Aidan. Bede remarks on the complete absence of private property at Whitby, which was not always the case at Continental monasteries.[22] The relative personal poverty of the monks and nuns of this double foundation did not, however, reflect on the intellectual life of the community. Hilda is most commonly remembered because of the famous men educated at Whitby—five of whom subsequently became bishops and one of whom, John of Beverly, was later canonized. Education at Whitby was however not the exclusive province of the male residents. Possibly on the model of the Continental double monasteries, Hilda extended literacy to women as well.[23] This is confirmed in the archaeological record, for styli were found at Whitby within the same precinct of huts within the monastic perimeter as were the remains of tools of traditionally feminine activities: spindle whorls, sewing needles, and hairpins.[24] This suggests a high level of literacy at Whitby, probably as a result of Hilda's personal inspiration, for Bede tells us she was also highly regarded as a counselor to nobility. It was thus consistent that she and her community were called upon to host the synod

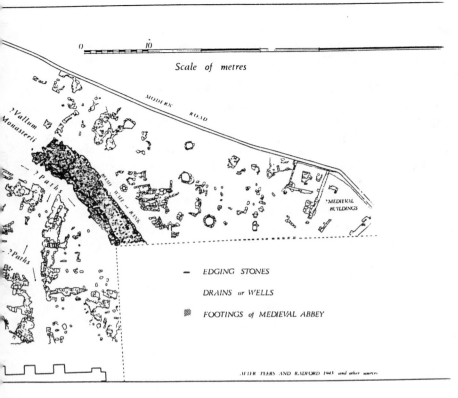

of 664, where she was numbered among the Celtic faction, true to the memory of Aidan of Lindisfarne.[25]

In light of the influence of Whitby as an ecclesiastical and cultural center, and of Hilda's Celtic associations, the findings of Peers and Radford's excavations become relevant to the question of the Celtic monastic plan. The structural remains found at Whitby were remarkably extensive and elaborate, but also badly scattered, so that interpretation of the findings has become somewhat controversial, as in many cases it is difficult to ascertain which rows of stones in the excavation plan are foundation lines and which are the results of the haphazard falling of buildings.[26] The density of the layout of the site also adds to the difficulties of interpreting the plan. Peers and Radford pointed out that no consistent plan was mentioned in early writings concerning Whitby. They suggested an arrangement similar to the monastery at Coldingham, where small individual cells, or *domunculae*, and communal buildings such as dormitories and refectories were clustered around an open space.[27] However, the excavation plan of Whitby shows no plaza, albeit some of the original construction is probably under the remains of the later Norman minster on the site.

In 1958 Philip Rahtz reexcavated Whitby and published a redrawn plan of the site in conjunction with Rosemary Cramp.[28] Cramp, whose excavations of Jarrow and Wearmouth produced evidence of rectilinear arrangements of structures following Continental models, interpreted the evidence from Whitby as showing buildings in rows flanking a major east-west roadway. This interpretation of Continental influence at Whitby was supported by the discovery at the site of large quantities of imported Continental pottery. However, it is difficult to see Cramp's rectilinear arrangement in Rahtz's excavation plan. What seems at first glance to be an east-west path is interrupted by strongly indicated north-south foundations at one point, and by groups of graves on either side of this masonry barrier. The path seems more clear to the east of the foundations and the graves here are also more sparse. The path may thus be interpreted to turn right at the interrupting wall and proceed along the side of the largest early building. This is, however, problematic as the relative ages of the various walls and foundations are difficult to establish. In any case, a clearly rectilinear layout such as Cramp found at Jarrow cannot be rigorously derived from the Whitby excavation plan. The buildings seem not so much to line up in rows as to cluster in blocks.

Modern knowledge of the early abbey at Whitby is incomplete due to the superimposition of the Norman abbey about 1067. Any understanding of the plan is thus likely to be flawed. One fragment, however, strikes a note of indubitable familiarity. To the northeast, along the periphery of the most densely occupied section of the site, is a curving section of an extremely thick, rubble-filled wall. The curve of its foundation suggests that this barrier once separated the monastery from the rest of the headland on which it is situated. The northwestern section of the site overlooks the bay at the mouth of the Esk River from a considerable altitude. Moreover, the western descent to the harbor town of Whitby is precipitous. The town itself is not early, and by imagining it away one may see the clear resemblances of Whitby—cliff site and encircling embankment—to Celtic sites in Ireland and England. At Whitby, these affinities of location and plan occur despite the evidence of strong links of trade to the Continent. These latter connections include not only the presence of imported pottery sequences, but also the elaboration of two of the *domunculae* into two-room bed-sitter arrangements complete with lavatory, and the widespread use of *opus signinum* flooring, both of which suggest the comparative luxury of Continental ecclesiastical life.[29] These connections are probably the result of Hilda's modeling of her community after the great Continental double houses, such as Chelles (where she had wished to study and where her sister resided), of the comparative wealth of the community due to Hilda's royal connections, and of the conformity of Whitby to Roman usage after 664. Nonetheless, Whitby was originally part of the *paruchia* of Iona, through Hilda's mission from Aidan of Lindisfarne. This link may serve to explain why the earliest elements—the choice of site and the use of a protective encircling embankment—are Celtic in flavor, indicating the strength of these traditions even in an otherwise completely Anglian foundation. Perhaps the site plan of

Whitby can thus best be seen as a merging of traditions, a synthesis of Celtic and Continental.

Despite the continuous tradition of monastic ground plans in the Celtic Church, the architecture of Celtic monastic communities varied substantially in Ireland and England, largely through differing degrees of contact with secular Anglo-Saxon and mainstream Christian ecclesiastical architecture. In this period, the Irish had two words denoting "church": *durthech* (a wooden, often oak, church) and *daimlaig* (a stone church) indicating the use of both types of structure.[30] Few ecclesiastical stone buildings survive from the earliest period of the Irish church, and of these the original function is controversial. Some of the dry-corbeled round *clochain*, or beehive, huts at Skellig Michael may have been places of devotion rather than houses, but archaeological investigation has been minimal. Another example is the boat-shaped so-called Gallerus Oratory in county Kerry, possibly a shrine, a hermitage, or a small church for public or monastic use. The oratory is constructed by the dry-corbeling method, but other contemporary constructions, such as the small chapel on Saint MacDara's Island, county Galway, probably use mortar in the core of the walls, and Temple na Skelling at Glendalough, slightly later, is mortar built. The increasing use of mortar, reflecting observation of mainstream European architecture, gradually replaces the dry-corbeling method in all but the most outlying areas of Ireland. However, the forms of the extant buildings—round, boat shaped, or rectangular with ridged roof and antas as at Saint MacDara's Island—show no particular affinities to Continental architecture.[31]

Wooden construction, in documentary sources and in the Irish archaeological record, included wickerwork, or wattles, and joined planks. Wooden structures were more typical of the Celtic Church than stone buildings, for when Bede described the church at Lindisfarne, he said it was "after the Irish method, not of stone but of hewn oak." Roofing was thatch or yew shingles, although these flammable substances were replaced with lead sheeting when financial opportunity arose.[32] Timber construction was also the medium most favored by Anglo-Saxon secular builders. The architectural joinery of the walls at the Northumbrian royal site, Yeavering, indicate the extent of the Angles' mastery of this medium.[33] However, there is no archaeological evidence from Ireland on which to base a comparison of practice. Cogitosus's seventh-century *Life of Saint Brigid* gives a description of the wooden church at Kildare as having had many ornamented windows and a carved doorway. However, this document does not give sufficiently clear information to allow a reconstruction of the building, although it was probably larger and had more and larger windows than the surviving stone buildings of the period.[34]

One form of building that may have carried over from the Irish tradition to Celtic foundations in England is the small rectangular chapel with projecting antas or corner buttresses. These stone buildings are usually small, high, and narrow, rarely over thirty feet in length. They have small, deeply splayed windows and unemphasized post-and-lintel doorways, the lintel sometimes marked with a cross. This formula occurs in Ireland at Saint MacDara's, at Fore, county Kerry, and at Clonamery, county Kilkenny.[35] The same type is seen in slightly larger scale at Cedd's chapel of Saint Peter-on-the-Wall at Bradwell in Esssex, although here, in keeping with southern English practice, an apse with porticus to north and south and a western porch was either included in the original construction or added later.[36] Documentary evidence and archaeological data concerning churches at other Celtic foundations in England are both scarce, and the degree of influence of Ireland on architecture in England is difficult to measure. The general proportions of the small, high-walled, rectangular churches of the north such as Saint John at Escomb, Durham, may be derived from Celtic architecture, but the foundations of these churches are undocumented and their affiliations are unknown.

The Portable Arts in the Celtic Church

The connection between the Celtic Church in Ireland and its offshoots in England is more clearly visible in the portable arts. This is particularly evident in the impact of traditional Celtic metalwork on early manuscript painting in the Anglo-Celtic milieu.

The Celtic metalworking tradition was already more than a millenium old when the Irish became Christians. Metalwork had developed more strongly than any other medium in northern Europe in the migration period because of its portability, its value as a sign of wealth and status, and its easy valuation as gift, bribe, ransom, or indemnity. Utilitarian as well as ceremonial metal objects were commonly ornamented in northern Europe, but the Celts brought this skill to an uncommonly high level of expertise in design and craftsmanship. Celtic techniques included both the addition of ornament in the initial casting of pieces in bronze and other metals, and the later engraving and enameling of the surface of the cast object. The possibilities of enamelwork were greatly extended by the introduction of millefiori, a Mediterranean craft imported through Roman-occupied Britain and quickly adapted by the Celts to their own tastes.[37]

The Celts, like the other tribal groups of northern Europe, were outside the mainstream of the Late Antique world and nonclassical in aesthetic outlook. Their decorative artisans concerned themselves primarily with the decoration of the surface of forms rather than with the forms themselves, demonstrating a preference for additive ornament over integral design. The Celts devised an ornamental vocabulary totally different from that of their Germanic neighbors in that it very rarely utilized human or animal motifs except in ritual contexts.[38] The predominant patterns are geometric even when organic in derivation; the ubiquitous spiral may be derived from a vine motif but lacks shoots, leaves, and fruit. The outwardly purely decorative spiral may have symbolic or metaphysical meaning in certain contexts, as on grave tumulus thresholds, but the motif is also used on utilitarian mirror backs and snaffle bits.[39]

Imported forms were quickly assimilated into Celtic decorative motifs, as for example the Roman *pelta,* or shield, motif, adapted as the enduring double spiral or trumpet.[40] It is unknown how these motifs were imported and where they were first adapted into the native ornamental vocabulary, but the method of their dissemination is evident. Patterns were transmitted between and within workshops by engraving them on slips or fragments of bone, such as those found at Lough Crew, county Meath, and at Lagore Crannog, county Meath.[41]

The Celtic traditions of metalwork and ornamentation were completely developed in the Celtic world before the advent of Christianity. With the conversion of the Celts in Ireland, these traditions continued both in the secular sphere and in the service of the new faith. Christianity brought with it a demand for new applications of metalworking: for plaques for the covers of manuscripts, and for chalices, patens, croziers, and the other paraphernalia of the new faith. As the Church was assimilated into the preexisting political and social structures of Irish culture, traditional motifs and techniques were used for the embellishment of ecclesiastical treasures. Only one factor might have stood in the way of this easy confluence of demand and ability. The Christian Church was essentially Mediterranean and its art figural, whereas Celtic metal-working was abstract. These opposites were reconciled in a unique if somewhat bizarre synthesis, as in the famous bronze Crucifixion plaque from near Athlone, county Westmeath (Dublin, National Museum). Probably originally part of a book cover, the plaque is dominated by the crucified Christ, flanked by the lance and sponge bearers below and by two angels above. The figures are flattened and distorted with large, simple heads facing forward in awkward contrast to profile bodies and grossly out of proportion to the diminutive and minimally indicated limbs. The artist is ill at ease with the image of the human body. However, the crudity of the figures lends them a certain primitive strength, heightened by the concentration of the artist on the ornament that covers the figures. Three trumpet motifs are symmetrically laid out across Christ's chest, his robe is trimmed with three vertical bands of interlace and key patterns, and the hem is edged with two bands of continuous wavelike spirals. These tightly controlled patterns not only draw the eye to the figure but also suggest the power and mystery of Christ. The angels are awash in pattern; triskelions and other complex multiple spiral motifs indicate the junctures of bodies and wings, suggesting swift wind-borne motion or supernatural energy. Thus the figures of the crucified Christ, his tormenters, and the angels—the basic ingredients of the imported model—have been reduced to near hiero-glyphs of human form, overlaid with the ornament of the indigenous Celtic tradition. Yet the resultant combination of aesthetics is not so awkward as one might expect. Instead, the harsh strength of the figures and the self-assured contained power of the ornamental motifs reconfirm the meaning of the model, if not its style. Moreover, if the Celtic copy does not emulate any element of classical naturalism from the model, it does incorporate elements of composition from the model that are more confluent with indigenous aesthetics. Principally these include the initial appearance, if not the absolute fact, of symmetry, and the iconic hierarchy of scale among the figures. This hieratic use

Bronze plaque from Athlone (Westmeath); Dublin, National Museum of Ireland.
(photo: National Museum of Ireland)

of scale parallels Celtic concepts of balance in ornament, where one motif is frequently a central and larger base for the outward radiation of smaller motifs.[42] In the Athlone plaque, Christian symbolism and composition were assimilated with typical ease into Celtic metalwork, even as the Church itself was made part of the culture as a whole.

The Development of Manuscript Illumination

The Christian Church also brought with it a demand for art work in media other than metal, of which the most alien was the writing and ornamentation of manuscripts. Celtic culture had been to this date largely nonliterate.[43] The written word, and the idea of the codex in particular, were basically foreign to Celtic culture. The Church, however, had constant need and use for the written word. Not only were Scripture and commentary vital to the transmission and understanding of the faith, but the codices themselves were part of the paraphernalia of the sacraments. Church tradition also demanded that codices be ornamented.

The study of the development of the earliest Irish illumination is hindered by problems of nonsurvival, and complicated by questions of date and provenance for almost all extant manuscripts. However, surviving examples most probably constitute a cross-section of the work produced and developmental trends can be traced by comparative examination of the extant fragments.

The earliest extant decorated codices of the Celtic Church are linked by their ornament with contemporary developments on the Continent. The majority of these codices have been definitely or speculatively linked with Bobbio, a foundation of the Celtic Church in northern Italy founded by the Irishman Columbanus. Moreover, it is likely that Bobbio, Luxeuil, and other Celtic missionary houses on the Continent served as points of transmission of the medium of manuscript decoration to Celtic craftsmen in Ireland and in northern England.

One manuscript certainly manufactured at Bobbio is a text of Jerome's *Commentary on Isaiah* (Milan, Ambrosian Library, MS S.45.sup.). This volume bears a Bobbio ex libris and number on the third page and a colophon on the second ascribing the manuscript to the hand of Atalanus, Columbanus's successor in the abbacy, who died in 622.[44] The decoration consists of an initial *N* on the second page. The main descender of the initial is elongated and filled with cross-hatchings, terminating at the bottom in a slim bifurcation ending in two abbreviated trumpet motifs. The shorter descender at right is also decorated with cross-hatchings and a single spiral terminus at the right of its base. The crossbar of the *N* is formed of two leaping fish that arch around spirals. The crossbar is also transformed into a cross by a vertical bar at its center, which also terminates in abbreviated trumpets. Above, three crosses trimmed with short curlicues and ending in trumpets are appended to the descenders of the initial at skewed angles, so that they essentially form a string of *X*'s.

Milan, Ambrosian Library, MS S.45 sup., Jerome, *Commentary on Isaiah,* **p. 2: N** *(by permission of the Directors)*

The spirals of this initial remind the observer of Celtic metalwork, but the other elements—the fish and the decorative use of crosses—are to be found in contemporary Italian manuscripts. Despite the subsequent apotheosis of the illuminated initial in insular art, the roots of the decoration of the initial are to be found in Late Antique manuscripts. The decorated hollow shafts of the descenders in this particular initial *N* have their earliest traceable ancestor in the *Vergilius Augusteus* (Rome, Vatican Library, MS Lat. 3256; and Berlin, Staatsbibliothek, Lat. fol. 416), a manuscript usually dated to the fourth century.[45] Here initials are already enlarged, and their hollow shafts are filled with enamel-like multicolor geometric patterns. By the sixth century, elaborated initials are found in both Eastern and Western manuscripts, and animal forms have been introduced. In the East, the most well-known example is the *Vienna Dioscurides* (Vienna, Nationalbibliothek, Med. Grec. 1), written in Constantinople about 512. Here (fols. 10v, 11r) are enlarged initials standing at the center of the column of text, surrounded by red dots, with fish occcasionally forming part of a letter.[46] Western Late Antique initials do not include red dotting, but the West, particularly northern Italy, develops the tradition of animal initials more strongly than the East. The *Codex Valerianus* (Munich, Staatsbibliothek, CLM 6224), probably written in northern Italy in the sixth or seventh century, not only continues the use of the ornamented hollow-shaft descender, but transforms it (fol. 128v) into a column on which birds perch. Elsewhere in the same manuscript, animals not only hover near initials but form parts of them, as for example fish forming the stems of letters (fol. 33v) or birds' heads their terminals (C on fol. 110r).[47] Fish letters are especially popular in Italy in this period.[48] Hence the use of the same motif in the Ambrosian Jerome manuscript from Bobbio cannot be the exclusive result of imported Celtic decorative caprice. Sufficient elements of Roman cursive script also occur in the paleographic analysis of this manuscript that the Bobbio writers and artists must have been familiar with contemporary Italian manuscripts—not surprising, given the location of Bobbio. From Bobbio, Italianate animal motifs in enlarged initials spread northward through Columbanus's other foundations. The earliest dated Luxeuil manuscript, of about 669 (New York, Morgan Library, M. 334), has elaborate initials comprised of fish and birds.[49]

The *Codex Usserianus Primus* (Dublin, Trinity College Library, MS A.4.15) is another early insular manuscript often, but inconclusively, associated with Columbanus's foundations. The fragments of these Gospels retain only one decoration—a cross modified as a Chi-Rho monogram, with appended alpha and omega, in reddish brown ink, framed by the explicit of Luke and the incipit of Mark (fol. 149v). Carl Nordenfalk has noted the similarities, both in form and in placement within the manuscript, between this emblem and crosses found in fifth-century Italian manuscripts such as the *Bologna Lactantius* (Bologna, Biblioteca Università, 701), and the *Paris Saint John* (Paris, Bibliothèque Nationale, Lat. 10439), and also the terminal cross colophon of the *Valerianus Gospels*.[50] These similar illuminations link the *Codex Usserianus Primus* with the northern Italian scriptoria and with Bobbio in particular, which is further borne out by intrusions of Roman cursive similar to those in the Bobbio Jerome in the developing insular script.[51] The codex was consequently probably executed at Bobbio and subsequently migrated to Ireland through the network of Columbanus's foundations, though it may also be an early example of Irish work under strong Continental influence.[52] Although the exact provenance of the *Codex Usserianus Primus* remains controversial, the importance of the Mediterranean prototypes is nonetheless inescapable. The association of this and other early manuscripts with Bobbio indicates the pathway of Italian

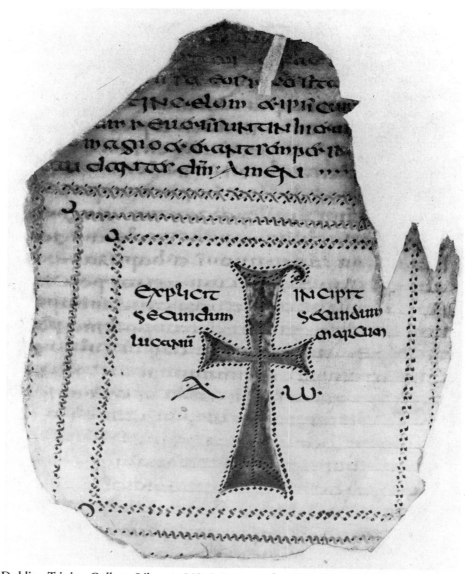

Dublin, Trinity College Library, MS A.4.15., *Codex Usserianus Primus*, fol. 149v: staurogram *(by permission of the Keeper of Manuscripts and the Board of Trinity College, Dublin)*

methods and motifs into what must be called insular art, regardless of the locus of execution.[53] Thus the centers founded by Columbanus on the Continent made a major contribution in the transmission of both the medium and the motifs of book decoration to Irish art. The contributions of other Celtic Continental foundations are more difficult to trace and have not yet been assessed.

The Ambrosian *Chronicon* of Orosius (Milan, Ambrosian Library, D.23.sup.) is more certainly a product of Bobbio.[54] The manuscript is remarkable for the complexity of its decoration, which has given rise to some controversy about its date. I believe, however, that it exemplifies the formative phase of insular illumination at Bobbio, following the Ambrosian Jerome and the *Codex Usserianus Primus* within a generation.

The verso of the opening folio of the *Chronicon* bears a full-page ornamental frontispiece, perhaps the earliest carpet-page in insular art.[55] The central motif is a rosette of eight petals in alternating shades of white and orange, surrounded in the corners by smaller rosettes. The rosette as a motif is very common in Late Antique art, but rare in insular art. Apparently the motif was available at Bobbio for reference in this manuscript, but either not exported to Ireland or not sufficiently popular in insular workshops to have survived in the extant handful of works. The patterned margins of the page are more instructive. A twisted rope or cable pattern, a guilloche, is used—a single thick rope at the left, or outer, edge of the page and two smaller cables separated by a yellow bar at the right, or inner, edge. The guilloche is the simplest and clearest form of interlace. It is commonly found in Mediterranean art, freqently in the borders of Late Antique manuscripts and Coptic textiles.[56] This motif developed simultaneously in several different areas around the borders of the Roman Empire, wherever an interface occurred between classical ornament and the more abstract motifs of nonclassical cultures. In the context of the rosette carpet-page of the *Chronicon*, it may well have been adapted along with the rosette from a single model, probably Mediterranean if not specifically northern Italian in origin.

Ambrosian D.23.sup. also contains some interesting initials. On the recto of the second folio, directly opposite the carpet-page, the opening words of the text, "praeceptis tuis pa[rui]," are significantly enlarged. The opening initial *P* is treated much like the *N* of the Bobbio Jerome. The descender is a hollow shaft, and the base terminates in a cross hatch design and modified trumpet spiral motif. Yet here the descender of the *P* is not merely elongated; it extends down the entire side of the page. Moreover, the following *R* is strangely written at an angle to suggest continuous diminution of scale toward the rest of the top line of letters, which are uniform in size. This may be an early form of insular diminution, where a large and sumptuously decorated initial will be followed by a row of progressively smaller letters. This phenomenon is common in all later insular manuscripts, as in the *Book of Durrow* (Dublin, Trinity College Library, MS 57, A.4.5), for example, the recto of folio 193.[57] In the *Chronicon*, the opening two letters are also sparsely decorated with red dots, possibly from the Byzantine tradition of initial decoration. Red-dot work is common in later insular initial decoration as well.[58] Here again, Bobbio is a possible point of transmission, although exclusivity is not only not provable but not probable.

Of early decorated codices associated with the insular school, none is more certainly executed and decorated in Ireland than the *Cathach of Saint Columba* (Dublin, Royal Irish Academy),[59] traditionally, if improbably, associated with the hand of Columba himself.

Milan, Ambrosian Library, MS D.23. sup., Orosius, *Chronicon*, fol. 1v: frontispiece
(by permission of the Directors)

Milan, Ambrosian Library, MS D.23. sup., fol. 2r: "Praeceptis tuis" *(by permission of the Directors)*

The *Cathach* is a fairly clear member of the Gallican recension of the Hieronymian Psalter; it does not show the use of Old Latin readings seen in later seventh-century Irish texts, such as the *Antiphonary of Bangor* (Milan, Ambrosian Library, MS C.5.inf.). Its proximity to the version of Jerome's text in use on the Continent in the sixth and seventh centuries suggests recent text importation.[60] However, the purity of the text does not give a date for the text's importation or for the manuscript itself, nor is it possible to prove the association of the *Cathach* with Saint Columba, which would give a secure date for the codex. Hence the question of date must be argued in terms of decoration and paleography.[61]

The opening initial to each psalm in the *Cathach* is enlarged and decorated. The initials are executed entirely in black ink, ornamented with reddish orange dots. There is only one zoomorphic initial in the codex, a *Q* (fol. 48r) which includes a fish with a cross above it. The use of red dots, animal forms, and guilloche in initials link this manuscript to the earlier codices associated with Bobbio. However, these imported motifs are here incorporated into illumination that bears for the first time the marks of a developing, distinctly insular, school. The principle of diminution is here becoming standard practice, and often the second and third letters of the sequence are ornamented. Another feature that later becomes an intrinsic part of insular illumination is seen here in nascent form: the distortion of the letters to create decoratively harmonious forms at the expense of legibility. For example, an *M* (fol. 21r) has become an elaborate double spiral.[62] This practice is a distinct departure from previous and contemporary practice elsewhere; decorated initials in Mediterranean manuscripts had always remained true to the original form of the letter. The spiral—the motif most beloved of Irish smiths—now begins to rule the written page as well, and places the codex convincingly in a Celtic milieu. The *Cathach* is part of a second phase of insular illumination. Rather than copying motifs directly from models from other cultures as in contemporary or earlier codices from Bobbio, the artist-scribe of the *Cathach* was willing to adapt these forms to indigenous Celtic taste.[63]

The *Cathach* is generally considered on paleographic grounds to have been executed in Ireland in the late sixth or early seventh century and to represent the earliest form of insular script in Ireland.[64] E. A. Lowe, commenting on the traditional attribution of the codex to Saint Columba, considered that such an early date, of about 560, was "paleographically possible," and that this script was the "pure milk of Irish calligraphy" in its formative stages.[65] However, dated comparative material is lacking, and Lowe's chronology is based on a theoretical regression of insular script to the hagiographically suggested date. Most scholars accept a date in the early 600s.[66] In any case, the manuscript is early, predating the *Book of Durrow* by at least half a century, and is probably the earliest decorated codex of reasonably certain Irish provenance.

The next phase in the development of insular illumination is the addition of bright color and the use of large-scale ornament in an indigenous style. In extant codices, this is first seen in a large fragmentary Gospels codex in

Durham (Cathedral Library, MS A.II.10, fols. 2–5; and MS C.III.13, fols. 192–95). All that remains of this codex is the end of the Gospel of Matthew and the beginning of Mark. The script is a pure Irish majuscule. The text however shows symptoms of derivation from not only the *Codex Usserianus Primus* recension, but also a southern English stemma, which suggests that the text was written in England, but either by an Irish scribe or by an Englishman trained in the methods of the Irish scriptoria.[67] The orthography also shows symptoms of "Irish spelling," of which the opening word of the Gospel of Mark is a startling example: "Initium," has become "Inititium."[68] On paleographic grounds, a date in the early seventh century is now generally accepted; the majuscule is evolving toward the mid-century *Book of Durrow*. The Irish majuscule is subsequently continued and perfected in the Northumbrian schools by the end of the century; the scribes of the Irish scriptoria do not show so high a quality and regularity of penmanship.[69] Durham A.II.10 also contains examples at the end of Matthew of an Irish miniscule of which certain connected letters' forms find parallels in the Echternach manuscripts, which were written either in Northumbria or in a transplanted Northumbrian scriptorium on the Continent.[70] The manuscript is most probably the product of an Irish scriptorium on English soil, perhaps the earliest surviving Irish illuminated manuscript from the missionary foundations of the Celtic Church.[71]

The two surviving ornamented folios of this scattered codex occur in Durham A.II.10, at the juncture of the two Gospels. The end of Matthew (fol. 3v) is marked by three connected D-shaped loops of broad-band interlace, containing the explicit of Matthew, the incipit of Mark, and the Lord's Prayer in Greek, transcribed to Latin letters. The beginning of Mark (fol. 2r) has a large, brightly colored monogram of the letters *INI*. Sadly, this is all the remaining ornament in the manuscript fragments. The codex probably had equally elaborate opening initials for the other Gospels and other framing devices for colophons, dedications, and other explicit-incipit junctions.

The monograph *INI* on the second folio develops further the principles of the initials of the *Cathach*. First, the three letters are fused together; the descenders of the *I*'s are separated from those of the *N* only by very narrow bands of guilloche, in complete disregard for legibility. The descenders terminate in elaborate trumpet spirals and are themselves subdivided into areas of color separated by narrow bands, suggesting at once both the subdivided and crosshatched descenders of initials in the Bobbio manuscripts and bright panels of insular enamelwork. The analogy to metalwork is carried a step further in the use of tiny, light red specks to line some of the rectangles and spirals. These resemble the infinitesimal gold beads used to outline areas of color or filigree in Celtic jewelry, as on the famous Tara Brooch (Dublin, National Museum of Ireland).[72] The crossbar of the *N* on the other hand, formed of two intertwined snakes, shows the impact of contact with Anglo-Saxon art. This interpretation is justified by a comparison to the three interlaced D loops on the verso of the third folio.

Interlace, or knotwork, is a staple motif in Late Antique decorative art.[73]

Durham, Cathedral Library, MS A.II.10, *Gospels,* fol. 3v: end of Matthew, D loops
(by permission of the Dean and Chapter of Durham)

Durham, Cathedral Library, MS A.II.10, fol. 2r *(by permission of the Dean and Chapter of Durham)*

Classical interlace commonly consists of a woven band comprised of a single continuous ribbon, usually arranged in a logical geometric pattern without breaks, and lacking zoomorphic elements. Durham A.II.10 is the earliest insular manuscript to make use of interlace more complex than the simple guilloche of the Bobbio manuscripts. The triple D loops are at first glance a direct borrowing of Late Antique border interlace. However, careful examination reveals progressive deviation from the classical norm. While the interlace here remains purely geometric and nonzoomorphic throughout, there is a progressive breaking up of the strands from the bottom loop upward. The interlace of the lowest loop consists of a single interwoven strand in the classical manner, but the top one is formed of eleven strands, separated by breaks in the pattern.[74] This tendency to use multiple strands and breaks to form more intricate, if less even, knotwork is a late anticlassical development. The same occurs in interlace in Coptic manuscripts.[75] This anticlassical interlace probably did not develop exclusively in Coptic Egypt; it more probably arose simultaneously at several points along the receding borders of the Roman Empire from the contact between late classical ornament and the art of nonclassical peoples. In Durham A.II.10 this evolution can be seen in progress. However, there may have been a foreign model for the A.II.10 D-loop interlace, with breaks and multiple strands already present, as such designs are frequently found in Coptic textiles. Interlace is completely absent from early Celtic metalwork. The earliest dated use is in certain molds for penannular and roundel brooches found at the Mote of Mark in Dumfries, a site dated in the late sixth or early seventh century, late enough for the availability of Coptic models through ecclesiastical channels.[76] The complexity of the interlace in A.II.10, in approximately the same period, also suggests a foreign model, wherein the premise of knotwork with breaks and multiple strands had already been explored. The unusual D-loop design suggests the use of a fabric border, possibly Coptic, as a model.[77] An essentially foreign motif is thus here adapted with ease into an insular manuscript. This indicates both the extent of use of imported models for book decoration in the early Celtic Church, and the familiarity of insular scribes with the process of adapting such models to their own purposes. Such a development is not entirely unexpected, given the extent of trade contact over several centuries between the Mediterranean and the Celtic world. Wide-band interlace continues to develop in the *Book of Durrow*, and on two carved stone crosses in Donegal, at Fahan Mura and at Carndonagh.[78]

The interlace of the D loops of A.II.10 is purely geometric, but in the initial on the second folio, the crossbar of the initial *N* is elaborated into two intertwined snakes. The use of animal forms is completely foreign to Late Antique geometric interlace but is a regular feature of knotwork in Anglo-Saxon metalwork, such as the gold belt buckle from Sutton Hoo. Here no evenly woven or consistently knotted patterns prevail; rather, a mass of serpents twist, tangle, and ferociously bite at one another—a design deriving its aesthetic force from chaotic disorder.[79] The similar snakes in A.II.10 add to the evidence of text and paleography further proof that the manuscript was executed in

Belt buckle, Sutton Hoo; British Museum *(photo: Trustees of the British Museum, by permission)*

England, albeit in a northern center of the Celtic Church. Yet the beasts of A.II.10 are not so disorderly as those of the belt buckle. Instead, they form a clearly planned rhomboidal knot, which indicates, like the D loops of the following folio, a familiarity with Mediterranean knotwork principles. In A.II.10 a relatively early illuminator of the Celtic Church in northern England adeptly combines Celtic spiral, Mediterranean knotwork, and Germanic zoomorphic ornament, all in the space of a single monogram. This creative synthesis of materials from three totally different cultures is perhaps the first signpost on the road to the Northumbrian Renaissance.

The *Book of Durrow*

The *Book of Durrow* (Dublin, Trinity College Library, MS 57, A.4.5.) is the earliest extant truly major illuminated insular manuscript. The codex, a Gospels text, bears a colophon (fol. 247v) in which the scribe of the manuscript asks for prayers for the scribe Columba. The area of the inscription shows signs of erasure and rewriting, and the tradition that the manuscript is by the hand of Saint Columba is extremely dubious; the manuscript may be either a copy of a work by the saint, or a pious forgery.[80] However, the presence of the erasures unfortunately tends to confirm the suspicion of forgery. An inscription including a dedication to Columba was recorded in 1677 on a tenth-century *cumdach*, or ceremonial casing of the codex, but the *cumdach* itself was lost in 1688. The manuscript was at the monastic center of Durrow, county Offaly, at least from the eleventh century forward, but how early the text came to Durrow, or if in fact it originated there is unknown.[81]

The *Book of Durrow* was rebound in 1954 by Roger Powell, but had been rebound at least once previously, at which time all the pages had been cut to single leaves. Powell's examination of the inner edges of the leaves demonstrated, however, that some parts of the manuscript were made up originally from single leaves.[82] Moreover, Powell discovered that the original composition of the manuscript included several defective or patched sheets. These observations suggest that the codex was manufactured under conditions of a shortage of vellum. This is not the case for later products of the insular school, such as the *Book of Kells,* and indicates that the *Book of Durrow* was made in a monastic center without vast resources, where every available calfskin would be processed and every salvageable piece, however small or torn, would be used, despite the apparent importance of the codex.

The *Book of Durrow* has a remarkably pure Vulgate text, purer than that of *Kells* and other late Irish Gospel books, but is not textually derived from the Vulgate stemma introduced to Northumbria at Jarrow and Monkwearmouth.[83] Moreover, *Durrow* shows the Irish tendency to use scattered Old Latin readings within the body of the Vulgate text. This strongly suggests an origin within the Celtic Church, but cannot be further used to deduce provenance, because codices were frequently sent from place to place in the Irish Church's missions to England and the Continent. The text of *Durrow* does, however, eliminate the possibility that it was written in a Northumbrian center with a strong Roman bias, such as Hexham, or one associated with the nearly Vulgate tradition of Jarrow and Monkwearmouth.

The script of *Durrow* is an Irish majuscule halfway between the script of Durham A.II.10 and that of the *Echternach Gospels* (Paris, Bibliothèque Nationale, MS Lat. 9389), which dates about 700. *Durrow* is consequently dated on paleographic grounds in the third quarter of the seventh century. The script of *Durrow* may also indicate Northumbrian associations, since both A.II.10 and *Echternach* have connections to or roots in that milieu, and the use of Irish majuscule declines in Ireland after *Durrow.* The layout of the text on the page follows Irish practice in the use of long lines rather than the bicolumnar arrangement found in Northumbrian codices at the end of the century. However, bicolumnar layout may have developed after the date of *Durrow* and so is no certain indication of provenance in this case. The similarities in the script to Durham A.II.10 suggest a parallel provenance for *Durrow* in the Anglo-Celtic missionary foundations of northern England.[84]

The *Book of Durrow* is the earliest extant fully illuminated insular codex, but probably not the first such codex ever made. The sophistication and technical expertise of its art did not develop instantaneously from the preliminaries of the *Cathach* and A.II.10. One must assume an intermediate series of lost, more experimental but less complex manuscripts. *Durrow* is not the child of A.II.10; it is a cousin at several generations' remove. The imported models and foreign influences have become more apparent, but at the same time a unified aesthetic has developed that freely incorporates both indigenous and alien motifs into a balanced and coherent whole.

The *Book of Durrow* has both text-associated ornament and full-page illuminations. The text-associated ornament is dominated by five major initials, one at the commencement of each of the Gospels, and one additional at the first mention of Christ's name in Matthew, where the Chi-Rho monogram is enlarged and decorated, subsequently an unfailing tradition in insular manuscripts. There are also small initials for the prefaces and the chapter lists. The canon tables are framed with panels of interlace and divided into a grid ornamented with red-dot and other colorful motifs. Full-page illuminations include six ornamental carpet-pages, four pages on which single Evangelist symbols are framed with interlace, and one page on which all four Evangelist symbols fill the reentrant angles of a large cross, the whole framed with a wide border of pattern.

The range of colors used in the illuminations of the *Book of Durrow* is severely limited, predominantly yellow, orange, black, and white, with green used infrequently. This is approximately identical to the range in Durham A.II.10, and suggests a relatively early date for *Durrow*, since a broader spectrum of hues is used in later manuscripts in both Ireland and Northumbria.

Most remarkable about *Durrow* is the quantity and quality of illumination in so small a volume. The codex measures only 245 by 145 millimeters. Insular ceremonial texts of slightly later date are considerably larger, if one may consider the *Lindisfarne Gospels* as fairly typical, and even Durham A.II.10, probably earlier, is a noticeable larger volume.[85] The scale suggests that the book may have been intended for private hands or for study, but the quantity of decoration, even of remote pages, suggests that *Durrow;* was intended to serve as the ceremonial Gospels of a community of high status. Its contradictory small scale, however, correlates the evidence of the occasional use of monofolia and of patched vellum; this is the product of a center without substantial wealth. Again, this suggests that the codex was not executed at one of the major Irish foundations that were under royal patronage and would not have had to skimp on scale or vellum in the interests of economy.

The initials of *Durrow* are more imposing and elaborate than those of Durham A.II.10, and at least equal in scale relative to the page, if not larger. For example, the descender of *IN* at the opening of John (fol. 193r) runs the full vertical length of the page, and an entire vertical third of the page is devoted to the descender and its framing space. Six lines of text are presented in progressive insular diminution. As though electrified by the presence of the monogram, they sparkle with myriads of framing red dots. The remaining eight lines are relegated to the lower right-hand corner, almost overwhelmed by the splendid monogram above. The insular departure from Late Antique models for decorated initials has become established by this time; ornament clearly dominates text. Moreover, the monogram itself is not only visually dominant because of scale, but it also draws the eye by the application of an incredibly intricate system of ornament. Descenders are filled with knotwork, framing occasional oblongs of solid color. The crossbar of the *N* and the descender terminals are filled with exceptionally refined spirals. By comparison, the monogram *INI* of Durham A.II.10 seems almost crudely simple. The source of *Durrow*'s refinement must be found in another medium—metalwork.

Dublin, Trinity College Library, MS A.4.5., *Book of Durrow*, fol. 193r: opening of John *(by permission of the Keeper of Manuscripts and the Board of Trinity College, Dublin)*

The exchange of motifs between metalwork and illumination is no surprise. Metalwork was the highest Celtic art form, and there was no apparent reason that the advanced ornamental compositions of metalwork should not be applied to the decoration of the written word. Indeed, one wonders why earlier manuscripts were not similarly treated. It may be that there was some question of suitability—of sumptuous ornament to the functional objects of an ascetic faith, or of a traditional secular craft to a religious object of foreign meaning and medium. It may be that metal Christian objects, such as the Athlone plaque, are the halfway point, combining indigenous style and technique with imported iconography, a bridge from secular metal to Christian illumination. There may also have been an eventual confluence of workshop traditions, as artisans trained in the traditional motifs of metal either joined or became affiliated with the monastic centers, or as the monks at some point chose to avail themselves of these motifs, either by copying from metal objects or by obtaining the patterns of the metal shops engraved on bone slips or possibly pieces of leather or wood.

One other question is prompted by the aggrandized and richly ornamented initials of *Durrow:* why is so much attention lavished on initials in the insular manuscripts, contrary to the moderate use of decorated letters in their probably Mediterranean ancestors; why does the initial dominate the page, almost obliterating the text with its visual histrionics? The Celtic love of ornament on all objects partially answers this question, but there is perhaps also a deeper reason. Writing was essentially foreign to pre-Christian Celtic culture. Christianity presented not only the new concept of the written word, but also the understanding of these words as the Word. The great insular initials can be understood as a tribute to the Word itself, manifested mystically in the written words of Scripture. This argument explains the location of a major initial—the Chi-Rho monogram—at the first mention of the name of Christ, the embodiment of the Word.

The carpet-pages of *Durrow* show both a similar distance from Mediterranean models and an equal familiarity with Celtic metalwork. The only earlier carpet-page in insular art is the rosette panel in Ambrosian D.23. sup. (fol. 1v), but there the motifs used are entirely Mediterranean. The origin of thoroughly insular carpet-pages, as seen first in *Durrow*, is difficult to determine. It has been suggested that the concept of the carpet-page was borrowed from illuminations or bindings of eastern Mediterranean codices, but there are no extant early ornamental carpet-pages. Later Eastern carpet-pages, moroever, bear little resemblance to the insular examples.[86] If closer Eastern models for insular carpet-pages existed, there is no surviving trace of them. Similarly, there are no extant examples of purely ornamental bindings resembling *Durrow*'s noniconographic carpets.

Insular carpet-pages have also been compared to Roman mosaic pavements, possibly still visible at Romano-British settlement sites in England at the time of the Anglo-Saxon conversion.[87] The Romano-British mosaic pavements and the insular carpet-pages have in common an extremely dense layout, using a complex subdivision of areas within areas, and the application of broad-band

Book of Durrow, fol. 1v: cross-carpet-page *(By permission of the Keeper of Manuscripts and the Board of Trinity College, Dublin)*

interlace as a frequent border and filler motif. Certain mosaics have remarkable parallels to the *Book of Durrow;* one at Frampton has inset crosslets, and one at Brislington has an overlay of nested squares, both similar to aspects of *Durrow's* cross-carpet-page (fol. 1v). However, the documents do not mention the observation of mosaics, nor are there examples of the direct transcription of extant pavement motifs into extant manuscripts. Nevertheless, problems of nonsurvival for art and documents for this period make consideration of circumstantial evidence imperative.

Not all Roman cities were abruptly abandoned and allowed to fall into ruin at the departure of the legions. Many continued to have sizable populations of romanized Britons, of which the better-educated and wealthier classes tried to maintain the forms of Roman culture.[88] Although the Anglo-Saxon invaders and settlers of England avoided abandoned Roman cities, as their culture was primarily agricultural and nonurban, this avoidance did not pertain to continuously inhabited Roman sites. As kingdoms became consolidated, Anglo-Saxon kings established courts in the larger cities. Edwin of Northumbria, for example, held court at York. Moreover, where Britons and Angles coexisted peacefully, Roman sites, and an understanding of their heritage, were gradually shifted from the former tenants to the new overlords. The Angles of Carlisle became so proud of "their" Roman heritage that when Saint Cuthbert visited them in 685, the reeve of the city and a group of citizens were delighted to give him a tour of the walls, culminating with a visit to a Roman fountain.[89] If mosaic pavements remained in the area, they would certainly have been known and admired. Reuse of Roman building materials for churches—as at Escomb and Corbridge—and the reuse of a Roman sarcophagus for an abbess of Ely indicate that the use of pavement patterns in Christian manuscripts would not have been considered inappropriate.[90] The question remains, however, whether mosaic pavements were available in Northumbria to provide a repertory of motifs for manuscript painting. In Northumbria as a whole, there were very few Roman villas, as compared to the concentration in southern counties; those few, most near York, were substantially less elegant than the comparable southern establishments. Tesselated pavements surviving in Yorkshire, at Aldborough and at Rudstone near Brislington, are relatively simple. Moreover, Yorkshire was the southernmost part of Northumbria, farthest from Iona and the Celtic Church, and least likely to provide models for the latter's art. Roman Carlisle, on the other hand, was a substantial walled town, with sufficient wealth and taste to harbor a mosaicist's workshop, but here there are no surviving mosaics.

The circumstantial evidence for contact and influence is at best inconclusive. The resemblance of the *Durrow* cross-carpet-page (fol. 1v) to the pavements of southern and central England is striking, particularly as concerns the mosaics of Brislington and Frampton, and cannot be completely disregarded. However, the pavements laid out on a grid pattern, and providing the closest parallels for the insular carpet-pages, are found outside England, notably in North Africa.[91] Consequently, it remains unclear whether the carpet-page is an insular in-

Book of Durrow, fol. 3v: spiral carpet-page *(by permission of the Keeper of Manuscripts and the Board of Trinity College, Dublin)*

vention, derived from locally available surviving Roman designs, or whether it was imported as a completely evolved concept in eastern Mediterranean manuscript sources. However, the carpet-pages of *Durrow* are not pure transcriptions of Mediterranean ornament. Unlike the frontispiece of Ambrosian D.23.sup., the *Durrow* carpet-pages show the intrusion of motifs from insular metalwork. The verso of the damaged third folio, for example, contains within a border of parti-colored interlace a series of discs, framed by trumpet and spiral motifs, and filled with very fine spirals and triskelion designs in black against the plain vellum of the page. These spiral patterns strongly resemble Celtic metalwork, for example, the designs engraved or chased on the backs of

Domnach Airgid; **Dublin, National Museum of Ireland** *(photo: National Museum of Ireland)*

Dark Age mirrors, including those found at Desborough, Northamptonshire, and Birdlip, Gloucestershire, both now in the British Museum. The spiral lines of the *Durrow* page are somewhat thinner and more elegant, reflecting perhaps the middle stage in the refinement of Celtic metalcraft between the British mirrors and the nearly microscopically fine line spirals in niello on the back of the eighth-century Tara Brooch. On this page and elsewhere among *Durrow*'s full-page illuminations, the interlace shows a significant increase in complexity over the triple D loops of Durham A.II.10. The *Durrow* interlace also finds close parallels in contemporary metalwork, as on the *Domnach Airgid*, a book shrine in the National Museum in Dublin.[92] Here the parallelism is so acute that the question of priority between media cannot be resolved.

One carpet-page in *Durrow* (fol. 192v) is distinguished by the use of zoomorphic interlace in its borders. This animal interlace, already noted in a much more basic form in the monogram of Durham A.II.10, is a fundamentally Germanic motif, transmitted to insular art from Anglo-Saxon metalwork. The presence of this motif suggests extensive contact between the center that produced *Durrow* and Anglo-Saxon lands. Saxon metalwork was being exported to Ireland in the seventh century and might have provided models for Irish illuminators of *Durrow*, but early Irish examples of zoomorphic ornament from this period are far weaker and show much less comprehension of the use of animal forms in interlace.[93] The *Durrow* animals, on the other hand, are a remarkably competent, fluid, and precise fusion of the ultimately Mediterranean regularized knotwork seen elsewhere in the codex and the ferocity of the biting, intertwined snakes of the Sutton Hoo belt buckle and other Anglian

Book of Durrow, fol. 192v: carpet-page with zoomorphs *(by permission of the Keeper of Manuscripts and the Board of Trinity College, Dublin)*

pieces—an effect that could not be achieved without an intensive comprehension of the art of both cultures. This suggests the close cooperation of Celtic and Anglo-Saxon craftsmen and points to a provenance for the manuscript at a Celtic site close to Anglo-Saxon soil.

Two carpet-pages of *Durrow* (fols. 1v, 192v) are distinguished by the central use of a cross motif. On the verso of folio 192, the cross is small, embedded at the center of a disc of multicolored interlace.[94] On the verso of the first folio, the cross is larger and double armed, and is the central motif of the design of the page. It is entrenched in an interlace pattern that also contains four small interlace stepped crosslets in the reentrant angles of the larger cross. One possible foreign source for such insular frontispiece cross-pages is Coptic cross frontispieces such as in the fifth-century Egyptian *Glazier Codex* in the Morgan Library.[95] Here an Egyptian ankh, executed in interlace, is the central motif of the page, flanked in traditional Eastern style with peacocks, doves, and foliate branches. In addition, the circular head of the ankh contains a dove bearing an olive branch. These symbolic creatures do not appear in the *Durrow* cross-carpet-page. However, the interlace of the cross shows a marked similarity to that of *Durrow*, showing both the anticlassical tendency toward breaks already examined in Durham A.II.10, and the equally anticlassical use of discontinuous coloration (in which a ribbon will change color as it passes behind another strand) found for the first time in insular illumination in the border of Durrow's carpet-pages. Later Coptic manuscripts frequently show large interlaced crosses as part of their decorative vocabulary, but the *Glazier Codex* is the only known extant example predating *Durrow*.[96] However, the anticlassical interlace of A.II.10 and *Durrow* and the idea of the cross-carpet-page come from a single cultural source. The extent of commerce and ecclesiastical contact with the eastern Mediterranean suggests rather a variety of available models, possibly including several of Coptic provenance, at work in *Durrow* and other insular manuscripts.

Book covers of imported manuscripts are another possible source for insular cross-carpet-pages. Ceremonial Gospel books were frequently covered with applied plaques of precious metals or ivory, decorated either with biblical scenes or with a large cross, and simpler books with leather or wooden bindings would be inscribed with a painted or applied metal cross. The elaborate bindings of the Gospels of Monza Cathedral, a gift from the Lombard queen, Theodolinda, are a famous example of ceremonial covers.[97] The front and back of this seventh-century binding are each dominated by a large cross and decorated with precious stones, antique cameos, panels of applied cloisonné, and gold bands bearing dedicatory inscriptions. The background is, however, a blank sheet of gold, without interlace or other filler ornament. A similar but more simple cross is seen on the cover of the Gospels volume in the book cupboard behind the scribe Ezra in the frontispiece to the *Codex Amiatinus* (Florence, Laurentian Library, (fol. V); painted from an Italian model in Northumbria in the late seventh century. However, no extant book covers or depicted volume predating *Durrow* shows the extensive background ornament or the *horror vacui* of Durrow's frontispiece cross-carpet-page. The combination of ornament and cross into cross-carpet-page must originate elsewhere, whether in insular or in foreign art.

The presence of foreign models in whatever form does not preclude the use of indigenous metalworking motifs on the cross-carpet-pages of *Durrow* any more than on the purely ornamented carpet-pages. On the cross-carpet-page (fol. 1v), the ends of the bars of the cross and their intersections are marked with small checkerboard squares, resembling inset millefiori cubes, and equally small blocks filled with key patterns and outlined with lighter colors, suggesting cloisonné enamelwork. These techniques had been perfected by Celtic metalworkers in preceding centuries, in the escutcheons of the hanging bowls. The ease with which these indigenous themes of ornament are inserted into a design possibly derived from an imported model is indicative of the degree to which Celtic illuminators felt both at home with foreign art and able to adapt it to suit native stylistic preferences. This relaxed attitude toward foreign objects is a natural consequence of earlier trade contacts with the Mediterranean world and the Continent. The cross-carpet-page as found in *Durrow* is probably an insular invention, amalgamating both foreign models such as the Coptic designs seen in the *Glazier Codex* frontispiece and the Gospel binding tradition, and the Celtic love of complex ornament and refined metalwork.

The evangelist-symbol pages of *Durrow* (fols. 21v, 84v, 124v, 191v) show a similarly assimilative spirit. The figures are shown full-length, lacking books, halos, and, excepting the Eagle, wings. Evangelist beasts in Mediterranean tradition fall into two fairly distinct categories. For the most part, they are shown half-length, protruding from clouds or from behind a prop, and bear one or more of the above-mentioned attributes. Evangelist symbols resembling those of *Durrow* are by far the minority, and are generally associated with or found in northern Italy. The most famous examples are the four Evangelist symbols in the sixth-century mosaics of the bema of San Vitale in Ravenna and those of the *Codex Valerianus* in Munich (fols. 12r, 82v).[98] However, as the San Vitale beasts are in an immobile medium and as the *Codex Valerianus* pages show the symbols as small decorations in the text column, neither of these examples provides a complete source for the *Durrow* pages, which show the symbols isolated at the center of an open page framed with interlace borders. Indeed, such grand treatment of the Evangelist symbols in any format is unprecedented in extant earlier manuscripts. Consequently, although northern Italy may have provided a model for the series of symbols, the origin—Italian or insular—of the concept of the symbol page is undeterminable. The stylistic treatment of the symbols, however, suggests that, whatever the source of the forms, they have been completely revised to suit insular taste. The figure of the Man of Matthew (fol. 21v) has been flattened into a two-dimensional bell shape. The only human features of this figures are a forward-facing head stuck awkwardly and without a neck at the top and two profile feet projecting below and aimed to the right. There is no suggestion of modeling, expression, or movement, except the direction of foot placement. The figure is not truly a representation of human form, but this is not necessarily due to lack of familiarity with the classical representational style of Mediterranean models or evidence of lack of skill in transmitting the gist of such a model. It was rather probably intended as a hieroglyph of human form, literally as the *symbol* of Matthew, the Man. Similar reductions of human form are found in pre-Christian Celtic metalwork

Book of Durrow, fol. 21v: Man of Matthew *(by permission of the Keeper of Manuscripts and the Board of Trinity College, Dublin)*

and in the earliest Christian stone carving in Ireland. Two enameled escutcheons in human form, probably Irish in origin, have been found at Viking
sites in Norway, one attached to a bucket in the Oseberg ship burial, now in the
Bygdö Museum, Oslo, and the other applied to a bowl found at Miklebostad,
now in the Bergen Museum.[99] These resemble the *Durrow* figure not only in
the reduction of physiographic detail and the enlargement of the head and eyes,
but also in the treatment of the torso as a planar area filled with enamelwork
and millefiori in a patchwork pattern. The checkerboard design of the *Durrow*
Man is probably borrowed directly from similar enameled figures, in light of
the preeminence of metalworking among Celtic craftsmen and the evidence of
its intrusion elsewhere in *Durrow*. Patchwork plaque figures also occur in early
Irish stone crosses, as metalwork designs were probably also available to
sculptors. The interlace of the Fahan Mura cross slab (county Donegal) bears a
marked resemblance to that of both Durham A.II.10 and *Durrow*. The slab
consequently can be dated to the third quarter of the seventh century. This slab
also shows two small figures very similar to the *Durrow* Man flanking the
cross. They are planar oblongs, patterned with squares, with tiny protruding
feet and enlarged heads. The type continues into the slightly later crosses of
county Offaly, most notably the eighth-century North Cross at Clonmac-
noise.[100]

The figures at Fahan Mura also resemble the Man of *Durrow* in the treatment
of hairstyle. In both, the front of the crown is shaved, and the hair grows to
shoulder length backward from the center of the crown. The Man of *Durrow*
includes the additional lifelike detail of stippling on the front of the crown,
suggesting the stubble of new growth. An unusual degree of detail is applied to
this particular feature where the rest of the figure is presented in very simple
terms. This detail is noteworthy because the Man of *Durrow* and the Fahan
Mura figures are tonsured in the manner of the Celtic Church. This detail, in
combination with an accepted date of 675 for *Durrow*, is of great importance in
determining the provenance of the manuscript. In 664, the Synod of Whitby
had established the orthodoxy of the Roman tonsure and the date of Easter, and
brought Lindisfarne, Whitby, and other eastern Northumbrian Celtic houses
into conformity. Southern Ireland had already been romanized in 635, but the
northern Irish held out for Celtic ways until Adamnan's reforms in 703, and
Iona until 716. Indeed, it was within the Columban *paruchia*, of which Iona
was the motherhouse, that the Celtic schism persisted longest and most intensely. *Durrow* must originate in a setting where such a demonstration of
resistance to Roman practice would be tolerated as late as 675, either northern
Ireland or Iona.

The other Evangelist-symbol pages of *Durrow* also hint at the provenance of
the manuscript. The joints of the Calf (fol. 124v) and the Lion (fol. 191v) are
decoratively articulated with spirals and scroll patterns. The animals are, however, otherwise naturalistically portrayed; the Calf particularly is close to a
study from life. As there were no lions available to the insular artist, naturalism
has been attempted in *Durrow*'s Lion by amalgamating the pose of a heraldic

Book of Durrow, fol. 84v: Eagle of Mark *(by permission of the Keeper of Manuscripts and the Board of Trinity College, Dublin)*

Book of Durrow, **fol. 124v: Calf of Luke** *(by permission of the Keeper of Manuscripts and the Board of Trinity College, Dublin)*

beast, possibly from an imported model, with the snout, glare, and snarl of a mastiff; with the result resembling an Alsatian. This bizarre combination of pattern and natural form against a plain vellum ground is closely analogous to

Book of Durrow, fol. 191v: Lion of John *(by permission of the Keeper of Manuscripts and the Board of Trinity College, Dublin)*

certain Pictish carvings of inscribed animals, the so-called Class 1 symbol stones, among which the Papil Lion, the Burghead Bull, and the Ardross Wolf are the closest parallels for the symbols of *Durrow*.[101] One possible means of transmission of this style from the Pictish north to other parts of the British Isles is the trade in metalwork. A hanging bowl with escutcheons in the form of stags with spiral joints was found near Lullingstone, Kent, probably as a result of sixth- or seventh-century trade with the Picts. However, the influence of Pictish carvings in *Durrow* suggests a greater geographic proximity of provenance of the manuscript to the carvings—either in Northumbria (which had a long, albeit occasionally hostile, border with Pictland) or at Iona (off the western coast of Scotland, originally established for the purpose of converting the Picts).[102]

The Eagle of *Durrow* (fol. 84v), unlike the Calf and Lion, is shown frontally, as in Roman legionary standards, rather than in profile. It shows a close resemblance to a type of Merovingian brooch in the shape of an eagle, inlaid with garnets. However, on the four-symbols page of *Durrow* (fol. 2r), a duplicate Eagle is seen, modified only by the addition of a halo, suggesting that the *Durrow* Eagle had a model in which Christian attributes had been added to the imperial formula. Nonetheless, the treatment of the feathers as scallops of bright, flat color indicates the free use of enamelwork design and colors in reworking an imported model.

Like the Man and Eagle, the *Durrow* Calf and Lion avoid natural coloration. The Lion is covered with a diaper pattern in red and green, and his outline and joint scrolls are bright yellow. The Eagle's feather scallops are equally unnaturally colored red and yellow, and the pinfeathers are executed to resemble incised metal plates. The lack of coloristic naturalism, the patterned flatness of the beasts, and their broad monochromatic outlines are plainly borrowed from insular enamel design, once again altering foreign models to local taste.

The four Evangelist symbols also appear together on a single page (fol. 24), where they fill the reentrant angles of a large cross. The symbols here are unusual in both their order and their form. Clockwise from the upper left are the Man, the Eagle, the Calf, and the Lion. Read in this sequence, the coordination of Evangelists to symbols is not in the Vulgate order but rather in the sequence established by Irenaeus, the second-century bishop of Lyons. Read counterclockwise, of course, the symbols are in the Vulgate order, but the Irenaean order persists also in the arrangement of the symbol frontispieces to the individual Gospels in *Durrow*—the Eagle precedes Mark, and the Lion appears before John. At least one source for *Durrow*'s Evangelist-symbol pages had the Irenaean sequence parallels, whether in images or in text.[103]

The forms of the Evangelist symbols on the four-symbols page of *Durrow*, particularly the Lion and the Calf, are also unusual. The Lion is seen frontally rather than in profile as on the single-symbol page, so that here no part of his hindquarters is visible. Thus he can be interpreted to be "upright"; reduced to a head, torso block, and forelegs, he is a cipher much like the Man. The process of reduction is taken further with the Calf, where the head perches on a trapezoidal torso that has lost all resemblance to the forequarters of an animal— a flat surface subdivided into blocks of interlace on dark ground. The Man is a close copy of his full-page counterpart, except for the addition of a single arm folded across his chest, and the Eagle is similarly identical to the full-page version with the addition of a halo. At a glance, all four symbols of this page seem to stand on two legs in an anthropomorphic manner, and to have been

Book of Durrow, fol. 2r: Evangelist-symbols page *(by permission of the Keeper of Manuscripts and the Board of Trinity College, Dublin)*

further designed to resemble the Man. Martin Werner has suggested a Coptic prototype for these zooanthropomorphic Evangelist symbols, possibly derived from the four animal-headed children of Horus. In a fresco in a narthex chapel at Saint Anthony in the Desert, the Pantocrator is flanked by four full-length, winged, clothed figures with human bodies and the heads of the four symbols. In an eleventh-century fresco at Faras, Nubia, half-length zooanthropomorphic figures inscribed with apocalyptic names fill the reentrant angles of the stepped Cross of Golgotha as a symbolic Christ in Majesty. In a separate Coptic iconographic tradition in manuscripts, medallion bust portraits of the four Evangelists sometimes surround an interlaced cross, very similar in composition to the *Durrow* page. It has been suggested that a conflation of these two traditions took place, which created a zooanthropomorpohic symbolic Christ in Majesty in which the association between apocalyptic symbols and Evangelists was established, and that an imported Coptic version of this composition was the model for the Evangelist-symbols page in *Durrow*.[104] Such a composition had been imported to England by the middle of the eighth century, for it forms the center of the highly complex iconographic program of the Wirksworth slab in Derbyshire, where the half-length figures closely resemble those in the Faras fresco.[105]

The suggestion of a Coptic model is marred by several problems. First, are the *Durrow* symbols truly zooanthropomorphic? Only the Calf is transformed into a flat trapezoid. The Eagle is certainly birdlike in morphology, although reduced to the stiff imperial formula; and the Lion is facing forward but not humanized, since it stands on its front paws and maintains furlike patterns. However, the viewpoint is unusual, as the full-length Lion is usually seen in profile. After attempting an experiment in rearranging the Lion to face forward, the *Durrow* artist may have then chosen the easier route of imitating insular metalwork when he drew the frontal-facing Calf in the same abstract manner as the Man. Why, however, would the artist be inclined to attempt to turn the animals to a forward-facing posture? The answer lies in the necessities of the composition. The profile full-length Calf and Lion, unlike the Man and the Eagle, require more horizontal than vertical space, not available in the reentrant angles of a cross on a vertically rectangular page without a reduction in scale. The easiest modification is to place the beast facing forward, so that it becomes primarily vertical. A different solution to the same problem is found in the *Book of Saint Chad* (Lichfield, Cathedral Library, p. 219), where the striding beasts are simply turned ninety degrees so that they seem to be running up the page. Thus one need not necessarily adduce a Coptic, zooanthropomorphic composition for *Durrow*'s "upright" beasts; they are sufficiently awkward to be original.

Lawrence Nees has suggested another possible model, a book cover with a cross flanked by four half-length, winged Evangelist symbols, in the *Durrow* or Irenaean order, held by a bishop in a fifth-century mosaic in an arcosolium in the catacombs of San Gennaro in Naples. [106] The mosaicist no doubt depicts an actual or typical cover of a ceremonial Gospels. The connections of the Celtic Church to the Mediterranean were sufficient that such a book cover might have been available as a model for *Durrow*. Nees further suggests a similar purpose for book cover and opening cross-page with Evangelist symbols. He points out

Lichfield, Cathedral Library, *Book of St. Chad*; p. 219; Evangelist-symbols page
(photo: Courtauld Institute of Art, by permission of the Librarian and Chapter, Lich-field)

that the four Evangelists were evoked with apotropaic intent in early Western medieval prayer, and that they might serve in these cases to protect the books from evil.

Suppose then that the artist or designer of the layout of the *Book of Durrow* decided that, since his product was to be a great ceremonial Gospels, he wished to include, for whatever reason, both a four-symbols page at the opening of the volume and individual symbol pages as well as carpet-pages at the opening of every chapter. He had available a book cover much like that in the San Gennaro mosaic or an illumination resembling it, perhaps a Coptic book with an interlace cross frontispiece and probably a set of full-length apocalyptic symbols, as well as a variety of sources for ornamental motifs. On the single-symbol pages, he adapted the full-length symbols to indigenous taste, transforming them with ornamental devices borrowed from Celtic metal craft and Pictish stone carving. He then decided to transpose these full-length types to the four-symbols page, borrowing the composition from the book cover, and modifying the symbols to suit the spaces available for them. Irenaean order was inherent either to decorations in the textual source for the Gospels or in the model—book cover or otherwise—for the four-symbols page. A Coptic interlace cross may also have been used for the four-symbols page and perhaps was also adapted for the cross-carpet-page, althouth there is evidence there of the use of other sources, whether imported eastern Mediterranean fabrics or manuscripts, or surviving Roman mosaic pavements in Britain.

What is most remarkable about *Durrow* is the ability of its artists to adapt so many different traditions and sources into a single aesthetically unified and consistent work. Hence the codex must be the product of a scriptorium where all these disparate elements were not only available, as a result of trade or occasional contact, but also familiar enough by frequency of contact to be easily and fluidly assimilated. *Durrow* must come from a center that was familiar with Celtic metalwork, and that had regular access to models for art transmitted on the ancient routes of trade and intellectual exchange from the eastern Mediterranean to the western Irish seas. These imported sources included elements from Coptic Egypt, the spiritual origin point of Irish monasticism. Hence the manuscript must be a product of a center associated with the Celtic Church; of a foundation, moreover, in which the old Celtic tonsure was not thought heretical in the third quarter of the seventh century. At the same time, however, the artists of *Durrow* knew not only Germanic, probably Anglo-Saxon, zoomorphic interlace, but perhaps also the incised carvings of the Picts, both of which suggest an origin outside Ireland, most probably in northern England. Moreover, the script of the manuscript and the possibility of the influence of Roman mosaic pavements on the carpet-pages both suggest a provenance on the eastern side of the Irish seas. The manuscript was made at a foundation without extensive wealth, where every scrap of vellum had to be used regardless of its condition and where codices were made on a reduced scale, but a monastic center that its inhabitants thought worthy of a major illuminated ceremonial Gospels manuscript. These factors suggest a missionary outpost of the Celtic Church, far from the open hands of Irish royal patronage, but nonetheless a significant center. Finally, there is the traditional attribution of the manuscript to Saint Columba and its history of association with Durrow, a Columban foundation. Collectively, all these factors point to a provenance at Iona, metropolis of the Columban *paruchia* in Ireland and England and fountainhead of the mission of the Celtic Church to the Picts, the Scots, and the Angles of Northumbria.[107]

Iona has yet to be excavated in detail. Preliminary excavations in the early 1970s revealed that the site benefited from the western seaways trade. A shard of North African red-slipped ware, discovered in a trial cutting, was dated by stratigraphic comparison between 550 and 650 and determined to be of rather recent manufacture at the time of burial. Unfortunately, this has been the only shard of pre-Viking date found in sealed deposit on the site. Other than this, little is known of life and art at early Iona, as the surviving stone crosses are much later in date.[108] However, the weight of evidence in the art and ornament of *Durrow* is strongly in favor of a tentative attribution to Iona.

It has been claimed that Iona was too poor a center to produce such a book, as it was established as a mission base without amenities on the frontiers of Celtic Christianity.[109] Iona's original purpose in 565 was certainly missionary, but by about 675, it may well have had all the amenities available at Irish Columban houses such as Durrow or Derry. It has also been asserted that Iona was less Celtic than other sites in Ireland because of its location outside Ireland proper, and that its monks were consequently incapable of so Celtic a codex as *Durrow*.[110] Yet the monks of Iona were the last northern adherents of the Celtic schism, more durable in their differences with Rome than even their Irish brethren. Indeed it is a tribute to the strength of will of the Irish monks of Iona that they were able to produce a codex that successfully combined so culturally and artistically complex a variety of sources without losing either its aesthetic unity, its perfection of craftsmanship, or its ultimately Celtic character.

The *Book of Durrow* is in a way the culmination of the process of the Christianization of Celtic art. It incorporates traditions of metalwork craftmanship inherent in Celtic art since the late Iron Age, but also freely utilizes models imported from the Mediterranean sources of Christianity. The ease with which these models are assimilated into a manuscript of remarkable unity suggests not only the strong ties of the Celtic Church to Italy, Coptic Egypt, and the eastern Mediterranean, but also the extent to which these ties were founded in ancient trade patterns. This ongoing trade lent familiarity to foreign models for art, making their adaption to native stylistic preferences easier and more successful.

On the other hand, the *Book of Durrow* is part of the beginning of another process, the development of art in Northumbria. *Durrow*, or works much like it, presented to Northumbrian artists the repertory of the art of the Celtic Church, both indigenous and imported, in a thoroughly integrated form. By inclusion of Anglian and Pictish motifs, moreover, it opened doors to a broader synthesis of traditions, which would later culminate in the major works of the Northumbrian Renaissance. Northumbrian art, however, also included the influence of the Roman Church, which was simultaneously evangelizing the Angles of Northumbria and providing a separate series of models for art.

The Roman Church in England: Imports and Emulation

The Roman Mission in Kent: Early Imports and Architecture

THE MISSION of the Roman Church to England, organized at the command of Gregory the Great and under the direction of Augustine, arrived in Kent in 597. There it encountered a Saxon culture already open to foreign trade in both luxury goods and common commodities. Moreover, a portion of the Kentish royal court was the émigré Christian entourage of the Merovingian princess Bertha, now queen of Kent. Augustine and his associates found the ground well prepared for the sowing of not only the new faith but also the artistic patrimony of the Mediterranean world of its origins.

Christianity had been introduced to England during the period of the Roman occupation. However, it had later receded almost entirely to the western areas of England where British hegemony lingered. A few old churches remained in Roman cities, but the extent of their continued use in the period immediately following the incursion of the pagan Saxons, Angles, and Jutes is difficult to determine. Bede mentions the old church at Verulamium near the site of the martyrdom of Saint Alban as being in use to his own day, but structural continuity is not certain.[1] Similarly he relates that Bertha and her chaplain Liudhard made use of an ancient church in Canterbury dedicated to Saint Martin, which had been built in Roman times, but the dedication to the patron saint of the Merovingian royal house suggests that the church may have had to be reconstructed and reconsecrated for this use.[2] Indeed, regardless of the constancy of trade contact with the Continent and despite the Christian practice of his own queen, Æthelbert of Kent insisted on meeting Augustine outdoors at first encounter, Bede tells us, so that Augustine would not be able to overcome him with magic in a confined space.[3] This suggests strongly that while Bertha's faith was tolerated as part of the conditions of her marriage contract, and that despite the extent of preexistent trade, the royal household was in other matters remarkably ignorant of the abilities and intentions of Christian priests.

Most if not all of the paraphernalia of the Christian service initially had to be imported, whether under the personal ownership of the earliest missionaries or through the supportive gifts of foreign clergy and royalty. The silver cross standard and the painted icon of Christ that Augustine brought with him to his initial meeting with Æthelbert were the beginning of an almost endless flood of foreign objects that the Roman Church imported for its own use. In 601, Gregroy sent Augustine several colleagues and assistants who brought with them all the necessities of the new faith, including the sacred vessels of the Mass, altar coverings, church ornaments, vestments, relics, and many books.[4] The *Gospels of Saint Augustine* (Cambridge, Corpus Christi College Library, MS 286) is an example of the early imports of the Church, possibly brought to England by Augustine himself.[5] Imported gifts also arrived as gifts to royal converts who would eventually lead their people to grace. Such, for example, are the unspecified gifts sent by Pope Gregory to Æthelbert of Kent at his conversion and the garments sent by Pope Boniface V to Edwin of Northumbria who was at the time vacillating about the new faith.[6]

The Roman Church needed suitable architecture in the early days of the conversion of the English. The scale of the churches was limited at first both by the small numbers of the faithful and by financial considerations. A sufficient number of early Kentish churches are known that some general statements concerning their form can be made. Of these, three are in Canterbury: Augustine's Saints Peter and Paul of 604, King Eadbald's Saint Mary of 620, modeled on Augustine's church, and Saint Pancras. In addition, there is evidence from Saint Mary, Lyminge, Saint Andrew, Rochester, and Saint Mary at Reculver, built by Egbert of Kent about 669.[7] In their number should also be included Saint Cedd's church of Saint Peter-on-the-Wall at Bradwell-on-Sea in Essex, which, although built by a Celtic churchman from Northumbria, is southern in form if not in proportions.

It is difficult to determine the precedents for Christian architecture available in England in Augustine's time. Bede mentions several churches of Roman date. Beside that at Verulamium and Saint Martin's in Canterbury, he also notes another church at Canterbury of Roman date later reconsecrated by Augustine to Christ.[8] He also specifies that after the persecution of the Christians under Diocletian and Heraclius, the ruined churches were restored.[9] This suggests that their number was not insignificant, but Bede does not describe them. A few structures may preserve fragments of Roman churches.[10] The Roman structure at Silchester, Hampshire, is the most elaborate possible Roman church in England, an apsidal structure oriented in early Roman Christian fashion to the west, with walled or arcaded aisle passages, narthex, and lateral

Cambridge, Corpus Christi College, MS 286, *St. Augustine Gospels*, fol. 129v: Evangelist portrait of Luke *(by permission of the Librarian and the Master and Fellows of Corpus Christi College, Cambridge)*

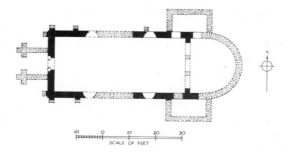

Plan of St. Peter-on-the-Wall, Bradwell-on-Sea (Essex) *(British Crown copyright, by permission of the Historic Buildings and Monuments Commission for England)*

St. Peter-on-the-Wall, Bradwell-on-Sea (Essex)

chambers. The Kentish churches resemble it in general layout, but there is no conclusive evidence that the Silchester structure was ever used as a church.[11] Moreover, there are no extant Roman-date parallels for the Silchester building anywhere near Canterbury. So the Kentish churches probably derived their form from other sources.[12]

The Kentish churches are related to contemporary and earlier Mediterranean church architecture in many aspects of their design. Their plan generally consists of a rectangular nave with a slightly stilted apse. The proportions of the Kentish apse are parallel to apses in North African churches at Biar el Kherba,

Tigzirt, and Announa. The Kentish apses, where known, tend to be semicircular both internally and externally, as at Saint Mary in Canterbury and Saint Pancras, or semipolygonal externally, as at Reculver and Bradwell.[13] Semipolygonal apses are found at Ravenna, Pomposa, and Grado and are ultimately derived from Byzantine sources. Reculver's and Saint Pancras's apses each contain a *synthronon*, or bench for the clergy, which occurs in both Rome and northern Greece, but which may have been transmitted to England via the Continent; parallel *synthronon* arrangements were found in a 1956 excavation of the east end of a mid-sixth-century church at Laubendorf (Kärnten), Austria.[14] The chord of the apse at three of the Kentish churches—Saint Pancras, Lyminge, and Reculver, and possibly at Saints Peter and Paul, Saint Mary at Canterbury, and Saint Andrew (where evidence is incomplete)—was marked off by a triple arcade. This was possibly also the case at Saint Peter-on-the-Wall, Bradwell. This arcade may have been a practical solution to the problem of a wide chancel arch, technically difficult for novice stonemasons.[15] On the other hand, the arcade has parallels in North Africa, as at Bénian and Tigzirt, and in isolated examples in Europe, as at Lugdunum Convenarum. Like its analogues elsewhere, the Kentish triple arcade may have served both as a structural support and as an iconostasis, possibly supporting wooden screens.[16]

From an examination of the remains at Reculver, H. M. Taylor has proposed that the altar was placed in front of the central arch of the triple arcade, here and in other Kentish churches.[17] This placement of the altar before the chord of the apse was not only similar to the arrangement of the sanctuary of the Basilica of Saint Peter in Rome, but was also common in the eastern Mediterranean, as in Basilica A at Nea-Anchialos.[18] However, the Kentish churches differed from these Mediterranean churches because they lacked both aisles and transepts, which were corollary in Mediterranean churches with the placement of the altar in front of the apse chord. The Kentish churches were usually flanked not by aisles, but by lateral chambers or porticus. These were often part of the original construction of the churches, although in some cases, as at Saint Andrew's Rochester, they were later additions.[19] Western porticus, serving as narthex or entry porch, were original at Saint Pancras and Saints Peter and Paul and added on later at Reculver. Reculver was eventually surrounded completely by these chambers much as Saints Peter and Paul was from the outset. At Saints Peter and Paul, there were three porticus on each side of the church as well as one to the west, but this quantity is unusual, and may have been determined by the intended use of the church as a burial space.[20] However, the most common arrangement of porticus was the placement of one on each lateral flank of the church at the junction of nave and apse, as at Reculver, Saint Pancras, Bradwell, and possibly also Lyminge. The paired porticus did make these Kentish churches cruciform in layout, but they cannot be interpreted as transepts because access to them was limited, through narrow doorways.[21] The placement of these porticus suggests that they functioned as the pastophories common in eastern Mediterranean churches and may indicate elements of Eastern liturgy in the Roman Church in England.[22] However, the arrangement of access to these chambers varies from church to church. Only at Bradwell, Saint Cedd's later church in Essex, can the classic Eastern arrangement be said to have pertained, with north porticus as a prothesis accessible only from the chancel and south porticus as diaconicon open to the nave for the reception of offerings. At Lyminge, the one remaining portal opened to the chancel; at Reculver, both were accessible from the chancel; at Saint Andrew, the one later porticus opened onto the nave, and the arrangement at Saint Pancras is unclear.[23] The liturgical function of the porticus probably varied considerably among the Kentish churches, which would naturally affect arrangements for access. The porticus were used for burial, and possibly also served as oratories for private devotion, or for storage, or as auxiliary spaces substituting for the absent aisles.[24] The early Kentish churches were parts of small monastic communities that served as missionary bases among a largely non-Christian laity, where local building was done largely in wood. Consequently, building in stone, on no matter how small a scale, was a major undertaking, without locally available technical skill or a large, devoted labor force. Augustine's associates and followers were able to import portable goods of the highest quality, but were probably forced by circumstances to build their churches themselves, with, at most, technical advisors from the Continent. It was not until a generation later that foreign stonemasons are documented in England.[25] The continuous aisle was probably beyond the technical expertise of the amateur builders of these communities. The porticus, essentially a simple lean-to room attached to the exterior wall of a two-cell church, was a more feasible solution to the need for auxiliary space for the collection of offerings, the vesting of clergy, and other functions peripheral to the Mass. Such solutions were tried elsewhere in the hinterlands of Christianity, probably under similar conditions: at the fifth-century church at Romainmoutier and the sixth- or seventh-century church of Notre-Dame-sous-le-Bourg, Saint Maurice d'Aguane (both in Switzerland), in the early-seventh-century cemeterial chapel of Saint Germain at Speyer, and at Allenberg in the South Tirol.[26]

The tone of the development of the art of the Roman Church in England was set by the earliest phases of the mission in Kent, where by necessity style was determined by the provenance of imports rather than by any indigenous frame of reference. The portable objects used by the Church here came from Mediterranean and Continental sources; and ecclesiastical architecture, while not portable, was imported in its medium—stonework—and in its forms—triple chancel arcades, stilted semicircular apses, and so on. These forms were borrowed with or without their original functions from ultimately eastern Mediterranean, North African, and Gallic sources. The art of the Roman Church in England was, like the Church itself, fundamentally an alien transplant, which would maintain in some sectors a strong separation from the indigenous culture until remarkably late in its history. This was not the case with the art of the Celtic Church in Ireland and in England, where the art of different cultures was readily assimilated to local taste. The separatism of the art of the Roman Church was founded partly in an association of the purity of the transmitted faith with the unaltered emulation of imported examples of its art. This deliberate stylistic self-isolation continued in Northumbria in two contexts: at the closely linked monastic centers of Jarrow and Monkwearmouth (founded by Benedict Biscop and perpetuated by his successor Ceolfrith), and at the foundations established or embellished by Saint Wilfrid at Hexham, Ripon, and York.

The Roman Church in Northumbria and the Foundations of Benedict Biscop

The Roman Church came to Northumbria in 625, much as it had come to Kent in 597, in the wake of a royal marriage—of Edwin of Northumbria to Æthelburh, a Christian Kentish princess. Paulinus, one of the early assistants sent by Gregory to Augustine to aid in the establishment of the Roman mission in Kent, was now consecrated bishop by Archbishop Justus for the combined purpose of accompanying the new queen to the north as her chaplain and of attempting the conversion of the Northumbrians. Paulinus's missionary campaign, at least according to Bede's account, proceeded with same secure inevitability that had characterized the conversion of Kent.[27] Thereafter the Northumbrian court remained at least nominally Christian and moreover provided well-endowed clergy, including the two most prominent patrons of the Late Antique spirit in Northumbria—Benedict Biscop and Wilfrid.

The life of Benedict Biscop, founder of the closely affiliated monastic communities of Jarrow and Monkwearmouth, is known through Bede's *Lives of the Abbots*.[28] Biscop Baducing in secular life was a noble-born Northumbrian who spent his youth as a soldier in the personal entourage of King Oswy. He prospered in this career, receiving landed estates for his service. However, at the age of twenty-five, he decided to pursue a religious vocation, and to embark upon this new life not by joining a local monastic house, but by traveling to Rome. His first journey, in 653, was a pilgrimage to see the shrines, churches, and martyria. Biscop certainly must have visited the major churches of Rome, including Saint Peter's, Santa Maria Maggiore, the Lateran, and Saint Paul-outside-the-Walls, as well as the shrines of the martyrs in the cemeteries and catacombs, which were at this time being extensively restored to attract pilgrims.[29] Biscop shortly returned to England, but traveled to Rome four more times: in 665, 671, 676, and 685. On his second journey, he left Rome to study for two years at Lérins, the famous ascetic community near Cannes. He received the tonsure at Lérins before returning to Rome briefly in 668. At this time, Pope Vitalian appointed him to guide Theodore of Tarsus, the newly appointed archbishop of Canterbury, to England. Biscop consequently became involved in the political life of the Roman Church in England. After many delays, Biscop brought Theodore safely to his new see in 669, and was awarded the abbacy of Augustine's house of Saint Peter in Canterbury. Bede's description of Biscop's third voyage, in 671, includes the first mention of his importation of a wide variety of religious books—some bought, some received as gifts, some collected earlier and left at Vienne. He also brought relics of the apostles and martyrs with him to England. On his return, he was given a grant of land by Ecgfrith of Northumbria, Oswy's son and heir, and used it to found the abbey of Monkwearmouth. In 681–82, he transformed a second royal estate at Jarrow into another monastic community, assigning its leadership to his follower Ceolfrith.

On his deathbed many years later, Biscop described to his followers and associates the rule he had had in mind in founding his monastic communities:

> You must not think . . . that this institute which I drew up for you was simply the impulsive voice of my heart, without any study having gone into it. What I have passed on to you . . . is nothing but a compilation of all the practices I learned from the seventeen monasteries that, in the course of my frequent travel abroad, I found out were the best.[30]

As with the rule of the life in his foundations, so the very buildings were the best available from foreign centers, but not from any single source. For his constructions at Monkwearmouth, Bede tells us, Biscop crossed the Channel to Gaul to obtain masons to build in stone, and later sent messengers to obtain glaziers.[31] Both the results of Rosemary Cramp's excavations at Monkwearmouth and Jarrow and the visible remains of early stonework amply demonstrate Biscop's intentions.[32]

The layouts of the communities at Jarrow and Monkwearmouth, known through Cramp's excavations, are very different from the more haphazard products of the Celtic Church in Ireland and Northumbria. In both of Biscop's foundations, most of the buildings are regularly oriented on the basis of the alignment to the major church of the site.[33] On the other hand, they cannot be said to be laid out according to a particular custom, for the layout differs between the two foundations, and certain buildings, such as Building D at Monkwearmouth, are irregularly sited. Nonetheless, Biscop's foundations show a general rectilinearity and affection for perpendicularity in the mutual siting of buildings that ultimately derive from Roman city planning and are evident in contemporary Continental ecclesiastical establishments. Moreover, the wealth in land of Biscop's monasteries parallels monastic holdings in Gaul. Monkwearmouth was given a basic land grant of seventy hides, and Jarrow of forty. These were not insubstantial pieces of property, as a hide was reckoned in Bede's day as a unit of land sufficient to support a family.[34] Moreover, the standing remains of Biscop's architecture in the churches at both sites and archaeological evidence of the monastic communities show that no expense was spared in the construction and embellishment of the monastic buildings, despite the individual poverty of the monks.[35]

The churches at Jarrow and Monkwearmouth have both been substantially altered in the intervening centuries since Biscop's masons from Gaul first set stone on stone. At Jarrow, the old church of Saint Paul was destroyed in 1782, and only part of the chapel of Saint Mary was preserved in the chancel of the

St. Paul, Jarrow (Tyne and Wear), chancel

St. Peter, Monkwearmouth (Tyne and Wear), view of west tower

modern church. However, a drawing of 1769 in the British Museum (BMK 12.47B) gives a further idea of the original church. Of Saint Peter's at Monk-wearmouth, only parts of the west wall of the nave and the first two stories of the entry porch tower at the west end date from the early Saxon period. However, the churches of both sites are known substantially from remnants in the fabric of the modern churches and from archaeological examination of their sites.[36]

It is known from Bede's *Lives of the Abbots* and the *Anonymous Life of Ceolfrith* that each site had one major church: Saint Peter at Monkwearmouth and Saint Paul at Jarrow. However, the documents also indicate that there was more than one church at each site, each of which had a separate chapel dedicated to the Virgin.[37] At Jarrow, this chapel survives in the chancel of the modern church, aligned on the east end of Saint Paul's; the two churches were joined by a tower built by Abbot Aldwin in the eleventh century. At Monkwearmouth the situation is slightly more complex. The *Life of Ceolfrith* refers to both an eastern porticus "to the east of the altar" where Biscop was buried, and to a separate church of Saint Mary.[38] Multiple-church foundations on the Continent, such as Tours and Bordeaux, served at least in part as models for the layouts of Biscop's monasteries—not surprising, given Biscop's reference to Continental sources for his foundations.

The proportions of Saint Peter at Monkwearmouth and Saint Paul and Saint Mary at Jarrow are typical of early Anglian stone churches in Northumbria. From the west nave wall it can be deduced that Saint Peter was 18.5 feet in internal width and thirty feet in internal height. According to excavated dimensions, Saint Paul at Jarrow also was 18.5 feet wide, and 165 feet in internal

St. John, Escomb (Durham)

St. Mary, Seaham (Nthld.)

St. Andrew, Corbridge (Nthld.), nave wall arch stone window

length. These measurements indicate churches of very much greater length and height than width. These proportions, on the smaller scale approximately equal to Saint Mary's, are paralleled in surviving Northumbrian churches at Escomb, Corbridge, and Seaham, and are probably derived more from indigenous secular wooden architecture than from any Continental prototypes. In addition, the churches of Monkwearmouth and Jarrow share with other Northumbrian churches such devices of masonry as the use of side-alternate quoining, as opposed to the long-and-short work found in the Kentish churches, and also the arch-carved single-stone window cap and the single-splayed window.[39] These similarities may derive from the diffusion of stonemasonry techniques from Biscop's foundations.[40]

On the other hand, Biscop's churches share a number of features that separate them from other extant Northumbrian churches. First, they may have had parallel porticus arranged as in the Kentish churches, flanking the junction of nave and chancel. When an arch collapsed in the transept of Saint Peter's in 1971, a shallow footing wall was found that indicated a northern porticus overlapping nave and chancel. A parallel southern porticus has been postulated by Cramp as having since been destroyed in the construction of the southern transept.[41] At Jarrow, the north wall of Saint Mary's has traces of an arched doorway close to the east end, suggesting a similar arrangement of porticus there. The absence of these chancel-wing porticus at other Northumbrian churches may indeed indicate the lack of established liturgical function for these auxiliary spaces; they must have been dispensable, particularly in financially constricted circumstances.

The internal arrangements of the churches of Biscop's foundations are most readily assumed to parallel the aisleless churches at Corbridge and Escomb. However, Biscop's churches may have had aisles. At Saint Peter's, the extant western porch was an early addition. It is not in bond with the original west nave wall but was present by 716 when the body of Abbot Eostrewine was translated from it to the chancel. Indeed, it may have been added to the western facade as early as 685, expressly for the burial of Eostrewine. The original western nave wall doorway is off center to the south, a displacement possibly designed to accommodate the grave of the abbot. This may indicate that the west nave wall was unfinished when the western porch was added and that its portal still could be placed to accommodate the burial in the porch.[42] However, within the early Anglian period, possibly at the time of Eostrewine's translation to the chancel, the western end of the church was rearranged. A new western nave door was cut, taller and in a centered position; a second story was added to the porch, and lower annexes were added to the north and south of the porch tower. The southern annex has been excavated, and was found to extend twelve to fifteen feet to the south of the external wall of the west porch. Cramp has suggested that these annexes opened into aisles, although no trace of these aisles has been found.[43] If there were aisles at Saint Peter's, were they open to the nave or enclosed wall passages? If open, were they longitudinally open as well, in traditional basilican fashion, or were they subdivided into a series of separate porticus chambers, as at Saints Peter and Paul at Canterbury? Neither of these questions can be answered from the present archaeological data. At Saint Paul's at Jarrow there may also have been aisles, for the nave walls in the 1769 British Museum drawing show distinct traces of arcading, which may have originally separated nave and aisles.[44] However, the date of these arcades relative to the wall structure cannot be determined from the sketch, leaving some of the same problems as at Saint Peter's. Did these arcades open into aisles or to a series of chambers along the nave walls? Moreover, the question of the date of these hypothetical aisles at Biscop's foundations is crucial. If aisles were original to Biscop's structures, then their founder may have required from his Gallic architects copies of those great basilican churches of Gaul and Rome which he had no doubt seen on his journeys.[45] If aisles, or rows of chambers, or wall passages were added to Monkwearmouth in conjunction with the 716 translation of Eostrewine and the hypothetically simultaneous reworking of the western facade of the church, then the addition postdated Wilfrid's remarkable churches at Ripon and Hexham and might have been an attempt by the monks of Biscop's foundations to bring their churches up to those high standards. The arcading in the British Museum drawing of Jarrow strongly resembles extant brick arcading at Brixworth, Northamptonshire, a church sometimes associated with Wilfrid, where aisles were immediately or later divided into a series of chambers, and where, moreover, a two-story western porticus was probably included from the start.[46] Do the Jarrow arcades postdate Brixworth, or does the influence run in the opposite direction? Without further data, one is left reconstructing hypothetical churches and cross-influences.

However, the churches of Jarrow and Monkwearmouth were more complex in internal arrangements than other contemporary churches in Northumbria. Galleries were included at both Saint Mary's at Jarrow and Saint Peter's at Monkwearmouth. At Monkwearmouth, the gallery was evidently against the western wall of the nave, supported by a huge L-shaped beam passed through the total thickness of the western wall seventeen feet above the nave floor. The magnitude of this beam and its integral unity with the western wall of the church indicate that the gallery was built or at least planned at the time of the first program of construction. The gallery was visible from the second floor of the porth tower through two round-headed windows, but probably accessible only from the nave via a wooden stair.[47] At Saint Mary's at Jarrow, a wall gallery was accessible via an exterior stair to a doorway placed high on the west end of the south wall. A jamb and part of an arched door head of this entrance are visible today near the later Decorated window. Round-headed entries in the later west wall, part of Abbot Aldwin's tower, are at the same level.[48] This gallery was thus like that at Saint Peter's—ranged against the west wall of the church—but could have been a later addition, as no part of it was integral to the body of the church.

For the most part, extant Continental examples of church galleries are later, as in the Carolingian church of Saint Peter at Jumièges and the ninth-century church at Oviedo in Spain, but the type probably came to England from the

Continent. Similar galleries at Hexham served to house hidden choirs.[49] The importance of the choir in the liturgy of Biscop's foundations is stressed by Bede, who tells us not only that Biscop brought John, the archchanter of Saint Peter's in Rome, to Monkwearmouth to introduce singing, chanting, and liturgical usage in accordance with Roman practice, but that in his final illness he had the regular psalms of the canonical hours sung antiphonally at his bedside.[50] Consequently, the galleries at Biscop's churches, like those of Wilfrid's, were most probably intended as choir lofts.

So imposing was the stonework of Biscop's churches and so impressive the accomplishments of their masons to contemporaries that Biscop's twin foundations became the center for the dissemination of stone architecture in the north. It is also evident that this stone architecture was closely associated with the orthodoxy of the Roman Church. When King Nechtan of the Picts decided in 710 to bring his nation into conformity with Roman liturgical practice, he sent to Ceolfrith, Biscop's successor in the dual abbacy, for architects to build him a church in the Roman style. The porch of the tower at Restenneth Priory, Angus, which resembles the western porch at Saint Peter's Monkwearmouth in form and proportions, is believed to be part of Nechtan's church. Restenneth was within Nechtan's private domain in Angus, and was later the center from which Boniface conducted his eighth-century campaign to bring the Picts into conformity with Rome. Nechtan borrowed not only the medium and some of the form of his church from the churches of his advisor's foundations, but also the dedication to Saint Peter, with its deliberate Roman associations. Documents also mention churches with the same dedication built by Nechtan at Invergowrie and Tealing.[51]

Biscop not only desired his foundations to be structurally the best and the most imposing possible in his remote circumstances, but he also wished them to be elaborately ornamented. His Gallic masons began the task with the application of carved stone church furnishings and architectural ornament. This process of decoration in stone must have appeared technically miraculous to Anglian contemporaries, accustomed to architecture in wood, and the introduction of stone carving at Biscop's foundations had far-reaching effects in the art of postconversion Northumbria.

The west porch of Saint Peter at Monkwearmouth and a collection of fragments from Jarrow now assembled in the north porch of Saint Paul give, no doubt, only a partial summary of the repertory of Biscop's stonemasons. At Monkwearmouth, the outer portal of the western porch was not designed to hold a door but rather to provide a rich visual preamble in carved stone to the building beyond. The round arch of the westward opening is supported on a pair of massive flattened and chamfered impost blocks, similar to those at the sixth-century baptistry at Venasque near Fulda and in other early Gallic constructions. These imposts rest on pairs of turned dwarf columns or baluster shafts, for which parallels have been found at Novaillé.[52] Similar balusters have been found in substantial numbers at Jarrow, but their function there is unknown. These elements distinctly demonstrate the stylistic influence of the

St. Peter, Monkwearmouth, west porch entrance

St. Peter, Monkwearmouth, west porch entrance colur

Gallic masons at Biscop's churches, for the prevalence of large numbers of columns—structural or ornamental—is a feature of every extant or documented Gallic church of the period.[53] At Monkwearmouth the paired balusters stand clear of the wall and are supported on stone shelves, the faces of which, toward the portal, are carved with shallow relief. These relief carvings are, however, not in any way related to the Mediterranean or Late Antique schools of ornament. Instead, they show paired serpentlike beasts with long beaks interlocked and tails intertwined in a guilloche—animal ornament reminiscent of the Sutton Hoo belt buckle or perhaps of the more orderly creatures of the *Book of Durrow.* It is odd to find this device in a structure that, in almost every other way, is so totally transplanted, so foreign to English soil. It may be that the stonemasons here took their inspiration from Anglian portable art, translating it into an alien medium and giving it unprecedented symmetry. However, it is also possible that Anglo-Saxon wooden architecture, like its later distant cousin—the stave church—was decorated with relief carvings, whether apotropaic or purely aesthetic, and that no building of the Angles was considered complete without them.

The collection of fragments at Jarrow shows more of the decorative vocabulary of the stonemasons from Gaul. Miniature baluster friezes (only 3.5 inches in height) and panels of simple interlace, wave patterns, chevrons, and cable moldings must have ornamented interior walls or imposts. The baluster frieze is ultimately a Roman motif, but the immediate model could be local or Gallic.[54] Some fragments of internal fittings, such as a horizontal panel showing a striding figure in a thicket of blooming vines, are possibly later additions, for

Jarrow, balusters

Jarrow, baluster frieze

Jarrow, interlace panel

Jarrow, chevrons, rope molding, wave pattern

Jarrow, panel, figure in a vine

the tubular drapery of the figure and the simplicity of the trilobate berries resemble the carving of mid-eighth-century crosses, such as that at Saint Andrew, Auckland, Durham. Equally elaborate, but nonetheless probably quite early by comparison, are a pair of bench ends from Monkwearmouth, carved with lions partly in the round, partly in relief. Both of these are left-hand bench ends, and may have served as armrests for the abbot's throne, with south German parallels, or as the ends of a *synthronon*, as at San Apollinare in Classe in Ravenna, or possibly as one of each of these, considering their leftward orientation. The stone-carving techniques used here are Gallic and probably cannot much postdate Biscop's introduction of foreign personnel.[55]

The churches of Biscop's foundations were further elaborated by the introduction of pictorial cycles. For Monkwearmouth, for the church of Saint Peter, Biscop brought from Rome a number of "painted representations"; probably icons on wood that he hung in his church for their didactic value.[56] On a board across the chancel arch, possibly in imitation of iconostases seen in churches of Eastern orientation in Rome, he placed an icon of the Virgin with the twelve Apostles. To the south wall, he applied a cycle of Gospel scenes; to the north, a series of scenes from the Apocalypse of Saint John. On his fifth journey to Rome, Biscop acquired pictures for the churches at Jarrow: for Saint Paul's, a series of typological parallels; for Saint Mary's, a cycle of the life of Christ. No doubt while in Rome he had been impressed with pictorial cycles such as the mosaics at Santa Maria Maggiore, or the murals at Saint Paul-outside-the Walls, but probably could not induce a workshop of artisans in either of these media to leave Rome for the edges of the known earth. Mosaicists and mural painters were at work in contemporary France as well, but none of these were apparently available to or within the financial means of Biscop, so portable panels were the most workable alternative.[57] Some fresco technique was, however, used to decorate the interior plaster of the churches and other buildings with simple patterns, primarily in red.

Biscop also called glaziers from the Continent, perhaps the first in England, although he may have been preempted by Wilfrid in the latter's restoration of York Cathedral. The use of this newly imported technique again demonstrates Biscop's desire to fit his communities into the mainstream of European culture and the Late Antique tradition. The colored and striped fragments from the churches and other buildings at his foundations are technically similar to Rhenish glass, which may indicate the provenance of the workshop.[58] The medium became popular quickly among the Anglians, for Bede discusses at length its usefulness for church vessels, lamps, and so forth, and a glass workshop practiced to a relatively late date at Jarow.[59] Nonetheless, the thirst for foreign examples of this strange and delightful medium continued at Biscop's foundations, for a glass vial with a metal base, probably from the Middle East and dating between the seventh and ninth century, was found at Monkwearmouth.[60]

In the construction of his monastic communities no less than in his churches, Biscop found the means to duplicate as closely as possible Continental standards of excellence. At Jarrow, two major stone buildings have been found south of and aligned with the church. Building A, possibly a refectory, was a long rectangular building, 91.5 by 26 feet in internal dimensions. It was extremely solidly constructed, with three massive buttresses along the south wall, which may indicate that it had two stories. This structure was originally

JARROW

Saxon

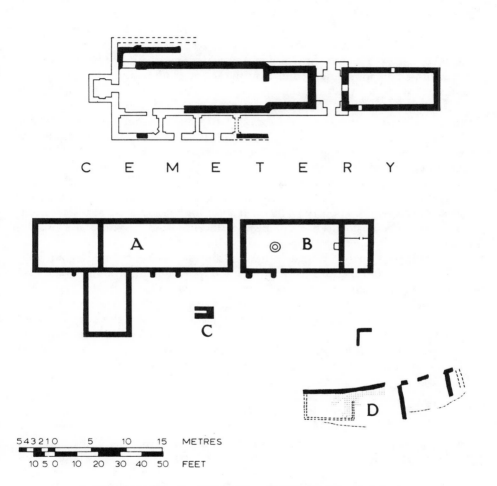

1. Site plan of Jarrow Abbey *(from R. Cramp, by permission)*

subdivided into two rooms, but the party wall was later removed. At some point, a southern annex was added, as a serving pantry or storage room. The floor of Building A was concrete faced with powdered brick—the *opus sig-ninum* common in Roman provincial buildings—and supported an octagonal red sandstone base, probably for a reading stand. This base was decorated with interlace and vinescroll in relief. The walls were internally faced with a creamy plaster, into which patterns were carved on the east wall. The south wall was lined with benches. All the windows were glazed—to the south with clear glass, to the north with colored lights. The building was roofed with small stone slates and finished with lead flashing. Building B, to the east of and aligned with A, measured 60 by 16 feet internally and was subdivided into a large room to the west and two small rooms at the east end. Cramp believes that this building corresponded to the east range in a Benedictine monastery, with the large room serving for assembly and possibly as a scriptorium and the paired small rooms as the private suite of the abbot or senior monk. It might also be suggested that the library might have been housed in the larger room, as it would be an appropriate adjunct to the scriptorium and well housed in this substantial stone structure. The private suite at the east end of Building B consisted of an oratory and a dwelling space, separated by a wooden screen set into a groove in the floor. The oratory had an *opus signinum* floor and a centrally placed stone that may have supported an altar. The living space was partially paved with flagstones and was provided with a lavatory. Yet, despite his intention of equaling the Continental foundations in solidity of construction, Biscop did not choose to emulate in his rule the more questionable individual wealth of individual Continental prelates. This aspect of Biscop's directions was scrupulously maintained at his foundations, for, at Bede's death, his entire personal effects were pepper, incense, and napkins; and archaeological traces of personal goods at Biscop's foundations are scarce.[61]

Elsewhere at Jarrow, Roman structural considerations prevailed in buildings with a variety of functions. A hut to the south of Building A found in the 1973 excavations had reused Roman *tegulae,* or roofing tiles, and *impices,* box tiles. Building D, between A and B and the stream to the south, was a stone structure set back into the natural slope on Roman-style footings and glazed with striped windows. It was apparently in use quite late, for a ninth-century bronze strap end was found inside its perimeter walls, along with a considerable amount of imported pottery of variable date. This latter indicates the long-standing connections of Jarrow to the Continent via commercial trade routes as well as through ecclesiastical channels.

At Monkwearmouth, the layout is considerably less clear.[62] Two buildings from the earliest period are known. Building B of Cramp's excavation plan was a long gallery leading south from and perpendicular to the nave of the church of Saint Peter. This 10-foot-wide gallery has been traced some 105 feet and continues unexcavated further southward. It was roofed in lead, plastered internally and externally, glazed, and decorated with baluster shafts, of which many fragments were found. The mortar of Building B is very similar to that in the earliest extant parts of the church, which suggests roughly synchronous construction. To this long passageway was attached Building A, an oblong building 10.5 by 12 feet in interior dimensions, which seems to have served primarily as a mortuary chapel or funerary oratory. Its floor was sunken a foot beneath the Saxon ground level, as in the sunken-floored huts of Anglo-Saxon secular sites;

MONKWEARMOUTH 1974

Saxon I
Saxon II/Norman

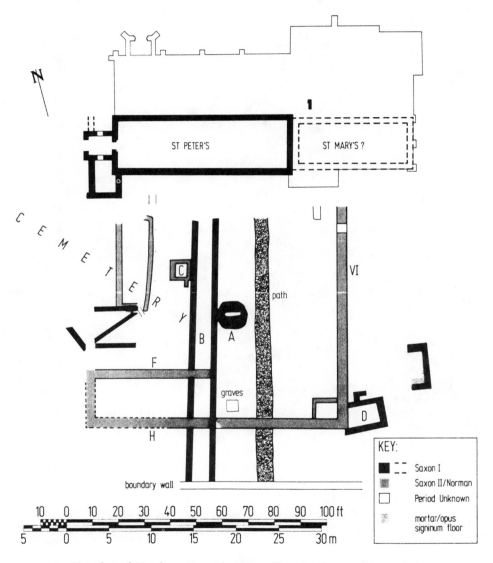

2. Site plan of Monkwearmouth Abbey *(from R. Cramp, by permission)*

Monkwearmouth balusters; Durham, Chapter Library *(by permission of the Dean and Chapter of Durham)*

its walls were also similarly wattle and daub, supported by stakes. Despite this primitive construction, however, the floor was finished in *opus signinum*. It was cut by nine burials with a deeper ossuary pit beneath them. In the west end, a deep rounded niche was cut in the wall, perhaps designed for a primary burial.

Rosemary Cramp has pointed out the similarity of Building B to the connecting galleries of Roman buildings and to later Benedictine cloisters. She finds Building A, on the other hand, reminiscent of the concrete tombs of the archbishops of Canterbury, and of Roman martyria, here partially translated into a vernacular idiom—the sunken-floored hut.[63] An alternative suggestion, is, however, possible for Building A. In the 1971 reconstructed general plan of Jarrow, the ground plan of Building A consists of five sides of an octagon to the west, rounded off to the east. The presence of even a partial octagon suggests serious symbolic intent in the design of this oratory, however small. The only other centriform building in early Anglo-Saxon England was the Church of Saint Mary at Hexham, built under Wilfrid's direction. Aldred of Rielvaulx describes this church as a round structure in the form of a tower, with four projecting porticus. Archaeologically, all that remains of Saint Mary's at Hexham are three bulb-shaped capitals with abaci and neck molds of the same stone, found in 1881 behind the Shambles in a narrow passage traditionally called Old Church, southeast of the abbey toward the Meal Market.[64] Aldred's description suggests a Greek-cross plan around a central tower.

In describing Biscop's ornamentation of the Church of Saint Peter at Monkwearmouth, Bede is very careful to note the location of the cycles on the iconostasis or on a specific nave wall, north or south. However, when he describes the cycle of the life of Christ at Saint Mary's, he says that Biscop intended them to be "hung for decoration all the way around the inside of the church of the Blessed Mother of God." This choice of words suggests that Saint Mary's at Monkwearmouth was centriform, and that Building A may be Saint Mary's.[65]

Centriform martyria, mausoleums, and baptistries were part of the vocabulary of Late Antique and Early Christian architectural symbolism. However, there may also have been a further tradition of centriform churches dedicated to the Virgin, and funereal or martyrial in intent. Hypothetical reconstructions of the church capping the tomb of the Virgin outside Jerusalem call for a centriform building. Descriptions of the structure at this site were, moreover, available in England in the seventh century in pilgrims' accounts of the Holy Land.[66] Further, at the time of Biscop's journeys to Rome, the Pantheon had recently been rededicated by Boniface IV in 608 as Santa Maria ad Martyres, which would have been enough in itself to provide symbolic precedent for Wilfrid's church at Hexham and possibly also Building A, on a smaller scale, at Monkwearmouth.

So far as archaeological and documentary evidence permit reconstruction, Biscop's constructions were architecturally and spiritually as akin to mainstream Late Antique architecture as their founder could command. Biscop's masons from Gaul, the heirs of Roman masonry secrets, were Jarrow's claim to legitimacy in the tradition of ecclesiastical architecture. Bede further notes that, in many cases, church furnishings that could have been manufactured on the site, such as church lamps and vessels, were instead imported, probably out of a preference for the purer and thus more legitimate craftsmanship of the Mediterranean basin and the Continent. Biscop, "like a merchant monk," imported vestments and cloths for the service of his churches as well.[67] Bede explains that many of the necessary items were not available in England, but the communities at Canterbury certainly could have supplied some of these needs, particularly after the establishment of Theodore of Tarsus as archbishop and the resultant strengthening of Canterbury as a center. Moreover, there were certainly adequate craftsmen among the Angles, Saxons, Britons, and Picts to supply patens, chalices, and any other metalwork Biscop's churches might have required. Benedict Biscop, like other clergy of the Roman Church in England before and after him, evidently preferred to obtain foreign supplies even at great expense and difficulty. These imported materials were so desirable because they were considered part of the traditions not only of the Roman Church herself but of the Late Antique world that was her origin and heritage. This clinging to the traditions of the late classical world barred the way at least temporarily of the easy assimilation of indigenous crafts and ornament that simultaneously fostered the unique development of the art of the Celtic Church in Britain and Ireland. The traditions of the emulation of Late Antique forms established by Biscop at his twin foundations were carried yet further under Ceolfrith, not however in architecture, but rather in manuscript illumination, in the *Codex Amiatinus.*

Ceolfrith was, like Biscop, a noble-born Northumbrian.[68] He entered monastic life at the age of eighteen at Gilling, during the reign of Oswy. He subsequently lived at Ripon under the rule of Wilfrid and in East Anglia under Botolph before coming to Monkwearmouth to assist Biscop at his foundation. Ceolfrith accompanied Biscop to Rome on the latter's fourth trip. On his return, he was made the abbot of the new community at Jarrow. Six months before his death, in 688 or 689, Biscop appointed Ceolfrith abbot of Monkwearmouth. Ceolfrith held the double abbacy for twenty-seven years, inheriting from Biscop not only the two foundations but also their remarkable libraries that Biscop had brought piecemeal from Rome and the Continent. Among these texts was a Bible in one volume or pandect, in the Old Latin translation. Ceolfrith decided to supplement this work by the manufacture of three pandects in the Vulgate translation, one for each of his foundations and the third as a gift to the see of Saint Peter. The pandect sent by Jarrow to the see of Saint Peter survives as the *Codex Amiatinus* (Florence, Laurentian Library).[69] The codex eventually came into the library of the monastery of Monte Amiato in Central Italy, possibly in the abbacy of Peter the Lombard in the early tenth century, where the colophon was altered. Peter's name replaced Ceolfrith's, and Monte Amiato claimed authorship of the *Codex.* The colophon, also recorded at Jarrow and independently preserved in the *Anonymous Life of Ceolfrith,* originally read:

> Corpus ad eximii merito venerabile Petri
> Quem caput ecclesiae dedicat alta fides,
> Ceolfridus Anglorum extremis de finibus abbas
> Devoti affectus pignora mitto mei
> Meque meos optans tanti inter gaudia patris
> In caelis memorem semper habere locum.[70]

The *Codex Amiatinus* is a massive (505 by 340 millimeters) volume. If Ceolfrith's other two pandects were equal to *Amiatinus* in scale, the three together required the skins of 1,550 calves for the vellum alone.[71] This figure is at first staggering, until one recalls that the twin foundations held 600 monks at the completion of the project in 716, and that they were closely connected to the royal house, from which they not only had received their initial land grants but also were continually supported with gifts of land and kind.[72]

The script of the *Codex Amiatinus* is a purely classical uncial, unlike the semiuncial favored by later Hiberno-Saxon scriptoria. This uncial, typical of Jarrow manuscripts, was apparently introduced to Northumbria at Biscop's foundations and nurtured there because of its Late Antique authenticity. The Jarrow uncial survived only in this particular classicizing environment and did not affect such neighboring scriptoria as Lindisfarne.[73]

The sources of *Codex Amiatinus* are remarkably clearly traceable. Bede, discussing the making of the three Jarrow Bibles, mentions that the library there already held a similar pandext, which, unlike the three new Bibles, was in the Old Latin translation rather than in the Vulgate. An examination of the first gathering of the *Amiatinus* indicates that this Old Latin pandect was the *Codex Grandior*, written at Vivarium and described by Cassiodorus in his *Institutiones*, which contained a plan of the Temple of Solomon and a series of diagrams comparing the arrangements of the books of the Bible by Saint Hilary, Saint Jerome, and Saint Augustine.[74] These diagrams and the plan appear in the prefatory gathering of *Amiatinus*. Moreover, Bede elsewhere mentions a plan of the Temple that he and his colleagues at Jarrow knew by casual reference, as "Cassiodorus's picture."[75]

Codex Grandior may not have been the only Cassiodoran text to migrate to Jarrow. Bede specified only that there was only one earlier pandect present, in the Old Latin translation, but he does not mention what other works were present to provide Vulgate text models for *Codex Amiatinus* and its fellows. The text of *Amiatinus* is remarkably pure and scholarly Vulgate, which stands at the head of an insular stemma including the *Lindisfarne Gospels* and, more remotely, the *Book of St. Chad* and the *Book of Kells*. John Chapman, the great early-twentieth-century Vulgate scholar, pointed out evidence in *Amiatinus* suggesting that the text model was the *Novem Codices*, a Vulgate Bible in nine volumes also compiled by Cassiodorus at Vivarium. On the table of contents of the *Codex Amiatinus*, on the verso of the fourth folio, the books of the Bible are given in the Vulgate order, but are subdivided into the nine groups of the Old Latin translation that Cassiodorus, in the *Institutiones*, noted that he maintained in the *Novem Codices*. Moreover, despite their Vulgate ordering, the number of listed books is the Old Latin seventy rather than the Vulgate forty-nine, a more workable arrangement given the large number of commentaries inserted in the *Novem Codices*. On the recto of the same folio in *Amiatinus*, a prologue again mentions the seventy books. Chapman believed that this folio, with prologue and table of contents, was taken from the first volume of the *Novem Codices*, which might then easily also provide a source for the near-perfect scholarly Vulgate of *Amiatinus,* with only the first quaternion, excluding the fourth folio, taken from the *Codex Grandior.*[76] However, a single text source for all of *Amiatinus* is not certain. The Gospels text in particular may have had other sources as well.[77]

The art of the *Codex Amiatinus* is as Late Antique, or as noninsular, as its script. In the first quaternion are included an author portrait identified by an inscription as Ezra transcribing the Law (fol. V), a table of contents under arcades on purple-stained leaf (fol. IV), and a two-page opening (fols. IIv, III) showing the plan of the Tabernacle of the Temple of Solomon. The head of each diagram of textual order (fols. VII, VI, 8) is ornamented with a roundel showing a bearded bust of God the Father for Saint Hilary, the Lamb as God the Son for Saint Jerome, and the dove of the Holy Spirit for Saint Augustine. A further diagram on a purple leaf, on the verso of the Saint Hilary diagram, concerns the books of the Pentateuch and was probably originally adjacent to the plan of the Tabernacle. Outside the first quaternion, there is only one other major illumination in *Amiatinus*, at the junction of the Old and New Testaments: a full-page miniature of Christ in Majesty (fol. 796).[78]

The plan of the Temple, the associated Pentateuch table, and the diagrams of text order were all probably copied directly from the *Codex Grandior*. The table of contents, on the other hand, was probably taken from the *Novem Codices*. As these are all basically diagrams, they show less of the stylistic niceties of the illuminator's art than do the author portrait and the Christ in Majesty. Nonetheless, they demonstrate the awareness of the Jarrow copyists of the practices of Late Antique illumination and their willingness to copy exactly the style and technique of their model. The use of purple-stained leaves for the table of contents and the Pentateuch diagram is reminiscent of the great purple codices of sixth-century Byzantium: the *Vienna Genesis*, the *Rossano Gospels*, and the *Sinope Gospels*. The use of silver framing and lettering in yellow orpiment on the table of contents to simulate gold are likewise similar to practice in Byzantine manuscripts. The use of gold and silver are otherwise extremely rare in insular illumination. One indeed wonders whether the editions of Cassiodorus's work to arrive in England were imperial presentation copies instead of the original scholarly volumes, perhaps also providing a model for the huge scale of *Amiatinus*. On the other hand, the library of Vivarium probably included comparably large and elegant volumes, and the title *Codex Grandior* suggests a large volume.

Other classicizing elements in *Amiatinus* include penned-in Corinthian capitals of the frame of the table of contents. Similarly, the attempted perspective of the altar, the table, and the supporting frame of the urn of the Holocaust in the Temple plan were probably copied line for line from the model, as perspective and modeling had no tradition in earlier insular art. The use of gesso and wash on the Temple plan, common in Byzantine codices but rare outside Jarrow in insular illuminations, are also imported techniques, necessary to the stylistic emulation of the model.

The tendency to copy exactly from the model in *Codex Amiatinus* finds its apotheosis in the portrait of the scribe. The couplet above him identifies him as Ezra: "Codicibus sacris hostili clade perustis / Esdras deo fervens hoc reparavit

CODICIBVS SACRIS HOSTILI CLADE PERVSTIS
ESDRA DŌ FERVENS HOC REPARAVIT OPVS

Florence, Laurentian Library, *Codex Amiatinus* **fol. V: Ezra Transcribing the Law**
(by the permission of the Director)

opus." The writer sits on a cushioned bench writing in a sizable codex couched on his lap. He wears the headdress and breastplate of a Hebrew priest, and a large halo. His feet rest on a footrest, and a nearby table supports an inkwell. Around him on the floor, a scholarly clutter of the implements of his trade includes an open book, a marking pointer, a pen, a pair of ink bottles, and a caliper for centering the text on the page. An open cupboard behind him contains nine volumes, a sand horn, and a scroll. The book covers are variously decorated; one on the fourth shelf from the top, on the left, bears a cross. The exterior of the cabinet is painted with a variety of Late Antique and early Christian decorative motifs. On the gable above, two peacocks flank a cross. On the cabinet front above the doors, urns and quadrupeds are arranged around a Chi-Rho emblem in a circle. Panels below the doors show a bird and a cross. The nine volumes suggest that the illumination was taken from the frontispiece of the *Codex Grandior.* If this is the case, the figure may be Cassiodorus, shown as Ezra because of his similar role in the transcription of biblical text, writing the *Codex Grandior* while the *Novem Codices* rest completed in the cupboard behind him.[79]

In this illumination, the artist has made a sincere effort to stay as close as possible to the Late Antique style and techniques of his model.[80] The face of the scribe is modeled by the use of shaded wash over gesso. This modeling technique is not found in earlier or subsequent insular illumination, but rather links *Amiatinus* to Greek manuscripts.[81] Further, the portrait of Ezra shows chipping and flaking that do not occur elsewhere in insular illumination but are common in Byzantine miniatures.[82] The stylistic treatment of the *Amiatinus* Ezra, however, has its closest parallel not in the Byzantine East but in Rome. Frescoes of the Forty Martyrs, the Annunciation, and Christ Healing the Blind Man executed under Pope Martin I (649–53) in Santa Maria Antiqua in Rome show similar facial modeling, albeit in a different medium, and parallel elongated, disjointed figural proportions. The style of these frescoes, however, has its roots in the eastern Mediterranean, in frescoes of about 650 in Hagios Demetrios, Thessaloniki, and in a Sacrifice of Jephtha's Daughter at the side of the apse of Saint Catherine on Mount Sinai. Given these elements of style and technique in the *Amiatinus* Ezra, it has been suggested that the artist who painted it was an Easterner who had come to Jarrow via Rome, or a Roman trained in Byzantine manuscript techniques.[83]

Nonetheless, the imported elements of technique and style in the *Amiatinus* Ezra do not necessarily imply a foreign artisan in Jarrow's scriptorium. Rather they suggest that the illuminators of Jarrow learned their craft through channels to the outside world separate from those of the Celtic illuminators, and that they did not alter their received knowledge in any way. Consequently, along with relayed information on gesso, washes, purple stain, and metallic paints, the Jarrow scriptorium also unfortunately inherited the processes that caused chipping and flaking. However, the *Amiatinus* Ezra also demonstrates various stylistic misunderstandings of its model.[84] The artist has muddled the drapery of Ezra's *tunica talaris.* Further, despite his grave attempts at perspective, he has failed to comprehend the structure of the collapsible table, the internal angles of the cupboard, or the treatment of the shadows of the sand horn and scroll in the cupboard. Also significant is the lack of external documentation of foreigners in Jarrow's scriptorium, particularly in Bede's *Lives of the Abbots,* where other visitors, from masons and glaziers to archchanters, are noted as evidence of Jarrow's sophistication. It is therefore probable that the Ezra artist was an Anglian monk of Jarrow, possibly one who had traveled with Biscop or Ceolfrith to Rome and had seen similar works in progress, but who had at best a good memory of techniques and a powerful model, rather than extensive training in a Roman scriptorium.

The miniature of Christ in Majesty is derived from a different model, less classicizing and naturalistic than that of the Ezra, and probably not from the Cassiodoran sources. Christ is seen seated surrounded by a circular gloriole of bands of color, the innermost of which is decorated with a broad ribbon pattern. Against a field of stars, a stern, haloed Christ is seated facing forward on a high-backed throne with cushion and footstool. He holds a book in his draped left hand while gesturing toward it with his right. He is flanked by a pair of standing angels with rods of office who bow in homage, bending just enough to be fitted into the circular gloriole. Outside the gloriole, the page is painted with broad horizontal bands of color. In each corner, holding a book in his covered hands, is one of the four Evangelists accompanied by his winged, full-length symbol. The Evangelists are arranged in canonical order counterclockwise from the upper left. The full-length symbols have their closest parallels in Ravenna.[85] The model appears to have been an impressionistic Late Antique work similar in style and general provenance to the minatures of the *Cotton Genesis* (London, British Library, MS Cotton Otho B.IV). In both cases the figures are somewhat brittle, with drapery picked out in gold and oddly prominent feet.[86] As the model for the Christ in Majesty was broader and simpler than that of the Ezra, the insular copyist was more adroit at reproducing it and has been able to include something of the stern power of the model as well as a basic delineation of its forms and composition. The model here may also have been more linear and decoratively stylized and consequently more accessible to Anglian stylistic sensibilities.[87]

The monks of the Jarrow scriptorium under Ceolfrith were more inclined to copy foreign models directly than were their predecessors who had been responsible for the architectural forms and ornamentation of Biscop's foundations. *Amiatinus* is truly an exotic hothouse plant, the offshoot of imported models transplanted directly from Mediterranean to insular centers.[88] The result is representative of Jarrow as a center where every stylistic and compositional consideration is directly borrowed from imported models, without the influence of indigenous motifs, crafts, or tastes. Such an isolated phenomenon was not destined to be long-lived. Just as a tropical plant is able to flourish in a hothouse in any climate but must adapt or perish in a northern environment, within a generation the art of the Jarrow scriptorium began to adapt to the indigenous formulas of insular illumination. The two earliest extant man-

Codex Amiatinus, fol. 796v: Christ in Majesty *(by the permission of the Director)*

uscripts of Bede's *Ecclesiastical History,* both probably from Jarrow—the *Leningrad Bede* of 730 and the *Cotton Bede* (London, British Library, MS Cotton Tiberius A.XIV), which is usually dated in the eighth century—use the elaborate initials of the Celtic tradition. Yet Jarrow was not without influence on later insular illumination, particularly as its models and products became progressively available to more assimilatively oriented centers such as Lindisfarne.

Art and Architecture under Wilfrid

Mediterranean culture and its artistic legacy were also forcibly transplanted to the foundations of Wilfrid, bishop of York and abbot of Hexham and Ripon. Wilfrid, however, was not a kindred spirit of Biscop, whose closest modern parallel is the eccentric English gentleman in fiction whose study is packed with the mementos of a dozen trips to some exotic and much-loved port of India or Java. Wilfrid was more the shrewd politician, and his emulation of Mediterranean, and particularly Roman, splendor was not so much a gesture of love and reverence as a statement of political affiliation and of powerful foreign alliances. In the early stages of his career, Wilfrid made his reputation as a fiery orator by speaking for the Roman Church against the stubborn but outmaneuvered Colman of Lindisfarne at the Synod of Whitby in 664. The details of Wilfrid's biography are recorded in the *Vita* by his friend and and admirer Eddius Stephanus.[89] Like Hilda, Biscop, and Ceolfrith, Wilfrid came of a noble Northumbrian house with royal connections. He began his education at Lindisfarne, but soon developed a longing to see Rome, and set out southward with Benedict Biscop in 653. Wilfrid, however, traveled only as far as Lyons. Here Archbishop Dalfinus took Wilfrid under his spiritual and political wing and familiarized him with the temporal powers of bishops in Gaul. Dalfinus offered Wilfrid a province of Gaul and Dalfinus's niece as wife, in the hope of establishing a powerful and permanent ally in the temporal sphere. This must have been a revelation to Wilfrid, who was accustomed to the appointment and relative control of bishops by secular monarchs and not the reverse. Moreover, the wealth of the churches and their prelates in Lyons and in Gaul as a whole must have been a shock to Wilfrid, who had just left the ascetic rigors of Lindisfarne. Despite Dalfinus's offer, Wilfrid nonetheless chose to continue to Rome, where he visited the shrines of the Apostles and martyrs and studied Church law with the archdeacon Boniface, who stressed *computatio* or chronological studies, pointing out the heresies of the Celtic Church. After leaving Rome, Wilfrid returned to Lyons for three years before taking ship for England. In his ten years abroad, he had learned two lessons that would affect the rest of his career: the primacy that Rome asserted for herself in decisions on doctrine and practice, and the wealth and power adhering both to Rome and to the Continental bishops.

The circumstances of his return to England immediately suggested to Wilfrid that the attitudes of the Church of Rome and her aristocratic clergy might be applicable even to this land of small monastic communities and tribal kingdoms without permanent courts. Alchfrith, Oswy's son and underking of Deira, was a longtime supporter of the Roman Church and had at one point wanted to travel to Rome with Benedict Biscop. He now welcomed Wilfrid as a papal messenger, "prostrated himself at the feet of [Wilfrid], received his message, and asked for his blessing." Even if Eddius exaggerates, as is his stylistic habit, it is clear that Wilfrid had the upper hand with Alchfrith from the outset. Eddius uses the biblical reference to David and Jonathan to describe the relationship of the young prelate and his royal patron. Alchfrith immediately set out to demonstrate his loyalty to Rome, first by evicting the Celtic monks from Ripon and giving it with three thousand acres to Wilfrid, and second by arranging for Wilfrid to be ordained priest by Agilbert, bishop of Wessex, whose Roman loyalties were unquestionable. Agilbert, Alchfrith, and Wilfrid together formed the Roman faction at Whitby in 664, possibly in the same year as Wilfrid's ordination. In the course of the disputation over the Northumbrian see of Colman of Lindisfarne, Wilfrid traveled to Gaul to be consecrated by fourteen Gallic bishops. On his return, Wilfrid "acted as a bishop in several areas," despite the fact that Chad held the diocese of Northumbria until Wilfrid secured that position under Theodore of Canterbury.[90] Once having secured his diocese, Wilfrid restored the cathedral at York, providing it with not only decorations and sacred paraphernalia, but also vast tracts of land. He also built an abbey church at Ripon and enriched it with gold and silver vessels and an altar cloth in imperial purple and gold. The consecration of this church was a major event for the Northumbria of its day, and Wilfrid seized the moment to press the cause of the Roman Church. King Ecgfrith was present as were his brother Ælfwine, foreign dignitaries, underkings, officials, and nobility. After the service of consecration, Wilfrid stood before the altar, read aloud a list of the lands already in his possession, and then enumerated formerly Celtic holdings and foundations, concerning which he thought "God would indeed be pleased" if they were added to his estates. The kings and officials consented, possibly overwhelmed by the splendor of the church and the consecration. The ceremony was followed by three days of feasting. Such munificence by a clergyman for the consecration of a monastic church was unprecedented in Northumbria, where ascetic Celtic Christianity had been the norm, but totally in keeping with Gallic and Roman practices. Wilfrid followed his work at Ripon with the yet more magnificent church at Hexham.

In 678 dispute arose between Wilfrid and Ecgfrith. The king had previous cause to dislike the prelate, who had encouraged Ecgfrith's first queen, Ætheldreda, to persist in remaining chaste throughout their twelve years of marriage.[91] By 678 Ecgfrith had married Iurminburgh, whom Eddius paints as an evil slanderer, but who may actually have hit close to the mark in pointing out to the king the growing power, wealth, and influence of Wilfrid. Somehow (through bribery according to Eddius), Archbishop Theodore was convinced to remove Wilfrid from his see, appointing three bishops in his place to divide his vast diocese and estates. Suddenly deprived of office and wealth, Wilfrid made a decision that demonstrated the power of the lessons of his youth. He set off for Rome to appeal to the Holy See. He presented his petition before Pope Agatho, claiming that he had been robbed of his see without having been condemned of any crime, and that this and the consecration of his three replacements were irregularities under canon law. The council granted his petition wholeheartedly. On his return to Britain, however, he found that Ecgfrith and his queen chose to disregard the papal decree in Wilfrid's favor. The king went so far as to order Wilfrid imprisoned and his property confiscated. He was held until his friend Æbbe, abbess of Coldingham, announced that his imprisonment was the cause of a severe illness of the queen. As a result, Wilfrid was released but exiled from Northumbria. Wilfrid took refuge in Sussex, where he converted the pagan king, Æthelwalh and received estates. Finally Archbishop Theodore, in his old age, made peace with Wilfrid and convinced Aldfrith, Ecgfrith's successor, to receive Wilfrid and restore his see. However, Wilfrid's opponents wasted no time in stirring up trouble between the prelate and the new monarch. Soon thereafter, Aldfrith insisted on honoring Theodore's earlier decree, removing Wilfrid from the episcopal throne of Northumbria. Wilfrid decided to appeal to Rome once more, which he did with identical results: exoneration of all charges and a papal decree of restoration. On Wilfrid's return to England, the Mercian king, Æthelred, and his appointed heir, Coenred, swore him their support, a gesture stemming more from their political rivalry with Northumbria than from any loyalty to Rome. Aldfrith, however, remained committed against Wilfrid to his deathbed, where his repentance was sincere but quickly nullified by his successor Eadwulf. However, Eadwulf reigned only two months, and his successor, the boy-king Osred, deeply under Wilfrid's influence, saw to it that the latter's see and possessions were restored by a synod held on the banks of the Nidd River. Wilfrid was finally reinstated as bishop of Northumbria, as he had so long desired, but he lived to enjoy his success for only eighteen months. He died at one of his monasteries in the Oundle valley and was buried at Ripon.

Beyond the miracles and the saintly character ascribed to him by Eddius, Wilfrid was a politically astute ecclesiastic, as full of the affairs of his day as the hermit saints of the Celtic Church were removed from them. Despite his gift for political intrigue, however, Wilfrid's ambition was not primarily personal. Like the Gallic bishops, he saw episcopal power as a means of pastoral function, placing bishops on a par with kings, allowing them to become a focus of strength and stability in troubled times.[92] Indeed, the bishops of Gaul, on whom Wilfrid modeled his career, provided the major threads of social continuity amid the coups and intrigues of the Merovingian dynasty. However, to provide such a focus of strength, Wilfrid had to establish an episcopal kingdom within Northumbria. Such a kingdom was doomed from the outset because its scale and wealth drew the envy of kings, abbots, and bishops used to smaller, more mobile, and less monolithic government. Moreover, Wilfrid's attempt to enforce the will of external authority—the Petrine authority of Rome—could scarcely anticipate welcome from the kings and bishops of Northumbria, who had proven willing at Whitby to accept Roman practices by their own decision but not necessarily by the fiat of papal decree. Wilfrid fell from power because he was unable or unwilling to relinquish or in any way compromise the lessons of his youth. These lessons of papal authority and of the value of ecclesiastical power are reflected equally in the grandiose ambitions of the architecture and art that Wilfrid commissioned.

Wilfrid's architectural projects at York, Ripon, and Hexham are fascinating but highly controversial problems for modern reconstruction. Of these three buildings, only the crypts of Hexham and Ripon remain partially intact. Fortunately, Eddius and later chroniclers described the churches at Hexham and Ripon. Moreover, Saxon stonework brought to light when the Norman abbey at Hexham was torn down and replaced before 1907 is recorded in a plan and general archaeological survey done between 1905 and 1908 by C. C. Hodges.[93] The plan, however, lends itself to a variety of possible reconstructions, and the medieval descriptions are so vague as to aggravate the controversies over these churches rather than to resolve them.

The restoration of the cathedral church at York was Wilfrid's first project. The earlier church of Edwin and Oswald was in poor repair, but Wilfrid undertook to restore rather than replace the building at hand. Edwin had begun to build a "greater and more magnificent church of stone" around the wooden church in which he had been baptised. This project was later completed by Oswald. Bede describes Edwin's church as follows: "The foundations were laid and he began to build this square church surrounding the former chapel."[94] The description suggests a simple quadrilateral or rectangular church, built without foreign masons such as Biscop subsequently employed at Jarrow. Edwin's church probably resembled the Kentish churches with which Paulinus and his associates were familiar. The church at York had porticus in the Kentish manner, for Bede notes that Edwin's head was laid to rest at York in the porticus of Saint Gregory.[95] Eddius describes how Wilfrid replaced the roof ridges of Edwin's church and had them coated with lead. The roofing material, probably thatch, was also replaced as it had become leaky with age, and the windows were glazed for the first time. The walls were whitewashed, and the interior of the building was decorated, although Eddius is not specific on the nature of the decorations.[96]

Documentary descriptions of Hexham and Ripon, on the other hand, indicate that Wilfrid was capable of more grandiose architectural efforts. Eddius describes Ripon, the first church Wilfrid built from the ground up, as "a church built of dressed stone, supported with columns and complete with porticus."[97] The key word in Eddius's description is *porticus*, which, as encountered in the Kentish churches and in Edwin's probably similar church in York, can be defined as a discrete auxiliary chamber, accessible from the main body of the church through a doorway and used for a variety of purposes including burial. However, the term is susceptible to a variety of definitions. Originally derived from *porta*, understood in classical architecture as a vestibule or entryway, often embellished with an open-sided porch or canopy on columns, *porticus* came to mean first an open colonnade, columned structure, or arcade, or additionally a vestibule, side space, or adjunct opening into the main body of a building. Medieval writers used the term with great freedom. Prior Richard of Hexham, in his description of Wilfrid's church of Saint Mary at Hexham probably used the word *porticus* in the sense of a separate chamber, as Bede did in describing the burial chambers at Saints Peter and Paul at Canterbury, the latter confirmed by archaeological investigation. However, when William of Malmesbury describes Duncan of Glastonbury's additions to a church, designed to make it as wide as it was originally long, he uses the expression *alas vel porticus*, "aisles or porticus," which has been interpreted as "side aisles."[98] Translators of Eddius have consistently read *porticus* in Eddius's descriptions of Wilfrid's churches as "side aisles," suggesting that Wilfrid's basilicas were modeled on the great aisled churches of Rome and the Continent.[99] However, the texts use the nebulous term *porticus* and, at Ripon, in the absence of archaeological information, no particular kind of space can be assumed. Moreover, mention of columns supporting the church does not necessarily indicate arcades, for in descriptions of contemporary churches on the Continent, supportive columns are frequently mentioned whether they hold up arcades or bolster the nave wall itself, as do the applied wall columns at Saint Pierre at Vienne. Consequently, the upper church at Ripon cannot be reconstructed from the documentary evidence alone.

Brixworth, Northamptonshire, sometimes associated with Wilfrid, preserves arcades that led to a row of porticus either original to the design or walled off from a continuous aisle very early.[100] Jarrow may have had either aisles or chambers accessible through arcades similar to those at Brixworth. The church at Wing, Buckinghamshire, may also have had aisles, but its date is indeterminate. Estimates of date for the aisled church at Lydd, Kent, have varied from the Roman occupation to the eighth century.[101] Hence there are no parallels elsewhere in England to determine with certainty whether Wilfrid's churches were aisled or flanked by rows of discrete chambers.

Of Hexham, Eddius is more eloquent, but equally difficult to interpret:

> At Hexham [Wilfrid] built a church to the glory of God and the honour of St. Andrew on land given by the saintly queen Æthelthryth. My poor mind is at quite a loss for words to describe it: the great depth of the foundations, the crypts of beautifully dressed stone, the vast structure supported by columns of various styles and with numerous *porticus*, the walls of remarkable height and length, the many winding passages and spiral staircases leading up and down. Without a doubt it was the spirit of God who taught our bishop to plan the construction of such a place, for we have never heard of its like this side of the Alps. Bishop Acca . . . decked out this superb edifice with splendid gold and silver ornaments, precious stones and silks and purples for the altars. What description could do justice to the fabric he installed?[102]

Other documentary information substantiates or contradicts Eddius's description. Prior Richard of Hexham comments that the walls were indeed high, *tribus tabulatis distinctos*, "in three stories," and that there were hidden galleries for choirs. He mentions moreover that the chancel arch was carved with reliefs, and that there were multiple oratories in the porticus.[103] Bede may possibly contradict Eddius on the role of Wilfrid's successor, for he tells us that Acca "enriched the fabric of his church . . . with all kinds of decoration and works of art. He took great trouble . . . to gather relics . . . and to put up altars for their veneration, establishing various chapels for this purpose within the walls of the church."[104] The word *ampliavit*, here translated as "enriched," can also be translated as "enlarged," "made wide," or "glorified," of which the first two imply structural alterations, not simple decoration.

Eddius used the hyperbole common to early Western church descriptions in describing Hexham. Consequently, reconstruction of the church from his description is difficult, given the additional oblique and contradictory comments of other writers. Fortunately, unlike Ripon, the Anglian structure at Hexham is to some extent known archaeologically through Hodges's plan. However, this plan is difficult to interpret. Hodges's criterion for establishing the generically Saxon date of the foundations in his plan was the nature of the mortar used in their construction. The use of his records implies acceptance of his judgment concerning the date of these walls, for the presence of the modern minster precludes the possibility of extensive excavation on the site, although some observations have been made possible by the recent restoration of the crypt.[105] Moreover, Hodges did not distinguish between those walls which were part of Wilfrid's original construction and those which might be a part of Acca's improvements. Finally, Hodges may not have noted all extant Saxon

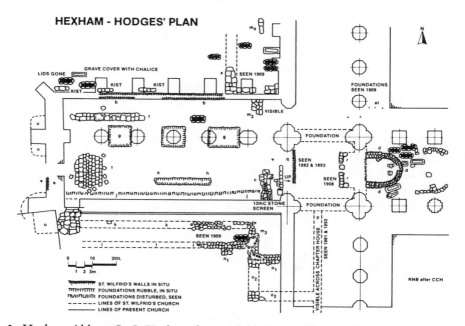

3. Hexham Abbey: C. C. Hodges plan, with his key and descriptive notes; walls and foundations are assigned the same letters as in Taylor and Taylor, *Anglo-Saxon Architecture*, 297 (*redrawn from Bailey, "Abbey Church" fig. 22; by permission of the author*)

walls, only those visible during reconstruction and in his rather haphazard excavation. Nonetheless, the reconstruction of the early Saxon church at Hexham on the basis of the documents and of Hodges's plan has been frequently attempted, due to the importance of Wilfrid and his architectural ambitions.

The Hodges plan shows three parallel sets of foundation lines for the nave. The innermost pair—*g* and *j*—differ in that *j* is unbroken, whereas *g* is divided into three massive rectangular blocks: *g1*, *g2*, and *g3*. The nave also includes an area of floor tile at its western extremity—at *t*—and a mysterious wall—*h*—that runs close to and parallel to *j* for a short distance roughly opposite the central block of *g*. Wall fragments east of block *g3* on both sides of the nave suggest lateral extensions enlarged or altered at several dates, particularly to the south. Wall *q* cuts perpendicularly across the nave slightly further east, and there is evidence of a step up directly in front of it. Beyond *q* to the east are the remains of a smaller apsidal structure delineated by walls *r* and *d*, oriented along the main axis of the church and with a door in its western wall.

Hodges believed the Saxon church to have been copied after Old Saint Peter's in Rome, with four aisles.[106] Later interpretations have, for the most part, reduced the number of aisles to two, in agreement with the majority of early basilican churches, but this arrangement is not compatible with the number of walls in Hodges's plan. H. M. and Joan Taylor suggested that the foundation lines *g* and *j* each supported the arcade piers of a four-bay nave, with a 23.5-foot interval between centers.[107] They offered two alternative reconstructions of the external perimeter of the nave. First, *f* and *k* might have been the external nave walls, in which case *b* and *l* delineated an external ambulatory, Eddius's "winding passages." On the other hand, *b* and *l* might have delineated a second pair of aisles, in which case they would have been the external nave walls, and *f* and *k* would have supported a second set of piers or columns. This latter reconstruction is more likely, as the line of *f* is broken by a grave, and repeats Hodges's original four-aisle plan. Prior Richard mentions hidden choirs singing from galleries, and the Taylors suggest that these galleries might have been located above the aisles and/or ambulatory, making up the additional two of Prior Richard's three stories, and possibly having an open view onto the nave. Such galleries had already been built in the eastern Mediterranean region, as at the Acheiropoitos in Thessaloniki, by Wilfrid's day. The Taylors' reconstruction suggests a lofty open basilica in an eastern Mediterranean idiom.

Recent evidence discovered by Richard Bailey and D. O'Sullivan during excavations at Hexham casts new light on Hodges's plan, which proved to be erroneous in several aspects.[108] Wall *j* continues past the thirteenth-century stone screen to the foot of the step in front of wall *q*. Wall *j* is also slightly north of the position indicated by Hodges, not underlying the present nave wall. Walls *j* and *g* are subsequently equidistant from the center of the nave. However, *j* is not so thick as *g*. Consequently, Bailey and O'Sullivan believe that these are not a matched set, and that *j* implies a Saxon solid-wall nave church like Saint Pierre at Vienne, whereas *g* must be later, possible post-Norman.[109] Bailey believes recent finds may indicate a continuous foundation wall, corresponding to *j*, on the north side of the church. However, despite the narrowness of *j*, and presumably of its northern counterpart, it is still possible to construe these walls as sleepers supporting a light superstructure on a colonnade as suggested in the Taylors' reconstruction of a four-aisle basilica.

Wilfrid's church may have had a transept at its eastern end. Hodges himself and many later writers have interpreted Hodges's foundations to indicate a long open continuous transept, resembling that at Old Saint Peter's.[110] The crypt at Hexham is now accessible by a stairway running westward up into the center of the nave, but this was not originally the only accessway. Wilfrid's crypt was also reached through two additional passages: one from the north started east of *m2* and debouched into a half-barrel-vaulted vestibule, and the other, from the south, began east of *m3* and gave direct access to the vaulted crypt chapel. A similar bicameral crypt with paired passages is all that remains of Wilfrid's church at Ripon, but the relationship of the paired passages there to the eastern end of the upper church cannot be determined.[111] Hodges's plan does not

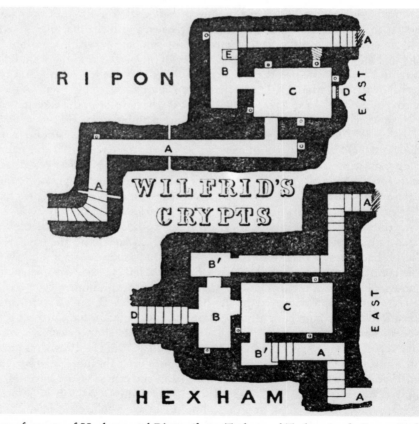

Plans of crypts of Hexham and Ripon (from Taylor and Taylor, *Anglo-Saxon Architecture*, 265; by permission of the publisher)

reveal how the northern and southern wings of the east end of Wilfrid's church were arranged, because it shows many remnants of walls of probably diverse date in both areas: *s* and *m4* to the north, *n1*, *n2*, *o2*, and *p* to the south. The complexity of the foundations in these areas indicates that here the church was altered over time to suit the changing needs of the community. Bede's statement that Acca *ampliavit* the church may indicate that he extended these north and south wings with the progressive addition of chambers for a variety of purposes. Indeed these foundations may be the remains of porticus added on to contain the altars "within the walls" that Acca installed for the veneration of his collection of relics. In Roman tradition, as at Saint Agnes-Outside-the-Walls and other cemeterial churches, martyria and mausoleums were often added to or clustered around the eastern ends of basilicas. Acca may have chosen to emulate this custom in his embellishment of Saint Andrew's.

In Saxon times the crypt at Hexham was not entirely subterranean, as the early nave floor was from three to six feet below its present level. The crypt supported a raised sanctuary accessible either by stairs to the west or via the top flight of the crypt passage stairs to north and/or south.[112] The sanctuary perimeter may have been extended into the nave at that lower level by a schola cantorum, an area screened off by low barriers for the exclusive use of the clergy or of singers at certain liturgical events. The mysterious wall *h* that runs parallel to *j* about halfway to the western end of the nave may have been a sleeper foundation for such a screen wall.[113] Wilfrid's interest in Roman chant, Eddius's role as instructor of chant, Acca's personal interest in maintaining it at Hexham, and its significance in later medieval accounts of the church indicate the strength of musical tradition at Hexham.[114] The architectural schola cantorum originated in Rome, but the date of its invention is uncertain.[115] The presence of wall *h* at Hexham may however indicate that the earliest examples predate Wilfrid's visits.

Early reconstructions of the east end of Wilfrid's church assumed on the basis of common basilican formulas that there was a shallow bowed apse in the center of the east end, delineated by wall *d*.[116] However, wall *q* cuts in a straight line across the sanctuary to the east of the crypt. The Taylors therefore postulated a square east end for the main church, and considered the small apsidal structure delineated by walls *r* and *d* as a separate oratory.[117] Hodges's plan indicates a raised area at the back of the sanctuary in front of wall *q* which may have supported a clerical bench or *synthronon*. The inner face of wall *d* supports a *synthronon* with a central throne, which would be redundant if wall *d* were part of the same structure as wall *q*. Further, wall *d* is surrounded by numerous graves, suggesting that this building served as a cemeterial oratory, parallel in function to Building A at Monkwearmouth. The placement of a secondary chapel on the main axis of the church parallels the arrangement at Jarrow. The existence of a small separate structure to the east of Saint Andrew's at Hexham is further confirmed in a twelfth-century compilation traditionally ascribed to Simeon of Durham, where it is mentioned that the relics of Saint Alchmund, during their eleventh-century travels, found an overnight resting spot *in porticu orientalem plagam ipsius ecclesiae Hagustaldensis,* "in a porticus in the eastern region of the same church in Hexham."[118] The vague reference to an "eastern region" suggests a detached structure rather than a part of the main church. This small oratory has been identified as Saint Peter's, another church in Hexham built by Wilfrid, but the association is unlikely, as Saint Peter's is more probably associated with foundations on a thoroughfare called Holy Island northwest of the abbey.[119]

The possibilities in reconstructing the various sections of the church of Saint Andrew at Hexham are so complex that it is easy to lose sight of the intent of the whole. However, the construction of the church was undertaken by Wilfrid with a single unified intent. Eddius's remark—"We have never heard of its like this side of the Alps"—gives some indication of Wilfrid's central idea. The statement is in part Eddius's use of traditional hyperbole. The basilicas of Gaul were certainly elaborate, and Wilfrid's knowledge of them from his travels may well have provided the inspiration for various parts of his church. The origins of several elements of Hexham's design can possibly be identified in the early churches of Lyons, where Wilfrid had lived under the patronage of Dalfinus. The martyrium of Saint Irene, built by Bishop Patiens about 470, is known from documents to have had a half-sunken crypt, a vaulted chamber for the housing of relics, which resembles the barrel-vaulted chapel of Hexham's crypt.[120] Even closer is Apollinaris Sidonius's description of the suffocatingly narrow crypt passages of Saint Just. A parallel for the upper church at Hexham might have been Bishop Patiens's cathedral basilica on the Saône, of which Apollinaris Sidonius describes the many columns separating nave from aisles, as well as the splendid revetments and decorations. Certainly there were also churches in Gaul that resembled Hexham in splendor if not necessarily in form, at Tours, Clermont, and Vienne, and among the sixth-century royal churches of Paris, notably Clovis's Saints Peter and Paul and Childebert's Saint Vincent. Eddius had been to Rome on at least one occasion—Wilfrid's second appeal to the papal see.[121] He had no doubt seen many Gallic churches and also the great Roman basilicas and was in a position to make comparisons from experience. Eddius was of course no architectural historian, but he would certainly have known churches as splendid as Hexham, possibly even some similar in design to Wilfrid's church, "north of the Alps." Yet his statement is not entirely hyperbole, but rather a statement of Wilfrid's intentions in the construction of Hexham.

The dimensions of Wilfrid's church of Saint Andrew at Hexham are well beyond normal Northumbrian scale, even as at Jarrow and Monkwearmouth. The church at Hexham, from the westernmost mapped point of wall *j* to the horizontal line of wall *q,* is over ninety feet in length, and from *b* to *l,* over sixty feet in width. It is probable that Wilfrid, like Benedict Biscop, imported stonemasons through his connections in Gaul. However, unlike his colleague at Monkwearmouth and Jarrow, Wilfrid did not stint to build on the scale to which his masons had become accustomed at home. Anglo-Saxon Hexham was comparable in scale to the churches of aristocratic bishops and of Merovingian royalty in France. Yet in Wilfrid's eyes, the scale of his church probably also had associations with the great basilicas of Rome.

A. W. Clapham's comparision of the crypts of Hexham and Ripon to Roman *confessio* crypts, and the further possible comparison to the winding passages and subterranean oratories of the catacombs of Rome, are instructive despite the availability of potential models at Lyons and elsewhere in Gaul.[122] Wilfrid had visited the shrines of the martyrs in Rome to collect relics, and had no doubt also made the pilgrims' round of the catacombs. The resemblance of the crypts of Hexham and Ripon to the Roman catacombs may indicate that the reuse of Roman ashlar in these crypts, when the churches themselves were built with rubble fill, may have been intended as symbol as well as structural advantage. To Wilfrid, devoted to the cult of relics, the crypts may well have been the most holy parts of his churches. The references of form to the Roman catacombs, and the reuse of Roman building material stressed the Roman authenticity of the relics housed there.

The ambitious construction of Hexham was, for Wilfrid, a statement of alliance with and expected protection from the Roman papacy, as well as of identity of status and wealth with the Continental bishops.[123] It was shortly after the completion of the minster at Hexham that Wilfrid's troubles with Ecgfrith and his observant queen began. The association with Rome is even more direct if the Hodges plan can be read to indicate a five-aisled basilica with a continuous transept and a crypt at its east end, a small-scale copy of the contemporary basilica of Saint Peter in Rome. Given the difficulties of the plan, however, such a reconstruction must remain hypothetical.

The furnishing that Wilfrid supplied to his churches at Ripon and Hexham served equally to conjure the power of the Roman Church both in Rome and in Gaul. The altar cloth used in the consecration of Ripon was the imperial purple and gold of the old empire and its heir, the Church. Moreover, these were the predominant colors, along with silver, used in the adornment of the church as a whole.[124] Also for Ripon, Wilfrid commissioned a Gospels codex "done in letters of purest gold on parchment all empurpled and illuminated and . . . ordered jewelers to make a case for them, also of the purest gold and set with precious gems."[125] This manuscript has not survived, but from its description, it resembled the great purple codices of Byzantium. Perhaps Wilfrid imported a purple codex to serve as model for text or illuminations, although such works were valuable and probably quite rare. In fact, Wilfrid's book was more precious than extant Byzantine purple codices, for these are written only in silver. The description of the binding brings to mind such sumptuous royal commissions as the covers of the Gospels of the Lombard queen Theodolinda made about 600 for Monza Cathedral (Monza Cathedral Treasury).

A comparison of Wilfrid's codex to Ceolfrith's pandects is instructive. Although the latter were massive and expensive projects and contained one or two purple leaves apiece, their primary goal was the reproduction of the best Vulgate text available along with Cassiodorus's famous illuminations, part of the scholarly legacy of the Roman Church. There is nothing intrinsically ostenta-

View of crypt chapel, St. Andrew, Hexham (Nthld.) *(by permission of the Royal Commission on Historical Monuments, England)*

tious about the *Codex Amiatinus* beyond the ambitiousness of the project and the scale of the codex itself. On the other hand, to Eddius, Wilfrid's biographer, the most striking aspect of the Ripon Gospels was their richness, with the reiteration of purple, gold, and jewels. The codex was obviously designed, like Wilfrid's churches, to make a particular impression of association not so much with Rome's legacy of scholarship as with her heritage of wealth and power.

It would be instructive to be able to examine the other structures of the monastic communities at Hexham and Ripon, but unlike Biscop's foundations, the sites of Wilfrid's churches are at the centers of modern towns, which limits excavation. However, both centers had substantial stone-carving workshops beginning in Wilfrid's period. Substantial collections of stonework from Ripon and Hexham are preserved at both sites and in the Chapter Library at Durham.[126] The richness of these carvings is very striking in comparison to the deocrative stonework at Jarrow and Monkwearmouth. Remarkably, neither Bede nor Eddius makes any mention of the stonework at Wilfrid's sites. Bede does mention that Acca decorated the churches at Hexham, and the Acca Cross at Hexham is traditionally thought to have stood at the head of his grave.[127] It has consequently been argued that the stone-carving workshops of Hexham and Ripon date from Acca's reign.[128] However, Bede does not specifically mention carvings among Acca's contributions. Bede's and Eddius's tendency to ignore the stone sculpture of Wilfrid's and other sites and to concentrate on the more colorful portable riches—metalwork, codices, embroidery, and so forth—probably reflects more their own taste and that of contemporary Northumbrian aristocracy than the absence or later date of stone-carving.[129] Moreover, stone-carving, at least of architectural ornament, most probably began during the construction of churches, while the stones were still conveniently at ground level and not yet fixed in the fabric of the building. The early date of Hexham's sculpture is also asserted by the medieval chronicler, Prior Richard of Hexham, who states:

> These same and the capitals of the columns which sustain them, and the arch of the sanctuary [Wilfrid] adorned with pictures and images and with many sculpted figures worked with relief from the stone, and pictures with a pleasing variety of colors and marvellous elegance.[130]

Consequently, the extant architectural ornament probably stems from the earliest period of the construction of the church.

The architectural sculpture of Hexham consisted of decorative elements including string courses, friezes, and imposts, as well as church furnishings such as screens, slabs, and bench ends. The extent of architectural ornamentation in stone at Hexham parallels contemporary usage in Lombardy and Visigothic Spain, but the motifs are derived from a wider variety of sources. These include not only contemporary stonework elsewhere, and the portable arts that served to transmit motifs, but also locally available stonework of the Roman period.

Hexham, *putto* slab

Hexham, *putto* slab; Durham, Chapter Library *(by permission of the Dean and Chapter of Durham)*

Rosemary Cramp has identified a group of carvings at Hexham as directly reused from local Roman sites. This group includes three fragments of what may have been a screen, decorated with naked *putti*, one with bow and arrow, cavorting in a vine.[131] These slabs are unique among carvings found at Anglo-Saxon sites both in the use of the Late Antique naked *putti,* and in the naturalism of the vine, which does not affect the local development of vine motifs on Anglian crosses. The elegance of composition and the Late Antique delicacy of relief carving in these fragments confirms Cramp's argument that these slabs are reused Roman work. They indicate that Wilfrid or his successor was aware of the Roman legacy of Northumbria and hunted among the ruins for more refined remains than simple, well-cut ashlar. Also in this category of reused Roman carving is a unique slab cut with a double-marigold rosette in shallow relief, in which careful modulation of degrees of relief suggests a Late Antique origin. Unlike the *putti* of the screen fragments, however, this motif was adopted by the Hexham masons, for it appears in a more crude state on a plain memorial cross from Hexham (Durham, Cathedral Chapter Library).[132]

Numerous string courses, friezes, and imposts at Hexham are decorated with motifs also seen at Biscop's foundations: balusters, interlace, and geometric and animal motifs. It is difficult to formulate in the mind's eye the total effect of all these elements in situ, but the roughly contemporary church at Ledsham, Yorkshire, shows the placement of similar imposts and stripwork, and can

Hexham, rosette slab

Hexham, rosette cross head; Durham, Chapter Library *(by permission of the Dean and Chapter of Durham)*

Hexham, animal friezes

Hexham, interlace panel

Hexham, baluster and chevron ornament; Durham, Chapter Library *(by permission of the Dean and Chapter of Durham)*

consequently give some idea of the impact of Hexham. Ultimately this ornamental treatment of architectural elements has its roots in the East, at Coptic sites such as Bawît and Apa Apollo, and has its reflection in tenth-century Armenian churches as at Ani and Aght'amar, but either or both northern Italy and Visigothic Spain were the probable points of transmission of this craft to Hexham. As at Jarrow, the Hexham balusters have precedents in local Roman work such as the Birrens altar, but other motifs at Hexham, including checks and volutes found on imposts parallel contemporary Lombard work. The animal friezes at Hexham in particular are more naturalistic than the snakes at Monkwearmouth and resemble motifs found on the ambo in the Church of Saints John and Paul in Ravenna.[133]

The stone-carvers' workshop at Hexham also produced a remarkable series of freestanding stone crosses, which constitute a unique subgroup among the Northumbrian stone crosses, among the few such subgroups to which an origin center can be assigned.

The origins of the standing stone crosses of England and Ireland are obscure and controversial. In Ireland, a clear progression, albeit with much, probably chronological, overlapping of types, can be traced: from incised crosses on rough slabs, as at Kilnasaggart, to relief crosses on trimmed slabs as at Fahan Mura, county Donegal, to slabs shaped into crosses and carved in relief on two or four sides, as at Carndonagh, county Donegal. Some of the interlace motifs used in these crosses may originate in Near Eastern or Coptic fabrics or in indigenous metalwork, but the origins of such motifs in the portable arts will not suffice to explain the introduction of relief carving in stone into Ireland. The beginnings of this evolution are, moreover, fairly late in Irish art.[134] A purely Irish origin of the stone cross is unlikely, as development in England is roughly simultaneous, if not earlier.

The chronological sequence of the stone crosses in England is much more difficult to determine. Unlike the Irish crosses that evolve gradually from simplicity to grandeur, the extant Anglo-Saxon crosses begin with several already perfected styles in the early to mid-eighth century. They experience a long heyday under a rich variety of influences, only to slip gradually into decline in the Viking period. In his early survey of the crosses. W. G. Collingswood postulated that the English crosses sprang from a single major influx of classical motifs and technical expertise centering around the crosses of Hexham and selected other monuments, and could be arranged chronologically in terms of the gradual failure of the classical prototypes.[135] These prototypes were entirely imported as the repertories of foreign craftsmen brought from Italy and elsewhere by Biscop, Wilfrid, and their unknown kindred spirits. The models were nurtured in isolation from the other crafts and imported motifs of their time by these foreigners and their native heirs, who over generations lost their initial contact with and feeling for Late Antique style. More recently, Rosemary Cramp has suggested that the models and technique of the crosses were initially not so much isolated imports as development from the architectural ornament of churches and that cross carving was a lateral offshoot that eventually became foremost in the medium.[136] This argument does not explain why the crosses at Hexham are so much more refined than the architectural carvings. Possibly the crosses are the work of the shop masters, who left the majority of the repetitive friezes and imposts to semiskilled assistants, but reserved for themselves the crosses, which allowed greater possibilities in design. Cramp has proposed further that different workshops probably received differing models and developed on individual timetables according to the varying dates of these imports. Major waves of model importation affected the style of crosses across England or started distinct schools such as that of Hexham or, in the later Mercian period, that of Breedon-on-the Hill, Leicestershire, but in other instances an individual monument may have borrowed freely from a locally available model without reference elsewhere.[137] Consequently stylistic proximity to imported models is no indicator of date as concerns the English crosses, except in the case of a recognizable school, where relative date can be suggested on the basis of evolution of motifs.

The Hexham crosses are dated in the early to mid-eighth century, on the basis of a statement in the *Historia Regum* of Simeon of Durham, who described the burial of Acca in 740 as follows:

Hexham, Acca Cross

Hexham, Acca Cross, detail

Outside of the wall at the east end of the church at Hexham . . . two stone crosses adorned with exquisite carvings were placed, one at his head, the other at his feet. On the one at his head was an inscription stating that he was buried there.[138]

The most elegant Hexham cross (Hexham I), now reassembled from four fragments in the south transept of Hexham Abbey, have been traditionally called the Acca Cross, and is presumed to have stood at the head of that bishop's grave.[139] It certainly does have "exquisite carving," as per Simeon's description, and if it was Acca's grave marker demonstrates the persistence of Wilfrid's standards of Late Antique craftsmanship half a century after his death. It once had an inscription, now almost totally lost, which begins, promisingly enough, with *A*, but all of the rest of the first line is lost to the end, a possible omega. The second line begins *SE* or *SC* and at the middle of the shaft

Acca Cross, Hexham, head

"UNIGENITO FILIO DEI" from the Nicaean Creed was at one time plainly legible. The inscription does not help us identify the cross as Acca's, nor do the find sites of the fragments, of which only one was found near the east end of the abbey church. There is also no precedent for the use of so richly carved a cross as a gravestone. Earlier grave markers were simple slabs marked with incised crosses, as for example the Hereberecht stone at Monkwearmouth and the early Lindisfarne gravestones. Again, this difference may indicate the distinctions in attitude between Wilfrid's foundations and other relatively more ascetic communities in Northumbria, or that the Acca Cross is misnamed and was never intended as a grave marker. The Acca Cross, which stands at the head of the Hexham series, may date from the abbacy of Wilfrid as easily as that of Acca.

Lindisfarne, Priory Museum, early tomb slabs *(British Crown copyright—reproduced with permission of the Controller of Her Britannic Majesty's Stationery Office)*

The carving on all four faces of the Acca cross shows a variety of delicate figure-eight vinescrolls. The vines interlace at their crossings, and their medallions are filled with symmetrical curls of vine and clusters of hanging grapes. The relief is shallow, and the vine and its fruit relatively naturalistic compared to other Anglian vinescrolls from Hexham and elsewhere. However, the vine has lost its leaves so as to make cleaner lines for interlacing patterns, except in the outside spaces between curves where small pointed leaves serve as contrapuntal fillers. The simplification of the vine and the stressing of interlacing at the crossings is not necessarily a sign of the influence of insular art, but could have been inherent in an imported model. The pattern resembles motifs used in bronze plates attached to the tie beams and the cupola mosaics in the Dome of the Rock, and in the mosaics of the Great Mosque in Damascus, and reflects eastern Mediterranean traditions.[140] Figure-eight vines of very similar design are also seen on pillars from a Visigothic structure now used to frame the entrance to a cistern of Islamic date at the Alcazar at Mérida. Further Visigothic parallels may also be seen in the treatment of impost blocks at San Pedro de la Nave at Zamora and at Saint Paul-Serge at Narbonne.[141] The Mérida panels also show similarities to the Acca Cross in carving techniques, most notably the use of very shallow, flat relief and very crisp, almost metallic, edges to the elements of the vine. Such technical elements could not be transmitted via an imported model alone and suggest the presence of at least one Visigothic master in the stone-carving workshops at Anglian Hexham.

The other Hexham crosses are similarly nonfigural, with few exceptions. Hexham II, called the Spital Cross because of its former location at Saint Giles Spital, Hexham, is now in the south transept of the abbey church. It has a simple figure-eight vine on one broad face, two curled single vines on the narrow faces, and a much worn Crucifixion with cup and lance bearers on the remaining broad side.[142] The proportions of the figures in the Crucifixion are somewhat bizarre, but they are by no means the bell-shaped, enamel-like men of the *Book of Durrow* and are thus probably copied from an imported model. The grape clusters of the vine here are thickened, resembling enlarged blackberries, and the vine is less delicate than that on the Acca Cross, indicating a probably later date. The Spital Cross was believed by Hodges to have been the foot cross from Acca's grave, but the stylistic differences with the Acca Cross make it unlikely that the two are from the same workshop at the same date. Moreover, associations of either cross with Acca are extremely tenuous. Another cross perhaps closer to the Acca Cross in date is Hexham III, now at Durham. One broad face here has a comparably delicate figure-eight vine, and the back has a simple volute vine like that of Hexham II. Here, however, the grape clusters are reduced to blossomlike arrangements centering around a single grape. This formula becomes a cliché in later crosses of the school, such as those from crosses from Lowther (Cumbria), Nunnykirk (Northumberland), Simonburn (Northumberland), and Heversham (Cumbria), which show a gradual decline of elegance and clarity.

By the establishment of the school of sculpture, Hexham remained, even after Wilfrid's death, a center for the promulgation of Mediterranean models. The strength of this tradition indicates the durability within the community of the precepts on which it had been established; the preeminence of Roman authority and the Mediterranean art associated with it. Whether these models were actually Roman or even Italian made little difference to Wilfrid, or to his heirs and colleagues in the Northumbrian foundations based closely on the authority of Rome. This was in part due to their northern perspective; they perceived the Mediterranean world as spiritually focused on Rome and her Church that had sent Saint Augustine to England and had triumphed at Whitby. It was to Rome that Wilfrid and Benedict Biscop had turned their steps, and from which they brought back many of their models for art. That these models were in fact from all the varied corners of the Mediterranean world is not however entirely due to any lack of artistic sensitivity on the part of the

Hexham Cross III, side view; Durham, Chapter Library *(by permission of the Dean and Chapter of Durham)*

Hexham Cross III, front view *(by permission of the Dean and Chapter of Durham)*

Cross shaft from Lowther, Cumbria, front; British Museum *(photo: Trustees of the British Museum, by permission)*

Cross shaft from Lowther, Cumbria, side; British Museum *(photo: Trustees of the British Museum, by permission)*

Cross shaft fragment at Heversham, Cumbria, front

Cross shaft fragment at Heversham, side

Anglo-Saxons, a "promiscuous eclecticism" (as T. D. Kendrick put it), or a "magpie attitude" (in Otto Demus's phrase).[143] Rome itself was, by 700, a magpie's nest of the odds and ends of Late Antique and contemporary Mediterranean art; eastern Mediterranean monastic communities in particular made Rome more Greek than it had been in Augustus's day. It is not surprising, therefore, that Anglo-Saxon travelers brought home the portable goods of the whole Mediterranean basin and thought them Roman, the visual essence of the see of Saint Peter and the triumph of the Roman Church.

Panofsky was thinking of the art centers such as Wilfrid's Hexham and Biscop's twin foundations when he wrote:

> Determined efforts to assimilate Latin models were made in England . . . where the classical tradition was always to remain a force more persistent and self-conscious . . . than was the case on the Continent.[144]

These efforts were made primarily at centers that identified closely with the Roman Church for spiritual or political reasons. Their nature was conditioned by the aspirations or ambitions of those who founded these centers and the establishment of their masons' shops and scriptoria. There are certainly differences between the art of Wilfrid's centers and that of Biscop's communities. However, the self-conscious maintenance of the purity of the model, in spirit if not in form, was a central factor in the art of all these centers. Here, in remote corners of England, is a renascence or reiteration of Late Antique traditions that one might well call a Northumbrian Renaissance.

The intention at these centers was to identify as closely as possible with Rome and her Church by emulating to the point of imitation all available imported models. This emulation deliberately excluded the creative assimilation of the model into indigenous styles or media. The Anglo-Saxons had no precedent for assimilative copying as did the Irish. Preconversion trade between Anglo-Saxon England and the Mediterranean had consisted largely of the importation of luxury goods that were accepted, hoarded, and used by those who could afford them, but they were rarely taken as models by native craftsmen. Thus there was no precedent for the amalgamation of foreign models and domestic taste. In the Christian era, the result was a transplanted emulative art that existed in rarified isolation in specialized Rome-oriented environments, without admitting the very existence of an indigenous aesthetic. Even here, however, it was impossible to exclude forever the artistic ideas of the surrounding insular world, originating in the Anglian secular tradition or in the developments of the Celtic Church. A small silver plaque (British Museum), found in an old house in Hexham, demonstrates that not even Wilfrid's Rome-away-from-Rome was secure from the vital innovations of art elsewhere in Northumbria.[145] Probably of eighth-century date, the plaque measures 10 by 7.5 centimeters and was probably part of a book cover or an altar frontal. It is incised from the front in an outline technique seen in late Roman Gaul and in certain Merovingian pieces such as the reliquary casket of Saint Mumma at Saint-Benoît-sur-Loire. However, its closest stylistic parallel is the reliquary

Engraved metal plaque from Hexham; British Museum *(photo: Trustees of the British Museum, by permission)*

coffin of Saint Cuthbert, made at Lindisfarne around 698. The latter combines a series of imported figural motifs with a linear technique in a stylistic mode emerging from the encounter of Mediterranean art with Anglian and Celtic styles. The Hexham plaque is crude, certainly an inferior piece of craftsmanship if compared to the Acca Cross or the *Codex Amiatinus*, but it has what they lack—a sense of creative innovation and exploration of the possibilities of stylistic synthesis.

[5]

Northumbrian Synthesis

THE ART OF POSTCONVERSION NORTHUMBRIA is richly diverse both in its sources and in the variety of responses to the available models and traditions. Besides the assimilative art of the Celtic Church and the emulative works of the Roman Church, there remains for consideration art either originating in politically more ambiguous centers or for which the workshop provenance is unknown. Here Celtic, Mediterranean, and native Anglian artistic traditions combine to produce the most creative synthesis of the Northumbrian period.

When the Synod of Whitby established the authority of the Roman Church in Northumbria, the Celtic Church lost both spiritual authority and royal patronage. Churchmen who would not conform to the edicts of Whitby abandoned their Northumbrian foundations for Northern Ireland, Pictland, and Wales where they could still practice their faith according to Columba's Rule. The Roman Church rapidly assimilated their deserted estates for their own foundations. At the consecration of Ripon, Wilfrid received the authorization of King Ecgfrith to take up abandoned Celtic holdings.[1] Elsewhere, however, the transition was less harsh. Bishop Colman of Lindisfarne, the leading spokesman for the Celtic faction at Whitby, left England for Ireland after his defeat, taking with him Celtic and Anglian followers.[2] Lindisfarne subsequently conformed to Roman usage in the date of Easter and the tonsure. Some changes were also imposed on Lindisfarne's structure of authority by external forces, if only temporarily. The abbot of Lindisfarne had previously also held the office of bishop of Northumbria under kings Oswald and Oswy. Now that office was divided and the diocesan seat of Northumbria was moved to York under the successive reigns of bishops Tuda and Wilfrid. However, the influence of the Celtic Church lingered at Lindisfarne. The new abbot, Eata, was appointed by Oswy at Colman's personal request. Eata had been "one of those twelve boys of English race whom Aidan . . . had taken and instructed in Christ."[3] Eata had been trained at Lindisfarne by its founder, the leader of the mission of the Celtic Church in Northumbria. Moreover, he had been abbot of Melrose, another Celtic foundation. Eata had no doubt conformed to the Roman Easter and tonsure when he was transferred to Lindisfarne, but the customs of man and community were otherwise fundamentally unchanged. In 678 Eata was consecrated bishop of Lindisfarne after Theodore deposed Wilfrid and divided the Northumbrian see to prevent the excessive concentration of authority in one bishop. Thereafter Eata held the offices of abbot and bishop simultaneously, as was the Celtic custom, and this tradition, once restored, was maintained at Lindisfarne to the end of the history of the foundation. The edicts of Whitby had not mentioned, let alone prohibited, this practice, so that its continuity at Lindisfarne was probably more custom than political gesture, but its continuity demonstrates nonetheless the depth of Celtic tradition ingrained in the fabric of the community. Although the consequences of Whitby are not so closely documented for other Celtic centers as for Lindisfarne, transition to Roman usage was most probably limited to the Whitby issues of tonsure and date of Easter alone. Certainly Whitby, Melrose, and Hartlepool were not transformed overnight into copies of Jarrow and Hexham. The continuity of practice at Northumbrian Celtic centers, moreover, was commended even by the staunchest advocates of Roman orthodoxy, who considered certain Celtic attitudes and virtues, predicated on the ascetic monasticism of Ireland, worthy of emulation. Bede retrospectively praised Aidan for his faith, generosity, and lack of worldly ambition, and similarly commended Colman and Chad.[4] No extensive outside pressure was applied to the Celtic monasteries to change their basic outlook, or to abandon the more harmless of their differences with the foundations of the Roman Church.

The Art of Lindisfarne

At Lindisfarne, the continuity of the premises of Anglo-Celtic monasticism is particularly striking. Bede describes the asceticism of this community as a moral lesson for the more decadent monastic foundations of his own day.[5] The intensity with which the monks of Lindisfarne maintained a state of spiritual grace by frugality and austerity is not surprising. Lindisfarne was the first Celtic missionary center established in Northumbria when Aidan came from Iona in 635 at the invitation of Oswald.[6] Aidan and his successors in the abbacy considered it their obligation as well as their custom to provide an example to the other foundations of their *paruchia*. Consequently Lindisfarne became the home of the most quintessentially Celtic saint to flourish in Northumbria after the Synod of Whitby. "Celtic" here implies adherence to the precepts of the Celtic Church rather than ethnic origin, for Cuthbert was a Northumbrian Angle.

Cuthbert's life is known through three early sources: the earliest *Anonymous Vita,* compiled at Lindisfarne around 698 and Bede's prose and verse *Lives,* based on the earlier Lindisfarne version.[7] Cuthbert entered monastic life at Melrose under Eata in 651, shortly assumed the rank of prior, and then followed Eata to Lindisfarne in 664. He spent much of his life as an anchorite on Farne Island and was noted for his fanatical asceticism. In 685, he was made bishop of Lindisfarne but assumed the office against his will and after only a year of active episcopal service, returned to Farne Island, to die there within a year. After his death, his cult developed rapidly and many miracles were ascribed to him both during and after life. In March 698, eleven years after his death, Bishop Eadbert permitted his exhumation and transfer from a stone coffin buried to the right of the altar in the church at Lindisfarne to a location above ground in the sanctuary. This occasion prompted the manufacture of a wooden reliquary coffin incised with figures, now in the Chapter House at Durham, and possibly the enclosure of Cuthbert's personal portable altar in a silver shrine with repoussé ornament. This event is probably also associated with the production of the *Lindisfarne Gospels* (London, British Library, Cotton Nero D. IV), dedicated to Saint Cuthbert. This manuscript reflects the ambiguous position of Lindisfarne—loyal to Rome in dogma and practice after Whitby, but essentially Celtic in spirit.

The *Lindisfarne Gospels* is a large (340 by 240 millimeters) and extraordinarily sumptuous Gospels codex. It is moreover remarkably complete, with the possible exception of one or more pages at the end. Its origin is known through an extensive colophon (fol. 259) written by the tenth-century Anglo-Saxon glossator of the manuscript, which reads in part:

Eadfrith, Bishop of Lindisfarne, wrote this book, at the first, in honor of God and St. Cuthbert and all the saints who are on the island, and Æthel-wald, Bishop of Lindisfarne, bound it on the outside and covered[?] it, as he was well able to do. And Billfrith the anchorite wrought the ornaments upon the outside and adorned this unalloyed metal, gilded over with gold and gems and also with silver[?] And Aldred, an unworthy and most miserable priest, with the help of God and St. Cuthbert, wrote an English gloss above.[8]

The Eadfrith to whom the codex is ascribed was Eadbert's successor in the see of Lindisfarne after the latter's death in May 698, shortly after the translation of the saint. The colophon is probably accurate, for a medieval forgery would more likely give Cuthbert himself authorship. It is generally believed that the composition of the manuscript predates Eadfrith's consecration in 698, for the duties of the bishop of Lindisfarne were not light.[9] Indeed it may have been the celebration of the completion of the codex honoring Cuthbert that prompted the translation of the saint's relics. However, the latest possible date for the manuscript is Eadfrith's death in 721, for it was customary for high clergy in the Celtic Church to copy sacred texts, as the *Life of Columba* attests, other obligations of office notwithstanding.[10]

Eadfrith's role was probably primarily that of scribe, but he may well be responsible for textual ornament as well, as the verb used in the colophon to describe his work is *writan* or *awritan*, which may mean either "to write" or "to draw." Moreover, another Northumbrian source demonstrates that scribe and illuminator in this period were frequently identical. A ninth-century Latin poem on the work of Ultan, an Irish scribe at Lindisfarne about 740, relates that he could "adorn books better than any modern scribe."[11] Lindisfarne no doubt dedicated its entire scriptorium to the production of this codex. Hence Eadfrith most probably had assistants who prepared the vellum, ink, quills, and pigments, and marked out the margins and lines of the pages. Nonetheless, the art of the codex is so unified in style that if more than one hand is present, there must have been a concerted effort to maintain the unity of the decorative scheme, implying a group of artists working very closely together.

Of the other participants in the manufacture of the codex, the binder Æthelwald succeeded Eadfrith as abbot in 721 and became bishop of Lindisfarne in 724. He had been at Lindisfarne in his youth but later spent time at Melrose, where he was first prior and then reigned as abbot from 705 to his succession at Lindisfarne in 721. If his binding of the *Gospels* preceded his abbacy, it must also have predated his sojourn at Melrose, which would suggest a relatively early date for the completion of the codex. However, binding is a far less time-consuming project than writing and illuminating; consequently the task could easily have been accomplished by an abbot or bishop, particularly with assistants to prepare the necessary materials. It may well be that at Eadfrith's death and Æthelwald's succession at Lindisfarne, the codex had just been completed, and was ready for binding. Billfrith the anchorite, who adorned the outside of the codex with fine metalwork, appears in the *Liber Vitae* in a list of the anchorites of Farne Island, in a position placing him chronologically in or near Æthelwald's reign. Æthelwald may therefore have suggested or commissioned the metalwork as an afterthought to his own binding. The metalwork has been thought to have been a *cumdach*, a metal book shrine in the Celtic tradition, such as that of the *Gospel of Saint Molaise* (Dublin, National Museum). Such a shrine would not have been inappropriate, as the *Lindisfarne Gospels* was closely associated from its making with the cult of Saint Cuthbert and came to be considered part of the relics themselves. However, neither Aldred the glossator nor later chronicles refer to the bindings as a shrine, and the colophon description, moreover, implies attached metalwork decorations rather than a separate case.[12]

The script of the *Lindisfarne Gospels* is a highly refined and even insular majuscule, probably typical of the Lindisfarne scriptorium of around 700.[13] The text is a member of the insular Vulgate stemma headed by the *Codex Amiatinus*, indicating the loan of a text model from Jarrow to Lindisfarne and demonstrating the close ties between these foundations after Whitby.[14]

The *Lindisfarne Gospels* is lavishly and extensively illuminated. The distribution of ornament generally follows and elaborates on the insular system established in the *Book of Durrow*. Major illuminated initials with subsequent insular diminution introduce each chapter and mark the Incarnation initial in Matthew (fol. 29r). Each Gospel is moreover opened with a cross-carpet-page and an

London, British Library, Cotton Nero D IV, *Lindisfarne Gospels,* **fol. 29r: incarnation initial** *(by permission of the British Library)*

Evangelist portrait. The latter includes the Evangelist symbol found alone in this position in the *Book of Durrow.* In addition, the sixteen-page canon-table sequence is illuminated with framing arcades. Both the author portraits and the canon arcades indicate the introduction of new models since the illumination of the *Book of Durrow* and represent a new phase in insular illumination.

The initials and cross-carpet-pages of *Lindisfarne* take further the fusion of ornamental traditions of the *Book of Durrow*. Insular metalworking traditions are ubiquitously used side by side with motifs of Late Antique design or illuminative tradition. The initials, as for example the Incarnation initial in Matthew (fol. 29r), are much richer and more complex than those in *Durrow*, reflecting contemporary trends toward elaboration and refinement in insular and particularly Celtic metalwork, as in the famous Tara Brooch (Dublin,

Lindisfarne Gospels, fol. 26v, cross-carpet-page *(by permission of the British Library)*

National Museum).[15] On the other hand, the Anglo-Saxon influence is more strongly felt here than in *Durrow*, reflective of the milieu and population of Lindisfarne around 700. This Germanic element is evident in the much more prevalent use of animal motifs, from the snarling hounds' heads that serve as terminals of descenders and framing elements, to the widespread use of friezes and blocks of animal interlace. The *Lindisfarne* animal interlace is made up of birds and hounds, of which legs, tails, and necks have been attenuated into fine ribbons, interwoven in a dense and complex lace knotwork. It occurs both in blocks and friezes in initials and cross-carpet-pages and as an overall background pattern to the cross on one particular carpet-page (fol. 26v). This animal interlace is at once more refined in the thinness of its parts and more ferocious in the behavior of the intertwined biting beasts than the rather staid broad-band hounds and snakes of *Durrow* (fol. 192v). Nonetheless, here as in *Durrow*, the regularizing influence of the Mediterranean knotwork has established control, balance, and evenness despite the ferocity of the animals themselves.[16] The successful fusion in the *Lindisfarne Gospels* of these three traditions—Celtic, Germanic, and Mediterranean—is evident even in a casual overview of the manuscript. Unlike *Durrow*, where the fusion in interlace is made feasible by the strict adherence to relatively simple broad lines and forms, in *Lindisfarne* unity is maintained even in extreme complexity by the total mastery of the artist of the various traditions, models, and styles at his disposal.

The decoration of the canon tables of the *Lindisfarne Gospels* further demonstrates the totally assimilative nature of this synthesis. In *Durrow*, the canon tables are arranged in grid frames—a simple functional device that carries over to at least one later insular manuscript, the *Echternach Gospels* (Paris, Bibliothèque Nationale MS Lat. 9389).[17] In *Lindisfarne*, however, the canon tables are arranged under arcades as in Late Antique manuscripts, here observing a pattern of a single larger arch over three or four smaller arches.[18] This design can also be seen in a sixth-century Latin Gospels in the Vatican (Vatican Lat. 3806, fol. 2v), and in the *Livinius Gospels* (Ghent, Saint Bavo), of about 800, of which the illusionistic style indicates close reliance on an early model.[19] Late Antique canon arcades show their origin in architectural form by the close emulation of pedestal and capital types, the use of architectural decorative motifs in the encompassing great arch, and the simulation of marble abstract swirls of color in the column shafts. Moreover, the solidity of the arch as an architectural form is occasionally demonstrated by the inclusion of birds—peacocks in the Vatican Gospels codex—that perch on the outermost set of capitals of the arcade.[20] The *Lindisfarne* canon arcades are derived from similar Late Antique types, but the exact prototypal form is difficult to trace. The *Codex Amiatinus*, too, has architectural canon arcades, but as the canon-table sequence there is a seven-page series, rather than the sixteen-page of *Lindisfarne*, it is unlikely that the *Lindisfarne* canon tables are borrowed from the same prototype as the *Amiatinus* arcades.[21] *Lindisfarne* probably follows an imported model with an illusionistic architectural framework and possibly with animal motifs as found in the Vatican codex. However, the *Lindisfarne* artist

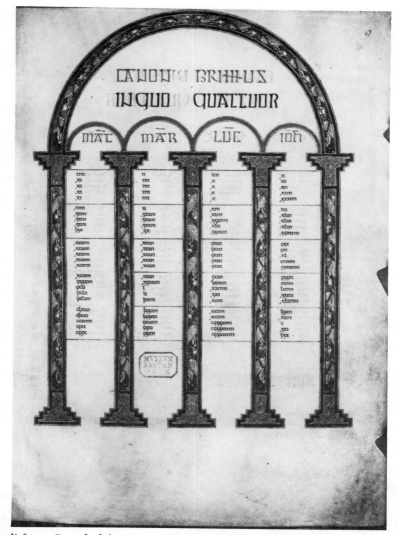

Lindisfarne Gospels, fol. 10r, canon tables *(by permission of the British Library)*

has completely transformed the model in all but its most basic structure. All effort at illusionistic solidity and three-dimensionality has been abandoned. Pedestals and capitals are here treated as flat blocks filled with fine geometric knotwork against a dark ground. Columns and great arch alike have been filled with friezes of interlaced birds and hounds. These animals are the successors of the naturalistic peacocks perched on the exterior of canon arcades in Late Antique canon tables, but no longer signal the solidity of the structure. They have instead been flattened and distorted to become part of a larger pattern that

Lindisfarne Gospels, fol. 25v: Evangelist portrait of Matthew *(by permission of the British Library)*

stresses the flatness and totally abstract nature of the arcade. These two-dimensional arcades, in losing their architectural pretensions, have become yet another field for the application of the insular metalworking motifs found elsewhere in the codex. The canon tables show an assimilative synthesis of forms parallel to that of the initials and cross-carpet-pages.[22]

The most complex question concerning the use of foreign models in the *Lindisfarne Gospels* pertains to the origins of the Evangelist portraits. Matthew (fol. 25v), with the inscription "O AGIOS MATTHEUS," sits facing right writing a codex on his knee. He is bearded and wears a tunic and pallium. His symbol, with the inscription "IMAGO HOMINIS," appears above his halo, a half-length angel with halo and book, blowing a trumpet. To the right, a bearded figure partially emerges from behind a curtain, holding a book in veiled hands. Mark (fol. 93v), inscribed "O AGIOS MARCUS," sits facing left, holding a book in his left hand while writing on a single leaf on a round-topped lectern. He is beardless, wearing a tunic and a chlamys. Above his halo, his symbolic lion, labeled "IMAGO LEONIS," is shown full-length with halo, wings, and a book, also blowing a trumpet. Luke (fol. 137v), inscribed "O AGIOS LUCAS," sits facing right, writing on a scroll in his lap. He is bearded and wears tunic and pallium. Above his halo, the Calf, "IMAGO VITULI," is depicted full-length, with wings, halo and book, its head awkwardly turned into the frontal plane. John (fol. 209v), inscribed "O AGIOS JOHANNES," is seated facing forward on a bench with a scroll across his lap and his right hand over his heart. From behind his halo flies his Eagle, labeled "IMAGO AE-QUILAE," wearing a halo and clutching a codex in its claws.

The first three Evangelists sit in semiprofile, in the act of writing. They are part of a tradition common in later Greek Gospels codices, which along with the Greek *agios* of the inscriptions suggests an eastern Mediterranean origin for these author portraits. However, the inscriptions may be an insular invention rather than part of any model, as the script and the names of the saints are Latinized and the spelling of *agios* also suggests local origin.[23] The use of the inscriptions in all four Evangelist portraits does not confirm the use of a single source for the series.

The most noted comparison for the *Lindisfarne* Evangelist portraits is the similarity of the Matthew to the Ezra in *Codex Amiatinus*. The two are so similar that they are probably derived from the same model.[24] This derivation is mutually independent, as the *Amiatinus* Ezra shows certain errors in copying the model, such as the width of the tunic sleeve emerging from under the chlamys, the treatment of part of the cushion under Ezra's thigh as part of the chlamys and peculiarities in the perspective of the front right bench leg, which are not repeated in *Lindisfarne* Matthew. However, the underdrawing of the Ezra, partially visible due to the flaking of paint, shows a closer affiliation to Matthew on these points, showing that they were correctly detailed in the model from which both miniatures were derived.

Two notable elements in the Matthew portrait do not appear in the Ezra: the figure behind the curtain and the Evangelist symbol. The mysterious interloper

Lindisfarne Gospels, fol. 93v: Evangelist portrait of Mark *(by permission of the British Library)*

behind the drapery is difficult to identify. The classical type behind the image is the portrait of the author with his muse. One example for the direct transition of this image into a Christian context is the Evangelist portrait of Mark in the sixth-century *Rossano Gospels* (Rossano Cathedral, fol. 121r), where the Evangelist is directed by an unidentified woman in a blue robe. However, the figure in *Lindisfarne* is neither female nor directing the course of the work, but hovers in the wings, peering reverentially at Matthew and almost timorously presenting a book with ritually veiled hands. For similar reasons the figure cannot be

Lindisfarne Gospels, fol. 137v: Evangelist portrait of Luke *(by permission of the British Library)*

Lindisfarne Gospels, fol. 209v: Evangelist portrait of John *(by permission of the British Library)*

Christ dictating the Gospels to Matthew, as suggested by a gold inscription on the opening page of the Gospel (fol. 27r)—"Ihs Xps Mattheus homo"—and by a line in the verses opening the colophon (fol. 259r)—"Mattheus ex ore Christi scripsit."[25] Christ would be identified at least by inscription or cross nimbus, and would in all likelihood appear more centrally placed, with Matthew receiving the Gospel at the foot of the throne, as in the *Coptic-Arabic Gospels* (Paris, Institut Catholique), or taking dictation while seated next to Christ, as in an ivory (London, Victoria and Albert Museum) in which Saint Peter dictates the Gospel to Mark.[26] The observing figure in *Lindisfarne* Matthew, on the other hand, hides nervously behind the arras like an anachronistic Polonius. However, the figure hints at his identity by presenting a small codex. His attitude is identical to that of the donor of a church in the ninth-century frescoes at San Benedetto at Malles.[27] He may be a scribe presenting a codex or a subordinate ecclesiastic deriving benefit from the presence of Matthew. The identity of the figure therefore must depend on its origin. It is possible that the figure is the addition of the Lindisfarne scriptorium, for as in the case of the canon arcades, the *Lindisfarne Gospels* artist freely altered models stylistically, and there is no reason why marginal iconographic additions could not be made as well. Hence the figure might have been intended as Saint Cuthbert, the most prominent local candidate for such honor, or as a portrait, perhaps even a self-portrait, of Eadfrith presenting his work to Matthew. On the other hand, the figure may have already been part of a Mediterranean model used in addition to or closely allied with the model of the *Amiatinus* Ezra, in which case Jerome as the Vulgate author, Cassiodorus, or earlier clerics or saints associated with this recension are equally possible identities for this mysterious figure.[28]

Bruce-Mitford has postulated that the four Evangelist portraits of the *Lindisfarne Gospels* have a single specific source—the Gospels volume of Cassiodorus's *Novem Codices*.[29] Under this theory, the resemblance of Matthew to Ezra reflects the derivation of Ezra from an Evangelist portrait, either the Matthew of the *Novem Codices* or a common ancestor. The Evangelist symbol and the observing figure would then have been included in the Cassiodoran Matthew portrait. Bruce-Mitford saw these addenda as reflected with greater accuracy in the eleventh-century *Copenhagen Gospels* (Copenhagen, Royal Library GKS 10–20, fol. 17v), possibly from Anglo-Saxon Canterbury. Here the half-length angel flies down from a cloud, and Matthew, writing on a round-topped lectern and seated on a slightly different bench, glances up from the page at the interloper behind the drapes, whose role in dictating or inspiring the Evangelist thus appears to be confirmed. There are also close similarities between the *Lindisfarne* Luke and his counterpart in the Copenhagen codex (fol. 82v), unfortunately the only other portrait of the series to survive in that manuscript. However, the parallel imagery of *Lindisfarne Gospels* and the *Copenhagen Gospels* may well have originated with *Lindisfarne*. The *Lindisfarne Gospels* must have been widely known and copied, in part because of its association with the relics of Saint Cuthbert. If the *Copenhagen* Evangelist portraits parallel those in *Lindisfarne*, they may be the only survivors of a tradition descending from the *Lindisfarne* types. *Lindisfarne* was the source of an insular tradition of illumination in at least one other composition, one of its cross-carpet-pages (fol. 26v), which served as the probable source of a very similar cross in the *Book of Saint Chad* (Lichfield, Cathedral Library, p. 220). The changes in the *Copenhagen* Evangelist portraits in both iconographic nuance and composition may consequently result from progressive alterations in a series of copies descending from the *Lindisfarne Gospels.*[30]

Did the *Lindisfarne Gospels* Evangelists have a single series of Evangelist portraits as a model? The Gospels volume of the *Novem Codices* may have been in Northumbria, perhaps even at Lindisfarne as a text model.[31] The extent of the illumination of the *Novem Codices* is unknown, but if present, the Gospel volume could have provided a series of Evangelist portrait models used by Eadfrith and his scriptorium. It is equally possible that other Gospel texts available at Lindisfarne provided a set of Evangelist portraits as a model.[32] However, if such a series existed, it was incomplete, and had to be supplemented by the model of the *Amiatinus* Ezra or a related work, such as a Cassiodoran Matthew portrait. There was more probably no one complete series of portraits available as a model. If so, the *Lindisfarne* Evangelists are a remarkable insular pastiche from a number of sources. The unity of the series may result not from a single model but from the internal stylistic consistency of Eadfrith's scriptorium and the *Lindisfarne Gospels* themselves. The similarities of Matthew to the underdrawing of the *Amiatinus* Ezra indicates that the first of these models was the Cassiodoran prototype of the Ezra portrait. However, several such models were available at Lindisfarne in this period, as demonstrated by a silver repoussé plaque applied to the portable altar of Saint Cuthbert at Lindisfarne, showing a semiprofile, seated Saint Peter.[33] Of the Evangelist portraits in the codex, Luke is perhaps closest to the seated Saint Peter of the altar, but the similarity is not sufficient to necessitate an identical model.

Furthermore, the forward-facing portrait of the Evangelist John in the codex was derived not from an author portrait, such as the front-facing Saint Luke in the *Saint Augustine Gospels,* but more probably from a Christ in Majesty much like that in the *Codex Amiatinus.*[34] John differs from the standard early Majesty type only in the placement of his hand over his heart; Christ enthroned usually makes a gesture of speech or blessing.[35] However, the gesture itself may have been borrowed from other sources as more appropriate to an Evangelist. Similar hand placement is found in later insular manuscripts, in standing Evangelists holding codices against themselves, as for example the Mark in the Irish *Book of Mulling* (Dublin, Trinity College Library, 60, fol. 35v), or the Luke of the *Saint Gall Gospels* (Saint Gall, Stiftsbibliothek, Codex 51, p. 128).[36] The scroll of the *Lindisfarne* John and the general configuration of the hand holding it could easily have been taken from the model used for the *Lindisfarne* Luke. The same gesture appears in the incised figure of John on the coffin reliquary of Saint Cuthbert. A line from the verse of Sedulius introducing the colophon (fol. 259r) explains why John was picked out from his fellow

Evangelists for such particular treatment. The poem notes that John's writing was considered extraordinary because of his unusual source of inspiration: *"Johannes in prochemio [sic] deinde extructuavit [sic] deo donante et spiritu sancto scripsit"* ("John subsequently uttered in his prologue the word that God and the Holy Spirit gave him").[37] John's purely metaphysical inspiration was unlike the sources of the other Evangelists who were instructed either by the incarnate Christ or by mortal men.[38] The colophon dates from the addition of the tenth-century gloss, but it may well be that the tradition of the special nature of John's inspiration had long been a part of the particular beliefs of the Lindisfarne community. The Evangelist John had special significance both for Saint Cuthbert and Lindisfarne and for the Anglo-Celtic Church as a whole. As a youth, Cuthbert had spent the last days of the life of his teacher, Boisil, reading with him a manuscript of the Gospel of John.[39] A copy of the Gospel of John in a seventh-century binding was found in Cuthbert's sarcophagus in 1104, placed there at the saint's initial burial in 687 or at his translation in 698.[40] The special treatment of John in the *Lindisfarne Gospels,* dedicated to Saint Cuthbert, is therefore appropriate. This Evangelist also had a particular political importance for the Anglo-Celtic Church, for, according to Wilfrid's biographer, Eddius, John was the authority cited by the Celtic Church at Whitby as giving apostolic sanction to their use of Irenaean computation of the date of Easter, as Irenaeus had been a student of Polycarp in Smyrna, and Polycarp had known John.[41] Cuthbert himself, however, had made it part of his life's work to bring the church at Lindisfarne into conformity with Roman usage. Consequently the special treatment of John in the *Lindisfarne Gospels* is not a statement of apostolic authority for the Celtic schism. The unusual singling out of John in *Lindisfarne* may be partly a nostalgic consideration of the Celtic origins of the foundation, but it is more probably an acknowledgment of the meaning of John for Cuthbert.

The use of multiple models rather than a single source series of Evangelist portraits helps to explain certain iconographic peculiarities of the *Lindisfarne Gospels,* particularly the treatment of the Evangelist symbols. These symbols are unusual in that they combine the full-length types without attributes, as used in the *Book of Durrow,* and the half-length types with books, wings, and halos more common in Late Antique art. It is possible that the fusion of types predates their use in *Lindisfarne.* Winged full-length symbols, already a partial synthesis, accompany the Evangelists in the corners of the Christ in Majesty page in the *Codex Amiatinus* (fol. 796v). The *Amiatinus* symbols, however, lack halos and only the Angel carries an attribute, a scroll, while the Evangelists themselves stand holding codices of their work in veiled hands. The Jarrow/ Monkwearmouth scriptorium that produced *Amiatinus* adhered closely to imported models in style as well as iconography, so the Evangelist symbols of the *Codex Amiatinus* probably originated in an extrainsular model. If such a partial fusion was available in the imported model of the *Amiatinus* page, then a similar and more complex synthesis of the full-length types with the attributes might have occurred in one of *Lindisfarne*'s foreign sources. However, such fusions are rare in Late Antique art, and there are no exact parallels anywhere for the *Lindisfarne* symbols. Alternatively, the synthesis of types may well be original to the *Lindisfarne Gospels*.[42] The trumpets of the Angel and Lion may have been borrowed from another source—an Apocalypse cycle such as that brought to England by Benedict Biscop.[43] The awkward addition of the trumpet to the Lion, floating without support in front of his mouth, suggests that the addition was a new insular invention. The turned head of the Calf also suggests that a model has been adjusted to the immediate requirements of the context.[45] Consequently, the models for the *Lindisfarne* Evangelists most likely lacked accompanying symbols, which were of necessity made up on the spot from several sources. These probably included the insular types established in the *Book of Durrow*, a half-length series with attributes or a partial fusion of this type with the full-length sequence, and certain elements from a locally available Apocalypse cycle.

The *Lindisfarne Gospels* demonstrates the willingness of Eadfrith and his scriptorium to adapt several sources into a new whole. The unity of the art of the *Lindisfarne Gospels*, like that of the *Book of Durrow*, was maintained by the strict imposition of a single style on a variety of models rather than on the unity of a single source. This is particularly the case in the Evangelist portrait series, where the models are entirely foreign, as in the transfiguration of the Late Antique style of the *Amiatinus* Ezra, close to its imported model, into the essentially insular *Lindisfarne* Matthew. The style of the *Amiatinus* Ezra is painterly and impressionistic, similar to contemporary mural painting in Rome. Through the application of washes of color, light and shade are used to give volume to form, using the fundamental modeling technique of classical painting. The *Lindisfarne* Matthew, although almost identical in composition, is radically altered in the treatment of space, color, and the reality of the object depicted. In short, the Matthew is the nonclassical stylistic antithesis of the Ezra. Despite the attempt at perspective in the bench, Matthew is essentially two-dimensional, a flattened form on a flat surface. No interest is shown in the modeling of the prototype. Facial features, drapery folds, and other elements have been reduced to planar areas of color with hard linear edges. The figure has taken on the hard flatness and linearism of insular enamelwork. Unlike the Man of *Durrow*, however, which primarily resembles Irish enamel figure plaques, the *Lindisfarne* figure stylistically approximates the sharp-edged birds, beasts, and men of the Sutton Hoo purse lid, with which the *Lindisfarne* Evangelist also shares an antirepresentational preference in the choice and distribution of color.[45] In the purse lid, the figures are entirely red except for the occasional blue millefiori insert as leg or midsection. The *Lindisfarne* Evangelist shows a similar disregard for color in the treatment of the pallium. Matthew's robe is green, but all its contours and folds are represented as thick bands and hooks of red. The comparison with the *Amiatinus* Ezra demonstrates clearly the confluence of classical and nonclassical art in Northumbria in this period. The lack of concern in *Lindisfarne* for both the spatial modeling and the naturalistic treatment of color in the model indicates the differences in attitude between

Lindisfarne and Jarrow. However, before assessing these differences, one must inquire whether the style of *Lindisfarne* is entirely the result of the imposition of Anglian metalwork traditions and aesthetics on Mediterranean models resembling the *Amiatinus* Ezra, or whether elements of that style as well were also imported through Mediterranean sources.

One stylistic source suggested by Carl Nordenfalk for the *Lindisfarne* Evangelists are ivories of the school that produced a series of plaques of the mission of Saint Mark to Alexandria, once associated with the cathedra of Saint Mark at Grado.[46] The ivories resemble the *Lindisfarne* Evangelists in compositional details, such as the similarity in placement of the small head above the halo of Mark between the arcade pillars in the fragmentary ivory of Saint Mark with a Codex in Milan (Museo del Castello Sforzesco), to the head of the angel above the halo of the *Lindisfarne* Matthew. Such minor parallels could be disregarded as fortuitous were it not for the very striking stylistic resemblance between these ivories and the *Lindisfarne* Evangelists. The Saint Mark ivories show a linear style in the rendering of figures and architecture unusual among Mediterranean ivories but analogous to the linear qualities of the *Lindisfarne* figures. In both, drapery is reduced to a system of surface lines, elaborated in the ivories into a double-fold system. In both, faces are flat expanses with the eyes rendered as double-line pointed ellipses. Noses are oblong tubes modeled only slightly by a planarized shadow on the near side and nostrils are depicted as simple hookings of the line of the nose. Beards and hair are ornamentally elaborated; older figures—Mark in the ivories and Matthew in the codex—have parallel locks, and younger men—the illuminated John, for example—have halos of tightly spiraled curls. However, the date of these ivories is problematic. Originally considered late sixth-century on the basis of their former association with the Grado cathedra, they have been redated to the middle of the eighth century because of stylistic parallels to eastern Mediterranean manuscripts and mosaics of that date, which would place them too late to influence the *Lindisfarne* Evangelists.[47] It is possible that earlier ivories of the same school or workshop as the Saint Mark ivories, dating to the last quarter of the seventh century and showing a formative stage of the same linear style, could have come north as book covers or independently. Such hypothetical ivories could have assisted the Lindisfarne scriptorium in translating Late Antique models, such as the model of the *Amiatinus* Ezra, into a linear idiom more in keeping with Anglian taste. One may even conjecture that there was an ivory author portrait, or partial set of Evangelists, available to Eadfrith and his co-workers.

However, the style of the *Lindisfarne* Evangelists is more probably an independent insular invention. The anticlassical treatment of ultimately Late Antique models, in both the *Lindisfarne Gospels* and the Saint Mark ivories, is part of a widespread early medieval phenomenon: transposition of classical models to a linear and unmodeled style more accessible to artists and local taste outside the Mediterranean littoral heartland of the classical tradition.[48] This development is the result of the independent responses of a variety of cultures with vernacular nonclassical traditions to the influx of unfamiliar classical

Christ Dictating the Gospels to St. Mark, ivory; London, Victoria and Albert Museum *(Crown Copyright Victoria and Albert Museum)*

models. These centers were not necessarily interconnected, and resemblances between their products are not necessarily the result of mutual influence, but rather of a common need to translate the classical model into a more accessible idiom. The Lindisfarne scriptorium itself is probably responsible for the stylistic transition between the model of the *Amiatinus* Ezra and the *Lindisfarne* Matthew. Such a hypothesis is more logical than the assumption that a Northumbrian artist would have preferred to use an imported ivory as a key in transforming the model of Ezra into a style closer to Anglian vernacular metalwork.

The style of the *Lindisfarne Gospels* Evangelists confirms the assimilative tendency already noted in the other elements of the ornament of the codex. The ability of Eadfrith and his scriptorium to combine diverse models and influences, both foreign and indigenous, with such stylistic continuity has led to a search for hypothetical single sources for the Evangelist series and foreign stylistic sources. However, the unique position of Lindisfarne as a center explains both the rich variety and the stylistic harmony of the *Lindisfarne Gospels*.[49] Politically on the frontier between the spreading Roman ecclesiastical empire and the Celtic missionary world, Lindisfarne was able to take advantage of the artistic traditions of both realms. From the Synod of Whitby forward, Lindisfarne's ties to the Roman Church provided the connection to Benedict Biscop's foundations to permit the transfer of the mutual model of Ezra and Matthew from Jarrow/Monkwearmouth to Lindisfarne. The strength of Lindisfarne's connection to the Roman Church after Whitby no doubt also contributed to the rate of influx of imported art to this remote northern center and hence to the variety of sources used in the Gospels. However, the foundational history of Lindisfarne linked it to the Celtic Church of Iona and the assimilative vernacular style of the *Book of Durrow*. Drawing on this tradition, the Lindisfarne scriptorium was able to absorb the new models into a unified vernacular synthesis, rather than transmitting the model by exact emulation of composition and style as had the artists of *Amiatinus*. The Lindisfarne synthesis was as much a part of the Northumbrian Renaissance as was the transplanted classicism of Jarrow and Hexham, for it incorporated many imported models bearing aspects of the Late Antique tradition. However, Lindisfarne added a significantly creative element to this renascence by adhering as well to the Celtic assimilative approach, both by translating the imported model into a vernacular style and by adding elements of indigenous ornament, particularly from the Anglian metalworking tradition.

Another object from Lindisfarne that demonstrates a similarly assimilative approach to imported models is the coffin reliquary of Saint Cuthbert (Durham, Chapter House). This wooden sarcophagus was made in 698 for the translation of the saint into the sanctuary of the church of Saint Peter. A detailed description of the translation is given in Bede's *Prose Life of Saint Cuthbert*, which mentions a "light casket" in which the monks of Lindisfarne placed the incorrupt body of their patron saint and which they set for veneration on the sanctuary floor.[50] This coffin became the reliquary in which the relics of the saint were transported during the wanderings of the Lindisfarne community in the Viking period, and thus came to Chester-le-Street and ultimately to Durham, where its fragments are preserved. These fragments are incised with figural motifs.[51] The lid shows a Christ in Majesty, with the throne of Christ surrounded by the four Evangelist symbols. One end of the coffin shows the Virgin and Child enthroned; one side shows the Twelve Apostles in two ranks;

Coffin of St. Cuthbert, ends: Virgin and Child and Two Angels; Durham, Chapter Library *(by permission of the Dean and Chapter of Durham)*

Coffin of St. Cuthbert, side: Apostles *(by permission of the Dean and Chapter of Durham)*

Coffin of St. Cuthbert, side: Angels *(by permission of the Dean and Chapter of Durham)*

Coffin of St. Cuthbert, lid: Christ in Majesty *(by permission of the Dean and Chapter of Durham)*

and the remaining end and side are incised with the six archangels. Here as in the *Lindisfarne Gospels*, foreign models have been subsumed in a unifying style even more abstract than that used for the Evangelist portraits in the codex. The medium of the coffin ornament, however, lends itself primarily to such linear treatment. Certain passages are awkwardly treated: the placement of the Virgin's right arm, and the absence of a bench under or behind her floating seated figure. The artist may have chosen here to avoid the difficulties of perspective by excluding rectilinear furniture. These observations suggest that the artist who decorated the coffin did not so much choose a style of linear abstraction, as did the Gospels scriptorium, but rather that he was forced to it by the exigencies of the medium and the complexities of imported models slightly beyond his capabilities. It may well have been that the most artistically gifted members of the community were drawn into or chose to join the scriptorium, and that the coffin, despite its importance, was ornamented by a craftsman of the second rank, possibly the carpenter who fitted the boards together. The tubular treatment of the drapery, however, indicates that the artisan of the coffin was aware of the development in the scriptorium. Moreover, the coffin was probably painted in bright colors, adding both visual richness to the otherwise minimal figures and also details to their otherwise huge, staring and inarticulate eyes and to the flow of their drapery. It remained for other and greater craftsmen to translate the richer style of the *Lindisfarne* Evangelists into relief, a more responsive and pliable medium.

Later Illumination in Northumbria and Elsewhere

As the assimilative or synthetic approach of Lindisfarne was more accessible to local taste and artists than the emulative style of Jarrow/Monkwearmouth and Hexham, later products of insular illumination followed Lindisfarne's lead. The treatment of drapery in later insular manuscripts develops rapidly away from Late Antique prototypes in such a radical manner that the green pallium with red fishhook folds of the *Lindisfarne* Matthew seems extraordinarily staid by comparison.

A manuscript closely associated with the *Lindisfarne Gospels* is a fragmentary Gospels codex at Durham (Cathedral Library, MS A.II.17).[52] T. J. Brown has argued on paleographic grounds that the scribe-artist of this badly damaged codex worked at Lindisfarne, possibly as the teacher of Eadfrith, but suggests a date slightly later than the *Lindisfarne Gospels* for the illuminations.[53] The argument of the identity of the hand is of course debatable, but the association of the codex with Lindisfarne is reinforced in several ways. First, C. D. Verey has demonstrated that the corrections in the *Durham Gospels* and in the *Lindisfarne Gospels* are by the same hand.[54] Furthermore, the manuscript was at Chester-le-Street with the community of Saint Cuthbert as early as the tenth century.[55] The text of the *Durham Gospels* is a mixed Italian Vulgate of good quality with scattered Irish readings.[56] The manuscript has two extant major

Durham, Cathedral Library, MS A.II.17, *Gospels,* **fol. 2r: initial** *(by permission of the Dean and Chapter of Durham)*

illuminations, the opening initials to John, "In principio" (fol. 383), and on the verso of the same folio, a Crucifixion showing a bearded Christ in a *colobium,* a long robe, flanked by the lance and sponge bearers below, and a pair of seraphim above the arms of the cross. The monogram, although badly scuffed, is comparable in both design and refinement to the parallel *Lindisfarne* initial.

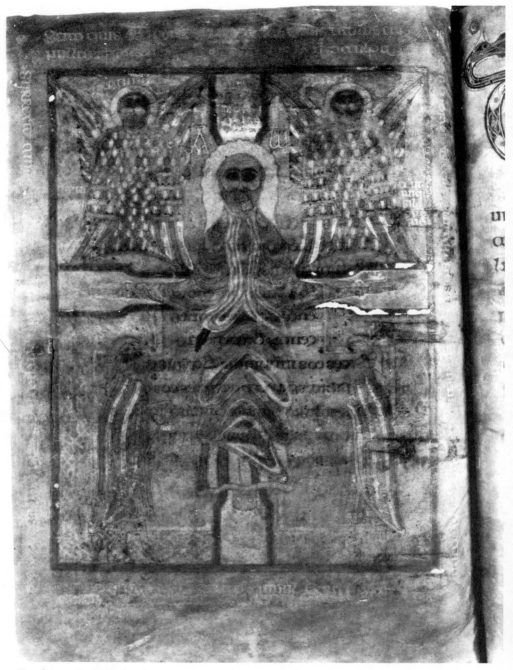

Durham, Cathedral Library, MS A.II.17, fol. 3v: Crucifixion *(by permission of the Dean and Chapter of Durham)*

However, the ornament here is less dense and overwhelming, as the codex was probably not intended for so major a purpose as the *Lindisfarne Gospels*. The motifs used here are generally similar to those in the *Lindisfarne Gospels*: lacertine animal friezes as fillers (albeit worked up more simply in black and white with bits of rose and blue and with green and black ribbon outline) and richly ornamented terminals built up around trumpet spirals and circle motifs. On this basis, the identity of the scriptorium as Lindisfarne is credible. However, the treatment of the colobium of the crucified Christ is strikingly different from the drapery formulas of the *Lindisfarne* Evangelists. In the latter, the general delineation of the basic Late Antique drapery patterns is left basically undisturbed, although coloristically altered and linearized. In the Durham Crucifixion, on the other hand, the color and line have taken over and the original flow of the garments is lost in an equally fluid but totally nonlogical flat patterning only vaguely related to representational draperies. Particularly interesting is the division of the colobium—both the sleeves and the fall from waist to knee—into scallops of flat color resembling shirred bunting. Given this development, artistically unthinkable without the prior experimentation of the *Lindisfarne* Evangelists, the illuminations of the *Durham Gospels* should, as Brown suggested, be placed at Lindisfarne, but after, rather than before, the *Lindisfarne Gospels*. The drapery of the *Durham Gospels* Christ is an early indication of the direction taken in subsequent insular manuscripts, such as the *Book of Saint Chad*.

The *Book of Saint Chad* (Lichfield, Cathedral Library) is a codex of which both date and provenance are controversial, albeit a date in the first half of the eighth century is generally accepted. The codex uses the Irish readings, juxtaposing Vulgate and Old Latin elements—the Old Latin passages descending from a text close to the *Codex Usserianus Secundus*.[57] The script is an insular majuscule close to the Lindisfarne group, and the layout of text on page—in spacing, scale, and placement—resembles the *Lindisfarne Gospels*. The question of provenance is complicated by the history of the codex. Welsh marginalia in the manuscript copy earlier documents associating the codex with the altar of Saint Teilo at Llandeilo-fawr, Carmarthenshire, as early as the late eighth century.[58] A ninth-century Latin inscription (p. 141) notes the exchange of the codex for "a good horse" by Gelhi son of Arithuid with one Cingal, and its donation to God and the altar of Saint Teilo. The price seems low for a large illuminated codex, suggesting that Cingal was not its legitimate owner, and that it had come into Wales through border raids into Mercia, such as those recorded in the *Brut y Tywysogion*.[59] The codex was at Lichfield in Mercia by the tenth century, as an inscription at the top of the first folio refers to "Wynsige presul," probably the Wynsige who was bishop of Lichfield between 963 and 973–5. Furthermore, a notice at the bottom of the fourth folio documents, in Mercian dialect, the settlement of a case in the reign of Bishop Leofgar (1020–27). H. E. Savage suggested that the codex's arrival in Lichfield was also the result of border raiding, this time by Mercians into Wales, as documented in the *Life of Saint Illtyd* in the reign of Edgar in 975, and

Lichfield, Cathedral Library, *Book of St. Chad*, p. 143: initial *(photo: Courtauld Institute of Art, by permission of the Librarian and Chapter, Lichfield)*

additionally in the *Annales Cambriae* in 965 and 983.[60]

The extant illuminations of the *Book of Saint Chad* consist of four major initials, two Evangelist portraits, a cross-carpet-page, and a four-symbols page. The four-symbols page shows a reliance on the traditions of the *Book of Durrow*. The initials are close to *Lindisfarne* in scale, complexity, and in some

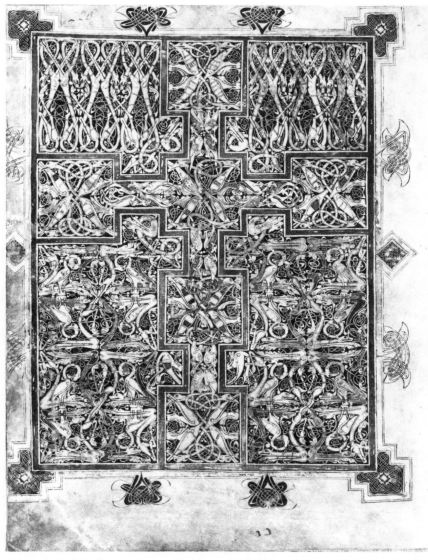

Book of St. Chad, **p. 220: cross-carpet-page** *(photo: Courtauld Institute of Art, by permission of the Librarian and Chapter, Lichfield)*

cases general layout, albeit they show a greater use of the spirals central to the repertory of Celtic metalwork. The primary resemblance to *Lindisfarne* is in the generic design of the cross-carpet-page (p. 220), which is close to the animal interlace cross-carpet-page in *Lindisfarne* (fol. 26v). In both cases, the spatulate-cross design extends to the internal frame of the page, and both cross and ground are filled with interlaced animals. The extrusive knots outside the

Book of St. Chad, **p. 142: Evangelist portrait of Mark** *(photo: Courtauld Institute of Art, by permission of the Librarian and Chapter, Lichfield).*

internal frame at the corners and around the borders are also similar. Consequently there must have been strong connections between the Lindisfarne scriptorium and the center that produced the *Book of Saint Chad.* Henry has suggested that the *Book of Saint Chad,* as the more experimental of the two codices, must therefore have been earlier.[61] However, the ornament of the *Book of Saint Chad* is clearly influenced by the development of art in Mercia in the second quarter of the eighth century. The most particular instance of this influence is the increasing concentration in the animal interlace on bilateral symmetry, both in the cross-carpet-page and in the paired beasts that flank the throne of the Evangelist Mark (p. 142). In Mercian art, as exemplified by the wall friezes at Breedon-on-the-Hill, animal forms are distorted not into the ferocious entanglement of Anglian metalwork, but into archly and heraldically posed and curiously elongated creatures frequently arranged in stylized facing or addorsed pairs.[62] The presence of Mercian elements of design in the *Book of Saint Chad* places them later than the *Lindisfarne Gospels*. H. E. Savage suggested that the Lichfield codex was made in Northumbria and came to the Mercian and Welsh Marches via the Northumbrian missions to Mercia in 653.[63] However, given the combination of Northumbrian and Mercian elements in the cross-carpet-pages, the codex was more probably executed in Mercia at a center with strong Northumbrian ties, and including Northumbrian-trained scribes in its scriptorium.

The Evangelist portraits in the *Book of Saint Chad* are considerably more abstract than those in *Lindisfarne*. The feet of both Mark (p. 142) and Luke (p. 218) are in a *contrapposto*, or striding, position, but this is the only indication as to whether the figures are seated or standing. Their bodies are obscured by masses of convoluted drapery folds with as little coloristic logic as was shown in the *Durham Gospels* Crucifixion. Mark's drapery can still be construed as a tunic and pallium, however bizarrely draped, but in Luke the artist has reduced the garments to an indistinguishable swirl of bunting. Drapery patterning similar to the *Saint Chad* Luke occurs in some later codices, as in the Crucifixion in the *Saint Gall Gospels* (Saint Gall, Stiftsbibliothek MS 51, p. 266), or in the Evangelist portraits in later small Irish Gospels such as the *Book of Dimma* (Dublin, Trinity College Library, MS 59; or London, British Library, Add. MS 40618 [fol. 21v]).[64] However, this degree of abstraction from the model must even in its own day have been considered extreme, for in most later insular figural illuminations the original drapery folds are at least as discernable in the overall design as in the *Saint Chad* Mark.

The thrones of the Evangelists in the *Book of Saint Chad* have also lost substance by comparison to the benches in the *Lindisfarne Gospels*. Both Mark and Luke are placed in front of rather than on seats that have been reduced to a few simple lines. Luke's bench consists of a broad horizontal bar behind the Evangelist's feet, which connects to risers on either side of the figure. These vertical bars terminate in hounds' heads, reminiscent of the lion bench ends of Monkwearmouth. It is possible to construe this arrangement as the footrest, legs, and armrests or sides of a throne, the back and seat of which are obscured by the drapery of the figure. The throne of Mark is, however, not so easily correlated with the parts of a real chair. Here the throne has been reduced to a simple grid behind the Evangelist. An oblong cushion is indicated by a flat oval above the lowest crossbar. The Evangelist is symmetrically flanked by a pair of

Book of St. Chad, p. 218: Evangelist portrait of Luke *(photo: Courtauld Institute of Art, by permission of the Librarian and Chapter, Lichfield)*

fantastically elongated beasts that tie themselves in knots at neck and tail. These may also be the descendants of lion bench ends, but their form has overtaken and all but obliterated their function, much like an insular initial. This reduction of thrones to abstract bars and grids may be due to the insular artists' lack of familiarity with perspective as used in Late Antique depictions of furniture as much as to a deliberate preference for abstraction and flatness. The beginnings of such a reduction can already be seen in the bench of the *Lindisfarne* John, where the artist, obviously ill at ease with the relation of vertical and horizontal elements, covers all the parts of the bench with bright bands and patterns of color.

Even at Jarrow, a similar transformation from Late Antique representation to insular abstraction can be seen in a manuscript of a generation later than *Codex Amiatinus,* the *Durham Cassiodorus* (Cassiodorus, *Commentary on the Psalms*

British Library, MS Add. 40618, *Gospels,* fol. 21v: Evangelist portrait of Luke *(by permission of the British Library)*

Durham, Cathedral Library, MS B.II.30, Cassiodorus, *Institutiones,* **fol. 81v: David Enthroned** *(by permission of the Dean and Chapter of Durham)*

[Durham, Cathedral Library MS B.II.30]), commonly dated in the second quarter of the eighth century.[65] This codex has two major illuminations—preceding Psalms 51 and 101. The first shows David enthroned as a musician (fol. 81v). The second depicts David standing on a two-headed snake, holding a spear and an orange ring framing an inscription of his name (fol. 172v). Carl Nordenfalk has attributed this codex to Jarrow on the basis of the resemblance

Durham, Cassiodorus, *Institutiones;* **fol. 172v: David Standing** *(by permission of the Dean and Chapter of Durham)*

of the frame of the standing David to that of the first miniature of the *Valenciennes Apocalypse,* a copy of a Jarrow manuscript.[66] Moreover, the importance of Cassiodoran manuscripts at Biscop's foundations makes Jarrow a likely candidate for the production of this codex, as does a medieval tradition that it was written by Bede. Both figures of David show the strong influence of the early school of illumination at Biscop's foundations which, in *Codex Amiatinus* and presumably also in Ceolfrith's other pandects, maintained the style of the available Late Antique models. Although the border motifs of the *Durham Cassiodorus*—including key patterns, interlaced beasts, and knotwork—are by this date purely insular, the figures retain a massive solidity and classical monumentality, uncommon in Northumbrian illumination, by their ponderous width and the arrangement of their tubular draperies, wrapped around them to emphasize their bulk. This is particularly true of the seated David, where washes are used to give weight and three-dimensionality to the figure. The standing David, by a different artist, reduces the form to a pattern of lines, but even here the contours are chosen so that the figure has the appearance of mass, however flattened.[67] Nonetheless, the artist of the standing David is moving toward insular linearism as a simpler solution to the problems of the figure than the modeling attempted by his colleague. However, the techniques of perspective are too complex even for the seated-figure master, who reduces David's throne to the familiar insular grid with animal-head armrest terminals. Thus, even at Jarrow, in the generation after *Amiatinus,* there is a movement away from the style of the Late Antique model toward a more insular style of linear abstraction. Here, however, the choice is a compromise between linearism and classical plasticity, which leans closer to abstraction only when the artist lacks the skill to maintain the tradition of modeling techniques.

The illumination of manuscripts documents the diversity of response in Northumbria to imported classical prototypes. The variety of results indicates that the emulative style of Jarrow/Monkwearmouth, as documented in the *Codex Amiatinus,* was only a fragment of this response. In illumination, only *Amiatinus* fits Panofsky's description of the northern English renascence as a classicism, "self-conscious either in the sense of purism or in the sense of romanticism."[68] However, the response of the artists of the *Lindisfarne Gospels* and their descendants to Late Antique models is not the result of a lack of comprehension but of innovative, spontaneous creativity. It is known from the *Codex Amiatinus* that direct stylistic emulation of Late Antique models was possible for insular artists. The products of other centers are the results of a sequence of choices to assimilate or adapt the model to local taste. Only some of these choices are the result of the difficulties of the model itself, such as the transformation of perspective bench to planar grid. Other developments, particularly in the treatment of the figure and its drapery, are more conditioned by indigenous insular traditions, both in metalwork and in earlier Celtic illumination. In this context it is useful to recall that manuscript illumination was a relatively new development in Northumbria in this period, and that many of the Anglian scriptoria had no tradition of copying as did Mediterranean centers of illumination. Moreover, the Northumbrian illuminators of Lindisfarne and related houses were the heirs of the broadly assimilative outlook of the artists of the Celtic Church. Emulative loyalty to the style of imported models had meaning only at centers with a particular loyalty to Rome, identified as the source of these models. Elsewhere, creative assimilation was at once a more practical and a more aesthetically accessible approach. The resulting naturally evolved synthesis varied from center to center and from codex to codex, conditioned only by the particular aims and desires of the illuminators and their superiors.

Northumbrian Stone Crosses

A similarly assimilative approach can be traced in many of Northumbria's stone crosses. However, very few Northumbrian crosses can be so easily linked with particular foundations as those of Wilfrid's Hexham. Most of them are or were originally sited in fairly remote areas, and only a few crosses can be linked on stylistic grounds to workshops at particular centers. The degree and nature of the assimilation of foreign models in insular art are conditioned by the attitude of the individual art-producing centers. In the case of the crosses, workshop provenance and consequently also foundational attitude are unknown variables. Nonetheless, analysis of function, style, and iconography of individual crosses can clarify the circumstances of their carving and the choice of and approach to models. Such analysis is only possible where the cross has survived entirely or nearly intact, and where the nature and treatment of models can be discerned. The Ruthwell Cross is a particularly revealing case. Panofsky cited this cross as comparable to the *Codex Amiatinus* in its deliberate and self-conscious use of classical models.[69] However, despite its transplanted Late Antique style, the Ruthwell Cross carries an iconographic program that is distinctly outside the mainstream traditions of the Roman Church in England. This program is explained by the location and function of the cross and the intentions of its makers.

The remote locations of the majority of Northumbrian crosses result from their intended function. The origin of the tradition of cross carving in northern England goes back to the beginning of the conversion period. The earliest insular crosses were simply standing slabs inscribed with crosses, set up by early missionaries to mark their presence and for propaganda purposes. An example is the Whithorn Cross of about 600, at the site of Candida Casa, Saint Ninian's missionary foundation on the Solway Firth in Galloway. There was at the same time a tradition imported by Irish missionaries of crosses used to mark the sites of important events in ecclesiastical history. This practice evolved in Ireland in the fifth and sixth centuries. In the *Book of Armagh*, Tirechan cites the description by Bishop Ultan of the meeting of two fifth-century saints: "Patrick went to the wall at Munco . . . and Secundinus was sitting apart under a leafy elm, and there is the sign of the cross to this day."[70] Adamnan's *Life of*

Columba similarly mentions crosses set up at significant sites by the wayside.[71] From the Irish, the Northumbrians also borrowed the use of crosses to mark the perimeter and major points of a monastic community.[72] In the *Prose Life of Saint Cuthbert*, Bede notes that the saint requested burial on the island of Farne: "When God takes my soul, bury me here close to the oratory, on the south side and to the east of that holy cross which I myself put up."[73] Cuthbert's cross was not funerary by original intent as were those marking the grave of Bishop Acca at Hexham, but its location gave the saint the means to orient his followers to the exact spot he intended for his burial. The raising of crosses primarily as funerary monuments was a practice of centers of Roman affiliation, as in the case of Acca's tomb at Hexham.[74]

Considerable numbers of Northumbrian crosses were, however, not associated with monastic sites. In northern England, during the mission of the Celtic Church, much of the evangelizing was done by itinerant monks, with or without affiliation with a particular monastic community. Many of these early missionaries founded small monastic communities of their own, and the direction and extent of their work can be traced in the surviving place-names of their foundations. Often, however, the community of the faithful was small enough in a given area that the construction of a church, let alone the foundation of a monastic community, was unwarranted. Such areas continued to be served by traveling clergy, who taught and provided the sacraments in the open air by the roadside. As the major Celto-Northumbrian ecclesiastical centers became established over time, the wayside ministry became part of their cure. Bede notes that Saint Cuthbert, while a monk at Melrose, particularly devoted himself to preaching in remote villages, often traveling an entire month on foot in the mountainous hinterlands of Northumbria, a predilection he acquired from his teacher Boisil. Thus the practice of roadside preaching that had evolved in the less-organized period of the missions became a function of the later, more institutional Celtic Church. Although Theodore of Canterbury tried to curtail the wanderings of unaffiliated clergy in order to simplify the imposition of Roman canonical practice, the use of the preaching stations by the institutional Church continued, as it was the only form of Christian contact available to the hinterlands population.[75] Stone crosses at these stations were sometimes carved with didactic scenes, functioning much as had the church frescoes of Paulinus of Nola, as a *biblia pauperum*, and as an inspiration and teaching device for the traveling clergy.[76]

The Ruthwell Cross was originally a didactic station marker. It is now located inside the parish church at Ruthwell in Dumfries, but was not originally associated with a church or even with the village of Ruthwell. According to a local tradition, recorded by John Craig, minister of Ruthwell, in his 1783 *Old Statistical Account of Scotland*, and later repeated by Dr. Duncan, minister in the early nineteenth century, the cross was brought from a site called Priest-woodside on the Solway Firth.[77] The name Priestwoodside suggests use as a preaching station predating the construction of any churches in the area. The Ruthwell Cross stood in the parish church in Ruthwell until 1642, when it was destroyed by order of the Reform Church of Scotland.[78] The cross was then thrown down, its shaft broken in several places and some parts deliberately damaged, particularly the transom and central medallion of the head, which were completely obliterated. The fragments were preserved by the minister of the period, Gavin Young, who had the sense and courage to hide them by burying them in the earth floor of the church. The fragments were then lost for some fifty years. Parts were seen in the churchyard by antiquarians of the seventeenth century.[79] In 1802 Dr. Duncan reassembled the fragments into a standing cross in the churchyard, using carefully chosen blank pieces of similar sandstone to fill lacunae, and commissioning the present transom and central medallion in a clearly modern style, distinguishing them from the earlier fragments. The ancient uppermost cross arm was restored above the new transom but in reverse, so that John the Evangelist with the Eagle, which belongs on the front or north side of the cross, now faces back, or southward. In the 1880s Reverend McFarlain arranged for the cross to be scheduled for

Bewcastle Cross, view of the whole

protection under the Ancient Monuments Act, and in 1887 an apsidal extension was built onto Ruthwell Church to contain the cross and protect it from further weathering. Despite its fractures and the effects of weathering, however, the Ruthwell Cross is remarkably clearly preserved.

The Ruthwell Cross is dated to the first half of the eighth century on the basis of the runes, the meter, and the language of the *Dream of the Rood,* the Anglo-Saxon poem inscribed on the borders around the panels of inhabited vine scroll on the lateral faces of the cross.[80] An earlier date, about 675, was once given on the basis of the runic colophon on the Bewcastle Cross, a closely related monument in the cemetery of the Church of Saint Cuthbert at Bewcastle, Cumbria. The Bewcastle Cross is a product of the same workshop that carved Ruthwell, although slightly later in its use of roll moldings and other elegant details. Bewcastle has three figural panels on the main or west face of the cross. In vertically descending order, these are John the Baptist with the Lamb, Blessing Christ on the Animals, and John the Evangelist with the Eagle. The first two use precisely the same models as were used for the identical subjects at Ruthwell, and the styles of the two crosses are overwhelmingly similar. Bewcastle's runic colophon has been long debated. Those who have claimed to be able, over the past three centuries, to decipher the runes read references to Alchfrith, King Oswy's son and underking of Deira, his Mercian bride Cyniburg, and possibly also to *"fruman gear Ecgfrithu,"* "in the first year of [the reign of] Ecgfrith," 671–72.[81] However, the Bewcastle Cross has never been sheltered from the elements, and the legibility and historical references of these runes are highly questionable.[82] The runic and epigraphic style of the *Dream of the Road* gives a far more acceptable date for both Ruthwell and Bewcastle around 750.

The Ruthwell Cross is decorated with panels of figural relief on front and back, and with an inhabited vinescroll of its sides. The panels and vinescroll show the extensive use of imported Mediterranean models, probably predominantly ivory devotional panels and book covers. Such sources would demonstrate both compositions and relief-carving techniques, supplementing both methods and motifs already developed in insular workshops producing architectural ornament. However, despite its use of both medium and models of immediate or only slightly removed foreign origin, the Ruthwell Cross is a purely insular product in its iconographic program. This program is remarkably sophisticated in its recombinative treatment of models to achieve a particular and immediate meaning for an insular audience, with strong political implications.

The front of the upper arm of the cross head, now at the back of the cross, shows the Evangelist John with the Eagle. The margins contain the remains of an inscription, "IN——UM," suggesting, by the allocation of space for lost letters, the first words of John's Gospel, "In principio erat verbum." The top scene on the north side of the shaft, constituting the lower arm of the cross has two defaced frontal figures—one with wings and the other holding a book— possibly the Evangelist Matthew with the Angel. Given this interpretation, the

Bewcastle Cross, front top: John the Baptist

Bewcastle Cross: Blessing Christ on the Animals

Bewcastle Cross, runic inscription

Bewcastle Cross: John the Evangelist

Ruthwell Cross, top front: John the Baptist

Ruthwell Cross, side, vinescroll

lost transom arms would probably have shown the Evangelists Mark and Luke with their respective symbols. On this basis, G. Baldwin Brown suggested that the central medallion contained a symbol of Christ that attracted the particular wrath of the Reformation more than the rest of the cross. One possibility is the Agnus Dei, particularly hated by the early Scottish reformers for what it considered its blasphemous idolatry of a lamb in lieu of Christ, equivalent to the Israelites' worship of the golden Calf.[83]

The top panel of the front of the shaft proper contains the figure of John the Baptist holding the Lamb.[84] The Baptist is elderly, with beard and long hair, and wears a *tunica talarica*, a mantle, and clogs or sabots. The Lamb has a nimbus and raises its right foreleg. The panel was broken and, although repaired, leaves the position of the Baptist's arms unclear. The composition has a prototype among the ivory reliefs of the sixth-century ivory cathedra of Archbishop Maximian in Ravenna, and a wall painting in the Egyptian monastic complex at Deir-Abu-Makar.[85] The inscription fragment— "ADORAMUS ET NON EUM"—is taken from the Agnus Dei: "Agnum Dei

Ruthwell Cross: Blessing Christ on the Animals

adoramus et non eum singillatim, totam vero Trinitatem." The Agnus Dei was introduced into the canon of the Mass at the fraction by Pope Sergius (687–701) and was known in England shortly thereafter.[86] In the context of the program of the cross, John is recognized as the prototypal ascetic, the "voice crying in the wilderness," living in the desert on locusts and honey.

The next panel below the Baptist shows Blessing Christ on the Animals, a variation of the standard Christ Standing on the Animals of early Christian art. Christ stands in an attitude of blessing, with raised right forearm, and holds a scroll in his left hand. He wears a cross nimbus, a long tunic and mantle, chin-length hair, and a mustache. His bare feet rests on twin creatures emerging from the lower frame of the panel. These animals have long snouts and prominent rounded ears, and they are placed with their heads together so that their snouts touch and their forelegs overlap. The scene is significantly differentiated from its standard formulation in that the beasts are identical rather than distinguished as the lion and the basilisk of Psalms 90:13.[87] Moreover, the inscription of the panel—"IHS XPS / JUDEX AEQUITATIS / BESTIAE ET DRACONES COGNOVERUNT IN DE / ESERTO SALVA[T]OREM MUNDI"—refers not to the Psalmist's triumphant Christ trampling the lion and the basilisk but to the less common motif of Christ in the wilderness during the temptation, to whom the animals ministered (Mark 1:13). Meyer Schapiro has traced this image not to the mainstream commentators who saw the beasts as emblematic of the temptations but to more remote sources both in the Old Testament and in the Apocrypha that predict or perceive Christ's harmony with the desert beasts as a fulfillment of messianic promise.[88] The ascetic in the wilderness comforted by animals was part of the standard symbolism in the eremitic monastic tradition and the associated hagiographic literature. Because of the strength of the eremitic tradition in the Celtic Church, such symbolic references are not uncommon in the lives of Celtic saints. For example, Saint Cuthbert was obeyed by crows and had his feet warmed and dried by a pair of sea otters on emerging from the ocean after a night vigil. The panel of Blessing Christ on the Animals on the Ruthwell Cross consequently shows an aspect of Christ strongly consonant with Celtic eremitic monasticism.

The next panel below the Blessing Christ shows Saint Anthony and Saint Paul the Hermit. The two saints divide between them a loaf of bread brought to them in the wilderness by a raven. The saints stand facing one another with the loaf of bread held between them. The inscription reads, "SCS PAULUS ET A[NTONIUS] FREGER[UN]T PANEM IN DESERTO." The motif is originally Egyptian; the earliest extant version of the scene is at Deir-Abu-Makar on the south wall of the south chapel of the old monastic church. Here, however, the raven gives the bread to Paul only, who is shown as an antitype of Elijah.[89] G. Baldwin Brown has suggested the transmission of the theme to insular art via Alexandrine ivories.[90] The legend occurs neither in the Athanasius's *Life of Anthony* nor in the early anonymous Greek *Life of Saint Paul the Hermit*. Its earliest extant recounting is in the *Martyrology* of Saint Jerome. Anthony, traveling in the wilderness, encounters Paul, who survives

Ruthwell Cross: Paul and Anthony

by being brought his daily loaf of bread by a raven. This day the raven brings a doubly large loaf of bread, which the saints consider divine recognition of their meeting. They quarrel as to who should break bread first; at last both hold it and break it together. These events are followed in the narrative by Paul's death and miraculous burial by two lions and Anthony's famous temptation. The Ruthwell Cross and Nigg Cross versions show the breaking of bread, but on the Irish crosses the saints receive with upraised arms the bread brought by the raven.[91] The scene has obvious reference to the Blessing Christ above, as Paul as the ascetic in the wilderness is provisioned by a raven, and Anthony subsequently undergoes a series of temptations in the desert. The scene, however, had broader implications for insular clergy, who practiced the ascetic monasticism ultimately inherited by the Celtic Church from the Antonine Fathers. It was an Anglo-Saxon tradition that Paul and Anthony were the first monks and the first founders of monasteries.[92] Moreover, in early Anglo-Saxon calendars, Saint Paul is consistently called the first hermit. However, the scene may have an additional and potentially political significance for the Celtic Church. The choice at Ruthwell and Nigg of the particular moment when Paul and Anthony break the bread between them may be an allusion to the Irish ritual of *cofractio,* or joint consecration. This ceremony was part of the liturgy of Iona and was practiced elsewhere in the Celtic Church, as recounted in Adamnan's *Life of Columba.* This unusual rite is also cited in a hymn on the Eucharist in the *Bangor Antiphonary,* beginning "quando communicarent sacerdotes," which associates the *fractio* with Paul and Anthony's loaf.[93] *Cofractio* may have come into Irish liturgy from the Antonine Fathers, either directly or via the ascetic centers of Southern France. It does not occur in the Roman rite, and was one of the minor heterodoxies of the Celtic Church, although not one specifically challenged by the Roman Church at Whitby. Its appearance on the Ruthwell Cross may consequently indicate the ambience of the design and the meaning of the program of the cross as a whole.

The next panel in descending order shows the Flight into Egypt. The donkey, much damaged and its legs totally obliterated, travels to the left. Before

Ruthwell Cross: Flight into Egypt

him is a circular object, possibly the remains of the head of Joseph but more probably a tree top. Mary sits facing forward on the donkey as on a throne, with the Child on her lap. Only the Child has a halo. The upper border is inscribed, " + MARIA ET IO——" but the rest of the inscription is lost. The design of the Flight has earlier formal parallels in one of the Adana medallions from Cilicia and in the *Rabūlā Gospels* (Florence, Laurentian Library, Cod. Plut. I, fol. 56).[94] The scene evokes wilderness and privation in accordance with the developing program, but also has other connections to ascetic imagery: in the Apocrypha, the Christ Child is worshiped and unharmed by the animals in the desert during the Flight.[95] Unfortunately, the panel at Ruthwell is so damaged that it is impossible to tell whether any such animals were included in the scene.

Below the Flight is a very badly damaged final panel. W. R. Lethaby wrote in 1912 of a possible Nativity with a coiled snake to the right, certainly an unusual iconographic combination.[96] The panel is, however, so totally obliterated that it is impossible to discern any figures, let alone a program, in the remaining irregularities of the surface.

The present south or back face of the cross was originally topped by the cross arm panel now facing north. This shows a large raptor, possibly an eagle, perched on a branch with one claw raised. This panel was framed with a runic rather than a Latin inscription, unfortunately now lost. The lower arm of the cross shows an archer aiming upward and to the right at a forty-five-degree angle, his quiver possibly at the right. The panel is damaged and the inscription here is also lost. These two images have been considered both separately and as a unit, with a resulting variety of interpretations both secular and sacred. Archers appear in inhabited vinescrolls in crosses at Saint Andrew, Auckland, Durham, slightly later than Ruthwell, and in ninth-century crosses at Sheffield and Bakewell. One of the reused *putto* screen fragments from Hexham shows a *putto* with a bow, which suggests that the motif of the archer in the vine may be derived from locally available sub-Roman Late Antique decorative reliefs. Eagles and other raptors appear frequently on Anglo-Saxon coins. The archer and the eagle at Ruthwell have been considered together as a secular hunt scene, as eagle hunts are a documented pastime of the period, illustrated in eighth-century manuscripts.[97] The inclusion of secular and even pre-Christian mythological material is common in Irish and in English Viking-period crosses, but is unlikely here where the selection of scenes is not only strongly Christian but also programmatic. In Christian terms, the archer alone has been interpreted as "the arrow that flieth by day" (Psalms 90:5), in which case the eagle might be construed as the protection of the Lord, "under His wings thou shalt trust" (Psalsm 90:4).[98] However, without the images of the transom and central medallion, this cannot be verified. The archer may also be a reference to a line in the *Dream of the Rood,* where the Cross itself is "wounded by shafts," and the bird alone can read as the eagle of the Ascension, as derived from Psalms 102:5: "Thy youth shall be renewed like the eagle's."[99] However, none of these explanations coherently fits the program thus far worked out. More applicable

Ruthwell Cross: Reconciliation of Mary and Martha

is E. H. Kantorwicz's theory that the archer is Ishmael, the son of Abraham and Hagar, who was sent into the wilderness at Isaac's birth, and where, after being miraculously provided with water, he survived as an archer (Genesis 21:1–21).[100] According to rabbinic tradition, Ishmael "aimed at birds," and lived as a penitent in the wilderness. The ascetic Ishmael would be an appropriate element in the Ruthwell program. The archer and bird of Ruthwell are also close in general composition to portrayals of Ishmael both in the Vatican Greek *Octateuchs* (Vatican, MS Grec. 746, *Octateuch* 8040; MS Grec. 747, *Octateuch* 4210) and in a later Anglo-Saxon manuscript, the *Heptateuch of Ælfric* (London, British Library, Cotton Claudius B.IV).

The panel below the archer shows two women embracing, and was long thought to be a Visitation. A reexamination of the marginal inscription— "MARTHA / MARIAE MR / DOMINNAE"—has indicated that the scene is the Reconciliation of Mary and Martha.[101] The original error was based on the formal similarity of the panel to early Visitations, from which it was no doubt derived, and on the presence below of the Annunciation, with which the Visitation is usually paired. Analagous Visitations include an Egyptian embroidery (London, Victoria and Albert Museum, no. 777), an illumination in the *Paris Homilies of Gregory Nazianzus* (Paris, Bibliothèque Nationale, MS Grec.

510), a lost fresco formerly in San Valentino in Rome, another of the Adana medallions from Cilicia, the eighth-century Ratchis Altar in Lombard Cividale, and a lost ivory from the cathedra of Maximian in Ravenna. On the other hand, the subject of the Ruthwell panel—the story of Mary and Martha—is extremely rare in early Christian art, and this particular iconography of reconciliation is unique. The closest textual source is Bede's *In Lucam Evangelium Expositio:*

> Duae quippe istae Domino dilectae sorores duas vitas spirituales quibus in praesenti sancta exercetur ecclesia demonstrant; Martha quidem actualem qua proximo in caritate sociamur; Maria ver contemplativam qua in Deo amore suspiramus.[102]

Bede observes that Mary and Martha represent the two life-styles reconciled in the Church, the contemplative and the active. This reconciliation is crucial to the program of the cross as many of the other scenes have dealt only with the eremitic contemplative path.

Ruthwell Cross: Christ in the House of Simon and Healing of the Blind Man

The next panel below the Reconciliation shows Christ in the House of Simon. Christ stands face forward, blessing with his right hand and holding a codex in his veiled left hand. The woman who washed Christ's feet is shown in profile on her knees to the left of Christ. She covers Christ's left foot with her right forearm and a long snakelike coil of hair. Her elongated fingers constitute a third of the length of her arm, but, in striking contrast to this crudity, the sculptor has rendered with extreme delicacy a strand of hair on the inner side of her face. The inscription reads: "ATTULIT —— BA / STRUM UNGENTI & STANS RETROSECUS PEDES / EIUS LACRIMIS COEPIT RIGARE PEDES EIUS & CAPILLIS / CAPITIS SUI TERGEBA[T]" (Luke 7 : 37–38). The theme is rare in art before the ninth century, and it appears that the model at Ruthwell was identical to that used for the Blessing Christ on the Animals on the front of the cross.[103] This explains the physically awkward position of the woman at Christ's feet and the cruder details of her arm, if the sculptor had to interpolate a kneeling figure into the corner of a prototypal single-figure composition.[104] In her form and, to some extent, in the meaning, she is analagous to the animals beneath Christ's feet, the sinful and demonic submitting to Christ. The association of the woman in the house of Simon with Mary Magdalen, exorcized of seven devils (Luke 8 : 2), and the Mary of the panel above, the sister of Martha (Luke 10 : 38–42), although never specific in the Gospels, was often used in support of monasticism by early writers, basing their argument on the story of Mary and Martha. The iconography of Mary Magdalen as a recluse begins in the eleventh and twelfth centuries as a result of a dispute over her relics, but the association of the foot washing in the house of Simon with the ascetic Mary the Egyptian is earlier. In the ninth-century *Anglo-Saxon Martyrology,* Mary the Egyptian is said to have spent thirty years as a penitent in the wilderness.[105] The Ruthwell Cross suggests that the legend was already established in the mid-eighth century, particularly in England where female ascetics were numerous. However, the awkward position of the kneeling figure at Ruthwell suggests that, although the hagiographic material was current, the pictorial motif was just evolving at the time the cross was made.

The lower three scenes on the back of the Ruthwell Cross, like the lower two of the front, are Christological narratives. Of these, the uppermost is the Healing of the Blind Man. Christ stands at left in semiprofile with a rayed nimbus and a mustache, touching the chin of the blind man at right with a rod. The inscription reads: "ET PRAETERIENS VIDI — / ANATIBITATE ET SA —— BINFI[?] ——RMI[TATE][?]," probably derived from the passage, "Et praeteriens vidit hominem coecum a nativitate et sanavit eum ab infirmitate" (John 9 : 1). The Ruthwell scene has specific formal parallels with a Syro-Egyptian ivory pyx in Bologna. The next panel shows the Annunciation. The Angel enters from the left, wearing a plain nimbus and long hair in ringlets. He raises his right arm across his chest in a gesture of greeting and allocution; his left arm is lost. The Virgin stands to the right, cringing slightly with her left hand at her throat in a motion that combines surprise, modesty, and terror. The

Ruthwell Cross: Annunciation

Ruthwell Cross: Crucifixion

gestures of these two figures indicate the sensitivity of which the Ruthwell sculptors were capable; the scene has a breathless grace foreshadowing late Gothic Annunciations. The borders at the sides of the panel have been badly damaged, but part of the inscription remains as "INGRESSUS—— TE—— BE——" from "Ingressus angelus ad eam dixit Ave gratia plena Dominus tecum, benedicta tu in mulieribus" (Matthew 1:28). Stuhlfauth has shown that this Annuniciation type is of Syro-Palestinian origin.[106] The placement of the Annunciation on the Ruthwell Cross is consistent with the location at the same level of the Flight into Egypt, another infancy scene, on the front of the Cross. It is also linked to the two scenes above. The Annunciation, as the moment of incarnation, was considered the origin of redemption; Bede, in the *In Lucam Evangelium Expositio,* refers to this moment as "exordium nostrae redemptionis."[107] Similarly, the woman in the house of Simon and the blind man are both redeemed by the direct intervention of Christ.[108]

The lowest scene on the back of the Ruthwell Cross is the Crucifixion. In this much damaged panel, Christ is presented on a Latin cross, of which the shaft is broader than the crossbar. He wears a short tunic or loincloth. The upper part of the panel is much eroded.[109] Round indentations above the cross arms suggest that sun and moon flanked Christ's head, and the remaining space below the cross arms would be sufficient for the lance and sponge bearer, who appear regularly in early insular Crucifixions, including the Athlone Plaque, the Hexham reliefs, and the illumination in the *Durham Gospels.*[110] Crucifixions on Irish crosses lack sun and moon, but provide parallels for Ruthwell in Christ's short tunic or loincloth, whereas in earlier Anglican Crucifixions, as in the *Durham Gospels,* Christ wears the longer colobium.[111] A similar barelegged Christ in a noninsular context is seen in a panel of a fifth-century Byzantine ivory casket in the British Museum.[112]

The program of the Ruthwell Cross is arranged as follows:

Front (north)	Back (south)
Four Evangelists and Their Symbols, Agnus Dei (?)	*Ishmael in the Wilderness (?)
*John the Baptist with the Lamb	*Reconciliation of Mary and Martha
*Blessing Christ on the Animals	*Christ in the House of Simon
*Paul and Anthony Breaking Bread	Christ Healing the Blind Man
*Flight into Egypt	Annunciation
(Nativity?)	Crucifixion

The scenes are divided into two groups. The second-to-lowest and possibly the lowest scene on the front of the cross and the three lowest scenes on the back are Christological narratives and were probably intended for didactic purposes much as were painted or mosaic Christological cycles in churches. However, the upper scenes are more iconic than narrative and provide the basis of a program. A consistent thematic unity has emerged from the preceding discussion. At least seven of the twelve panels (those marked above with asterisks) are directly linked to the subject of monasticism and particularly to the ascetic eremitic monasticism that was the legacy of the Celtic Church. Moreover, the artist has probably gone to the trouble to invent a composition for at least one if not two of the scenes. He has somewhat awkwardly added the figure of the crouching woman to the Blessing Christ model to produce the Christ in the House of Simon, and he probably also transposed a Visitation into the Reconciliation of Mary and Martha, although it is possible that that transition had already been made in a model. The necessity for inventing new compositions suggests a single literary source for Ruthwell's program. No single liturgical work, lectionary, or homily has yet been found to be a source of the entire Ruthwell program, although some of the same and other ascetic subjects were frequently used as readings for Lent in England and elsewhere in the medieval period. There are, furthermore, no liturgical pericopes for Dumfries for this period, so an association of the cross program with a locally available lectionary cycle for Lent is speculative.[113] On the other hand, the use of ascetic themes at Ruthwell may have had an entirely nonliturgical basis. The Strathclyde region, which includes Ruthwell, was more resistant than the rest of Celtic-converted Northumbria to Roman orthodoxy. This conservatism was not due to a preponderance of nonconforming Irish clergy in the area, for even Iona had conformed in 715. Strathclyde, Galloway, and most of southwestern Scotland had its own ancient church, based in the ancient British kingdom of Rheged and similar to the Irish Church in heterodoxy and ascetic traditions. The Church of Strathclyde had its own centers of learning, such as Saint Ninian's Whithorn, which had been made a see by the Northumbrians in 731, and several other foundations along the Solway Firth. The Strathclyde Church also had its own hagiographic literature. The life of Saint Kentigern (518–603), the major missionary to the Strathclyde region, was that of a model hermit saint. His biography is preserved both in the early anonymous *Apostolic Life*, and in a twelfth-century life by Jocelin. Meyer Schapiro has suggested that the life and acts of Kentigern may be the basis of Ruthwell's program, as the *Lives* narrates Saint Kentigern's repetition of many of the ascetic acts of Christ, John the Baptist, and Mary the Egyptian.[114] Kentigern also raised many crosses at preaching stations, so that the Ruthwell Cross may be commemorative of his work, or even a replacement of an early perishable cross set up by the saint himself.

The choice of Saint Kentigern as the tacit subject of the Ruthwell Cross would have had political implications in the post-Whitby period. Kentigern not only was a paragon of Celtic messianic eremitism, but also, through two particular acts, became a plausible standard for the independence of the Celtic Church, in and out of Strathclyde, from the authority of Rome. According to the hagiographic sources, Kentigern went to Rome and met Gregory the Great, who gave him freedom from episcopal authority, an act that could be construed as giving him and his Church in Strathclyde apostolic autocephaly. In a second politically freighted moment, Kentigern met and exchanged staves with Columba, the Irish missionary saint. At Whitby, where Columba's staff was kept as a holy relic, Wilfrid, the champion of the Roman faction, had demanded whether those present acknowledged the authority of Rome and Saint Peter, to whom Christ had expressly given earthly dominion over his churches, or of Columba, who had no such authority. Kentigern's equal exchange of staffs with Columba made Columba, although never specifically apostolic, to some extent Kentigern's peer, thus refuting Wilfrid's assertions of Roman primacy at Whitby. This circuitous argument would certainly have appealed to the more adamantly conservative members of the Celtic faction in Strathclyde. Schapiro has consequently argued that the Ruthwell Cross is to some extent a political statement; by honoring Kentigern, it makes a gesture against the decisions of Whitby in favor of the independence of the Strathclyde Church. However, the Ruthwell Cross lacks any specific reference to Kentigern. Eremitic or ascetic subjects may well occur on the Ruthwell Cross for the same reason that they were stressed in the formulation of the Kentigern legend—eremitic monasticism was fundamental to the nature of the Celtic Church both before and after the imposition of the edicts of Whitby. Consequently the use of these motifs at Ruthwell need not be a direct reference to any particular saint. Second, the reflection of Kentigern's quasi-apostolic status on the decisions of Whitby is not mentioned in any contemporary sources, although the beleaguered Celtic prelates at Whitby and their conservative later colleagues in Strathclyde might have found it very useful. Oblique references to the life and acts of Kentigern may or may not be present at Ruthwell, without necessitating the interpretation of the cross as a political manifesto.

The Ruthwell Cross can be understood as having a program centering on the ascetic aspects of the life of Christ and his close associates, and of their prototypes and later emulators. The cross may have had a specific meaning for a Strathclyde audience because of the parallels between these historic figures and the life of Saint Kentigern, and would consequently have served as a reminder of the continuity of the ascetic tradition in the local Celtic Church. Nonetheless, the inclusion of the Reconciliation of Mary and Martha can be construed as compromise, as symbolic of the progressive reconciliation in Strathclyde as in Northumbria and elsewhere of the Celtic monastic and contemplative Church and the Anglian/Roman episcopal and more temporal Church in this turbulent period.

The Ruthwell Cross has a plainly insular program, yet the stylistic associations of its figural and ornamental sculpture are Mediterranean. The relief is powerful; the legs of Christ in the House of Simon panel and those of the eagle on the back of the cross head are fully undercut. This plasticity is lost in later crosses that are further from the importation of the Mediterranean prototypes both in time and in style, and adopt a variety of degrees of stylized flatness and linearized abstraction. At Ruthwell, details have been dulled by weathering, but the figural proportions are for the most part correct. Moreover, the artist seems comfortable working in figural relief on the monumental scale, as the figures are on average about two feet in height, beyond the scale of metalwork and ivory. The figures are slender and heavily draped; anatomical features are often suppressed in favor of an elaboration of folds. This suppression of anatomy and an angularization of movement are variations on the classical style already seen in earlier and contemporary Mediterranean art. The stylistic models are mostly eastern Mediterranean in origin, as are the compositions. Stylistic comparisons for Ruthwell's figural reliefs have been made specifically to two monuments in Ravenna: the fifth-century Pignatta sarcophagus in San Francesco, and the sixth-century ivory cathedra of Maximian in the Cathedral Treasury. The Pignatta sarcophagus, probably Ravennate in origin, has a Blessing Christ on the Lion and Basilisk similar in proportions, placement, gesture, and drapery to the analogous panels at Ruthwell, but is more refined in technique and anatomical form. The cathedra shows similarly slender figures but the modeling here is livelier than at Ruthwell. The Maximian cathedra also provides the closest Mediterranean parallel for the inhabited vinescroll seen at Ruthwell and on the back of the Bewcastle Cross, although with variations toward a conventionalization of vine curves, greater use of leaves to conceal the vine, and more baroque variability of modeling.[115] The Maximian chair has been linked with equal probability to the imperial workshops of Constantino-

Bewcastle Cross, back, vinescroll

Bewcastle Cross, side, figure-eight vine

ple, with the Byzantine Levant (predominantly Syria), and with contemporary Alexandria. It can be dated to the 540s at the latest by its association with Maximian, the first archbishop of Ravenna. Similar ivories could have provided stylistic and compositional models for the Ruthwell Cross.

The technical sources of the stone-carving techniques of Ruthwell are more difficult to trace. As the style of the Ruthwell and Bewcastle Crosses is so close to that of their classical prototypes, early scholars—notably G. F. Browne, A. K. Porter, Martin Conway, and Josef Strzygowski—believed Ruthwell to be the product of foreign artists, whose indigenous students were responsible for later, less refined crosses.[116] However, the Ruthwell carvings include details that make attribution to foreign craftsmen difficult; for example, the crudity of the added figure of the woman in the House of Simon panel, which would not have occurred if the artist were more familiar with the style rather than working from a relatively unfamiliar model. Other elements at Ruthwell also demonstrate that the workshop was indigenous. The birds can be linked to Anglo-Saxon *sceatta* coins, a source unlikely to be chosen by foreign artists. The vinescroll, classical in its basic form, nonetheless delights in the interplay of the linear spirals of the stem and the playful ferocity of the animals intertwined in it rather than in the naturalistic depiction of leaves, fruit, and branches—aspects giving the vine a peculiarly northern flavor. The Ruthwell workshop was most probably indigenously Northumbrian. Considering the iconography of the cross, the workshop was probably based at a center with strong ties to the heritage of the Celtic Church and possibly also with the life of Saint Kentigern.[117] The relief-carving techniques used here were acquired both from earlier workshops producing architectural ornament and from observation of foreign models. The artists may also have examined late Roman reliefs found in the area, such as the *Dea Brigantia* (Dumfries Museum) from nearby Birrens.[118] Local continuity of carving tradition from the Roman period onward cannot be demonstrated, but the introduction of Mediterranean models may well have sparked an awareness of locally available antiquities.

Panofsky was correct in comparing the stylistic classicism of the Ruthwell Cross to the *Codex Amiatinus,* another insular work so thoroughly emulative of its models that it, too, has been considered the work of deliberately imported or immigrant foreigners. Yet at Ruthwell this style is juxtaposed with a sophisticated program that is not only intensely insular and possibly local in meaning, but also a potential statement on contemporary ecclesiastical politics. In this the Ruthwell Cross is entirely opposite *Amiatinus,* where classical style is used to signal loyalty both to the Roman Church herself and to her aesthetic legacy. The Ruthwell Cross is essentially divided in its treatment of the models, appropriating the style but altering the meaning by the choice and juxtaposition of scenes and sometimes by the alteration of the model itself to produce a new composition. From this viewpoint, the Ruthwell Cross is closer in temperament to the *Lindisfarne Gospels,* where the composition and symbolic content of the models was maintained or recombined to suit an imported concept of illumination, the Evangelist portrait, but where the politically ambiguous nature of the foundation allowed the style of the model to be altered to accord with indigenous aesthetic preferences. Both monuments rely heavily on foreign models, yet introduce local elements to produce a synthesis in keeping with their own needs. The assimilative attitude necessary to such synthesis was the legacy of the Celtic Church, surviving after Whitby in centers of Celtic origin throughout Northumbria. Assimilation is inherent in the earlier art of the Celtic Church, of which the *Book of Durrow* is but one extant example. Such Celtic prototypes must have provided paradigms to the next generation for the imposition of stylistic unity on a variety of sources. The ecclesiastical politics of the period after Whitby left centers such as Lindisfarne and the workshop source of Ruthwell in ambiguous positions, newly Roman in practice, but Celtic in foundational temperament. In such centers strict adhesion to the style or particular meaning of a foreign model was significantly less imperative than at foundations such as Hexham and Jarrow, where the transplantation of

Hoddam cross shaft fragment; Edinburgh, National Museum of the Antiquities of Scotland *(photo: National Museum of the Antiquities of Scotland, by permission of the Director)*

Rothbury I, cross head, front; Museum of Antiquities of the University and Society
of Antiquaries of Newcastle upon Tyne *(by permission of the Keeper)*

foreign forms and ideas was paramount. Each Anglo-Celtic center was consequently able to adapt imported models stylistically or iconographically to its own needs, and the results vary considerably among these centers. Therefore, an "Anglo-Celtic style" cannot be strictly identified, for the works of Lindisfarne, Ruthwell, and their kindred are each the product of a particular center and a particular set of needs and circumstances.

As in manuscripts after *Lindisfarne*, so it is in the crosses after Ruthwell; once the essential step of altering the model has been taken, the distance from model to insular work increases rapidly and sculptors like illuminators move toward the linear abstraction of forms that has its roots in the insular metal-working tradition. This development is particularly apparent in the treatment of drapery patterns and of the inhabited vine. Both the cross shaft from Hoddam, Dumfries, (Edinburgh, National Museum of Scotland), and the cross-head fragments of Rothbury, Northumberland (Newcastle upon Tyne, University Museum), especially Rothbury I, retain the depth of relief of Ruthwell. Rothbury I may be a later product or offshoot of the Ruthwell workshop, for the identical formulation is used for Christ Healing the Blind Man; Christ's right hand here is holding back his sleeve while his left hand is raised across his body to touch the blind man's eye.[119] The vinescroll on the back of the same fragment links Rothbury to another example of east-central Northumbrian carving, the Jedburgh Slab, Borders (Jedburgh, Abbey Museum), a panel probably originally used as a screen or furnishing in a church. Both in the Rothbury fragment and in the Jedburgh slab, the vine is considered not so much as an organic plant but as a long series of spirals in which various animals are trapped: at Rothbury a clearly represented cow; at Jedburgh, a variety of birds, and a lively pair of squirrels. In these two cases alone, the animals are treated with a whimsical sweetness not traceable elsewhere: the cow daintily taking the vine in her teeth and the squirrels gripping it gingerly with their forepaws while they turn to eat a particularly succulent berry or gnaw determinedly at a vine shoot while staring nervously at the viewer. The vine details are also treated similarly and the depth and technique of carving are comparable, so that one may consider Rothbury I and the Jedburgh slab the products of a single workshop, possibly a generation after Ruthwell. The inhabitants of the vinescroll elsewhere, as at Morham, East Lothian, maintain the ferocity of the beasts in the vine at Ruthwell, although here, too, the vine has been simplified to stress its curvilinearity. A similar linearization can be traced in the descendants of the Hexham vines, both single and double vinescrolls at Heversham and Lowther, Cumbria (the latter in London, British Museum); Saint Vigeans, Angus; Aberlady and Abercorn, East Lothian; and Bewcastle, particularly noticeable in the increasing treatment of the shoots of the vine as purely geometric spirals and in the use of complex interwoven junctures in the figure-eight vine that begin to resemble interlaced knotwork.

The political decline of Northumbria begins with King Ecgfrith's loss of the Battle of Nechtansmere, fought at Dunnichen Moss, Forfar, against the Picts in 686.[120] Early chronologies of the crosses consequently dated the North-

Rothbury I, back; Museum of Antiquities of the University and Society of Antiquaries of Newcastle upon Tyne *(by permission of the Keeper)*

Jedburgh slab, Jedburgh (Borders); Abbey Museum *(photo: National Museum of the Antiquities of Scotland, by permission of the Director)*

umbrian crosses of better quality in the period before this political watershed, and saw the poorer crosses as later products of a politically induced decline. The political fortunes of Northumbria never again attained their previous status after Nechtansmere, but the kingdom did not slide into oblivion overnight. In 710 the Northumbrians, under the ealdorman Bertfrith, fought a battle against the Picts in central Scotland between the rivers Canon and Avon, maintaining their territorial claims in the north. In 731 the Anglian see of Whithorn in Galloway was founded, possibly to minister to the northern regions formerly administered by the see of Abercorn, which had been discontinued after Nechtansmere. In 750 the Northumbrians occupied Kyle, and in 756, in league with the Picts, they conquered the British at Dumbarton. Although Bede complained of a decline in learning in his own day (around 730), there seems to

Cross shaft fragment, Morham (E. Lothian); Edinburgh, National Museum of the Antiquities of Scotland (*photo: National Museum of the Antiquities of Scotland, by permission of the Director*)

Breedon-on-the-Hill (Leics.), wall frieze

Breedon, wall frieze

have been a revival therafter, for his teaching was continued by others at Jarrow after his death, and his pupil Egbert founded the minster and school at York in 735, training in his turn the noted theologian Alcuin.[121] The verses and runes of the *Dream of the Rood* date the Ruthwell Cross in the mid-eighth century, and the crosses that follow it must be later. Other Northumbrian crosses can be dated still later on the basis of the presence of new influences from noninsular art. These new models arrived via the art of Mercia, the Middle Anglian kindgom in ascendancy as Northumbria entered its long decline and began to lose control of the political hegemony established under Oswald and Oswy.[122] The remarkably rich and stylistically diverse assortment of wall plaques, friezes, and other decorations at Breedon-on-the-Hill, Leicestershire, and related works at Caistor, Peterborough, and Fletton represent Mercian carving at its finest. The wall friezes at Breedon take the inhabited vine as their fundamental motif, but its treatment is at once more delicate and more conventionalized

Breedon, wall frieze

Breedon, wall plaque: dancing prophets

than at Ruthwell and elsewhere in earlier Northumbrian work. The friezes are extensively undercut to give a lacelike airiness to the wall surface. The spirals of the vine have been reduced to an almost purely linear abstraction and the birds and beasts have assumed a heraldic stiffness, often arranged in symmetrical facing or addorsed pairs. The heraldic effect is emphasized by bowing the animals' chests into gracefully exaggerated curves, elongating their legs, necks, and tails, and interlacing these various parts with the vine. Both the conventions and the delicacy of Mercian art is derived from ornament in portable

Croft Cross fragment, Croft (N. Yorks.)

St. Andrew Auckland Cross, Bishop Auckland (Durham)

Easby Cross, Easby (N. Yorks.); London, Victoria and Albert Museum (*Crown Copyright Victoria and Albert Museum*)

goods from the Near East, particularly from Sassanian Persia. However, despite their entrapment in the stiff ornamental patterning of the vine, the Mercian animals retain the ferocity of their pre-Christian Anglian metalwork ancestors, creating a subtle but powerful tension between the beasts' staidly con-

Ormside Bowl; York, Yorkshire Museum *(by permission of the Senior Keeper of Archaeology)*

ventionalized forms and the rapaciousness with which they glare at one another and tear at the fruit of the vine with hooked beaks and teeth. The effects of this style in Northumbria are already being felt in the rough summetry of the Jedburgh slab, but truly come into their own in later crosses at Escomb in Durham; Croft, Melsonby, and Easby in North Yorkshire (the last in London, Victoria and Albert Museum), and Saint Andrew Auckland in Durham. All these northern crosses must consequently fall into the late eighth or early ninth century. Vine motifs traveled via itinerant workshops and through the portable arts. A fine example of the Mercian style in metalwork—the Ormside Bowl (York Museum)—was found in Yorkshire and, by its stylistic similarities to the Breedon carvings, indicates that by the early ninth century, the patterns of taste in secular as well as in sacred art in Northumbria were being set by developments elsewhere in England. Similarly, a strongly classicizing style developed

Cross fragment, Reculver (Kent); Canterbury Cathedral, Crypt Museum

Reculver Cross fragment

Rothbury Cross, shaft fragment, now font stem, Rothbury (Nthld.)

in the cylindrical cross shaft at Reculver, Kent (Canterbury, Crypt Museum), reminiscent of Carolingian ivories and illuminations, and was soon adapted in Northumbria in an octagonal shaft now serving as a font stem at Rothbury, Northumberland.[123] The ninth-century Wharfedale, West Yorkshire, crosses at Otley, Collingham, and later at Ilkley, maintain the monumental style and deep relief of Ruthwell, possibly because of the influence of available sub-Roman reliefs, but the ornamental motifs show the heraldic stiffness and posturing of Mercian influence.[124]

Nechtansmere was not the end of Northumbrian culture, although it did mark the watershed between the rise and decline of the political fortunes of the nation. The secular culture continued unaffected for a while, as did the ecclesiastical arts. Ecgfrith was killed at Nechtansmere and was succeeded by his younger half-brother Aldfrith, a highly cultured and educated nobleman who had studied in Ireland during his years of exile while his brother ruled. This scholar-prince was destined to become a patron of the arts and of the monasteries that fostered them. It was in his reign that yet another synthesis reached fulfillment—the assimilation of the achievements and models of the art of the Northumbrian churches with the ancient and traditional secular world of Anglian kings and warriors.

[6]

Secular Traditions in Northumbria

IN THE CONVERSION PERIOD, three distinct secular traditions can be traced in Northumbria: the British, the Anglian, and the Roman. These secular traditions included such societal patterns as the rites and symbols of kingship, and lingering pre-Christian ritual and mythology. Two indigenous insular traditions coexisted from the Anglo-Saxon invasion forward; the older British or Celtic patterns underlying the more recently imposed culture of the Anglian rulers. Roman traditions, on the other hand, were imported; either lingering as the detritus of the occupation period, or arriving through trade or as part of the intellectual or artistic baggage of the Christian faith. These three mutually distinct secular traditions had a profound impact on the development of Northumbrian secular art in the postconversion period.

Secular Syncretism and the Survival of the Heroic Tradition

The indigenous secular traditions of Northumbria, as of Anglo-Saxon England as a whole, are difficult to trace. Most documentation of the period is ecclesiastic in origin and focus, and secular life and traditions are rarely discussed at length. However, the documents do occasionally make passing reference to secular life at court and elsewhere, and take parenthetical if condemnatory notice of pagan recidivism at all social levels, from the apostasy of kings to the amulets of peasants. Furthermore, the archaeological exploration of Anglo-Saxon sites has revealed substantial evidence on secular life and customs, and helps determine the value of the documentary references.

The Anglo-Saxon invasions of England, particularly in the north, superimposed a Germanic ruling class on a well-established British Celtic culture, but this transfer of political control did not disrupt Celtic cultural practices. Some Celtic patterns of usage were adopted unaltered by the new Anglo-Saxon overlords, particularly in Northumbria where the Anglican rulers constituted a minority in a predominantly Celtic population. The Northumbrian Angles inherited at least one royal and ceremonial center from their Celtic subjects: the occupation of Yeavering—the *ad Gefrin* of Edwin's conversion—is continuous from the Celtic into the Anglian period of domination.[1] Some of the paraphernalia of court practice may also have been inherited by the Anglian rulers from their British predecessors. The controversial hanging bowls found at Saxon secular sites are possibly the legacy of British traditions of court hospitality or ceremony. However, the absence of extensive reliable data on specific court practices in either culture makes specific continuities difficult to trace.

The legacy of the Germanic pagan and heroic tradition among the Anglo-Saxons is also known only in fragments. Surviving documentary evidence on the nature and organization of pagan Anglo-Saxon religion is sparse, mostly in the form of passing references to gods and heroes such as Woden, Thunor, Tiw, and Weland in place-names, medical charms, and poetry.[2] The similarities of these divinities to the Norse gods have frequently tempted scholars to project details of the later Norse material back onto the Anglo-Saxons, who were culturally linked to the Scandinavian peoples. However, it is impossible to determine which aspects of later-documented sagas are ancient mythology and which are the embellishments of later poets and chroniclers. Only one relatively complete saga, *Beowulf*, survives from the Anglo-Saxon period, providing a glimpse of court life, particularly architecture and furnishings.[3] *Beowulf* also mentions in passing the names of heroes who must have been well known to listening audiences of the period, suggesting a rich saga tradition now lost except for this exemplar. *Beowulf* survives because, unlike the rest of the Anglo-Saxon secular tradition, it was committed to writing. However, *Beowulf*'s writer was a Christian, who no doubt expurgated any pagan material in the preceding oral tradition, leaving only the hero's personal feats.

Whatever religious and heroic traditions predated the advent of Christianity in Anglo-Saxon England, there is no lack of evidence of their partial survival into the Christian period. The conversion of the Anglo-Saxons was not thorough and irreversible, despite Bede's descriptions of mass baptism. The old traditions were strong enough that apostasy was frequent even at the courts where Christianity first took root. Eadbald of Kent, son of and successor to King Æthelbert, refused to accept the Christian faith, and his entire court reverted to pagan practice on his example.[4] This reversion is surprising, since Eadbald's mother was the Christian Merovingian princess Bertha, and Eadbald, unlike most Anglo-Saxon princes of the period, had been exposed to Christian faith all his life. Moreover, the twenty-year residence of Augustine and his successors at Canterbury made the revival of paganism in Kent particularly improbable. Eadbald's apostasy may however have been a matter of convenience, for his first overtly pagan act on his accession in 616 was to marry his father's second wife.[5] However, elsewhere the Church was less entrenched, and the shift of power to a younger generation occasioned less pragmatically motivated apostasy. The three sons of Sabert of the East Saxons, who collectively inherited their father's throne in 616, denounced the new faith and drove out the missionary Mellitus and all his followers.[6] In 616 the political situation of the Roman Church in England looked so grim that Archbishop Lawrence, Augustine's successor, contemplated abandoning the mission entirely. Moreover, even where kings and their courts accepted Christianity, their will was not always that of the people. Even after Eadbald relented, the people of London refused the mission of Mellitus.[7] People more remote from courts and religious centers returned to paganism at moments of crisis until much later in the century. Saint Cuthbert's "field mission" was designed to dissuade the Angles of the more distant hinterlands of Northumbria from the use of "incantations or amulets or any other mysteries of devilish art" in combating the plague.[8]

Pre-Christian traditions flourished in Anglo-Saxon England, not only in cases of individual royal and mass popular apostasy. There was also a strong tendency toward a much more durable syncretism, combining the new faith with older traditional beliefs. This was initially condoned by the Roman Church as a means of encouraging conversion. Gregory the Great's letter to Mellitus suggests that pagan temples, feasts, and other customs should be amalgamated into the practices of the Church while being denied their old meaning.[9] However, the Anglo-Saxons viewed this continuity differently than did their foreign evangelizers, perceiving this amalgamation as proceeding from their traditions toward the new faith rather than the reverse. For example, according to Bede, the feast of the Resurrection of Christ was given the name of Eostre, after a goddess whose rites had been celebrated in the spring.[10] The strength and longevity of syncretism in England are most easily measured by the frequency of edicts of the Church and secular laws of Christian kings against acts of overt paganism. The *Penitential* of Theodore of Canterbury, written between 669 and 690, gave the proper penances for making offerings to trees, springs, stones, and rocks, for sacrificing, for practicing incantations, for the use of magical parchments *(ligaturas)*, for the casting of lots, for auguring according to the flight of birds, for indulging in ritual feasts at pagan shrines, and for burning grain either on graves or in houses to guard them against evil spirits or to exorcise their inhabitants.[11] In 695 the *Laws* of Wihtred of Kent outlawed idols, setting fines for their possession and worship.[12] The 747 Synod of Clovesho forbade priests to recite Scripture with the tragic intonations of secular bards.[13] Later documents continued these prohibitions, indicating the continuity of forbidden practices and beliefs as late as the eleventh century.[14]

The most graphic example of the active continuity of pagan ritual in a Christianized context is Bede's description of the temple at the seventh-century court of Rædwald of East Anglia, which contained both a Christian altar and another altar for sacrifices to pagan divinities.[15] The burial at Sutton Hoo, which has been associated with Rædwald, readily shows evidence of such syncretism. The tomb contains evidence of the presence of Christianity, both the silver spoons inscribed "Saulos" and "Paulos" and the set of imported nested silver bowls, each decorated with bands of ornament laid out in a cross. The tomb may have been a cenotaph, perhaps honoring a king who had become Christian but whose court and followers resolutely demanded traditional burial with grave goods. However, recent analysis of phosphoric deposits on metal objects in the ship burial, particularly the sword blade, indicates the possible

Ceremonial whetstone, Sutton Hoo; British Museum *(photo: Trustees of the British Museum, by permission)*

presence of an inhumation.[16] The often-cited resemblances of the Sutton Hoo ship burial to the funeral of Scyld in *Beowulf,* and the presence of additional smaller boat burials at Sutton Hoo suggest the practice of ship burial was an ancient heroic-age pattern locally established and maintained over several generations.[17] Moreover, despite the evidence of the spoons and silver bowls, other objects found at Sutton Hoo speak strongly of the pre-Christian religious functions of royalty. Of these the most significant is the large ceremonial whetstone, sometimes called the scepter; found across the west end of the burial chamber. This remarkable stone bar is quadrilateral in section, two feet in length and weighs over six pounds. Although it is made of the same kind of stone used for the practical whetstones found in other Anglo-Saxon sites, it shows no evidence of ever having been used as a whetstone, and indeed because of its scale can hardly have been intended for practical use.[18] Moreover, the Sutton Hoo whetstone has been carved with ornament that suggests a ceremonial purpose. Each end of the bar terminates in a spherical red knob, surmounted by a conical projection. One of these knobs, probably the base, retains a saucer-shaped bronze terminal attached to the conical projection and knob. Small human faces are carved in relief on all four faces of the bar below the knobs at both ends. At the saucer end three of four of these faces are bearded and two have mustaches, but other heads are beardless and have long hair and slightly more delicate features, possibly depicting women. A separately found terminal, an iron ring fixed by Y-shaped arms on a bronze cone-shaped pedestal and supporting a bronze stag, is believed to be the upper terminal of the scepter.

In 1945 R. L. S. Bruce-Mitford pointed out that the Sutton Hoo whetstone is plainly ceremonial, and cannot be directly compared to the functional whetstones found in Swedish sites, such as the ship burials at Vendel and the mounds at Old Uppsala.[19] He argued that this whetstone served as a scepter, a form borrowed from the Romans via Merovingian court usage, as seen in a signet of Childeric I. However, the use of a whetstone as a scepter has no classical associations. Such a practice has been speculatively linked with more local cults of gods and heroes, including Thunor and Weland the Smith. The whetstone would also be an appropriate attribute for a king, both as battle leader and as giver of swords.[20] However, neither such pagan religious or royal symbolic associations can be documented. Whetstones have been found in occasional pagan Saxon graves, but these have been functional hones without ornament found in common graves, whereas the Sutton Hoo find context is royal.[21] On the other hand, Bruce-Mitford has pointed out a group of whetstones carved with heads at at least one end that were probably ceremonial like that at Sutton Hoo.[22] Only one of these was found in an Anglo-Saxon grave, at Hough-on-the-Hill, Lincolnshire. The other three are from the Celtic north and west, and one of these, from Lochar Moss, Dumfries, is comparable in scale to the Sutton Hoo example. The example from Hough-on-the-Hill is also large, but the heads here lack the refinement of carving found in the Celtic examples and at Sutton Hoo. The whetstone at Sutton Hoo is consequently probably associated with Celtic rather than Germanic royal practice, an example of paraphernalia taken over in the same way as royal sites such as Yeavering. The meaning of such Celtic royal whetstones is open to speculation. The ceremonial usage of whetstones may stem from their association with smiths, considered magic workers in Celtic mythology. An eighth-century hymn invokes God's aid against the the spells of "women and smiths and druids."[23] The magic of human smiths was associated with the powers of the divine smith—called Goibhniu in Ireland and Gofannon in Wales—who was the provider or host of the otherworld feast, the *Fledh Ghoibbnenn*, or "Feast of Goibhniu," which rendered feasters immortal.[24] The stag, too, had primarily Celtic rather than Anglo-Saxon mythological associations.[25] If the symbolic meaning of the whetstone at Sutton Hoo goes back to the mythology of subject Celtic peoples rather than to that of their Anglian overlords, it may have been included in the ship burial as an appropriate piece of equipment to carry into the Otherworld. On the other hand, if the whetstone was already part of royal iconography by association with the divine smith in the Celtic kingdoms, it could have been assimilated by the Angles as a symbol of royal authority.[26] The scale and sophistication of the Sutton Hoo whetstone, whether Anglo-Saxon or British in manufacture, would be further explained if the king buried here was Rædwald, the only East Anglian king to extend his power beyond the confines of East Anglia and to hold widespread authority over the Angles, Saxons, and Britons south of the Humber.[27] The whetstone would surely have been recognized as a symbol of authority by Britons and Anglo-Saxons alike and consequently would be the ideal insignia of an overking. However, if the stone was such a major symbol, why did Rædwald's successors allow it to be buried with him rather than keeping it in sight to maintain the claims of the dynasty? Perhaps the whetstone held too many pagan associations for his successor, the pious Earpwald, to condone its use. On the other hand, Rædwald's followers, sensing the end of an era, may have buried the stone with their lord rather than see it fall into the hands of those who would consider it blasphemous—or worse, an insignificant antique trinket.

Other objects in the Sutton Hoo burial may also hold pre-Christian religious meaning. The early Anglo-Saxon kings universally traced their genealogies back to various gods, usually Woden.[28] Later ninth-century monastic chroniclers extended these ancestor lists back beyond Woden to biblical characters.[29] However, in the early period of syncretism to which Sutton Hoo evidently belongs, Woden was remembered as the father of the gods and as the god of kings and warriors, as the evidence of Anglo-Saxon place-names confirms.[30] The descent of kings from Woden gave them authority over freemen and warriors. Divine ancestry consequently played a major role in the symbolism of royal trappings, as confirmed by finds at Sutton Hoo. The shield, found directly to the north of the whetstone and hence in a ceremonial context, had gilt bronze fittings that had been repaired several times before the date of burial, indicating that the shield was an heirloom of considerable age.[31] Many of these repairs were to metal animal-head trim around the perimeter of the shield, suggesting that the shield was carried in battle, as much for its totemic or apotropaic value as for its effectiveness as armor. The shield fittings included a raven (symbol of Woden) as well as a winged dragon and various other emblems. The decoration of the shield parallels Scandinavian examples, particularly shields found in the earliest boat graves in the Swedish cemetery at Vendel, dated to the sixth century.[32] The age of the shield was symbolically significant as well, for it provided a physical link between the Sutton Hoo king and his heroic and/or divine ancestors. An ancient sword with similar connotations is mentioned in *Beowulf*.[33]

The Sutton Hoo helmet, also found close to the west end of the ship burial, and the sword, found near the center of the keel line, near the possible locus of interment, are also thoroughly Swedish in type. The helmet, similar in construction to examples from boat graves at Vendel and Valsgärde in Sweden, was covered with thin bronze plates with stamped motifs, closely resembling examples from Vendel, showing warriors fighting and performing possibly ritual dances.[34] R. L. S. Bruce-Mitford has proposed that all three—sword, shield, and helmet—may be Scandinavian rather than local copies of foreign types. This is not improbable, as there is no further evidence of these types in England, and as the Wulfingas, who held the throne of East Anglia, were descended from a Scandinavian royal house.[35] The presence of Scandinavian warriors' equipment at Sutton Hoo signifies at once the concern of the East Anglian dynasty with its origin and genealogy, as connected with the cult of kingship, and the importance of the burial as the end of an era. Once buried, like the whetstone, the shield, sword, and helmet were no longer available to future generations as material symbols of royal status.

Additional mythological symbolism can be discovered in the recurring animal motifs decorating the Sutton Hoo objects. The eyebrow ridges of the helmet terminate in gilt boars' heads. The same beast decks the ridge of the Anglo-Saxon helmet from Benty Grange, Derbyshire, (Sheffield Museum).[36] Boars also ornament the two cloisonné shoulder clasps from Sutton Hoo, as well as a sword blade found in the Lark River in Cambridgeshire, and various brooches, buckles, harness mounts, and other items from the royal burial ground at King's Field, near Faversham, Kent.[37] The boar has been linked with the cult of kingship in Anglo-Saxon England, and indeed most of the boar-decorated objects come from sites with royal associations.[38] George Speake has shown that the use of this symbol is based on the claims of Anglo-Saxon kings to descent from Woden, as Saxo Grammaticus states in the *Gesta Danorum* that the boar and the boar's head in particular were Woden's emblems.[39] Speake has also traced both the raven on the shield, and the eagles on the Sutton Hoo purse lid to the Woden cult. Moreover, he has proposed that the interlaced snakes on the great buckle and the dragon on the shield were also associated with Woden as the god of death and the dead. Hence they are appropriate symbols for a king both as descendant of Woden and as warrior, and suitable for burial imagery as well. Of course it may not be necessary to consider every use of an animal motif to be symbolic, as it is conceivable these themes were used at another level purely as ornament. On the other hand, it is difficult to determine when a symbolic meaning is not present. Given the northern pagan outlook wherein nothing in nature was considered fortuitous, it may well be that symbolism in animal motifs is ubiquitous and that the idea of "pure ornament" was limited to geometric patterning such as knotwork and key patterns.

The ship burial at Sutton Hoo was a royal burial of particular circumstances, and has many attributes specific not only to the cult of kingship but also to the moment of transition from the pagan to the Christian era. However, burial with grave goods of a person of at least partial Christian faith is not peculiar to the royal circumstances at Sutton Hoo. It was once believed that the date of lesser Anglo-Saxon burials could be determined by the presence or absence of grave goods, since the disappearance of grave goods was thought to represent the watershed between pagan and Christian burials. However, the excavations of Audrey Meaney and Sonia Hawkes of Saxon cemeteries in Hampshire and elsewhere have determined that burial with grave goods continued well into the Christian era.[40] The determining factor in judging whether a particular grave is Christian is now whether it is aligned on an east-west axis, in preparation for the appearance of Christ in the east at the Last Judgment. Burials with Christian alignment, however, often hold substantial amounts of grave goods, as at Winall, near Leighton Buzzard, Hampshire. Unlike the hinterlands of Northumbria, Winall was not a pagan refugium area but was closely under the supervision of a bishop. Winall became part of the see of Winchester and part of the estates of the minster of Winchester either at the foundation of the see in 648 or at the installation of Bishop Wini in 660 under King Cenwealh. The population, to judge from the alignment of graves, was Christian, but the inclusion of grave goods indicates that conversion did not imply immediate abandonment of tradition, although whether goods burial was continued for religious or sentimental reasons is unclear. In the north, the practice continued to a later date; at Garton, Humberside, grave-goods burial can be dated by coins into the eighth century. The termination of the deposit of grave goods at Garton dates only from the transition of interment from extramural cemeteries to the minster yard, between 740 and 760.[41] The longevity of the grave-goods tradition, in conjunction with extramural burial, may have originated in the pagan Anglo-Saxon cult of the dead. The Anglo-Saxons were particularly afraid of revenants, and in the pagan period took special care that the dead should not "walk." Favorite possessions were put into graves as a matter of course. Food offerings were common, including joints of meat, ducks' eggs, nuts, and oysters. The Byzantine silver platter at Sutton Hoo, for example, contained ox bones.[42] Vessels filled with drink a custom first established in Scandinavia, are also conspicuously numerous in Anglo-Saxon inhumations. Often dogs and horses, as well as the occasional female servant, were sent with their masters into the otherworld.[43] More drastic methods were also used. In Mercia and northern Wessex, and among the Hwicce along the Welsh Marches, half-burned burials have been found. Corn was burned on graves elsewhere to bind the malicious spirits of the deceased. In other areas, decapitated skeletons and independently buried skulls have been found, although some of the skulls were doubtlessly battle trophies. By far the most common method of protecting the living from the dead, however, was to bury the latter in open spaces far from human habitation.[44] Either the later transition to burial in holy ground must have of itself provided sufficient safeguards against the return of the dead that all other methods, including the burial of personal possessions, could be safely abandoned, or the Church could now maintain sufficient control that goods burial became difficult.

Some of the goods found in these late goods burials show decorative motifs of which the iconography is either the secular material of sagas or perhaps the remnants of pagan methology. An example is the cylindrical bronze workbox found in grave 42 of the Anglo-Saxon cemetery at Burwell, Cambridgeshire.[45] The repoussé ornament on the barrel and lid has been dated about 650 to 675 by stylistic similarities to contemporary manuscripts, which places the burial in the postconversion period. The lid of the box shows a man killing a dragon. The image is probably from a saga or mythological source, and its presence may have served an apotropaic as well as a decorative function.[46]

The strength of pre-Christian religious practices in postconversion England was reinforced by marginally syncretistic traditions maintained by churchmen themselves. Although the initial Christian missionaries to England and Ireland were foreigners, their successors in the upper ecclesiastical hierarchy were often recruited from the native noble class, steeped in the imagery of secular power and its non-Christian associations. Their *Lives* characterize Benedict Biscop and Wilfrid as members of the *gesith*, or personal troop of housecarls of the Northumbrian king.[47] The spirit and symbolism of the heroic tradition, and concomitant fragments of pre-Christian mythology, were consequently preserved in the writings, actions, and art of churchmen.

Allusion to saga themes in insular hagiography is not limited to the Anglo-Saxons, but was shared by and perhaps originated in early Irish *Lives*.[48] The treatment of the saga motifs in Anglo-Saxon hagiography is somewhat different, however, as here references to secular heroes are scarce but the acts of the saints themselves are described in the terms usually applied to saga heroes. This is particularly true of Felix's *Life of Guthlac*, not only because Guthlac had been a noble and a mercenary soldier before he accepted religious vocation, but also because the *Life* was commissioned from Felix not by the clergy but by Ælfwald, king of East Anglia.[49] Elsewhere, references to ancient heroic tradition are more tacitly implicit in the deeds of saints. In Ceolfrith's departure from Jarrow and Monkwearmouth, described in the Anonymous *Life*, the sorrow of the monks of his communities at leave-taking and his repeated exhortation—"My Christ, be gracious to that company! O Lord Almighty, watch over that band of men!"—sounds more like the separation of a king from his small band of comrades than an abbot leaving a monastic complex housing more than six hundred monks.[50] Saint Willibrord, the Anglian missionary to the Frisians, had a similar ecclesiastical *gesith*.

Anglian clerics were not averse to the traditional sagas that were part of their own ethnic background. Most extant documentary fragments of Anglo-Saxon heroic tradition survive because they were recorded in the literate monastic environment.[51] Anglo-Saxon poetry of the Christian period makes frequent mythological allusions to illustrate points of theology, and consequently preserves odds and ends of pagan mythology. The early poem *Deor*, in advising the patience of Job in the face of adversities imposed by God as tests of the faithful, provides one of the earliest sources on the trials and revenge of Weland the Smith. Anglian churchmen sometimes enjoyed heroic tales more thoroughly than their stricter brethren could countenance. When some of the Lindisfarne monks came to Farne Island to share a Christmas feast with the eremitic Saint Cuthbert, and took to "feeling convivial and telling stories *(fabulae)*," their ascetic host interrupted to warn them "to be earnest in prayer and vigils and to be ready against all temptation."[52] A more direct warning to the Lindisfarne community came in the famous letter of 797 from Alcuin to Bishop Hygebald of Lindisfarne, admonishing the monks for having a harpist rather than a lector in the refectory:

> It is fitting to listen to the discourses of the Fathers, not the poems of the heathen. What has Ingeld to do with Christ? Narrow is the house; it will not be able to hold them both.[53]

Alcuin went so far as to suggest that the sack of Lindisfarne by Vikings in the previous year had been divine retribution for the heathen entertainments enjoyed by the monks. The paired serpents decorating the west door jambs of the porch of the Anglian church of Saint Peter at Monkwearmouth are significant in this context. They are the only element of purely indigenous design in all the extant carving at the site; but their symbolic intent is unknown, and they have usually been considered purely decorative. The double-headed serpent also appears on the iron crest of the Sutton Hoo helmet, and has been considered a protective motif in Anglo-Saxon animal symbolism.[54] The position of the Monkwearmouth reliefs around a doorway suggests that they, too, may have been apotropaic in intention, perhaps comparable in style and function to reliefs used on nonsurviving secular wooden buildings.[55] Hence even at early Monkwearmouth, when the focus of the community was on the emulation of the Roman Church and her art, it is possible that the Anglian monks were nonetheless so bound by their ancient traditions that they could not consider their church finished or "safe" without the inclusions of these biting, intertwined snakes at the doorway. Given the possibility of such quasi-pagan symbolism at Monkwearmouth, in a romanized Christian context, one might well expect a more forceful version of the same syncretistic outlook, in combination with the Anglian heroic tradition, to dominate the art of the secular court of Northumbria. However, Celtic and Germanic heroic and mythological traditions were not the only secular traditions available to the Northumbrian in the conversion period. Roman secular traditions, both the imagery of Roman authority and the classical mythological motifs, were available to the Northumbrian courts as well, and served as a visual resource for its craftsmen.

The Anglo-Saxons and Classical Secular Tradition

The traditions of the Roman world came into Anglo-Saxon secular culture through three channels. First, some remnants of Romano-British culture from the occupation period survived, preserved in the customs of the Britons and also in the visible physical remains of the Roman occupation. Second, trade with the Continent provided the preconversion Anglo-Saxons with occasional contact with luxury goods from the Late Antique Mediterranean world, although the Anglo-Saxons were less broadly familiar with these materials than were their Celtic neighbors and subjects. Third, the Church became the bearer of much of the literary paraphernalia of the secular and mythological traditions of antiquity. Despite the paganophobia of many churchmen, the collected books of the church carried forward fragments of classical mythology and made them available to the secular Anglo-Saxon world and its artists.

The majority of preconversion Anglo-Saxons were dimly aware of the legacy of the Roman occupation. Chance finds of utilitarian pottery and class were commonly reused. Intaglios and coins were pierced for use as weights or jewelry; Roman skillet handles, strap ends, and rings (usually enclosed in a special pouch or bag) are common finds in pagan Anglo-Saxon women's graves. Graves were marked with stacked Roman tile at Lackford, Suffolk and with column sections at Clovedon Hill, Lincolnshire.[56] These reused objects must

Assorted early Anglo-Saxon jewelry incorporating Roman coins; British Museum (*photo: Trustees of the British Museum, by permission*)

be considered apart from imported Mediterranean exotica such as Coptic bronze vessels, accessible only to the upper classes, whereas the detritus of Roman Britain was freely available to any Saxon farmer plowing a field in the right spot.

However, the legacy of Roman Britain was more influential among the ruling classes. The Anglo-Saxons had originally come to England in the fourth and fifth centuries as federates of the Roman Empire, serving as tribal mercenary units in the late Roman legions and in the early post-Roman British forces. Like federates elsewhere in the employ of the Roman military, the Anglo-Saxons became aware of the trappings of Roman imperial power and of the legitimacy adhering to the claims of those who adopted these symbols. In establishing their own kingdoms they therefore borrowed extensively both concepts and material forms from the vast storehouse of Roman imperial tradition.

Anglo-Saxon kings appropriated the use of various portable standards from Roman imperial symbolism. The classic example is Bede's description of the practices of Edwin of Northumbria:

> So great was his majesty in his realm that not only were banners *(vexilla)* carried before him in battle, but even in time of peace, as he rode about among his thegns, he always used to be preceded by a standard-bearer *(signifer)*. Further, when he walked anywhere along the roads, there used to be carried before him the type of standard which the Romans call a *tufa* and the English call a *thuf.* [57]

Bede took his terminology from Vegetius's *Epitoma Rei Militaris* (3.5), probably the abbreviated version included in the *Etymologies* of Isidore of Seville, "Muta signa sunt aquilae, dracones, vexilla, flammulae, tufae, pinnae." [58] In this context, Isidore's *tufae* was probably a misreading of Vegetius's *flammulae rufae* denoting "red banners." However, Anglo-Saxon has the independent form *thuf,* a tuft of leaves or vegetation, which may have also applied to a standard decorated with leafy branches. The Roman *vexillum* consisted of a spear from which a square banner was hung vertically, a sparse device suitable as a standard in battle. A Roman *signum,* carried by the mentioned *signifer,* was a more elaborate standard appropriate for processions and triumphs, usually showing in descending order the legionary eagle, a plaque with an inscription and a wreath or fillet surrounding discs ornamented with titulary smbols. This terminology and precise form may have been known to Edwin, as Isidore was known in Irish centers in his day. On the other hand, Edwin may have used a variety of standards, later given their terminology by Bede. Whatever the names and forms of his standards, however, Edwin had sufficient precedent and models for their use. Already in the post-Roman period of British hegemony, the *draco* had been borrowed by the British for military use; the pendragon, or "great dragon," was the standard of their leader. The *segn* or standard, may have already been sign of kings and heroes in Anglo-Saxon heroic tradition, as Beowulf was presented with a gilded metal *segn* as a part of his reward for killing Grendel. [59] However, this may be a later interpolation in the epic based

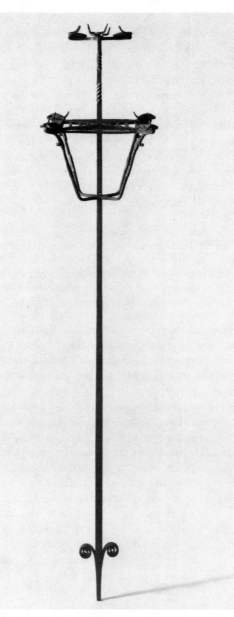

Ceremonial standard, Sutton Hoo; British Museum *(photo: Trustees of the British Museum, by permission)*

on postconversion royal practice. On the other hand, depictions of Roman insignia abounded both on coins and in legionary reliefs in England, and were available as models. One of the earliest English coins was a copy of the gold *solidus* of Honorius, showing the emperor holding a *vexillum*. Edwin's use of this type of standard therefore had both precedent and potential models.

Two possible Anglo-Saxon standards have been preserved. One is the controversial iron standard from Sutton Hoo. The standard was found across the west end of the burial chamber directly beside the ceremonial whetstone. Its find location suggests a ritual purpose, and its form precludes most suggested practical applications, as a torchholder, flambeau, lamp stand, or portable rack for armor.[60] The standard is five and a half feet high and retangular in section. It has a short spike and two flanking volutes at the bottom, to hold it upright in soft ground. At the top, a four-armed iron plate is set horizontally, each arm terminating in an abstract ox head turned inward. Eleven inches lower, the shaft passes through a square iron grille with ox heads at its corners. These corners are connected by four converging iron rods to a smaller horizontal iron plate set lower on the shaft, producing a light cagelike structure. Such a cage could have been used as a holder for ferns or bracken, possibly forming a *thuf* like that carried ahead of Edwin. However, the description of Edwin's *thuf* suggests portability, whereas the Sutton Hoo standard is made of iron and is cumbersome to carry. On the other hand, court usage may have varied between East Anglia, where Edwin had been Rædwald's guest, and Edwin's Northumbria, and the scale, weight, and elaboration of the *thuf* would have been accordingly differentiated. Edwin's succession to Rædwald in the role of overking, as noted by Bede, also suggests continuity of court protocol and symbolism beteen East Anglia and Northumbria.[61]

Another possible standard comes from a site in Northumbria that is otherwise associated with Edwin and may represent one of the types of standards mentioned by Bede. This device was found at the Northumbrian royal complex at Yeavering. Excavated by Brian Hope-Taylor, the royal complex at Yeavering shows several stages of destruction and reconstruction, notably in its great hall.[62] This building probably reached its greatest extent in Edwin's reign, paralleling Heorot, Hrothgar's "high and horn-gabled" hall in *Beowulf*, both in scale and grandeur. At the doorway of the hall as rebuilt in Edwin's reign, and aligned precisely on the hall's east-west axis was found a grave of the same period. The grave contained a skeleton with a javelin or spear shaft across its chest, the flattened skull of a goat at its feet and a bronze-bound wooden shaft running from a point at the head of the grave to a sharply ridge-backed animal terminal, possibly a goat, sheep, or crested bird, at the foot. Close to the animal terminal were a pair of horizontally set cross arms. Both the fragile substance of the shaft—wood rather than iron—and the crossbars suggest that this object was ceremonial rather than functional as weapon or implement. However, if it was a standard, it is of relatively poor quality compared to the iron standard of Sutton Hoo. Hope-Taylor has consequently suggested that the shaft in the grave may be a substitute token made for burial rather than the original ceremonial object that it emulates, and that the figure buried in the grave may be Edwin's *signifer*, who carried Edwin's insignia before him in peacetime progresses through his realm. On the other hand, the lightness of the grave standard makes it ideally portable as the *thuf* mentioned by Bede. Alternatively, the figure may be a doorkeeper, and the staff his rod of office. The custom of a doorkeeper was established in early Welsh law:

> From the time when the king enters the hall until each man goes to his lodging, the doorkeeper is not to go from the door further than the length of his arm and his rod.[63]

The royal center of Yeavering was a British ceremonial center before the advent of the Anglo-Saxons, and some of the local protocol, including the Celtic usage of door wardens, may also have been assimilated by the new landlords. Doorkeepers were, however, also a part of Anglo-Saxon court practice, for in *Beowulf* the arriving hero and his companions are challenged at the door of Heorot by a member of Hrothgar's *gesith*, who demands to know their identity and origin before admitting them to the royal presence.[64] Hrothgar's warrior performs a function that may well have been regularized as a permanent office with suitable ceremonial equipment at Edwin's court. Moreover, the possible goat's head at the feet of the figure and the possible identity of the animal terminal of the staff as a goat link the figure and his office to the site, as "Yeavering," or *ad Gefrin*, denotes "the hill of the goats." The possible warden in the grave may therefore have been linked to the place rather than to the traveling court. If he was a doorkeeper, then the shaft in his grave is still a ceremonial device related to court protocol, if not one specifically mentioned by Bede.[65]

Yeavering however also includes a structure for which all references point to a continuing awareness of Roman secular tradition. This structure, set at the center of the complex, was a wood-and-wattle replica of a single *cuneus* or wedge-shaped section of a Roman theater, with sixteen ranks of seats or steps at its greatest capacity. The whole structure was aligned and focused on a tall post, in front of which a small raised platform may have supported a seat facing the benches. A wood-and-wattle wall in an arc behind the post and two shorter walls radiating on either side of the small platform worked as sound baffles, allowing the voice of someone seated on the platform to be heard to the last row. These walls also served as visual limits, focusing the attention of the audience on the figure on the platform.[66]

A *cuneus* is a section of a Roman stone theater or amphitheater, as seen in Britain at Verulamium. The translation of the *cuneus* into wood at Yeavering is by no means unique, as Trajan's Column shows an entire wooden amphitheater and archaeological evidence of others has been discovered at Vindonissa in Switzerland and at Carnuntum in Austria.[67] However, as Hope-Taylor has demonstrated, Yeavering's *cuneus* is probably derived from stone architecture, and from theaters rather than amphitheaters, since a single deep bank of seats compensates better for the windy conditions on the hill. The small focal platform is reminiscent of stages in the Romano-Celtic theaters of western Gaul, and more local models may have included a hypothetical theater at York, another known only from inscriptions at Brough, Humberside, and possible theaters at Carlisle and other Roman centers along Hadrian's Wall. The presence of a *cuneus* at Yeavering reveals the extent to which the Anglian kings of Northumbria were aware of and perpetuated Roman secular tradition.[68]

The theater structure at Yeavering does not however date originally from the Anglo-Saxon period of site occupation. Technologically it belongs to the group of buildings that Hope-Taylor considers to represent the British ceremonial center that occupied the site before the advent of the new Germanic overlords. It was however first enlarged and later restored after a fire during the Anglian period, so that its importance and possibly its function were continuous despite the shift of political control.[69] It probably served as an assembly building, used in all likelihood for regular formal proceedings as part of the function of Yeavering as a royal administrative center. Because of the harsh climate of Yeavering's setting this outdoor structure was probably not used on a daily basis but perhaps seasonally. Eventually its use may have fallen into conjunction with the arrival of the Anglian mobile court, which one would imagine wintered in more hospitable surroundings, perhaps at York. As Hope-Taylor has pointed out, the focus of the *cuneus* on a platform suitable for a single orator suggests that its use was not for the operation of some romantically conceived democratic moot but rather for the address of a group by a single individual, either a person of authority or his representative. Moreover, the open windy setting also suggests that long discussion of these announcements was not intended.[70] Consequently the Yeavering assembly building was used from British times forward for the promulgation of the decisions of persons in authority. The *cuneus*, with its associations with Rome and Roman centralized authority, was ideally suited to this function. Doubtless the Anglo-Saxon heirs of its British builders were aware of the Roman origins of the formal theater, for they maintained the structure and enlarged it to suit the needs of the court. This structure exemplifies the continuity of Roman secular forms through British culture into Anglo-Saxon royal usage for the purpose of legitimizing authority and rulership by association with Roman tradition.

A strong awareness of Roman secular tradition is evident among the Anglo-Saxons in the period from the invasion to the conversion. Not only Roman architectural forms but also Roman sites and objects were used, with full knowledge of their historical implications. The pagan Anglo-Saxons generally avoided abandoned Roman cities, preferring to settle in rural areas. They were, however, well aware of the Roman ruins scattered across the land, which were far more numerous and conspicuous in their day than now. The early Anglo-Saxon poem, "The Ruin," describes the deserted Roman fortifications as seen through Anglo-Saxon eyes:

Wonderful is this wall of stone, wrecked by fate.

The city buildings crumble, the bold works of the giants decay.
Roofs have caved in, towers collapsed;
Barred gates have gone, gateways have gaping mouths;
Hoarfrost clings to mortar.[71]

However, elsewhere the Roman structures remained in use. In some cases, as at Portchester, the walls of towns were used occasionally as defenses in time of war. In other places continuous occupation of Roman towns by romanized Britons eventually drew first the control and then the occupation of Anglo-Saxons, who over generations came to see the Roman remains as part of their heritage. The pride of the citizens of Carlisle in the Roman underpinnings of their city is evident in the tour of the walls given by Waga the reeve to the visiting Bishop Cuthbert, culminating with a visit to a Roman fountain.[72]

The reuse of Roman objects and building materials was also common in the early Anglo-Saxon Church. Bede notes that the coffin used to house the translated bones of Ætheldreda, abbess of Ely, was a white marble sarcophagus from Roman Grantchester.[73] In the later Saxon period antique pottery and glass were frequently rededicated for liturgical use, using a particular ritual blessing devised for the purpose: "Benedictio super vasa reperta in locis antiquis."[74] Similarly, Roman building materials were frequently reused in churches, particularly for such technically difficult passages as tower and chancel arches or turned columns.[75] A visible legionary inscription on a block of stone used in the nave wall of the church at Escomb, Durham, demonstrates that this use was fairly indiscriminate. The use by the Church of Roman occupation-period materials side by side with more recently imported Late Antique models for art led the secular population to believe in the historical unity of the Roman secular world and the origins of the Christian faith.[76] After the conversion period, the Church also provided literary sources on Roman authority and its verbal and physical trappings, which the Anglo-Saxon rulers quickly adopted as a demonstration of legitimate entitlement. In the Mercian period of ascendancy, perhaps in competition with contemporary Carolingian aristocracy, there was an increasing tendency to use Roman titles. In Mercian charters, nobles and officials were called *tribuni, praepositi,* and *viri consulares,* and a witness to a 742 charter of Æthelbald of Mercia signs as "Offa the patrician," in the presence of four *duces.*[77] Similarly Caesar was incorporated into the East Anglian regnal lists in the eighth century, legitimizing the East Anglian kings directly, although Caesar is somewhat oddly listed here as a descendant of Woden.[78] Coinage as elsewhere in northern Europe was derived from Roman fourth-century coin types still available through trade. Early *sceattas* in general copy Roman coins, with the bust on the obverse never that of the minting king but always of the Roman emperor of the model, and with a rough transcription of the decorative motif on the reverse, usually reduced to an abstract pattern.[79] Intaglios and cameos were also valued as in the pagan period, although they were not considered magical until later in the Middle Ages.

Anglo-Saxon contact with pagan Roman mythology came largely through literary sources imported by the Church. Both the Celtic and the Roman Church valued classical learning highly and provided educated churchmen with access to antique sources and literacy in Latin and Greek. Not all the texts available, however, were theological or necessarily even Christian. Early insular writers considered it a demonstration of erudition to show off their knowledge of obscure classical references by the frequent use of quotations, from which the contents of their libraries can be pieced together.

Despite its widespread fame, the classical scholarship of the early Celtic Church varied greatly in depth and quality.[80] The Greek used by Columba, Cummian, Adamnan, Columbanus, and other was not fluent, but rather a collection of individual words and phrases gleaned from glossaries, grammars, and conversation books of which the primary language was Latin. On the other hand, knowledge of Latin Christian literature was widespread and often profound. Moreover, a few writers demonstrate a thorough awareness of selected Silver Age authors and poets. Columbanus, the founder of Luxeuil and Bobbio, makes frequent references in his verse letters to classical mythology, as do Adamnan of Iona; Muirchú, the biographer of Saint Patrick; and the anonymous author of the *De duodecim abusivis seculi*.[81] Of these, Adamnan was foremost in general classical learning, quoting both Vergil and Horace extensively, as well as other sources.[82] Orthography indicates that certain other texts, notably works of Petronius and Caesar, were transmitted by Irish scribes, in Ireland or at Irish Continental foundations.[83] These Continental missions maintained close links to parent foundations in Ireland, providing the contacts through which texts might travel to and from Ireland.

Despite the availability of a humanist tradition in Ireland, however, most dedicated clerics preferred to concentrate on patristic writers rather than on pre-Christian relics of the Silver Age authors. Consequently most references to pagan mythology and other pre-Christian classical material, like Greek quotations, are taken from grammars, textbooks and general sources such as Isidore's *Etymologies* rather than primary works. Nonetheless the references are widely varied and demonstrate a lively interest in the ancient gods and legends. Early Irish hymns include casual metaphoric mention of classical mythological figures such as Scylla and Charybdis, the Sirens, Circe, the nine daughters of Orcus, Medusa, the three Fates, and locations such as Tartarus, Acheron, Styx, and Phlegethon.[84] Such free use of essentially pagan classical citations is unusual in the pre-Carolingian Christian West as a whole. Such freedom may have been permitted Irish clerics because the Church had quickly become entrenched in Irish society and apostasy was rare. The Irish do not transmit the usual early Christian slanders concerning the pre-Christian classical world; Columbanus refers to Sappho as *inclyta vates troiugenarum*, "the famous Troyborn prophetess," without stigma.[85] Moreover, the twin passions of the Irish secular culture of the period for learning and bardic poetry and for heroic myth made the classical material appealing. Moreover, the Irish writers were attracted to classical mythological references much as they were to Greek and Latin quotations, as a pedantic demonstration of erudition.

Ireland was famous in the early period as a center of Latin patristic scholarship and attracted many students from abroad. These included such future worthies as the Frank Agilbert, later bishop of Wessex and then of Paris; Egbert, who brought Iona into conformity with the Catholic Easter; and Aldfrith, later king of Northumbria, who acquired a high reputation as a scholar and poet in Ireland.[86] However, the ease with which Irish Christian scholars accepted and toyed with Latin pagan references drew hostile comment from at least one English writer, Aldhelm, abbot of Malmesbury and later bishop of Sherbourne. Writing to a young scholar named Wihtred who was contemplating travel to Ireland in order to study there, Aldhelm warned of the dangers of certain kinds of knowledge:

> What, think you, does it profit a true believer to inquire busily into the foul loves of Proserpine, to desire to learn of Hermione and her various betrothals, to write in epic style the ritual of Priapus and the Luperci? Beware, my son, of evil women and their loves in legend.[87]

Bede, too, spoke out strongly against classical pagan writers and called for the expurgation of pagan references in grammars and textbooks.[88] On the basis of these two writers a more puritanical approach to the classical tradition might be anticipated at the centers of the Roman Church in England. This was, however, not the case.

Classical learning had long roots in England. Already in the 630s the devout King Sigbert invited Felix, a Burgundian cleric, to found a school on the Gaulish model in East Anglia.[89] Felix established the school by bringing in teachers and masters from Canterbury, where Augustine had started an earlier academy. These early schools taught primarily reading, writing, and Scripture to the children of the nobility at the elementary level, but despite the low level of their academic ambitions, they laid the necessary groundwork for the great later institutions of Canterbury and York. The arrival at Canterbury in 666 of Archbishop Theodore and his assistant Hadrian was however the formal beginning of classical studies in England. Theodore was the last student known to history of the ancient School of Athens, and a formidable scholar in a wealth of disciplines; Hadrian, born in Byzantine North Africa and trained in Byzantine southern Italy, was as fluent in Greek as he was in Latin.[90] Rather than choosing to languish intellectually in the pastoral care of the Anglo-Saxons, these two founded a school of sacred and secular studies without rival in all of contemporary northern Europe. Their reputation alone must have drawn their fellow scholars, just as it drew great numbers of students.[91] The curriculum of the Canterbury academy is well known from contemporary descriptions. Bede notes that graduates were amazingly fluent in both Latin and Greek, and that studies included poetry, astronomy, and calendric calculation as well as Scripture and exegesis.[92] Aldhelm, who had previously studied with the Irishman Maidulf in Wessex, came to study at Canterbury and was overwhelmed by the availability of new subjects for inquiry, expressing his astonishment in his correspondence. He sent his regrets to the bishop of Winchester at being unable to accept an invitation to a visit over Christmas, as he scarcely had enough time for all his subjects of study: Roman law, literature, poetic meter, music theory, arithmetic, and astronomy.[93] Aldhelm also wrote to a colleague, Ehfrid, to congratulate him on his completion of six years' study in Ireland, but also inquired why it was necessary to study in Ireland when excellent teachers of Greek and Latin are now available at Canterbury.[94] Bede also praised the scholarship of the graduates of Canterbury: Tobias, later bishop of Rochester; Albinus, Hadrian's successor as abbot of Saints Peter and Paul in Canterbury and colleague of Bede; and Oftfor, bishop of the Hwicce.[95] The impact of Canterbury was also felt in the secular sphere by the introduction of first Roman and later Greco-Byzantine law to England, which affected the development of the late-seventh-century law codes of Ine of Wessex and Wihtred of Kent.[96]

It is surprising, therefore, to find Aldhelm repudiating the secular classical tradition as taught in Ireland. However, an examination of his own works reveals that his bias was not anticlassical but anti-Irish.[97] This view is confirmed by an examination of Aldhelm's riddles. Writing in a secular context, Aldhelm clearly feels himself free to use classical mythological references with great ease. On the Pleiades, for example, he writes:

> Daughters of rugged Atlas men of old
> Have called us. Seven are we indeed, though one
> Scarce visible. We roam the vaults of heaven
> But also pass beneath grim Tartarus.[98]

Elsewhere, Aldhelm mentions the pagan gods directly, although he is cautious to let his readers know that they are no longer divine, as in the riddle on the moon:

> Not Jupiter, old Saturn's cursed son,
> Fathered us, he whom songs of poets call
> The mighty one; Latona bore us not,
> Feigned mother of us, both on Delos isle.
> I am not Cynthia, and my brother's name
> Is not Apollo.[99]

Elsewhere, Aldhelm mentions in passing Titan, Mars, Romulus, the Fates, Circe, Scylla, the Minotaur, the Eumenides, Vulcan, the Cyclops, Zephyr, Styx, and Lethe.

The Canterbury academy thus not only taught antique meter but also provided Aldhelm and others with access to such plainly pre-Christian resources as Ovid's *Metamorphoses*, the *Fasti*, and the *Amores;* Pliny's *Natural History;* and Vergil's *Aeneid* and the *Georgics*.[100] Other Anglo-Saxon riddlers, notably Tatwine, the ninth archbishop of Canterbury; Hwætberht, abbot of Jarrow and Monkwearmouth; and Willibrord, the Northumbrian missionary to the Frisians; had a more limited repertory of classical references, probably through the writings of Porphyry.[101] An examination of Bede's writings shows that a selection of books comparable to those used by Aldhelm was nonetheless available even in remote Northumbria. The primary sources in Bede's library must have included the *Epistles* and *Satires* of Horace, the *Natural History* of Pliny, and the *History* of Orosius, and may have also contained Lucan's *Parsalia,* and works by Livy, Lucretius, and Vergil, although it is debated whether Bede had an *Aeneid.* Bede used these works in addition to quotations and selections from grammars and textbooks, through which Bede knew, for example, fragments of Terence.[102] Bede was evidently not opposed to the use of pagan literature as historical source material.

Pre-Christian classical sources available in monastic libraries gradually filtered from ecclesiastical channels into the hands of the educated secular nobility, who were already aware of the useful implications of association with Roman authority and were eager for further information on secular Rome. This was particularly true of Aldfrith, king of Northumbria from 685 to 705, after his half-brother Ecgfrith. Aldfrith had been a student in Ireland and knew more of the classical tradition than its useful legitimizing symbols of power. Bede notes the breadth of Aldfrith's learning, and Alcuin refers to him as both *rex* and *magister.*[103] Even after he was called from a life of scholarship to the Northumbrian throne, he continued to collect books assiduously. Adamnan presented him with his *De Locis Sanctis,* a description of the sacred spots of the Holy Land, which Aldfrith had copied and widely distributed.[104] Aldhelm dedicated the *Riddles* to him, not as patron but as fellow scholar and friend from earlier days in Wessex, and sent him a collection of books.[105] More hungry for knowledge than for land, Aldfrith bartered eight hides of land to Ceolfrith and the Jarrow community in exchange for a book on cosmography, possibly illustrated. In all probability, Aldfrith selected men of similar interests for his entourage, for the intellectual sophistication of the king is reflected in the art associated with his court. Similar levels of literacy and artistic appreciation may have been attained at other Anglo-Saxon courts, but documentary evidence elsewhere is sparse. Moreover, Aldfrith's repute is so highly endorsed by the intellectuals of his day that the man and his court must have been extraordinary—an Anglo-Saxon prototype of the court of Charlemagne.

The availability of classical literary sources in the Northumbrian court is borne out by the use of *damnatio memoriae* in the Northumbrian regnal lists. The Northumbrian genealogies omit the names of two early kings who ruled between Edwin and Oswald: Osric of Deira and Eadfrid of Bernicia. Bede notes that the kingdom was divided at Edwin's death between these two young men: Osric as nephew of Edwin receiving the familial province of Deira and Eadfrid, son of Edwin's predecessor Æthelfrith, continuing his father's Bernician dynasty. Both had been baptized—Osric by Paulinus and Eadfrid at Iona—but at their accessions, both reverted to their ancestral paganism. Bede notes that divine justice was swift; both were killed within the year and the throne of a reunited Northumbria was passed to Eadfrid's saintly brother Oswald. Bede then remarks, "So all those who compute the dates of kings have decided to abolish the memory of those perfidious kings and to assign this year to their successor King Oswald, a man beloved of God."[106] This omission of names probably constitutes a formal *damnatio memoriae* in the Roman sense.[107] Bede refers to "those who compute the dates of kings," as to holders of a specific office, and implying that the introduction of Roman tradition was theirs. Bede is also not specific as to when the decision to exclude Osric and Eadfrid from the regnal list was made, but if the idea was literary in derivation, and if the keeping of lists was, as seems probable, a court function rather than a responsibility of the ecclesiastical community, the choice fits the humanistic court of Aldfrith. Not only would sources have been available at Aldfrith's court, but the application of such a Roman literary conceit to secular Northumbrian history would have been considered appropriate. Aldfrith's court is moreover a more likely setting for such quasi-Carolingian classical literary conceits than the courts of the celticized warrior Oswald, his highly political but nonintellectual successor Oswy, or the latter's warlike and nonclerical son Ecgfrith.

The Franks Casket

Given the literacy and intellect of the king, Aldfrith's court was an ideal environment for the patronage of art and literature. However, there are no works that can be definitively linked to Aldfrith. Moreover, because of the ecclesiastical viewpoint of Bede and most other documentary sources of the period, there are no descriptions of life at Aldfrith's court that might reveal what kinds of art and literature might have been produced there. However, works that freely fuse the classical and Anglo-Saxon heroic traditions are ideal candidates for attribution to this highly literate secular enclave.[108] Such hypothetical associations must remain tentative, but in at least one case, the Franks Casket (British Museum), there are no other environments of the period that provide so likely a venue of manufacture. The Franks Casket includes in its decorative program scenes from the various traditions of the Anglo-Saxon secular worlds: Germanic heroic imagery, elements from Roman mythology and imperial history, and Christian iconography. These diverse subjects not only coexist without difficulty but also form a unified program of particular significance to the Anglo-Saxon aristocracy.

The Franks Casket is a whalebone treasure box made in Northumbria about the year 700. It was discovered in the mid-nineteenth century in a private home in Auzon, near Brioude (Haute-Loire), by the antiquarian Mathieu of Clermont-Ferraud.[109] The casket, which had served an Auzon family for generations as a sewing box, had lost its silver fittings and had been wrenched apart, so that the right side was missing. Mathieu purchased the remaining panels, which then passed through the hands of a Parisian dealer into the collection of the antiquarian Sir Augustus Franks, from whom the casket takes its name. In 1867, Franks gave the box to the British Museum. Franks was also first to recognize the Anglo-Frisian runes on the box and to determine the Anglo-

Saxon origins of the casket. The right side of the box was eventually found in a bureau drawer of the same house in Auzon and was purchased by L. Carrand of Lyons, passing at his death to the Museo del Bargello in Florence. In 1890 Sven Söderberg of Copenhagen noted the relationship of the Bargello fragment to the sections in the British Museum. With the aid of photographs, and later with a cast of the Bargello panel, the British Museum staff has been able to reassemble their pieces into a unit probably identical in size and arrangement to the original.[110] Most of the lid is however still missing.

The Franks Casket as a personal treasure chest has a classical prototype—the *loculus*, a private ivory storage box for gold.[111] The casket is nine inches wide and seven and a half inches deep, approximating a modern cigar box in dimensions. It may originally have had small legs. The casket body, excluding the bottom and lid, is in eight pieces, four carved wall panels and four vertical corner piers. The uprights have mortises or grooves into which the larger plaques are fixed by projecting tenons. These tenons are secured in the grooves by wooden pegs passing through the three thicknesses of bone. On the outside of the box at the points of juncture corresponding to the tenons and pegs, a flat rectangular area is left uncarved. These were originally covered with silver fittings, possibly ornamented with repoussé or incised designs, and the pegs were driven through the silver and given a capping of silver, possibly gilt. The bottom of the box is plain, in three blank panels fitted into grooves in the bases of the side panels, without posts or screws. The top of the box was orginally fitted on in the manner of a pill box, as there is a rebate around the top of the box body.[112] Of the lid, only the central panel survives, with a round uncarved area at its center that probably had a knob or handle to lift the lid.

Franks Casket, front: Weland's Revenge and the Adoration of the Magi; British Museum *(photo: Trustees of the British Museum, by permission)*

The front of the Franks Casket is carved with two scenes, separated by a short strip of guilloche enclosed in a rectangular frame. At the right is the Adoration of the Magi. The Virgin and Child are seated at the right on a high-backed throne with footstool. The figures are hidden below the waist by a speckled cloth of honor hung between the posts of the enclosing structure. The Virgin and Child seem at first glance to be frontally posed, a classic *Hodegetria* type, yet their eyes and the double contour of the Virgin's side indicate a quarter turn toward the approaching Magi at left, and the confused series of contours at her left were probably intended to delineate the Virgin's lap and her arm, raised to beckon the Magi to approach.[113] Both Virgin and Child have haloes; the Child's halo is inscribed with a cross. The Child, in fact, appears only as a haloed head and shoulders at the center of the Virgin's lap. To the left and above the Virgin's throne is the star of the Magi, shown as a huge rosette. Below is, perhaps, an S-curved branch, and below this, a confused group of lines, possibly depicting a duck, a ewer or other vessel, a sacrificial animal, or a debased version of a model showing the dove of the Holy Spirit. The kings enter from the left. They wear short tunics, leggings, and short capes with clasps at the shoulder. They enter in order of age, indicated by length of beard. The eldest kneels before the throne and the two behind him bow their heads reverently. They carry their gifts in long-stemmed vessels. The first carries gold in balls or coins; the second brings frankincense, indicated by the smoke rising from his vessel's shallow basin; and the third brings myrrh, not the processed valuable, but the living plant. Above the heads of the first two kings is a flat rectangular blank area on which the word *maegi* has been incised in runes. Above the bowed back of the last king is a triple knot, or *triquetra,* also seen elsewhere on the casket. Also seen in mythological scenes on several stones in Gotland, this knot in northern European pagan art signifies the intervention of Odin in Scandinavian areas, or Woden in the Anglo-Saxon context, in the affairs of men. This symbol of the Woden cult is probably deliberately included here as many of the other scenes on the casket are overtly pagan.

On the left side of the front of the Franks Casket is a scene from the story of Weland the Smith. Place-names indicate that the Weland material was current in the Anglo-Saxon context, and his trials are also mentioned in the eighth-century poem, *Deor.* The story is preserved most completely in two Norse sagas, the *Volundarkviða,* part of the Older Eddic cycles of 1000, and the *Thið-rekksaga,* dating to the Court period about 1250, but the extrapolation of the legend from these later sources to the Franks Casket is extremely difficult.[114] The story in the sagas concerns the vengeance of Weland the Smith on King Nithad. Weland and his two brothers Egil and Slagfað are warriors and smiths who marry swan maidens. Swan maidens are one of the traditional forms of Valkyries—the sometimes monstrous bringers of death in battle, but also the promised brides of the afterlife. The three swan maidens leave Weland and his brothers to fulfill a mission in the south. Weland's brothers follow their wives, but Weland remains behind alone, crafting golden rings. Once when Weland is briefly away from his forge, King Nithad and his band of followers find

Weland's hoard of rings and steal one. Weland, assuming that his wife has returned and taken the missing ring, does not suspect the theft. Nithad's warriors later return and seize the smith and his rings, bringing both to the king. Nithad orders Weland hamstrung and installs him at an island smithy where he is forced to work for the king's enrichment. Weland plots and carries out a gruesome revenge. He invites the king's son (or two sons, as the number varies among the sagas) to visit his smithy on some pretext. There he beheads him and fashions a drinking cup from his skull, which he presents to the unknowing king. Nithad's daughter Baduhild has been given one of Weland's golden rings. The ring breaks, and she goes to the smithy to have it repaired. Weland gives her drugged beer; when she is half-conscious, he rapes and impregnates her. He then transforms himself into a bird, or puts on artificial wings, and escapes, first hovering over Nithad's hall to relate the horrible details of his revenge, which the unhappy Baduhild confirms.

The scene on the left half of the front of the Franks Casket shows the essential elements of Weland's revenge and escape. At the left, Weland works at his forge, his legs bent and crippled by his injuries. Weland is barechested and wears only a short kilt, and an armband on his right wrist. At his feet is the headless body of Nithad's son. Weland stands before an anvil and holds in his left hand the skull of the prince in an enormous pair of tongs. With his right hand he extends the cup of drugged beer to the cloaked and hooded Baduhild, who reaches for it eagerly. On the wall behind Weland hang two hammers and possibly a semicircular saw, which might however be the opening of the forge. There are also several enigmatic shapes on the wall that have not been deciphered. Behind Baduhild, between two leafy branches, stands another female figure in a hooded cloak, carrying a flask. She has been interpreted as Baduhild's maid, but it is more likely that this is Weland's swan maiden assisting his revenge on Nithad.[115] Her presence augments Weland's supernatural abilities and facilitates his revenge. The association of the swan maiden or Valkyrie with foliage is echoed elsewhere on the Franks Casket and in Norse legend.

At the extreme right of the Franks Casket Weland scene, a figure catches birds. In the late saga versions of the Weland story, his brother Egil, known in sagas as an archer, comes to Nithad's court in disguise to assist Weland's revenge, and shoots birds to bring feathers to Weland to make the wings for his escape. This figure has consequently been identified as Egil. Yet this figure does not shoot birds but grabs at them barehanded. The earlier literary sources do not mention Egil; Weland transforms himself into a bird and hides in Nithad's flock.[116] When the revenge is discovered, Nithad attempts to seize Weland but in the uproar grabs only true birds, allowing Weland to fly free. The figure on the Franks Casket has two birds by the neck and one trapped on the ground. Above and (if perspective of scale holds) far away, a single small bird can be seen flying away. Hence the scene on the Franks Casket encompasses both Weland's vengeance by murder and dishonor and his escape.

The inscription on the front of the Franks Casket, unlike those on the other sides of the casket, does not refer to the scenes but to the substance of the casket itself. A rough translation of the runes reads:

> Whalebone;
> The flood cast the fish up upon the life-mountain;
> The mighty one was sad when he was cast up.

The inscription starts up the left side, then runs across the top, down the right, and in reversed letters (or mirror writing) across the bottom from right to left. "Whalebone" obviously refers to the casket's material. The next line may be construed as a description of the event by which the material was made available. *Fergenberig*, "life-mountain," has been understood as descriptive of the actual place, or even as a place-name.[117] However, a more convincing argument has been made that the third line is a kenning for the death of the whale.[118] In Anglo-Saxon inscriptive tradition, death and other calamities are never mentioned directly, so that disaster will not descend by sympathetic magic on the writer, the reader, or the owner of the inscribed object. The use of mirror writing has the same purpose. The "mighty one" can be understood to refer to the whale itself. However, it may refer instead to the power of the "life-mountain," possibly a kenning for a divinity. So little is known of Anglo-Saxon pagan worship that an exact association with a particular cult is impossible, although the use of the triple knot on the Franks Casket indicates a continuing reverence for Woden.

The surviving fragment of the top of the casket may also be taken from the Weland saga. The runic border is lost, but a single personal name, "Ægili," in the picture itself has been linked frequently to Weland's brother Egil.[119] The scene, however, does not correspond to any event in the extant saga material on Egil. The figure marked "Ægili" stands at the right of the central circle, originally the base for the handle of the casket's lid, in a gate to an enclosure, which he is defending against an attack from the left. He is armed with a drawn bow; at his feet is an extra arrow. Behind him in an *aedicula* is a seated woman seen in profile, holding another arrow for the archer; possibly Egil's swan maiden wife, Olrun. The *aedicula* is flanked by columns filled with quilloche

Franks Casket, lid: Ægili's Defense *(photo: Trustees of the British Museum, by permission)*

and capped by an arch. Above and below the female figure are entwined pairs of animals. Above, two birds' heads grow outward along the inside of the arch from a single body. Below, a base is formed by a similar arrangement of dragons' heads. These creatures may serve as apotropaic door wardens, as may be the case in the similar porch reliefs at Saint Peter at Monkwearmouth.

At the left of the plaque, several warriors approach with raised swords, defending themselves with their shields from a hail of arrows. One in chain mail, at the lower left, has turned to flee. Two larger warriors and one smaller one advance intrepidly. At their feet, a nude, half-length figure is impaled by an arrow. Just under the edge of the circle at the center of the panel, another man is bent over with long hair streaming over his face; his right hand clutching an arrow shaft embedded in his chest, and his left hand clasped to his forehead in a dramatic gesture of shock and pain. The air is thick with arrows and with dots, which are also found inside the enclosure, possibly rocks thrown for defense. Above and below the central circle are two nude figures with shields, probably the dead who have already been stripped of their armor for trophies. Opinion on the mythological context of this plaque has varied widely, but in the absence of inscriptions, no interpretation can be valued as more than pure speculation.[120] Tentatively, the scene should probably be titled The Defense of Ægili's Burh, and left at that.

The left side of the Franks Casket shows a scene from classical mythology—the suckling and discovery of Romulus and Remus. The runic inscription reads:

Far from home,

Franks Casket, left side: Romulus and Remus (*photo: Trustees of the British Museum, by permission*)

> Romulus and Remus, two brothers,
> The she-wolf raised them in the area of Rome.

The panel shows one united scene. At the center, in a densely wooded grove, the wolf lies on her side while the brothers nurse lying on the ground beside her. Lacking an understanding of foreshortening, the artist has tipped this group into the vertical plane. The composition is unique among depictions of the Romulus and Remus story. Usually the wolf stands while the infants suckle from beneath. This standard Roman emblematic formula was known in England in the Anglo-Saxon period both in Romano-British occupation-period relics and in domestic *sceatta* coinage of about 650. However, the Franks Casket artist has either reinterpreted the scene for himself or turned to a now-lost model type. A second wolf lurks in the woods above, and pairs of spear-bearing warriors at left and right kneel reverently before the nursing trio. This scene corresponds neither to the story as told in Livy (*Liber* 1.4), where a single shepherd, Faustulus, discovers the twins with the wolf and takes them home to his wife, Acca Laurentia, to be reared, nor to the alternative version, transmitted by Dionysios of Halicarnassus, in which a group of hunters find the wolf and her nurslings in a cave, drive her off by shouting and waving, and then take the children to Faustulus and his wife.[121] Both of these versions have independent traditions in art, but the Franks Casket scene is based on neither. Not only has the scene been altered, but so has been the meaning. As Alfred Becker has demonstrated, the panel invokes the cult of the twin brothers, a devotion that manifests itself in ancient Greece in the Dioscuri Castor and Pollux, in Roman mythology in Romulus and Remus, and in Christian adaptation in either the paired saints Peter and Paul or in various pairs of brother saints, such as Cosmas and Damian. The brother gods were universally revered in the pre-Christian classical world as protectors of travelers and warriors. The cult of Romulus and Remus was moreover continued directly in the Christian period; the *Hieronymian Martyrology* lists a "sanctus Romulus" commemorated on 11 October.[122] The port city of San Remo in Italy had in the medieval period a twin city, San Romulo, now a ruin some eight hundred meters up the coastal cliff above San Remo; the two serving together, significantly, as beacons for ships entering the port. In Anglo-Saxon England the cult of the twins was confluent with the legends of Hengist and Horsa, heroic figures of the Anglo-Saxon invasion period, whose shrines were associated with groves.[123] Hence it is not odd to find the Roman pair in a grove, their number stressed by the wolves, the paired warriors and the symmetrical arrangement of trees around them. The warriors kneel reverently, invoking the divine brothers, rather than driving the wolf away as they do in the classical narrative, and repeating the gesture of the Magi on the front of the casket.

The back panel of the casket shows a scene from Roman history, the conquest of Jerusalem under Titus. The marginal inscription runs up the left side, across the top and down at the right:

Franks Casket, back: Titus's Sack of Jerusalem *(photo: Trustees of the British Museum, by permission)*

> Here fight
> Titus and the Jews, here flee
> The inhabitants of Jerusalem.

The inscription is partly in Latin and partly in the vernacular. The line concerning the flight of the inhabitants is in Latin, either because the artist carelessly lapsed from translation into the language of the model, or, as is more likely, because he tried to make the defeat more distant from the writer, reader, and owner by putting it in an unfamiliar or at least a foreign language. The use of Latin here may consequently be another example of the Anglo-Saxon use of euphemism and other methods for avoiding the transference of disaster by sympathetic magic from written word to reality.

The narrative is shown in two registers, although this division is broken by an architectural unit at the center that extends to the full height of the picture zone. In the upper left quadrant, a group of warriors approach the central structure. The fifth from the left, unlike the rest, has a helmet with a noseguard and carries a sword rather than a spear, with which he cuts down an enemy soldier fleeing before him, who has crumbled to one knee and dropped his sword. This heroic figure may be intended as Titus himself. Little figures in flight assist one another in climbing over the roof of the central structure. At the right in the top register are a series of refugees with packs, flasks, and walking sticks. Some look back over their shoulders, and one carries a woman on his back. The central structure is an arched *aedicula* standing three stories high; a single arch is carried by three levels of columns. Inside the arch at the center is a small round-headed niche, surrounded by animal emblems; above, two linked bird's heads with a single body; at the sides, two complex animals, possibly lions, with interlaced tails; and below, two horselike animals back to back. G. Baldwin Brown suggested that this is the shrine of the Ark of the Covenant in the Temple of Jerusalem with the shrine left open after the sack of the city.[124] The structure may also, however, be construed as the city gate, or as a hieroglyph of the entire city with the Temple at its center.[125] A scene of judgment fills the lower left quadrant. A central figure sits on a high seat, with a small figure, probably a scribe, in a subordinate position at his feet. The scribe extends a cup and a scroll to an unarmed man standing at the right who unrolls a parchment. Behind him stands a soldier with a spear. At the left two men wrestle; the one at left has seized the other by the hair and the one at right has grabbed at his opponent's arms. The scene probably narrates Fronto's judgment of the Jewish prisoners, as narrated in Josephus (*De Bello Judaico* 6.9).[126] At the lower left corner of the panel, beneath the rectangle left blank by the lost silver fitting, is the word *dom*, "judgment." In the right lower quadrant, three figures with staffs and short traveling capes lead five figures in long cloaks off to the right. The five are empty-handed; the central one, a woman, wears a heavy neck ring or yoke. The scene is explained by the word *gisl*, "hostages," in the lower right corner.

The subject of the right side of the Franks Casket in the Bargello is by far the most problematic aspect of the casket. The narrative is in three distinct scenes, distinguished by the convention of placing outermost figures of adjoining scenes back-to-back. At the extreme left, a polymorphic monster sits on a half-ovoid shape confronting a spear-bearing warrior. The monster has a horse's head and hooves, human clothing and sitting posture, wings, and a snake's head protruding from its mouth. In its hands or front hooves it holds foliate

Franks Casket, right side: A Heroic Death; Florence, Museo del Bargello *(photo: Trustees of the British Museum, by permission)*

branches over its shoulder and in front of its face. The warrior, in a striding stance and wearing a kilt and a heavy cloak, carries a shield ornamented with concentric circles on his left arm and a spear, point upward, in his right hand. His head is covered with a helmet with a noseguard and a forward-leaning animal crest, possibly an eagle.

In the central scene, a naturalistic stallion stands in a wooded grove. Beneath his hind legs is a bird in flight, and under his belly and between his forelegs are two triple knots or *triquetrae*. Above his back is the word *risci* and below his forelegs, the word *wudu*. Below his head at right is a mound containing a probable shrouded human head and torso. At the right stands a female figure, cloaked and hooded, bearing a raised staff and confronting the stallion. Between them at mutual eye level is a chalice and above their heads are written the runes, *bita*. Between the horse's left foreleg and the mound is a piece of foliage that could be, but is probably not, a Chi-Rho, the monogram of the first two Greek letters of the name of Christ, and above and behind the hooded figure to the right is a branch roughly in the form of a Greek cross. It is, however, difficult to imagine a Christian meaning for this scene.

At the extreme right of the panel is a symmetrical group of three figures. The two outer cloaked and hooded figures turn toward and violently seize the central figure by the forearms and shoulders. The central figure is hoodless and mouthless, stands facing forward, and appears to have just dropped an object to the lower right between itself and the figure to its right. These three figures may be female by the costume, the long skirt and full cloak, but the runes of the margin do not assist in this determination.

The marginal inscription here is particularly difficult because the writer has substituted variant runes for all the vowels. These are not naturally occurring vowel runes from an earlier form of the *futhorc* or local practice, but rather deliberately invented forms used to encipher or somehow obscure the contents of the passage from our understanding. The inscription reads:

> Herhos sits on the hill of injury.
> She works misery, as Erta commanded her.
> They created grief, sorrow, and anguish of heart.[127]

It is evident from the outset that the runes and the pictures must be somehow related.[128] Alfred Becker's is the only interpretation using all the aspects of the right side of the casket, including the inscription, as a plausible unit.[129] "Herhos" is the monster figure at left; she sits on a mound and appears before the warrior as a sign of his imminent death. Her polymorphic anatomy is similar to that of monsters in Norse mythology, but she can be most closely linked to the *waelcyrge* of the Anglo-Saxons. The *waelcyrge* are the mythological predecessors of the Norse Valkyries, but they are not yet the warrior maidens of the sagas; rather, they are both corpse demons and brides of the afterlife. The snake issuing from the monster's mouth is a statement of imminent death to the warrior, enabling his enemies to overcome him. She hides behind her branches, temporarily postponing the hero's death; his end will come on the instant that he sees her face. The warrior whom the monster confronts has occasionally been understood as the Erta who condemned her to this role, but is more likely her victim. It is not necessary that the warrior be identified with any particular historical or mythological person. He is more the generic hero, who suffers the fate of the courageous, and the runes do not identify him. At the center, the mound is open to give a view down into the warrior's grave, where he lies already wrapped in a winding sheet. The horse is not mourning his master but is his means of transportation to the afterlife, as in numerous illustrated stones in Gotland, Sweden. Although this is not the eight-legged horse belonging to Woden/Odin, other emblems of that god are present; the triple knots and possibly also the raven, sometimes but not always the god's bird, which serves first, like the Valkyries, to choose the dead, and then as a guide into the otherworld. The name Erta means "the instigator," and hence might be a reference to Woden/Odin himself. The woman with the staff at right may well be the Valkyrie again; transformed into the promised bride of the hero's afterlife. She carries a chalice of forgetfulness, to revive the hero from the stupor of death and to obliterate the memory of his death and his regrets. In the Norse *Edda*, the Valkyries are beautiful, not monstrous, and when they enter Valhalla with the dead heroes, they serve as the handmaidens of Odin. Whether the death goddesses in the Anglo-Saxon myths were associated in this capacity with Woden is difficult to determine. The staff or wand carried by the woman in the central scene of the right side of the Franks Casket may be a variation on the theme of the branches in the first scene, but no association of such rods with Valkyries remains in the Norse material or in Anglo-Saxon fragments, so its function here is problematic. *Wudu,* "woods," refers to the venue of the scene in a grove but may also be a sacred site in reference to Herhos and her branches. Groves were frequently used as pagan cult centers among the Anglo-Saxons, as the prohibitions in postconversion laws and edicts demonstrate. Moreover, Herhos may be a variant of *herh-os,* or "wood godhead." *Risci* is a branch or staff, an allusion to the attribute of the seated monster or to the woman's rod, or both. *Bita* is a form of the verb *bitan,* "to wound or cut down." The word may refer either to the warrior's death in battle or to a death with a spear made from a branch from the sacred grove, since the "T" rune of *bita* springs from the top of the woman's rod and is shaped like a spearhead. The spear is also an attribute of Woden and may imply the god's involvement in the warrior's selection for a heroic death and felicitous afterlife.

The group at the right is more difficult to decipher but may be linked to the third line of the inscriptive verse. The outside figures are probably the "creators of grief," agents of death in Herhos's service. The absence of a mouth on the central figure may indicate that the person is dead; the mouth which serves as the gate of the soul at the time of death has completed its usefulness and has vanished.

The use of the variant runes thus becomes clearly purposeful; the subject is sorrow and death, and by Anglo-Saxon tradition, the reader, the writer, and the owner of the casket must be shielded from the imminent actualization of the written word. Similarly the warrior is given no specific name or mythological association, and in the scene at left does not quite yet confront the monster of his fate. The scene is a promise of heroic death, as yet unfulfilled.

The amalgamation of these various scenes into a program was not considered possible until recently. As late as 1972, Lawrence Stone spoke for the mass of earlier scholars when he considered the combination of images on the Franks Casket and the variety of their probable sources to be symptomatic of the "intellectual promiscuity" of the period as a whole.[130] However, the study of Northumbrian ecclesiastical art has revealed the deliberate nature of its iconographic and stylistic choices, and the continuing application of the old standards of chance combination to a secular work of the same period and provenance is inappropriate. Moreover, the investigations of Alfred Becker have suggested that the Franks Casket has a complex and highly reasoned program, as intellectually tightly woven as that of comparable Christian art, despite its secular source and syncretistic approach.[131] Becker considers the Franks Casket in the category of early medieval magic-working objects, most of which are found in Scandinavia and its sphere of influence. In these objects, the important factor is not the realism or representative qualities of the image itself, but rather the sympathetic influence of the scene's meaning and content on the beholder. The Franks Casket differs from the bulk of these objects by the variety of its themes and their sources, and in the complexity of their mutual effect. The entire box functions programatically for the protection of both the owner and the contents of the casket, and magically invokes for the owner a life heroic and triumphant in all its aspects. The front deals with the creation and defense of wealth, in the story of Weland; and with its acquisition through the generosity of others, in the gifts of the Magi. The creation aspect is strengthened by the inscription, which deals with the manufacture of the casket itself in terms of the forces of life and death. Anglo-Saxon objects are frequently labeled with the name of the material of which they are made, giving them a sort of material inviolability. The Magi themselves, their presence strengthened by their label, were considered magicians in the early Anglo-Saxon period, prompting Bede to state in the *In Matthei Evangelium Expositio* (1.2): "Magi non propter magicam artem sic nominantur sed propter aliquam philosophiam."[132] Despite the Church's efforts to the contrary, however, the Magi appeared universally as apotropaic symbols, sometimes without the Virgin and Child, on brooches, fibulae, and other personal articles.

Furthermore, as Becker has determined, words serve throughout the Franks Casket to strengthen the meaning of the pictures. The alliterated consonants of the marginal inscriptions are significant, as each rune of the *futhorc* or runic alphabet had a symbolic or magical meaning as well as a phonetic value. On the front of the casket, *gifu*, "gift," suggests generosity and ownership, and *feod*, "wealth," has a particular connotation as the ownership of portable goods such as money and jewelry. Romulus and Remus, guardians and givers of strength to travelers and warriors, are ringed by verses stressing *os*, or "godhood," *ur*, or "ox," and *rad*, or "riding," a journey. This side of the casket evokes the protection of the twin gods on the owner while traveling, which considering the mobility of the Northumbrian nobility must have been a frequent activity. The Titus panel stresses the desired victories of the owner in battle, the flight of his opponents and his consequent right to sit in judgment, gain treasure and take hostages, thereby gaining power, wealth, fame, and honor. According to Germanic law, the goods of the conquered are forfeit to the conqueror, and aggressive acquisition by this means was considered a virtue in rulers. The *solidi* of Titus, bearing his imperial portrait, became amulets in the northern regions of the former Roman Empire because of his successful conquests. The alliteration here stresses *tyr*, the name of the Anglo-Saxon war god, as well as *feod* and *gifu*. The lid of the casket preserves no runes, but the theme is the successful defense, possibly with divine aid, of one's home and goods. The defender here is strengthened by the presence of his name, and although he is absent in the fragmentary sagas extant today, one may assume that he was known for his archery and his able defense of his home. The implicit invocation is that the casket owner may fight as successfully as his worthy prototype. The lid also specifically refers to the successful protection of the contents of the casket from theft. The right side of the casket suggests a heroic death and happy afterlife for the owner of the casket, but the runes themselves are enciphered to prevent their immediate effectiveness. Nonetheless, the first verse stresses *hagal*, "fate," the forces of destruction, later simply equated with misfortune. The second verse evokes *eh*, "horse," and *ac*, "oak," references to the scenes of the panel. The third verse, on the other hand, stresses *sigel*, the sun rune, image of life and counterbalance of evil.

According to Becker's analysis, the Franks Casket was programmatically devised as a portable magical system of protection for the owner, wishing him the accumulation and protection of material wealth, victory in battle, protection at home, safety on the road, and an eventual heroic death and afterlife. This program places the Franks Casket securely in a syncretistic secular milieu, where the official faith is Christianity but belief in sympathetic magic and traditional heroic values are still maintained.[133] The runic inscriptions of the Franks Casket place it both paleographically and linguistically in Northumbria about the year 700.[134] The variety of sources used in its program confirm the runological evidence, and the program demands a secular context. It has been suggested that the Titus scene and possibly also the Magi and Romulus and Remus were taken from the volume of cosmography, possibly a world chronicle acquired by Aldfrith from Jarrow.[135] It is possible that Aldfrith's book was an illustrated Latin version of an Alexandrian chronicle. Evidence for a tradition of Late Antique illustrated Latin chronicles is found in the incomplete *Barbarus of Scaliger* (Paris, Bibliothèque Nationale MS Lat. 4884), in which spaces were left in the text for illustrations. Furthermore, the arrangement of the Titus scene in registers strongly suggests a Late Antique manuscript source, paralleling, for example, battle scenes in the *Milan Iliad* (Milan, Ambrosian Library, Cod. F.205.inf., pict. XX–XXXI), of the fourth or fifth century. Of the Franks Casket scenes, the Titus panel is consequently most closely linked to a potential manuscript source. The use of such a manuscript source in Anglo-Saxon secular art is exceptional and strongly supports the association of the Franks Casket with Aldfrith's manuscript and hence with his court. The Adoration of the Magi, on the other hand, has been linked to the Byzantine *Nikopoia* and *Platytera* types of the Virgin and Child, which suggests importation via portable personal items on which these images were popular, as on the Attalans fibulae at Trier, or Palestinian pilgrim souvenirs such as the Monza ampules.[136] The scene of Romulus and Remus has no extant parallels in art, and may equally easily be either a new invention or a copy, whether from the hypothetical chronicle or another unknown source.

However, despite the use of foreign models, the Franks Casket remains as resolutely insular in style as it does in program. The style of the casket is completely northern, crude in its figural proportions and placements and its linear, unmodeled relief, yet it shows considerable vigor in depicting scenes of action, movement, and emotion. Despite its provenance in or near the Northumbrian court at the height of the Northumbrian Renaissance, the Franks Casket remains distinctly free of the classicizing stylistic influence of foreign models, even those which it may have appropriated for its program. Its closest purely Christian parallel is the wooden coffin of Saint Cuthbert, but the latter has a clearly classicizing undertone, however domesticated or diminished, which is absolutely lacking in the Franks Casket. Once again as elsewhere in Northumbria, as in the *Lindisfarne Gospels* or the *Book of Saint Chad*, stylistic choices are made in the Franks Casket that are appropriate to its milieu and meaning. Here an indigenous quasi-hieroglyphic style similar to that of the Sutton Hoo purse lid is appropriate to the syncretistic program of the casket. The Franks Casket also reflects concerns similar to those of the Sutton Hoo ship burial, both in symbolism and in sources.

The fundamental syncretism of the Franks Casket may suggest pushing its date back into the conversion period, possibly to the reign of Edwin. However, the runological evidence and the hypothetical association of the Titus scene at least with a codex arriving in the secular milieu in the reign of Aldfrith places the manufacture of the Franks Casket in the court of the Northumbrian philosopher king, between 685 and 705. Moreover, the syncretism of the Sutton Hoo period, although less outspoken at a later date, was slow to disappear from the Anglo-Saxon secular culture. Aldfrith's court had not only the probable intellectual sophistication to accept a syncretistic program of this nature without fear of damnation, but would also be able to appreciate the complexities and depth of symbolism of the Franks Casket program. The Franks Casket is not merely an example of the art of the early Anglo-Saxon syncretistic secular world but also representative of the intellectual concerns of the apex of that culture in Northumbria. Its style cannot therefore be dismissed as "primitive," nor its program as "intellectually promiscuous." Both must be considered the products of well-reasoned choices in a creative climate where other options, of transplanted classicism or of a more consistently Christian program, were chosen in other contexts.

The Franks Casket encapsules the cumulative concerns of the secular Anglo-Saxon world in the postconversion period. It represents both the survival of the pagan and heroic Germanic traditions and their fusion with the Christian faith. It also reflects the affinity of the Anglo-Saxon nobility for Roman imperial traditions as well as for more purely mythological subject matter available through the Church. As such the Franks Casket is a paradigm of the encounter of the Anglo-Saxon secular culture with the foreign ideas of Rome and the Christian Church, and of the final mutual assimilation that is the culmination of the Northumbrian Renaissance.

The Parameters of the Northumbrian Renaissance

THE POSTCONVERSION FLOWERING of the arts in Northumbria has been called a Northumbrian Renaissance. The term *renaissance* is often taken literally as a rebirth of the traditions of classical antiquity. Yet the art of seventh- and eighth-century Northumbria was neither a mimetic recapitulation of the Late Antique followed by stylistic degeneration into renewed isolation nor a haphazard foraging by Dark Age nostalgics among the relics of the past. Northumbrian art clearly reflects both the diversity of influences on its development and the deliberately chosen responses of various factions and centers to those influences. It has been convenient in the past to shrug off the complexity and diversity of the Northumbrian Renaissance with such generic and slightly pejorative phrases as "promiscuous eclecticism," suggesting that the evolution of Northumbrian art was the result of random combinations of models, artists, and patrons, and that no deeper understanding of the period as a whole is possible or even necessary.[1] Yet it has become increasingly evident in recent decades that the critical issue in the history of early medieval art is the survival and dissemination of Late Antique traditions and models and the degree and nature of the receptivity of the art-forming centers of the early medieval period toward the legacy of the classical past. Consequently, a general theory of the internal dynamics of the Northumbrian Renaissance is useful, not only for the study of the development of art in England, but also as a possible basis for the understanding of variations in receptivity elsewhere.

What then was the Northumbrian Renaissance? First, is the phrase "Northumbrian Renaissance" acceptable on geographic grounds? We must acknowledge that the primary impulse for art in early Anglo-Saxon England came from the kingdom of Northumbria. This is not entirely because most extant works of the period are directly or circumstantially connected with Northumbria, nor because we have so many major documentary sources, including Bede's monumental *History*, that focus primarily on this region. Absolute political stability cannot be expected in a Dark Age kingdom with two rival dynasties and hostile neighbors, but the relative calm of the reigns of Edwin and Oswald and the serenity of succession from Oswy forward speak eloquently for the continuity of leadership remarkable by comparison to the intrigues of the Merovingian Franks or the political tumult of Lombard Italy. The size and strength of Northumbria in its heyday was sufficient to command a kind of Anglo-Saxon high kingship for three of her kings in succession, a phenomenon not repeated elsewhere.[2] Northumbria was also an intellectual leader. Canterbury had Theodore, Hadrian, and their students; Malmesbury had Aldhelm; but no other region had an honor roll so long as that of Northumbria: Benedict Biscop, Ceolfrith, Wilfrid, Colman, Hilda, John of Beverly, Aidan, Cuthbert, Bede, Egbert, and Alcuin of York. It is of course possible that important evidence from elsewhere is lost. However, all signs indicate that Northumbria was both a sufficiently politically stable and intellectually gifted environment to permit the concentrated florescence of artistic endeavor demonstrated by the surviving works. Consequently we are not in error to speak of a Northumbrian Renaissance, however grandiose the phrase may seem.

Second, the diversity of the art produced in Northumbria in this period must be explained. Initially, it seems most logical to subdivide the works as "Roman" or "Celtic" along the lines of ecclesiastical politics. However, most of the significant works postdate Whitby, so that in point of fact no major work other than the *Book of Durrow* can be considered the unalloyed product of the Celtic Church in England. Moreover, *Durrow* was most probably neither written nor illuminated in Northumbria. Nonetheless, the historical or actively political allegiances of the various northern centers to either the Roman or the Celtic Church have substantial bearing on the receptivity of the art produced at those centers to foreign models. Romanized centers such as Monkwearmouth, Jarrow, and Hexham remained emulative as long as possible. They gave in to indigenous stylistic tendencies over time only as the transplanted Late Antique preferences of their founders began to give way to the environmental pressures of local taste. On the other hand, at centers such as Lindisfarne where orthodoxy followed the decision of Whitby by royal fiat, the old Celtic ascetic ideals lingered along with the equally culturally embedded assimilative attitude toward foreign ideas and models for art. The interaction of the "Celtic" and "Roman" attitudes was crucial to the development of Northumbrian art. Indeed the synthesis of foreign models and indigenous style or iconography in the *Lindisfarne Gospels* and the Late Antique models made available through the Roman Church and the adaptive attitude of the Celtic tradition.

The ecclesiastical art of Northumbria in this period may be best understood if subdivided into three modes, which reflect both the confronted tendencies of the two Churches and their later fusion in the Northumbrian milieu. The *assimilative mode* was developed in the art of the Celtic Church, such as the *Book of Durrow* and its probable descendants in Celtic foundations in Northumbria. Here imported concepts such as the illuminated Evangelist symbol were rigorously subjected to the aesthetic criteria of the indigenous culture and more or less lost their visual identity with the foreign models that originally inspired them. The *emulative mode* was inherent in the art of the Roman Church, such as Wilfrid's basilica at Hexham or the *Codex Amiatinus*, in which imported models were closely copied. Here the preferences of the essentially foreign culture behind the model were not only accepted but promulgated as evidence of identity with that foreign culture, either because of a belief in the superiority of the art and ideals of that culture, or because political advantage was to be gained by such self-identification. The *synthetic mode* was the result of the confrontation between these two approaches. In the *Lindisfarne Gospels*, the Ruthwell Cross, and elsewhere, a synthetic approach permitted the artist to use the imported model as desired, borrowing directly the iconographic or stylistic elements that appealed and altering form or meaning to local taste on aesthetic and/or ideological grounds. This approach was not the eclectic equivocation of artistic immaturity. It was instead the result of both a thorough understanding of the form, meaning and cultural attachments of the imported model and an equally profound sense of the value of indigenous traditions, and demanded that the artist be the equilibrator of these two forces.

The *synthetic mode* is taken further in the Anglo-Saxon secular culture, where the basic premise of the imported models, their association with the Christian faith, was modified by the syncretism of the secular community even at its highest levels, and by the persistence of the heroic tradition. In secular art, imported symbols of power were amalgamated into the indigenous tradition in order to be effective either as symbols or as magical devices. Moreover, foreign models for art had to be stylistically adapted to appeal to the secular patron, who—steeped in the heroic traditions of his ancestors—preferred the strangely powerful hieroglyphic style of their art over the fragile shortlived classicism of churchmen.

The identity of centers and even more of their individual founders and leaders was also a decisive factor in the development of art. The reconstruction of historical personalities is impossible, even with the most accurate records, all the more so at 1,300 years' distance. However, the intentions of individuals and groups are often recorded in their deeds and more graphically in their art. The lack of unity in the approach to imported models in the Northumbrian Renaissance makes necessary the consideration of the nature of particular art-forming centers and the effect of the intentions of the individuals who founded these centers on their collective temperament and their art. The three modes outline only the first level of possible response to the model, for the motives of groups and individuals vary as much within modes as between them. The emulative efforts of Wilfrid, for example, were differently directed than those of Benedict Biscop. It is useful to consider that within every mode there are *submodes* that take their character from the ideals of centers that produced them, and even more from the motivations of the individuals who founded these centers and directed or themselves undertook the production of art. Moreover, the ideals of centers changed slightly over time, particularly as strong-minded successors to the founders, the Accas and Ceolfriths, brought their own stamp to the art-forming attitudes of their communities. Several submodes can therefore be discerned within the art of a single center over time.

In the consideration of possible general models of cultural interaction, a theory of modes consequently provides only the first level of understanding of the process of artistic borrowing between cultures and is limited in its usefulness. However, it does provide an initial means of classifying the responses in one culture as a whole to a major influx of models for art from another culture, and can possibly be used in other contexts as a generic ethno-historical/art-historical model. The study of the Northumbrian Renaissance further demonstrates that artistic interaction between cultures is not an isolated phenomenon but should be studied in the context of such conditioning factors as patterns of trade, political history, and the attitudes of significant individuals. These factors determine in large degree the receptivity of various factions, groups and centers to imported models for art and their responses, whether assimilative, emulative, or synthesizing.

Finally there is the question as to what parts of the Northumbrian response to Late Antique models may be classified correctly as a renascence. Those who construe a renascence in the arts as an awakening of artistic sensibilities and the intelligent fusion of models and new formulations will find the phrase "Northumbrian Renaissance" wholly appropriate to most if not all the major works of the period. On the other hand, for purists such as Erwin Panofsky who define a renascence as a revitalization of the classical or Late Antique tradition in its most unadulterated forms, only the emulative art of Jarrow, Monkwearmouth, and Hexham, and the stylistically emulative elements in synthetic works such as the Ruthwell Cross are truly classicizing enough to fit the term.[3] To those one might bow and therefore consider the *Lindisfarne Gospels* and similar works part of a separate "Northumbrian Synthesis." However, perhaps it is the concept of a renascence that requires redefinition. The Carolingian renascence and even the Italian Renaissance included in their art elements that were products of their own times and of the cultures that gave them birth rather than the purely archaeological substance of classical antiquity. It may well be that Eadfrith and his colleagues considered the Evangelist portraits in the *Lindisfarne Gospels* to be a commentary on the Late Antique model rather than a rejection of it. If so, these Evangelist portraits are no less the products of a renascence than Brunelleschi's Pazzi Chapel, which despite its general dependency on the classical proportional and decorative formulations of Vitruvius Pollio is, after all, not structurally or aesthetically identical to any known Late Antique structure. In accepting the *Lindisfarne Gospels* and other examples of the synthetic mode as participants in the Northumbrian Renaissance, we simply admit the validity of a creative as well as a mimetic response to the late classical tradition in early medieval art.

Appendix
The Text of the *Lindisfarne Gospels*

THE TEXT of the *Lindisfarne Gospels* is a member of the insular Vulgate stemma headed by the *Codex Amiatinus*. John Chapman believed that this stemma was derived from the seventh volume of the Cassiodoran *Novem Codices*.[1] The presence of at least two other volumes of the *Novem Codices* at Jarrow has been demonstrated to the satisfaction of a consensus of text scholars by Pierre Courcelle.[2] However, T. J. Brown has postulated that the Gospel text of *Amiatinus*, *Lindisfarne*, and the rest of their stemma may have a non-Cassiodoran antecedent, a liturgical Gospel codex with Neapolitan associations.[3] In 1891 G. Morin published Edward Bishop's observations that the quasi capitularies appended to the *capitularia lectionum* of Lindisfarne include the two distinctly Neapolitan feasts of San Gennaro and of the dedication of the basilica of Saint Stephen.[4] A similar listing occurs in another Gospels codex in the British Library (Royal I.B.VII), which is also closer to *Lindisfarne* than any other member of this particular insular stemma. Moreover, the Gospels *capitularia lectionum* of *Lindisfarne*, Royal I.B.VII, and *Amiatinus* share similar liturgical rubrics. Chapman suggested that the Neapolitan liturgical material might have migrated north in the Cassiodoran text prototype. However, as Brown has correctly indicated, the *Novem Codices* constituted a study Bible, and probably lacked liturgical apparatus such as quasi capitularies.[5] Brown therefore suggested that the text of the insular Vulgate Gospel stemma and its liturgical apparatus were derived from a Neapolitan Gospel codex, although he agreed with Courcelle's hypothesis that parts or all of the *Novem Codices* may have indeed been present at Jarrow.

A marginal note included in the *Echternach Gospels*, (Paris, Bibliothèque Nationale MS Lat. 9389), a close member of the same stemma as the *Lindisfarne Gospels* and paleographically attributed to Lindisfarne, gives some indications concerning the textual prototype:

Promendaui ut potui secundum codicem de bibliotheca eugipi praesbiteri quem ferunt fuisse sci. hieronimi indicatione .ui p. con. bassilii u.c. anno septimo decimo.

The note indicates that in 558 an individual who does not name himself emended this Gospels text, using a codex that had allegedly belonged to Saint Jerome and was currently part of the library of a priest named Eugippius. The reference is probably to the Eugippius who was abbot of Lucullanum between about 510 and 535. This abbot was known to Cassiodorus who describes him in the *Institutiones* as a formidable text scholar:

Virum quidem non usque aedo saecularibus litteris eruditem, sed scrip-turarum divinarum lectione plenissimum.

It is thus evident that Cassiodorus was familiar with the scholarship of Eugip-pius and may have in addition known his library. Vivarium was not far from Naples, and Cassiodorus, a text scholar himself, certainly availed himself of the resources of his region. Chapman suggested that the notice in the *Echternach Gospels* was an addition by Cassiodorus himself, a notation on the sources used in the composition of the Vulgate Gospels in the seventh volume of the *Novem Codices.*[6] Certainly, the pedigree of such a source would have appealed to Cassiodorus's intention of producing a pure text. Chapman went on to suggest that the "Promendaui ut potui" was written with particularly Cassiodoran orthography and formulas of speech, but this analysis has since been discounted by the analysis of J. M. Heer.[7] On this basis, Brown has postulated that the addition of the notice of emendation must have occurred in the descent of the text source at Naples, also near Eugippius's Lucullanum, and traveled north with the Neopolitan model to England.

On the basis of the preceding arguments, Brown's analysis of the insular Vulgate Gospel stemma has led him to postulate that the imported source was a non-Cassiodoran Neapolitan Gospel text available at Jarrow/Monkwearmouth and at Lindisfarne around 700. However, it remains possible that the source of the Vulgate text was indeed the seventh volume of the *Novem Codices,* and that the Neapolitan source was adduced for the liturgical material alone, to substan-tiate the bare bones of Cassiodorus's study text, in the Northumbrian centers. This hypothesis may explain one of the more puzzling aspects of the insular Gospel stemma, the use of a variety of canon-table sequences. *Amiatinus* uses a seven-page sequence, whereas the *Lindisfarne Gospels* uses a sixteen-page sequence similar to that found in the Neapolitan *Codex Fuldensis* of Saint Victor of Capua (Fulda, Landesbibliothek, Codex Bonifacianus III), and Royal I.B.VII uses a twelve-page series. Brown suggested that the Neapolitan source lacked a canon sequence, because of the variation within the insular stemma, particularly between the otherwise closely allied *Lindisfarne* and Royal I.B.VII.[8] He proposed that *Amiatinus* used the seven-page series because of the needs of a pandect for compaction and postulated that the origin of this sequence was Cassiodoran, either the *Codex Grandior* or the seventh volume of the *Novem Codices*. He then theorized that the rest of the insular stemma borrowed sequences from a variety of sources. Finally, Brown agreed with his coauthor of the *Lindisfarne Gospels* 1956 facsimile commentary volume, R. L. S. Bruce-Mitford, that the sequence of Evangelist portraits in the codex was derived from a series of portraits in the seventh volume of the *Novem Codices*. Brown thus not only accepted the presence of the Cassiodoran Vulgate Gospels text at Jarrow/Monkwearmouth for use in the *Amiatinus* but believed it was also available as a model to the artists of *Lindisfarne*. However, he did not accept it as a textual source for *Lindisfarne*. In effect, he suggested that Eadfrith and his colleagues had on hand Cassiodorus's revised text of the Gospels, one of the finest Vulgates available, and yet deliberately chose to use another text source, a Neapolitan Gospels codex, partly because the latter contained needed liturgical apparatus and partly because it was a "better" text. However, although one may assume the relative excellence of Cassiodorus's Gospels, there is no indication whatever as to the quality of the Neapolitan model. Brown assumes that the "Promendaui ut potui" notice gives the pedigree of the Neapolitan codex. However, it has not been clearly demonstrated that this notice could not have arrived in the *Novem Codices* text. The orthography and phraseology of this notice, as Heer has demonstrated, cannot be proven to be specifically Cassiodoran, but neither can they be conclusively shown to be non-Cassiodoran. Indeed, this notice may well be, as Chapman stated originally, evidence on the methods of Cassiodorus in the research and development of his Vulgate. As both Chapman and Brown concluded, the final resolution of the insular Vulgate conundrum must await the next complete reediting of the Vulgate Gospels. However, one cannot on the basis of Brown's arguments conclusively exclude the seventh volume of the *Novem Codices* from paternity of the insular Vulgate Gospels stemma.

Brown has written at length on the ability of insular scribes to distinguish quality between texts; why would it not therefore be possible for them to combine texts to their own advantage? The Lindisfarne scriptorium may well have chosen to use the Vulgate text of the *Novem Codices* gospels, adding the necessary liturgical material from a secondary Neapolitan source, and also borrowing from that source a sixteen-page canon series more appropriate to the lavish scale of the *Lindisfarne Gospels* than to the less decorated Jarrow pandects, which called for the shorter seven-page Cassiodoran series. The use of a twelve-page sequence in Royal I.B.VII may be an attempt at compressing the *Lindisfarne* sixteen to save vellum, as Royal I.B.VII is generically a less ambitious project than *Lindisfarne*. The absence of the Neapolitan quasi capitularies in later insular Gospels of the same stemma seems to indicate that the Neapolitan liturgical source traveled separately from the Gospel text archetype. This may also explain the subsequent variation of insular canon tables, adduced along with liturgical addenda from a variety of models in preference over the abbreviated seven-page Cassiodoran canon sequence in the text archetype.

Notes

ABBREVIATIONS

Bede (Colgrave and Mynors)

Bede, *Ecclesiastical History of the English People,* ed. Bertram Colgrave and R.A.B. Mynors. Oxford Medieval Texts (Oxford: Oxford University Press, 1969).

Henry, *IAECP*

F. Henry, *Irish Art in the Early Christian Period (to A.D. 800)* (Ithaca: Cornell University Press, 1965).

Chapter 1. Secular Trade Routes and the Anglo-Saxon Invasion

1. Leslie Alcock, *Arthur's Britain: History and Archaeology, A.D. 367–634* (Harmondsworth: Penguin Books, 1971), 197; maps 5, 6; fig. 12; idem *Dinas Powys: An Iron Age, Dark Age and Early Medieval Settlement in Glamorgan* (Cardiff: University of Wales Press, 1963), 50; Charles Thomas, "Imported Pottery in Dark Age Britain," *Medieval Archaeology* 3 (1959): 89–111 See also Sean P. O'Ríordáin, "The Excavation of a Large Earthen Ringfort at Garranes, co. Cork," *Proceedings of the Royal Irish Academy* 47 (1942): 77–150, for the establishment of the typology of imported pottery in the British Isles; and also C. A. Ralegh Radford, "Imported Pottery at Tintagel, Cornwall: An Aspect of British Trade with the Mediterranean in the Early Christian Period," *Dark Age Britain: Studies Presented to E. T. Leeds,* ed. D. B. Harden (London: Methuen, 1956), 59–70, for its extension to present usage.

2. Bernard Wailes, *Some Imported Pottery in Western Britain, A.D. 400–800: Its Connections with Frankish and Visigothic Gaul,* Ph.D. diss., St. Catherine's College, Cambridge, 1963, 1: 48–72.

3. Elizabeth Dawes and Norman H. Baynes, *Three Byzantine Saints* (Crestwood, N.Y.: St. Vladimir's Seminary Press, 1977), 217.

4. The account states that the ship from Alexandria was blown off course by a storm and made landfall in Britain. However, Leontius, the writer of the *Vita,* does not seem to indicate that the act of trading with the Britons in this manner way anything unusual in the period. (ibid., and see also J. N. Hillgrath, "Visigothic Spain and Early Christian Ireland," *Proceedings of the Royal Irish Academy* 62 [1962], 178–79.

5. Hillgarth, "Visigothic Spain," 178–79.

6. E. G. Bowen, *Saints, Seaways and Settlements* (Cardiff: University of Wales Press, 1969),

76–77. See also J. N. Hillgarth, "The East, Visigothic Spain and the Irish," *Studia Patristica* 4 (1961): 445–45, mentions several points of contact.

7. A. R. Lewis, *The Northern Seas; Shipping and Commerce in Northern Europe, A.D. 300–1100* (Princeton: Princeton University Press, 1958), 89.

8. Wailes, *Some Imported Pottery,* 1: 171–87.

9. Lewis, *Northern Seas,* 129.

10. Isidore of Seville, *Etymologies,* as cited in Lewis, *Northern Seas,* 129.

11. C. A. Ralegh Radford, "The Celtic Monastery in Britain," *Archaeologia Cambrensis* 3 (1962): 1–12, discusses the prevalence of Gallic pottery at Tintagel, North Cornwall.

12. Wailes, *Some Imported Pottery,* vol. 2, pls. 172, 173, 174, and oral communication with the author. For a differing viewpoint on the origin of E ware, see David Peacock and Charles Thomas, "Class E Imported Pottery: A Suggested Origin," *Cornish Archaeology* 6 (1967): 35–46. Peacock and Thomas prefer the Saintonge area, near La Chapelle des Pots, over the Paris basin, Wailes's suggested origin for E ware. At present, Wailes argues strongly for his original suggestion of the Paris basin.

13. Alcock, *Arthur's Britain,* 233.

14. Alcock, *Dinas Powys,* 185–86; Radford, "Celtic Monastery"; R.L.S. Bruce-Mitford, "The Pectoral Cross," in *The Relics of St. Cuthbert,* ed. C. F. Battiscombe (Oxford: Oxford University Press, 1956), 308–25.

15. N. K. Chadwick, *The Age of the Saints in the Early Celtic Church,* University of Durham Riddell Memorial Lectures, 32d ser. (Oxford: Oxford University Press, 1961), 13.

16. A. R. Lewis, "La commerce maritime et les navires de la Gaule occidentale, 550–750," *Études mérovingiennes,* ed. R. Crozet (Paris: A. and J. Picard, 1953), 192–3.

17. Ibid., 192–93; Wilhelm Levison, *England and the Continent in the Eighth Century* (Oxford: Clarendon Press, 1943), 7–8; *Vita Filiberti abbatis Gementicensis et Heriensis,* in *Passione vitaque sanctorum aevi Merovingici,* ed. B. Krusch and W. Levison, Monumenta Germaniae Historica: Scriptorum rerum Merovingicarum (Hanover: Hahn 1896), 3 : 28–29.

18. Lewis, "Le commerce maritime," 193; Levison, *England and the Continent,* 7; *Vita Eparchii reclusi Ecolismensis,* in *Passione vitaque sanctorum aevi Merovingici,* ed. B. Krusch and W. Levison, Monumenta Germaniae Historica: Scriptorum rerum Merovingicarum (Hanover: Hahn, 1896), 3 : 559.

19. Levison, *England and the Continent,* 8, quotes a charter of Dagobert I in 634 for the trade fair of St. Denis, mentioning "saxones.", See also: Annethe Lohaus, *Die Merovinger und England,* Münchener Beiträge zur Mediavistik und Renaissance-Forschung, vol. 19 (Munich: Arbeo-Gesellschaft, 1974),52, who quotes a similar charter of Charibert III in 710, and also the *Vita* of Richard of Centula, who died in the reign of Dagobert I (629–39), and who "ultra mare in Saxonia predicavit."

20. C.H.V. Sutherland, *Anglo-Saxon Gold Coinage and Currency in Light of the Crondall Hoard* (London: Oxford University Press, 1948), 25, quotes Strabo (4.199) that the major exports of Britain in the period of Roman occupation were wheat, cattle, gold, silver, iron, hides, slaves, and hunting dogs. These were quite likely standard products of the post-Roman period as well.

21. Bede, *An Ecclesiastical History of the English People,* ed. B. Colgrave and R.A.B. Mynors, Oxford Medieval Texts (Oxford: Oxford University Press, 1969), 134–43; hereafter cited as Bede (Colgrave and Mynors).

22. K. Hughes, *Early Christian Ireland: An Introduction to the Sources* (Ithaca: Cornell University Press, 1972), 37; and N. K. Chadwick, *The Celts* (Harmondsworth: Penguin Books, 1970), 83–84.

23. F. Henry, *Irish Art in the Early Christian Period (to A.D. 800)* (Ithaca: Cornell University Press, 1965), 3, 46–48; hereafter cited as Henry, *IAECP,* and Alcock, *Arthur's Britain,* 210.

24. M. de Paor and L. de Paor, *Early Christian Ireland* (London: Thames and Hudson, 1978), 26.

25. Henry, *IAECP,* 71.

26. De Paor and de Paor, *Early Christian Ireland,* 28–29.

27. Hughes, *Early Christian Ireland: Sources, 229–39,* provides an overview of the hagiography

sources.. See also de Paor and de Paor, *Early Christian Ireland,* 27–30 for a capsule biography of the saint and for evidence of survival of paganism after Patrick's mission.

28. Henry, *IAECP,* 1–16; *Treasures of Early Irish Art, 1500 B.C. to A.D. 1500,* ed. P. Cone (New York: Metropolitan Museum of Art, 1977). See also N. K. Chadwick, *Celts,* passim, on conservativism in social structure in early Ireland; de Paor, and de Paor, *Early Christian Ireland,* 73–109, on secular life, and Hughes, *Early Christian Ireland: Sources,* 43–80, on legal structure.

29. See Peter Hunter Blair, *Introduction to Anglo-Saxon England* (Cambridge: Cambridge University Press, 1956), 3–24; and R. Ian Jack, *Medieval Wales* (Ithaca N.Y.: Cornell University Press, 1972), for historiographic bibliography and discussion of British sources.

30. See Gildas, *De Excidio et Conquestu Britanniae,* in *Chronica Minora Saeculi IV, V VI, VII,* ed. T. Mommsen, vol. 3, pt. 1, Monumenta Germaniae Historica: Auctores Antiquissimorum (Berlin: Weidmans, 1893), 13:85; and F. Kerlouégan, "Le Latin du *De Excidio Britanniae* de Gildas," in *Christianity in Britain, 300–700,* Conference on Christianity in Sub-Roman Britain, Nottingham, 17–20 April 1967, ed. M. W. Barley and R. P. C. Hanson (Leicester: Leicester University Press, 1968), 151–76, for linguistic analysis.

31. F. Lot, *Nennius et l'Historia Brittonum,* Bibliothèque de l'Ecole des Hautes Etudes Sciences Historiques et Philologiques, vol. 263 (Paris: H. Champion, 1934); D. Dumville, "Nennius and the *Historia Brittonum,*" *Studia Celtica* 10–11 (1975–1976): 78–95.

32. *The Anglo-Saxon Chronicles* ed. and trans. G. N. Garmonsway (London: Dent; New York: Dutton, 1960), 12–13, for which the manuscript sources are the *Parker Chronicle* (A) (Cambridge, Corpus Christi College, MS 173), and the *Laud Chronicle* (E), also called the *Peterborough Chronicle* (Oxford, Bodleian MS Laud 636), for the year 449 forward; J. Williams ab Ithel, ed., *Annales Cambriae,* Rolls Series, Chronicles and Memorials of Great Britain and Ireland during the Middle Ages, vol. 20 (London: Longman, Green, Longman and Roberts, 1860), from London, British Library, Harley MS 3859; see also Bede 1:15 (Colgrave and Mynors, 48–53)

33. B. Hope-Taylor, *Yeavering: An Anglo-British Centre of Early Northumbria,* Department of the Environment Archaeological Reports, vol. 7 (London: HMSO, 1977), 276–282.

34. Lohaus, *Die Merovinger und England,* 26–27.

35. Ibid., 10. Lohaus suggests that Liudhard instigated Gregory the Great's mission of Augustine to England from Rome.

36. Ibid., 16–17; see also Ernulf, bishop of Rochester, *Textus Roffensis:* ed. Peter Sawyer (Copenhagen: Rosenkilde and Bagger, 1926).

37. J. D. A. Thompson, *Inventory of British Coin Hoards, A.D. 600–1500,* Royal Numismatic Society, Special Publications, vol. 1 (London, 1956); and C. E. Blunt and R. H. M. Dolley, "The Anglo-Saxon Coins in the Vatican Library," *British Numismatic Journal,* 3d ser., 8 (1955–57): 449–58.

38. N. Åberg, *The Anglo-Saxons in England during the Early Centuries after the Invasion* (Uppsala: Almqvist and Wiksells, 1926), 90–106.

39. Richard Avent, "An Anglo-Saxon Variant of a Merovingian Rounded Plaque Buckle," *Medieval Archaeology* 17 (1973): 126–28.

40. G. C. Dunning, "Trade Relations between England and the Continent in the Late Anglo-Saxon Period," in *Dark Age Britain: Studies Presented to E. T. Leeds,* ed. D. B. Harden (London: Methuen, 1956), 218–33; and J. G. Hurst, "The Pottery," in *The Archaeology of Anglo-Saxon England, ed. David M. Wilson (London: Methuen, 1976), 311–13.*

41. J. Strzygowski, *Koptische Kunst,* Catalogue générale des antiquités Égyptiennes du Musée du Caire (Vienna: A. Holzhausen, 1904), cat. nos. 9044, 9047, 9068, 9118.

42. Åberg, *Anglo-Saxons,* fig. 187.

43. Ibid., fig. 191.

44. Ibid., fig. 189; see also *Victoria History of the Counties of England: Buckinghamshire,* ed. William Page (1905; reprint, London: Dawson's, 1969), 1:202.

45. Åberg, *Anglo-Saxons,* 103–5.

46. A. O. Curle, *The Treasure of Traprain* (Glascow: Maclehose and Jackson, 1923).

47. R. L. S. Bruce-Mitford, *The Sutton Hoo Ship Burial: A Handbook,* 2d ed. (London: British Museum, 1972), 65–66; Charles Green, *Sutton Hoo: The Excavation of a Royal Ship Burial,*

2d ed. (London: Merlin Press, 1968), 74; Ernst Kitzinger, "The Sutton Hoo Ship Burial V: The Silver," *Antiquity* 14 (1940): 40–50; idem, "The Sutton Hoo Finds III: The Silver," *British Museum Quarterly* 13 (1938): 118–21. See also E. C. Dodd, *Byzantine Silver Stamps* (Washington, D.C.: Dumbarton Oaks, 1961), 58–59.

48. Bruce-Mitford, *Sutton Hoo: Handbook*, 66; C. Green, *Sutton Hoo*, 74; Kitzinger, "Ship Burial V," 50–62; idem, "Sutton Hoo Finds III," 121–22.

49. Kitzinger, "Sutton Hoo Finds III," 121–22. The cymatium motif resembles that on a silver amphora from Poltawa.

50. Kitzinger, "Ship Burial V," 52; idem, "Sutton Hoo Finds III," 122–24.

51. Bruce-Mitford, *Sutton Hoo: Handbook*, 66–68; idem, *The Sutton Hoo Ship Burial* (London: British Museum, 1975), 1:683–717.

52. Bede 1.32, 2.10, 2.11 (Colgrave and Mynors, 114–15, 170–71, 174–75).

53. Bruce-Mitford, *Sutton Hoo: Handbook*, 68; Green, *Sutton Hoo*, 75. Kitzinger, "Ship Burial V," 52–62, discusses possible routes of importation. Kitzinger, "Sutton Hoo Finds III," 124–26, discusses parallel find of set of spoons as part of Lampsacus treasure, bearing names of apostles. The Mildenhall Treasure (British Museum) also contains spoons with Christian symbols.

54. R. E. Kaske, "The Silver Spoons of Sutton Hoo," *Speculum* 52 (1967): 670–72.

55. Bruce-Mitford, *Sutton Hoo: Handbook*, 68–69.

56. A. F. Griffith, "An Anglo-Saxon Cemetery at Alfriston, Susex," *Sussex Archaeological Collections* 57 (1905): pl. 29.

57. Bruce-Mitford, *Sutton Hoo Ship Burial*, "Who Was He?" 1:688–90.

58. Bruce-Mitford, *Sutton Hoo: Handbook*, 65–66.

59. F. Graus, *Volk, Herrscher, und Heiliger im Reich der Merovinger* (Prague: Nakladatelstvi Československe Akademie věd, 1965), passim; B. Young, *Merovingian Funeral Rites and the Evolution of Christianity: A Study in the Historical Interpretation of Archaeological Material*, Ph.D. diss., University of Pennsylvania, 1961.

60. D. M. Wilson, *Reflections on the St. Ninian's Isle Treasure*, Jarrow Lecture (Jarrow: The Rectory, 1970); A. Small, ed., *St. Ninian's Isle and Its Treasure* (Oxford: Oxford University Press, 1970).

61. Bruce-Mitford, *Sutton Hoo Ship Burial*, "Coins and the Date of Burial," 1:578–88; P. Grierson, "The Dating of the Sutton Hoo Coins," *Antiquity* 26 (1952): 83–86. The Merovingian coins at Sutton Hoo, Grierson has suggested, were probably not acquired in the normal course of trade. No two were of the same mint, and the coins were probably assembled as a collection, possibly with ritual connotations.

62. R.L.S. Bruce-Mitford, "The Sutton Hoo Ship Burial," *Proceedings of the Suffolk Institute of Archaeology* 25 (1949–51): 1–78, esp. 19. Such a traditional pagan monument to the secular fame of a royal Christian convert is not unique if, as according to José Ruyschaert, the Arch of Constantine has similar implications (see José Ruyschaert, "Essai d'interprétation synthétique de l'Arc de Constantin," *Atti della Pontificia Accademia Roma* 79 [1962–63]: 79–100).

63. Bruce-Mitford, "Sutton Hoo Ship Burial," 41.

64. Bruce-Mitford, *Sutton Hoo Ship Burial*, 1:66.

65. A. Meaney, *A Gazetteer of Early Anglo-Saxon Burial Sites* (London: G. Allen and Unwin, 1964), 13–21; and A. Meaney and S. C. Hawkes, *Two Anglo-Saxon Cemeteries at Winall, Winchester, Hants.*, Society for Medieval Archaeology Monograph Series (London, 1970), 4:50–55.

66. Bede 2.5 (Colgrave and Mynors, 148–51). For discussion of the origin of the term *bretwalda* and its symbolic or real content, see Patrick Wormald, "Bede, the *Bretwaldas* and the Origins of the *Gens Anglorum*," in *Ideal and Reality in Frankish and Anglo-Saxon Society: Studies presented to J. M. Wallace-Hadrill* (Oxford: Basil Blackwell, 1983); M. Deanesley, "Roman Traditionalist Influences among the Anglo-Saxons," *English Historical Review* 58 (1943): 129–30; Bruce-Mitford, "Sutton Hoo Ship Burial," 13–14.

67. Bede 2.15 (Colgrave and Mynors, 188–91).

68. Bruce-Mitford, *Sutton Hoo Ship Burial*, 1:683.

69. Bruce-Mitford, *Sutton Hoo: Handbook*, 58.

70. See note 30, above.

71. D. Longley, *Hanging Bowls, Penannular Brooches and the Anglo-Saxon Connection,* British Archaeological Reports, vol. 22 (1975).

72. Ibid., 14, 35–36.

73. For discussion of the provenance of the hanging bowls, see T. D. Kendrick, "British Hanging Bowls," *Antiquity* 6 (1932): 161–84; F. Henry, "Hanging Bowls," *Journal of the Royal Society of Antiquaries of Ireland* 66 (1936): 209–246; idem, "Irish Enamels of the Dark Ages and Their Relation to the *Cloisonné* Techniques," in *Dark Age Britain: Studies Presented to E. T. Leeds,* ed. D. B. Harden (London: Methuen, 1956), 71–88; H. Vierck, "*Cortina Tripodis:* Zu Aufhängung und Gebrauch südrömischer Hängebecken aus Britannien und Irland," *Frühmittelalterliche Studien* 4 (1970); 8–52; E. Fowler, "Hanging Bowls," in *Studies in Ancient Europe: Essays Presented to Stuart Piggott,* ed. J. M. Coles and D.D.A. Simpson (New York: Humanities Press, 1968), 287.

74. Vierck, "*Cortina Tripodis,*" 13–14; also used in Roman kitchen practice as *mortuaria.*

75. Henry, *IAECP,* 35.

76. Vierck, "*Cortina Tripodis,*" 24.

77. Ibid., 37–38, fig. 11.

78. Ibid., 39, fig. 11.

79. Henry, "Irish Enamels," 81; Vierck, "*Cortina Tripodis,*" 28.

80. Longley, *Hanging Bowls,* 14–15.

81. Ibid., 15–16.

82. Henry, "Irish Enamels," passim.

83. Ibid.; and also Henry, *IAECP,* 35 and 68, who notes millefiori rods found by O'Ríordáin at Garranes and millefiori rods and molds for casting bronze bosses found by Hencken (1934–36 Harvard Archaeological Expedition to Ireland) at Lagore Crannog.

84. Alcock, *Arthur's Britain,* 233–34.

85. Longley, *Hanging Bowls,* 30–32; L. Laing, "The Mote of Mark and the Origins of Celtic Interlace," *Antiquity* 49 (1975), 98–108; R. B. K. Stevenson, "Pictish Art," in *The Problem of the Picts,* ed. F. T. Wainwright (Edinburgh: T. Nelson, 1955), 106–12.

86. Longley, *Hanging Bowls,* 32–33.

87. Ibid., 36. Despite the growing trend to consider the Anglo-Saxon invasion of England as a progressive colonization, dominated in the archaeological record by evidence of agrarian coexistence, one must not underestimate the importance of Gildas and the *Gododdin,* and the cultural disparity and mutual violence of action and sentiment of Celt and Anglo-Saxon that they reflect.

Chapter 2. Historical Circumstances of the Northumbrian Renaissance

1. For the art and culture of the Picts, see Wainwright, *Problem of the Picts;* I. M. Henderson, *The Picts* (London: Thames and Hudson, 1967). For an overview of their culture and the extent of their territory, see Charles Thomas, *Britain and Ireland in Early Christian Times, A.D. 400–800* (London: McGraw-Hill, 1971), 42–53 and maps, 46.

2. A. Dornier, ed., *Mercian Studies* (Leicester: University of Leicester Press, 1977).

3. Blair, *Anglo-Saxon England,* 43; idem, *Northumbria in the Days of Bede* (New York: St. Martin's Press, 1976), 27. The evidence cited here for the employment of Saxons by the Romans as mercenaries along the northern frontier of Roman Britain suggests the possibility that the invitation of the British chieftains to Anglian and Saxon mercenaries in the fifth century was not so much an act of desperation as an emulation of the practices of their own former legionary overlords, and that the gradual development of Saxon settlements in England may have a small but real foundation in the Roman period.

4. Blair, *Anglo-Saxon England,* 43; *Anglo-Saxon Chronicle,* 18–19; Parker and Laud Chronicles for 560; D. P. Kirby, "Northumbria in the Time of Wilfrid," in *St. Wilfrid at Hexham,* ed. D. P. Kirby (Newcastle upon Tyne: Oriel Press, 1974), 18, pedigree I.

5. Blair, *Anglo-Saxon England,* 43–44; Bede 5.24 (Colgrave and Mynors, 562–63).

6. Blair, *Days of Bede,* 28; idem, *Origins of Northumbria* (Gateshead: Northumbrian Press, 1948).

7. Hope-Taylor, *Yeavering*, 276–324; K. H. Jackson, *The Gododdin* (Edinburgh: Edinburgh University Press, 1969).

8. Bede 1.34, 2.2 (Colgrave and Mynors, 140–43).

9. Ibid., 2.2 (176–81).

10. Blair, *Days of Bede*, 42. This triad is not in the historically questionable collection of Iolo Morganwg, and Blair does not cite his source.

11. Bede 2.12 (Colgrave and Mynors, 176–81).

12. Ibid., 2.15 (188–91)

13. Ibid., 2.12 (176–83).

14. Ibid., 1.25 (72–77).

15. Ibid. Here Bede mentions that at their first contact with the court of Kent, Augustine and his associates had with them a silver cross standard and an icon of Christ painted on wood.

16. Bede 2.12 (Colgrave and Mynors 180–81).

17. Ibid., 2.13 (182–87).

18. Ibid., 2.14 (186–87).

19. Ibid., 2.16 (192–93).

20. Ibid., 3.1 (212–15).

21. Ibid., 3.3 (218–19).

22. J. T. McNeill, "The Christian Mission in Scotland: St. Columba," *The Celtic Churches: A History, A.D. 200–1200* (Chicago: University of Chicago Press, 1974), 87; Hughes, *Early Christian Ireland: Sources*, 222, on Adamnan's *Life of Columba*, and 235, on the *Irish Life of Columcille*. See also A. O. Anderson and M. O. Anderson, *Adomnan's Life of Columba* (London: T. Nelson, 1961); W. Stokes, *Lives of the Saints from the Book of Lismore* (Oxford: Clarendon Press, 1890), lines 655–1119.

23. De Paor and de Paor, *Early Christian Ireland*, 49; Henry, *IAECP*, 64–65; J. Raftery, "Ex Oriente," *Journal of the Royal Society of Antiquaries of Ireland* 95 (1965): 193–204.

24. F. E. Warren, *The Antiphonary of Bangor* (London: Harrison and Sons, 1893), 2:28; also quoted in Henry, *IAECP*, 64.

25. Hughes, *Early Christian Ireland: Sources*, on Muirchu's *Vita*, 229–32; on the Tripartite *Vita*, 239–43; and McNeill, *Celtic Churches*, 69–70.

26. McNeill, *Celtic Churches*, 69–70. For the traditional, contradictory view, see de Paor and de Paor, *Early Christian Ireland*, 49, for the possible connection of Patrick to Lérins.

27. N. K. Chadwick, *Age of the Saints*, 22–23.

28. M. Dillon and N. K. Chadwick, "Secular Institutions: Early Irish Society," *The Celtic Realms* (New York: Weidenfeld and Nicholson, 1967), 92–109. See also Hughes, "The Secular Laws," *Early Christian Ireland: Sources* 43–64, for the primary sources on kinship, social status, and property holding. The complexity and all-inclusivity of this legal system makes self-evident the possible consequences of separation of self from kin group and social caste.

29. Bede 3.4 (Colgrave and Mynors, 222–25); K. Hughes, *The Church in Early Irish Society* (London: Methuen, 1966), 130–33; McNeill, *Celtic Churches, 70.*

30. N. K. Chadwick, *Age of the Saints*, 26–32. This was not the first incident of a power struggle between episcopal and monastic authorities. Documents from fifth-century Gaul give evidence of hostility between bishops and abbots of new ascetic communities, particularly in the election of new bishops. Pope Celestine's decree *Cupremus Quidem* (25 July, 428) takes issue with the practice of appointing foreign monastic clergy over local candidates.

31. Bede 2.2, 5.23 (Colgrave and Mynors 134–37, 560–61).

32. H. Mayr-Harting, *The Coming of Christianity to Britain* (New York: Schocken Books, 1972), 103–5, presents a clear summary of the issues of *computatio* that surrounded the English Easter question.

33. Bede 3.2 (Colgrave and Mynors, 218–21), narrates the foundation of Lindisfarne. Oswy succeeded to the throne of Bernicia after Oswald was killed by the Mercians in the Battle of Maserfelth, probably modern Oswestry on the Welsh Marches, on 5 August 642. At that time, Oswin, of the line of Edwin, attained the throne of Deira. Shortly thereafter, however, Oswin was

betrayed to and murdered by Oswy, who had inherited Bernicia from his brother. Oswy thus reconsolidated the Northumbrian kingdom and became the third Northumbrian ruler of England (Bede 3.9, 3.14 [Colgrave and Mynors, 240–43, 254–57]).

34. Bede 2.9, 2.20, 3.15, 3.25 (Colgrave and Mynors, 162–65, 204–5, 260–61, 294–97).

35. Ibid., 3.25 (294–97).

36. Symbol of Matthew, the Man, in the *Book of Durrow* (Dublin, Trinity College Library, A.4.5 fol. 21v. See also Luke (Fulda, Landesbibliothek, Cod. *Bonifatianus* 3, fol. 33v.); and possibly the Crucifixion (Christ, lancebearer, and spongebearer) (Durham, Cathedral Library, A.II.17, fol. 383v.).

37. See Bede 3.25, 3.26 on the Synod of Whitby and the conformity of Lindisfarne, 5.21 on Ceolfrith's advice to Nechtan concerning Pictish orthodoxy, and 5.22 on the conformity of Iona under Egbert (Colgrave and Mynors, 296–311, 532–55).

38. Bede 5.21 (Colgrave and Mynors, 548–49). The biblical source is Acts 8.

39. L. Hardinge, *The Celtic Church in Britain* (London: Society for Promoting Christian Knowledge, 1972), 194–96. Hardinge makes reference to the use of tonsure as a mark of status in pre-Christian Celtic society without citing a source.

40. Mayr-Harting, *Coming of Christianity*, 164.

41. Bede 3.25 (Colgrave and Mynors, 298–309); C. W. Jones, *Bedae Opera de Temporibus* (Cambridge, Mass.: Medieval Academy of America, 1943), for Bede's work on *computatio;* Aldhelm, *De Controversia Paschali,* Monumenta Germaniae Historica: Auctores Antiquissimorum, ed. W. R. Ehwald (Berlin: Weidmans, 1919), 4:485–86; Theodore of Canterbury, *Penitential,* in J. T. McNeill, *Medieval Handbooks of Penance: A Translation of the Principal Libri Poenitentiales and Selections from Related Documents,* Records of Civilization vol. 29, (New York: Columbia University Press, 1965).

42. Hardinge, *Celtic Church,* 73–101.

43. Mayr-Harting, *Coming of Christianity*, 164.

44. Ibid., 112; McNeill, *Celtic Churches*, 158–59.

45. Bede 2.19 (Colgrave and Mynors, 198–203).

46. McNeill, *Celtic Churches,* 110–111; Hardinge, *Celtic Church,* 23–25.

47. Bede 5.15, 5.21 (Colgrave and Mynors, 504–7, 532–53); Hardinge, *Celtic Church,* 25.

48. Hardinge, *Celtic Church,* 27–28.

49. Bede 2.2 (Colgrave and Mynors 134–41).

50. Ibid., 2.4 (144–47).

51. Ibid., 2.5, 2.6 (150–57).

52. Ibid., 3.15–17 (260–65).

53. Ibid., 3.25 (294–97).

54. Ibid., 2.20 (206–7).

55. Agilbert subsequently became bishop of Paris. Later he retired to the women's convent at Jouarre in the Marne Valley, east of Paris, ironically one of the foundations of Columbanus, that outspoken champion of the Irish Easter. Agilbert's sarcophagus is still to be seen in the crypt at Jouarre, and is one of the most enigmatic works of Merovingian stone carving, possibly incorporating Eastern style elements and iconography. See also J. Hubert, J. Porscher, and W. Volbach, *Europe of the Invasions* (New York: G. Braziller, 1969), 77.

56. Eddius Stephanus, *Life of Wilfrid* 24–34, 45–65, in *Lives of the Saints,* trans. J. F. Webb (Harmondsworth: Penguin Books, 1965), 156–68.

57. Bede 3.25 (Colgrave and Mynors 296–69).

58. Ibid., 3.25 (306–7).

59. Mayr-Harting, *Coming of Christianity*, 107–9.

60. Another documentary source, the badly damaged runic inscription on the Bewcastle Cross, may possibly refer to the fate of Alchfrith. Early antiquarians of the nineteenth century, including Dr. Maughan, rector of Bewcastle, and G. Stephens, the noted early runologist, suggested that the much-weathered inscription could be made out as a dedication of the cross as a memorial to Alchfrith, set up in "the first year of Ecgfrith's reign" (673 or 674), by "Hwaetred," and possibly "Olufwulf," the latter possibly identifiable as Aldwulf, king of East Anglia. Other names read

elsewhere on the cross include "Cyniburg," the daughter of Penda of Mercia who married Alchfrith of Deira in an attempt by Oswy to mingle the royal lines of the two nations and bring to an end a series of costly wars in the 650s (Bede 3.21 [Colgrave and Mynors, 278–79]), and possibly also "Cyniswitha," Penda's queen, and "Wulfhere," his younger son and leader of a revolt against Oswy in 658–59. Speculation on the meaning of these fragments tends to the melodramatic—Alchfrith involved with an uprising of Mercians and southern rulers against his father. Unfortunately, as R. I. Page noted in 1960, all that is legible today is the diphthong "lcfri" in the main inscription, and the name "Cyniburg," which is a common Anglian feminine given name. Moreover, the early readings were sufficiently controversial in their own day that one must consider them unreliable as documentation, despite the tantalizing possibilities. Finally the absence of further mention of Alchfrith in Bede, who even discusses Northumbrian kings whose names had been dropped from the king lists because of their shameful acts (Bede 3.1 [Colgrave and Mynors, 214–15]), suggests that Alchfrith's end was obscure rather than infamous. H. Bütow, *Das Altenglische Traumgeschichte vom Kreuz* (Heidelberg: C. Winter, 1935), gives a complete survey of the early bibliography on the Ruthwell and Bewcastle crosses. See also R. I. Page, "The Bewcastle Cross," *Nottingham Medieval Studies* 4(1960): 36–57.

61. Bede 3.28 (Colgrave and Mynors, 314–17).

62. Eddius 14 (Webb, 146–47).

63. Bede 3.28 (Colgrave and Mynors, 314–17).

64. Ibid., 1.27 (86–89).

65. Eddius 15 (Webb, 147). Ironically, in the previous chapter, Eddius calls Chad "a Celt but a truly devout servant of God and a great teacher," apparently echoing Bede, and, directly after the "thief" remark, he is valuable concerning Chad's humility and his willingness to do penance for his "fault" at having been used by "those Quartodecimans."

66. Two previous heresies had taken root in England, the Arian and the Pelagian. In sending Theodore, Vitalian was following the example of the bishops of Gaul who had sent Germanus of Auxerre and Lupus of Troyes to England in 429 to quell an outbreak of Pelagianism. See Bede 1.8, 1.10, 1.17–22 (Colgrave and Mynors, 34–37, 54–69).

67. Eddius 14 (Webb, 146–47).

68. Bede 4.2–3 (Colgrave and Mynors, 334–47).

69. Eddius 14–15 (Webb, 146–48).

70. Bede 4.2 (Colgrave and Mynors, 334–35).

71. Eddius 34, 39, 58–59 (Webb, 167–68, 171–72, 194–96).

72. Bede, *Lives of the Abbots*, in *Anglo-Saxon Saints and Heroes*, trans. C. Albertson (New York: Fordham University Press, 1967) 225–42, narrates the foundation of Jarrow and Monkwearmouth by Benedict Biscop, and details the ideals of their founder.

73. See Chapter 5 on the *Lindisfarne Gospels* and the *Codex Amiatinus*.

74. Theodore of Canterbury, *Penitential*, in McNeill, *Medieval Handbooks of Penance*, 206–7.

75. Eddius 15 (Webb, 148).

76. Hardinge, *Celtic Church* 22–23.

77. A poem allegedly by the Welsh poet Taliessyn, translated by Archbishop Ussher in the seventeenth century, puts in a nutshell the attitude of the Welsh Church before conformity:

> Wo be to that priest yborn
> That will not cleanly weed his corn
> And preach his charge among:
> Wo be to that shepherd (I say,)
> That will not watch his fold alway
> As to his office doth belong:
> Wo be to him that doth not keep
> From Romish wolves his sheep
> With staff and weapons strong.

78. Hardinge, *Celtic Church*, 25–26.

79. Ibid., 20.

80. Bede 5.21 (Colgrave and Mynors, 552–53).

81. E. John, "The Social and Political Problems of the Early English Church," in *Land, Church and People: Essays Presented to H. P. R. Finberg*, ed. D. Thirsk, supplement to *Agricultural History Review* 18 (1970): 39–63; discusses continuing political crises with secular authorities.

Chapter 3. Art in the Early Celtic Church: The *Book of Durrow* and Its Context

1. Bowen, *Saints, Seaways and Settlements*. Toponymic evidence for the progress of the missionaries follows the distribution of imported pottery.

2. Hughes, *Early Christian Ireland: Sources*, 82–89; Ludwig Bieler, ed., *The Irish Penitentials*, Scriptores Latini Hiberniae, vol. 5 (Dublin: Institute for Advanced Studies, 1963).

3. Hughes, *Early Christian Ireland: Sources*, 82–83.

4. W. Rutherford, *The Druids and Their Heritage* (London: Gordon and Cremonesi, 1978), 41.

5. Rutherford, *Druids*, 84; Henry, *IAECP*, 21.

6. Henry, *IAECP*, 58–59.

7. Ibid., 76–84.

8. Henry, *IAECP*, 81, 135, fig. 17.

9. *Anonymous Life of Cuthbert* 3.1, in *Anglo-Saxon Saints and Heroes*, 51–5.

10. Bede, *Life of Cuthbert* 17, *Lives of the Saints*, 95.

11. P. Rahtz, "Buildings and Rural Settlement," in *The Archaeology of Anglo-Saxon England*, ed. D. M. Wilson (London: Methuen, 1976), 49–98; P. V. Addyman, "The Anglo-Saxon House," in *The Anglo-Saxons: Studies in Some Aspects of Their History and Culture Presented to Bruce Dickins*, ed. P. A. M. Clemoes, (London: Bowes and Bowes, 1956), 273–307.

12. Henry, *IAECP*, 52, fig. 2, a and b.

13. Bede 4.3 (Colgrave and Mynors, 336–39).

14. Bede 5.2 (Colgrave and Mynors, 456–59).

15. R. Cramp, "Anglo-Saxon Monasteries of the North," *Scottish Archaeological Forum* 5 (1973): 104–8; R. Reese, "Recent Work at Iona," *Scottish Archaeological Forum* 5 (1973): 38. Neither Lindisfarne nor Iona has yielded evidence of monastic layout.

16. Bede 3.19 (Colgrave and Mynors, 270–71); Cramp, "Monasteries of the North," 104–8.

17. R. Cramp, "Monastic Sites," *Archaeology of Anglo-Saxon England*, 203–5.

18. Ibid., 201–41; Charles Thomas, *The Early Christian Archaeology of North Britain: The Hunter Marshall Lectures Delivered at the University of Glasgow in January and February, 1968* (Oxford: Oxford University Press, 1971), lists Scottish monasteries using the *rath* plan: Applecross (Wester Ross), Kingarth (Bute), and Abercorn (Lothian).

19. Bede 4.23 (Colgrave and Mynors, 406–7). Hartlepool, or *Heruteu*, was founded by Heiu, according to Bede the first Northumbrian woman to take religious orders, with the blessings of Aidan of Iona. Bede makes plain in his text that Northumbrian noblewomen entered religious life when widowed or not in a position to make an advantageous marriage. Often they founded new communities with funds from royal relatives.

20. C. R. Peers and C. A. Ralegh Radford, "The Saxon Monastery at Whitby," *Archaeologia* 89 (1943): 27–88.

21. Bede 4.23 (Colgrave and Mynors, 406–7).

22. Ibid. (408–9).

23. F. Masai and B. Bischoff, "Il monachesimo Irlandese nei suoi rapporti col Continente," in *Il monachesimo nell'alto medioevo e la forma della civiltà occidentale*, Settimane di Studio del Centro Italiano di Studi sull'alto Medioevo, Spoleto, 4 (1957): 138–72, with appended discussion by M. Werner and G. Parisi.

24. Cramp, "Monastic Sites," 228.

25. Bede 3.25 (Colgrave and Mynors, 298–99).

26. Peers and Radford, "Saxon Monastery at Whitby," plan.

27. Bede 3.25 (Colgrave and Mynors, 420–27).

28. Cramp, "Monasteries of the North," 112–14.

29. *Opus signinum*, or powdered-brick flooring, also occurs at Jarrow and Monkswearmouth. This Late Antique method for inexpensively finishing an earthen floor survived at Anglo-Saxon centers with awareness of Roman traditions and practicalities.

30. Henry, *IAECP*, 84.

31. De Paor and de Paor, *Early Christian Ireland*, 56–60, pl. 9.

32. Bede 3.25 (Colgrave and Mynors, 294–95).

33. Hope-Taylor, *Yeavering*, 124–49.

34. Hughes, *Early Christian Ireland: Sources*, 228; M. Esposito, "On the Earliest Latin Life of St. Brigid of Kildare," *Proceedings of the Royal Irish Academy* 30 (1912):307–26.

35. Henry, *IAECP*, 84–86, pls.22, 23, show cross lintels at Fore (Westmeath) and Clonamery (Kilkenny).

36. H. M. Taylor and J. Taylor, *Anglo-Saxon Architecture* (Cambridge: Cambridge University Press, 1965) 1:91–93.

37. *Treasures of Early Irish Art;* J. Brailsford, *Early Celtic Masterpieces from Britain in the British Museum* (London: British Museum, 1975); Sean P. O'Ríordáin, "Roman Material in Ireland," *Proceedings of the Royal Irish Academy 51(c) (1947):35–82; Henry, IAECP,* 13–14.

38. Exceptions to this general rule include two groups objects. First, a group of primitive stone heads of unknown purpose, one from Tanderagee (co. Armagh) now in Armagh Cathedral, another from Boa Island (co. Fermanagh) (Henry, *IAECP*, pls. 3,2). The importance of the disembodied or severed head in pre-Christian Celtic religious practice is discussed by Diodorus and Strabo, on the authority of Posidonius (M. Dillon and N. K. Chadwick, *The Celtic Realms* [New York: Weidenfeld and Nicholson, 1967] 295–96). Indeed, there is an entire tradition of naturalistic head sculptures in Celtic Gaul, culminating in the first century B.C., both in the area of the mouth of the Rhone and in central Gaul. It is possible that the Irish examples are related to a similar cult practice. See also Henry, *IAECP*, 7–8. Second, a group of metalwork animal figures, such as the boar from the crest of the helmet found at Benty Grange (Derbs.), and the stag from the top of the ceremonial whetstone found at Sutton Hoo, are apparently emblems or totems of secular authority and carry over to the royal practices of Anglo-Saxons.

39. P. MacCana, *Celtic Mythology* (Feltham: Hamlyn, 1970), 34.

40. Henry, *IAECP*, 70.

41. Ibid., pls. 7, 8; *Treasures of Early Irish Art*, pl. 39.

42. Henry, *IAECP*, 14–15.

43. Hughes, *Early Christian Ireland: Sources*, 165–90; Dillon and Chadwick, *Celtic Realms,* 206; N. K. Chadwick, *Age of the Saints* 13. The literature of the secular society was preserved in oral tradition in the case of trained bards. In Britain, a stone-carving script, *ogham*, was evolved for inscriptions, in emulation of Roman legionary markers.

44. J. J. G. Alexander, *Insular Manuscripts: Sixth to the Ninth Century* (London: Harvey Miller, 1978), 27.

45. C. Nordenfalk, *Die spätantike Zierbuchstaben* (Stockholm: Egnellska, 1970), 69, pls. 17–23.

46. Ibid., pls. 31–32. The red-dot tradition is apparently continued in the East, for enlarged initials with red dots also occur in the *Armenian Gospels* (Jerusalem, Armenian Patriarchal Library 2555, fol. 192r) of the tenth or eleventh century.

47. Nordenfalk, *Die spätantike Zierbuchstaben*, pls. 47–8.

48. Ibid., pls. 61–67.

49. Ibid., 212–16, fig. 68.

50. C. Nordenfalk, "Before the *Book of Durrow*," *Acta Archaeologica* 18 (1947): 149.

51. E. A. Lowe, *Codices Latini Antiquiores* (Oxford: Clarendon Press, 1935), 2:271.

52. Nordenfalk, "Before *Durrow*," 149; Henry, *IAECP*, 62; D. Wright, commentary in A. Dold and L. Eizenhöfer, "Das Irische Palimpsest-Sakramentar in Clm. 14429 der Staatsbibliothek München," *Texte und Arbeiten* 53–54 (1964): 36–37; E. C. R. Armstrong and R. A. S. MacAlister,

"Wooden Box with Leaves Indented and Waxed Found near Springmount Bog, co. Antrim," *Journal of the Royal Society of Antiquaries of Ireland* 6th ser., 10 (1920): 160. Henry, while accepting a possible Bobbio provenance for the *Codex Usserianus Primus,* also compares the staurogram to an inscribed cross on the Loher Slab (Kerry). She finds their similarity coincidental, but they may have models of similar provenance, or the *Codex* itself may have been the vehicle of importation for the motif. Wright believes the *Codex Usserianus Primus* was written in Ireland, based on paleographic similarities to the Psalter inscribed on the Springmount bog tablets, although he agrees with Lowe and Nordenfalk on the Late Antique and Italianate roots of the *Codex.* The bog tablets themselves may have been copied from imported codices, but Wright conversely conjectures that the similarity places *Usserianus Primus* in Ireland. He sees the *Codex* as representing an early phase of illumination in Ireland, in which imported models were emulated without alteration before a native style evolved. However, other early Irish manuscripts made significant changes in received motifs without hesitancy.

53. F. Henry, "Les débuts de la miniature irlandaise," *Gazette des Beaux Arts* 6th ser., 37 (1950): 22.

54. Alexander, *Insular Manuscripts,* 28. The manuscripts is no. 52 in the Bobbio inventory of 1461, bears a Bobbio ex libris of the fifteenth century, and was given by the monks to the Ambrosian Library at its foundation in 1606.

55. Ibid.; T. J. Brown et al., *Evangeliorum Quattuor Codex Lindisfarnensis,* ed. T. D. Kendrick (Olten: Urs Graf Verlag, 1956), 2 :113–15, pls. 10a, b, d. Alexander gives a full analysis of color use in this illumination.

56. Dedication page of the *Vienna Dioscurides* (Vienna, Nationalbibliothek MS Med. Gr. 1, fol. 6v), made in Constantinople about 512; Hare Nibbling a Bunch of Grapes, textile fragment from Egypt, private collection (C. Schug-Wille, *Art of the Byzantine World* [New York: Harry N. Abrams, 1969] 134).

57. Alexander, *Insular Manuscripts,* pl. 19.

58. Ibid., 11; Lowe, *Codices,* 3 :328; Henry, *IAECP,* 63 n. 1; Wright in Dold and Eizenhöfer, "Irische Palimpsest-Sakramentar." The date of the *Ambrosian Chronicon* has been debated. Lowe believed the text seventh century and the illumination a later addition. This is unlikely, on the basis of the integration of initials and text and the awkward handling of insular diminution, which probably indicates an early date, as does the legibility of the initial monogram. Also, the rosette is uncommon in insular illumination and indicates close links to a Late Antique model rather than reliance on indigenous aesthetics, as is common in later codices. The use of pink is also common in Late Antique codices and rare in insular illumination. Wright places the *Chronicon* in his early emulative phase along with the *Codex Usserianus Primus,* but does not note the experimental enlargement of initials or insular diminution, nor does he credit Bobbio as a significant point of transmission of Late Antique ideas to insular art.

59. Henry, *IAECP,* 58–60; Alexander, *Insular Manuscripts,* 28–29, no. 4; *Betha Colaim Chille: The Life of Columcille, Complied by Manus O'Donnell in 1532,* ed. A. O'Kelleher and G. Schoeperle (Urbana: University of Illinois Press, 1918), 14 :182–83.

60. Henry, *IAECP,* 60; Warren, *Antiphonary of Bangor,* 2 :39. Henry points out that St. Finnian of Moville is supposed to have brought a Gospels text to Ireland from Rome, and she speculates that he may also have brought a Vulgate Psalter that St. Columba or a contemporary may have copied into the *Cathach.*

61. Alexander, *Insular Manuscripts,* 29.

62. Ibid., pls. 4, 5.

63. Wright, in Dold and Eizenhöfer, "Irische Palimpsest-Sakramentar," 36–37.

64. T. J. Brown et al., *Codex Lindisfarnensis,* 2 :112–13.

65. Lowe, *Codices,* 2 :266.

66. T. J. Brown et al., *Codex Lindisfarnensis,* 2 :112–3; Henry, *IAECP,* 61; Henry, "Les débuts," 27–28; Wright, in Dold and Eizenhöfer, "Irische Palimpsest-Sakramentar," 36–37. Wright pushes his date up to the 630s, and Henry at one point pressed for a date of ca. 640, to allow the codex to postdate the Bobbio manuscripts.

67. Alexander, *Insular Manuscripts,* 29–30; Lowe, *Codices,* 2 :147; R. A. B. Mynors, *Durham*

Cathedral Manuscripts to the End of the Twelfth Century (Oxford: Oxford University Press, 1939), 17–18; T. J. Brown, "Northumbria and the *Book of Kells,*" *Anglo-Saxon England* 1 (1971): 227–29.

68. Henry, *IAECP,* 165.

69. A. A. Luce et al., *Evangeliorum Quattuor Codex Durmachensis,* (Olten: Urs Graf Verlag, 1960), 2:94–95.

70. Henry, *IAECP,* 166.

71. Another possible candidate is the Irish palimpsest sacramentary in Munich (see Dold and Eizenhöfer, "Irische Palimpsest-Sakramentar," 34–40).

72. *Treasures of Early Irish Art,* pl. 32.

73. A. M. Hadfield, J. S. Wacher, and D. J. Viner, *Cirencester: The Roman Corinium* (Gloucester: British Publishing Company, 1975), 34, show examples of interlace in Romano-British mosaic borders. Interlace is also common in Coptic textiles, which preserve a repertory of Late Antique decorative motifs. W. Y. Adams, "Celtic Interlace and Coptic Interlace," *Antiquity* 49 (1975): 301–3, suggests that Celtic art may have been the source of Coptic interlace, although the reverse is usually conjectured. P. W. Joyce, *A Social History of Ancient Ireland* (London: Longmans, 1903), 1:551, discusses possible transmission to Ireland from Byzantine and Lombard sources. G. Haseloff, "Fragments of a Hanging Bowl from Bekesbourne, Kent, and Some Ornamental Problems," *Medieval Archaeology* 2 (1958): 72–103, considers Bobbio responsible for the transmission of this and other ornamental motifs, but more probably they were transmitted from the Mediterranean basin to Ireland via a number of centers and media.

74. J. Romilly Allen, *Celtic Art in Pagan and Christian Times* (London: Philip Jacobs, [1904]), 259–30, considers breaks to originate in Lombard art.

75. H. Bober, "On the Illumination of the *Glazier Codex,*" in *Homage to a Bookman: Essays on Manuscripts, Books and Printing Written for Hans P. Kraus,* ed. H. Lehmann-Haupt (Berlin: Mann, 1967), 31–40, discusses at length the interlace of the earliest extant Coptic cross frontispiece.

76. Laing, "Mote of Mark," 68–108.

77. Ibid.; G. F. Mitchell, "Foreign Influences and the Beginnings of Christian Art," in *Treasures of Early Irish Art,* 59.

78. Henry, *IAECP,* 125, dates these crosses in the first half of the seventh century, as direct descendants of the inscribed crosses of Inishkeel and Drumhallagh, both also in Donegal. Eighteenth-century dates for these crosses given on the basis of technical developments, cannot explain stylistic similarities to A.II.10 and *Durrow.* R. A. S. MacAlister, "The Inscription of the Slab at Fahan Mure, co. Donegal," *Journal of the Royal Society of Antiquaries of Ireland* 59 (1929): 89–98, gives text evidence for an early date for the cross slab.

79. B. Salin, *Die altgermanische Thierornamentik,* 2d ed., trans. J. Mestorf (Stockholm: K. L. Beckmans, 1935), classifies Germanic zoomorphic ornament; the belt buckle fits into Salin Style II. S. O. Muller, *Dyreornamentiken i. Norden* (Copenhagen: Thieles, 1880), is Salin's major source.

80. Alexander, *Insular Manuscripts,* 32, suggests also that the scribe was a Columba other than the saint, but William O'Sullivan, formerly Keeper of Manuscripts at Trinity College Library, Dublin, believes that the notations *C* at the bottoms of folios 11 recto and 52 verso are more probably quire marks than scribal signatures. Luce, *Codex Durmachensis,* 2:17–25, suggests that the model of Durrow was in Columba's hand and possibly the source of the colophon.

81. Alexander, *Insular Manuscripts,* 32; the codex was removed from Durrow in the seventeenth century and was given to Trinity College in 1661.

82. R. Powell, "The *Book of Kells,* the *Book of Durrow,*" *Scriptorium* 10 (1956): 12–15.

83. J. Chapman. *Notes on the Early History of the Vulgate Gospels* (Oxford: Clarendon Press, 1908), 162–80; F. C. Burkitt, "*Kells, Durrow* and *Lindisfarne,*" *Antiquity* 9 (1935): 33–37.

84. Ludwig Bieler, "The Paleography of the *Book of Durrow,*" in Luce, *Codex Durmachensis,* 2: 94–95.

85. The *Lindisfarne Gospels* measures 505 × 340 mm; Durham A.II.10 is 385 × 250 mm.

86. C. Nordenfalk, "An Illustrated *Diatessaron,*" *Art Bulletin* 50 (1968): 119–40; M. Schapiro et al., "The Miniatures in the Florence *Diatessaron* (Laur. MS Orient 81)," *Art Bulletin* 51 (1969): 494–531; C. Nordenfalk, "The *Diatessaron* Miniatures Once More," *Art Bulletin* 55 (1973): 532–46. Nordenfalk has suggested that the model for the cross-carpet-page in *Durrow* is an early copy of the

Diatessaron of Tatian of which a sixteenth-century copy survives in Florence (Biblioteca Medicea-Laurenziana, MS Orient 81, fol. 127v). As Schapiro et al. have demonstrated, the late date of the Florence manuscripts and fundamental compositional dissimilarities limit this initially striking comparison to a bizarre case of the impact of Western manuscripts in the East, or of equifinality.

87. T. D. Kendrick, *Anglo-Saxon Art to A.D. 900* (London: Methuen, 1938), 101–5.

88. Alcock, *Arthur's Britain*, 166–75.

89. *Anonymous Life of Cuthbert* 4.8 (*Anglo-Saxon Saints and Heroes,* 70); Bede, *Life of Cuthbert* 27 (*Lives of the Saints*, 105).

90. Bede 4.9 (Colgrave and Mynors, 394–95).

91. Schapiro et al., "Florence *Diatessaron*," 519.

92. Henry, *IAECP,* pl. 55.

93. Ibid., 170–71; Kendrick, *Anglo-Saxon Art*, 100–101; Bruce-Mitford, *Codex Lindisfarnensis*, 2:111–12.

94. Alexander, *Insular Manuscripts*, pl. 22.

95. Bober, "Illumination of the *Glazier Codex*," 47–49.

96. M. Werner, "The Four Evangelist Symbols Page in the *Book of Durrow*," *Gesta* 8 (1969): 3–17.

97. W. Bakkes and R. Dölling, *Art of the Dark Ages* (New York: Harry N. Abrams, 1969), 18–19.

98. Alexander, *Insular Manuscripts*, 31, figs. 17, 18, pl. 31.

99. Henry, *IAECP,* 75, colorplate B, pl. 91.

100. Ibid., 143–47, pls. 52, 54.

101. Henderson, *Picts*, 121–27; R. B. K. Stevenson, "Pictish Art," in *The Problem of the Picts*, ed. F. T. Wainwright (Edinburgh: T. Nelson, 1955), 106–8; R. B. K. Stevenson, "Sculpture in Scotland in the Sixth to Ninth Centuries A.D.," in *Kolloquium über spätantike und frühmittelalterliche Skulptur,* Heidelberg, 1970 (Mainz: P. von Zabern, 1972), 68–74; Charles Thomas, "The Interpretation of the Pictish Symbols," *Archaeological Journal* 120 (1963): 31–97. Thomas dates these stones to the Late Iron Age, in the first to third centuries B.C., whereas Henderson sees them as coeval with and influential on *Durrow*, and Stevenson considers the stones to be influenced by *Durrow* and later manuscripts.

102. K. Hughes, *Early Christianity in Pictland*, Jarrow Lecture (Jarrow: The Rectory, 1970), suggests that there may have been scriptoria in Pictland capable of producing the *Book of Durrow*.

103. Luce, *Codex Durmachensis*, 2:11; Henry, *IAECP,* 172–73; T. J. Brown et al., *Codex Lindisfarnensis*, 2:6 n.1. Henry and Luce believe the Irenaean order points to available Irish Gospels texts mixing Vulgate and Old Latin forms, an Irish origin for *Durrow;* whereas Brown and Bruce-Mitford broaden this context to include Celtic foundations in northern England. However, Irenaean order could also have reached Ireland or England via a poem included in the prologue to Juvencas's fourth-century *Historia Evangelica* (see Nordenfalk, "*Diatessaron* Miniatures, 542–43). This text could have reached Celtic foundations from Juvencas's Spain via the western seaways trade (see J. N. Hillgarth, "East, Spain and Irish," 442–56; idem, "Visigothic Spain," 167–97). However, the same text was available in England, as for example in Bede's library (see J. D. A. Ogilvy, *Books Known to the English, 597–1066* [Cambridge, Mass.: Medieval Academy of America, 1967]). Nonetheless, the Irenaean order was more probably transmitted to *Durrow* via a Gospels text rather than via the remote intellectual conceit of a Juvencas prologue.

104. Werner, "Evangelist Symbols Page," 6–13.

105. R. W. P. Cockerton, "The Wirksworth Slab," *Derbyshire Archaeological Journal* 82 (1962): 1–20.

106. L. Nees, "A Fifth-Century Bookcover and the Origin of the Four Evangelists Symbols Page in the *Book of Durrow*," *Gesta* 17 (1978): 3–8; M. Werner, "The *Durrow* Four Evangelist Symbols Page Once Again," *Gesta* 20 (1981): 23–33.

107. Kendrick, *Anglo-Saxon Art*, 101–5, believed *Durrow* was made in Ireland and exported to the northern Celtic foundations; R. L. S. Bruce-Mitford, review of M. de Paor and L. de Paor, *Early Christian Ireland, Medieval Archaeology* 2 (1958): 214–17, thought *Durrow* Northumbrian; Wright, in Dold and Eizenhöfer, "Irische Palimpsest-Sakramentar," 37, also considered *Durrow*

Northumbrian; W. R. Hovey, "Sources of the Irish Illumination," *Art Studies* 6 (1928): 105–20, considered *Durrow* a product of Ireland with no northern English connections; Luce, *Codex Durmachensis*, 2:45–52, also considered *Durrow* probably the product of Durrow in Ireland, as did his coauthors of that text with the exception of Bieler, who considered a Celtic foundation in northern England possible; Henry, *IAECP*, 173, considered *Durrow* a product of the Columban *paruchia*, whether in Ireland (Durrow, Derry) or northern England (Iona).

108. Reese, "Recent Work at Iona," 33.

109. Luce, *Codex Durmachensis*, 2:40–41, 52–53.

110. Ibid., 52–53.

Chapter 4. The Roman Church in England

1. Bede 1.7 (Colgrave and Mynors, 34–35).

2. Ibid., 1.26 (76–77).

3. Ibid., 1.25 (74–75).

4. Ibid., 1.29 (104–5).

5. F. Wormald, *The Miniatures of the Gospel of St. Augustine* (Cambridge: Cambridge University Press, 1954) 102. The codex is written in a sixth-century Italian hand and was in England by the seventh century to serve as a textual model for a *Gospels* codex (Oxford, Bodleian MS Auct. D.II.14). The illuminations of the *Gospel of Saint Augustine* consist of two full-page miniatures: one an Evangelist portrait of Luke framed with small scenes of the miracles of Christ and the other divided into twelve small scenes of the Passion. The style of these illuminations is close to that in the sixth-century *Vienna Genesis* (Vienna, Bibl. Nat. Theol. Gr. 31) particularly in the small scenes—in the movements and gesture of the figures, in their general proportions, and in the minimally described settings. However, the *Gospel of Saint Augustine* illuminations do not utilize the Late Antique iconographic references and elements of landscape found in the Vienna codex. Moreover, the figures here, with the exception of the larger St. Luke, lack the sprightly posture of the *Vienna Genesis* figures and the elegant use of highlighting that make the latter seem to dance across the page. The artist of the *Gospel of Saint Augustine* is consequently most probably working in a scriptorium remote from the eastern Mediterranean sources of the *Vienna Genesis* but must have had access to models from that vicinity.

6. Bede 1.32, 2.10 (Colgrave and Mynors, 110–11, 170–71). The gifts to Edwin were "a robe embroidered with gold and a garment from Ancyra."

7. Saints Peter and Paul was the abbey church of Saint Augustine's monastery, built by King Æthelbert in 602 (Bede 1.33 [Colgrave and Mynors, 114–15]). It served as a burial church not only for the archbishops of Canterbury but also for the royalty of Kent, on the model of Saint Denis. Saint Mary, Canterbury, was built by King Eadbald of Kent in 616 in honor of his conversion (ibid., 2.6 [156–57]). It was later joined to the cathedral by Wulfric's rotunda before being subsumed in the Norman church. Saint Mary at Lyminge was built by Æthelburh, Æthelbert's daughter and queen to Edwin of Northumbria, after the latter's death at Hatfield in 633 and her retirement to the south. St. Andrew, Rochester, was the cathedral of the bishops of Rochester, a see held at one point by Paulinus, the missionary to the Northumbrians. Saint Mary at Reculver, according to the *Anglo-Saxon Chronicle*, was built around 669 by King Egbert of Kent for "Bassa his mass priest" possibly a court chaplain (see *Anglo-Saxon Chronicle*, 34–35).

8. Bede 1.33 (Colgrave and Mynors, 114–15).

9. Ibid., 1.8 (34–35).

10. B. Cherry, "Ecclesiastical Architecture," in *Archaeology of Anglo-Saxon England*, 157; E. Fletcher, "Early Kentish Churches," *Medieval Archaeology* 9 (1965): 16–18; M. Deanesley, *The Pre-Conquest Church in England* (Oxford: Oxford University Press, 1961), 137–39. Part of the church of Saint Martin at Canterbury may be of Roman date, as the brick used for its construction is Roman and it has an *opus signinum* floor. However, Roman brick was commonly reused in Anglo-Saxon structures, and *opus signinum* occurs throughout the early Anglo-Saxon period, as at Jarrow. Deanesley has suggested that the double-apsed plan of Canterbury cathedral as rebuilt

under Eadmer in the Late Saxon period may reflect the form of the Roman church on the site. A chamber inserted into the northwest corner of the colonnades of the public baths at Caerwent may have been a small church with a narthex.

11. A. W. Clapham, *English Romanesque Architecture before the Conquest* (1930; reprint, Oxford: Clarendon Press, 1964), 1–29; J. M. C. Toynbee, "Christianity in Roman Britain," *Journal of the British Archaeological Association*, 3d ser., 16 (1953):1–24.

12. The ancient church at Lydd, Kent, has been thought to be Roman in date, but the evidence is inconclusive. It was excavated in the 1920s by Canon Livett. This project revealed a three-bay, aisled basilica, of which only the northern arcade is known and the southern projected, with apse and narthex. The scale and elaboration of Lydd is inconsistent with early Anglo-Saxon usage, hence Cherry ("Ecclesiastical Architecture," 157–58) considers it possibly late Roman. However, as Fletcher has demonstrated ("Early Kentish Churches," 11), certain elements at Lydd, such as the originally single-splayed impost profiles, parallel the first rebuilding of Saint Martin's at Canterbury in the Augustinian period, and a Saxon date for Lydd cannot therefore be ruled out. However, the open-aisled basilican plan, lacking in the other Augustinian churches but perhaps paralleling such controversial northern structures at Wilfrid's Saint Andrew's at Hexham, suggests an even later date, perhaps around 700. Stone-by-Faversham, Kent, also has a church of possibly Roman date but noncontinuous usage.

13. At Reculver, the footer is semicircular while the riser is semipolygonal.

14. H. M. Taylor, "The Position of the Altar in Early Kentish Churches," *Antiquaries' Journal* 53 (1973):55–57; Deanesley, *Pre-Conquest Church*, 140; R. Krautheimer, *Early Christian and Byzantine Architecture* (Harmondsworth: Penguin, 1965), 107, 537.

15. Fletcher, "Early Kentish Churches," 24–26.

16. Clapham, *English Romanesque Architecture*, 29. Lugdunum Convenarum is now Saint Bertrand de Comminges, on the Franco-Spanish border.

17. Taylor and Taylor, "Position of the Altar," 52–56.

18. Krautheimer, *Early Christian Architecture*, 129, fig.75.

19. Bede 5.23 (Colgrave and Mynors, 556–57).

20. Ibid., 1.33, 2.3, 2.5 (114–15, 142–45, 150–51); Fletcher, "Early Kentish Churches," 26–28; C. A. R. Radford, "Roma e l'Arte dei Celti e degli Anglo-Sassoni dal V all' VII secolo D.C.," *Roma e le Province*, Istituto di Studi Romani vol. 17 (Rome, 1938), 3:11. The medieval chronicler Goscelin reports that the north porticus at Saint Mary Lyminge was used for the burial of the founding abbess, Æthelburh. Precedent for burial in lateral chambers of a church is found in Paulinus's description of his church at Nola in about 400, where this space is called a *cubiculum*.

21. H. M. Taylor, *English Architecture in the Time of Bede*, Jarrow Lecture (Jarrow: The Rectory, 1962), 11–13.

22. Deaneslay, *Pre-Conquest Church*, 147.

23. Clapham, *English Romanesque Architecture*, 29; and Fletcher, "Early Kentish Churches," 26–31, suggest that the arrangement of porticus at the Kentish churches reflects the evolution of the English rite.

24. Cherry, "Ecclesiastical Architecture," 160–68.

25. Bede, *Lives of the Abbots* 5 (*Anglo-Saxon Saints and Heroes*, 229–30).

26. Cherry, "Ecclesiastical Architecture," 164–68.

27. Bede 2.9–14 (Colgrave and Mynors, 162–89).

28. Bede, *Lives of the Abbots* 1–14 (*Anglo-Saxon Saints and Heroes*, 223–42).

29. P. Llewellyn, *Rome in the Dark Ages* (London: Praeger, 1970), 173; C. Cecchelli, "La pitture dei cimetarii cristiani dal V al VI secolo," *Corsi di Cultura sull'Arte Ravennate e Bizantine* (1958):45–56.

30. Bede, *Lives of the Abbots* 11 (*Anglo-Saxon Saints and Heroes*, 237).

31. Ibid., 5 (229–30).

32. R. Cramp, "Jarrow Church," *Archaeological Journal* 133 (1976):220–26; idem, "Monkwearmouth Church," *Archaeological Journal* 133 (1976):230–37; idem, "Excavations at the Saxon Monastic Sites of Jarrow and Wearmouth," *Medieval Archaeology* 13 (1969):21–66; idem, "Decorated Window Glass and Millefiori from Monkwearmouth," *Antiquaries' Journal* 1 (1970):327–35;

idem, "Monasteries of the North," 104–24.

33. Cramp, "Monastic Sites," 234.

34. Bede, *Lives of the Abbots*, 4–7 (*Anglo-Saxon Saints and Heroes*, 229–32).

35. Cramp, "Monasteries of the North," 123. The poverty of the monks is borne out by the absence of meat bones in early strata of the sites; the diet of the monks seems to have depended largely on fish and shellfish from nearby rivers.

36. Taylor and Taylor, *Anglo-Saxon Architecture*, 1:338–49, 432–48; E. Gilbert, "Anglian Remains at Jarrow Church," *Proceedings of the Society of Antiquaries of Newcastle-upon-Tyne*, 5th ser., 1(1951–56):311–33; Cramp, "Jarrow Church," 220–26; idem, "Monkwearmouth Church," 230–37.

37. *Anonymous Life of Ceolfrith* 25 (*Anglo-Saxon Saints and Heroes*, 261); Bede, *Lives of the Abbots* 9 (*Anglo-Saxon Saints and Heroes*, 235); Cramp, "Jarrow Church," 220–26.

38. *Anonymous Life of Ceolfrith* 18, 25 (*Anglo-Saxon Saints and Heroes*, 257, 261).

39. Taylor and Taylor, *Anglo-Saxon Architecture* 1:172–76, 234–38, 534–36, 734; 3:939–57; C. F. Innocent, "Romano-British Precedents for Some English Romanesque Details," *Journal of the Royal Institute for British Archaeology*, 3d ser., 15 (1908): 649–50, suggests that arch-carved window lintels were derived from door heads of gateway guardhouses along Hadrian's Wall.

40. Stonemasonry had been used earlier in the church constructed under Edwin at York, probably built by Paulinus and his associates with local labor, but the technique did not take root in Northumbria at that time. Wilfrid's Hexham and Ripon may predate Biscop's foundations, but did not become centers of technical dissemination of stone construction as did Jarrow and Monkwearmouth.

41. Cramp, "Monkwearmouth Church," 230–37.

42. Taylor and Taylor, *Anglo-Saxon Architecture*, 1:432–48.

43. Cramp, "Monkwearmouth Church," 230–37.

44. Gilbert, "Anglian Remains," 311–33.

45. E. Mâle, *La fin du paganisme en Gaule et les plus anciennes basiliques chrétiennes* (Paris: Flammarion, 1950) 123–87.

46. Taylor and Taylor, *Anglo-Saxon Architecture*, 1:108–14.

47. Cramp, "Monkwearmouth Church," 230–37.

48. H. M. Taylor, "The Rediscovery of Important Anglo-Saxon Sculpture in Pre-Conquest Churches," in *Anglo-Saxons*, 137–58.

49. Cramp, "Monkwearmouth Church," 230–37; quotes Prior Richard of Hexham, who describes choir arrangements at Hexham as follows: "An immense multitude of men could be there on all sides of the main building of the church, though no one of them could be seen by anybody from below."

50. Bede, *Lives of the Abbots*, 6, 12 (*Anglo-Saxon Saints and Heroes*, 231, 239).

51. Bede 5.21 (Colgrave and Mynors, 532–33); W. D. Simpson, "The Early Romanesque Tower at Restenneth Priory, Angus," *Antiquaries' Journal* 43 (1963):269–83.

52. R. Cramp, *Early Northumbrian Sculpture*, Jarrow Lecture (Jarrow: The Rectory, 1966), 4; E. Gilbert, "Some Problems of Early Northumbrian Architecture," *Archaeologia Aeliana*, 4th ser., 42 (1964): 65–83, sees parallels between the west porch at Monkwearmouth and the decorated narthex of certain Syrian churches, but the resemblance is more in the choice of ornamental motifs than in structure.

53. Mâle, *Fin du paganisme*, 123–187; Mayr-Harting, *Coming of Christianity*, 156, sees a link to eastern Mediterranean, specifically Coptic, architecture.

54. Innocent, "Romano-British Precedents," 649.

55. A. W. Clapham, "Two Carved Stones at Monkwearmouth," *Archaeologia Aeliana*, 4th ser., 28 (1950) 1–6; R. Cramp, *The Monastic Arts of Northumbria* (London: Arts Council of Britain, 1967) 24, pl. 45b.

56. Bede, *Lives of the Abbots*, 6 (*Anglo-Saxon Saints and Heroes*, 231–32); cf. Deanesley, *Pre-Conquest Church*, 175.

57. Mâle, *Fin du paganisme*, 160–71.

58. Cramp, *Monastic Arts*, 13; idem, "Decorated Window Glass," 327–35; idem, "Monastic Sites," 239.

59. Bede, *Lives of the Abbots* 5 (*Anglo-Saxon Saints and Heroes*, 230); Cramp, "Monasteries of the North," 122.

60. Cramp, *Monastic Arts*, 13, n. 20.

61. Cramp, "Monasteries of the North," 119–24.

62. Ibid., 114–19.

63. Ibid., 117, 119.

64. Taylor and Taylor, *Anglo-Saxon Architecture*, 1:98.

65. Bede, *Lives of the Abbots*, 9 (*Anglo-Saxon Saints and Heroes*, 231–32); Cramp, "Monkwearmouth Church," 230–37. Excavations in 1866 at the junction of the present nave and chancel of Saint Peter's at Monkwearmouth showed a widening of the old church to the east, which would seem to indicate the original presence of a square chancel slightly wider than the nave. However, if that chancel was the same proportionate dimensions as the usual Northumbrian chancel-chapel (such as at Jarrow, Escomb, Seaham, and Hoddam), then there would be no room at the site for even a small detached chapel to the east where Cramp believes Saint Mary's was located, parallel to the arrangement at Jarrow. Cramp consequently assumes that Saint Peter's lacked the usual eastern square chancel. However, the documents on Monkwearmouth do not place Saint Mary's to the east of the main church as they do at Jarrow. If Building A is Saint Mary's, then the archaeological evidence and comparison to other Northumbrian churches allow Saint Peter's to have had a square Northumbrian chancel. See also Taylor and Taylor, *Anglo-Saxon Architecture*, 1:234–38, 543–46; "Hoddam," in Royal Commission on the Ancient and Historical Monuments and Constructions of Scotland, *Seventh Report, with Inventory of the Monuments and Constructions in the County of Dumfries* (Edinburgh: HMSO, 1920), 93–104.

66. Krautheimer, *Early Christian Architecture*, 78, and note 14; T. Töbler and A. Molinier, *Itinera Hierosolymitana et Descriptiones Terrae Sanctae* (1879; reprint, Osnabrück: Zeller, 1966), 157–58.

67. Bede, *Lives of the Abbots* 5 (*Anglo-Saxon Saints and Heroes*, 230).

68. *Anonymous Life of Ceolfrith* 1–40 (*Anglo-Saxon Saints and Heroes*, 247–71).

69. *Anonymous Life of Ceolfrith* 39 (*Anglo-Saxon Saints and Heroes*, 270–71); Alexander, *Insular Manuscripts*, 32–35; H. Blum, "Über den *Codex Amiatinus* und Cassiodor's Bibliothek in Vivarium," *Zentralblatt für Bibliothekswesen* 64 (1950): 52. R. L. S. Bruce-Mitford, "The Art of the *Codex Amiatinus*," *Journal of the British Archaeological Association*, 3d ser., 32 (1969) 6–7, suggests that the codex was not originally intended as a gift but was destined for the libraries of the twin foundations, on the basis of a verse found at the bottom of fol. IVv:

> Hieronyme interpres variis doctissime linguis
> Te Bethelehem celebrat, te totus personat orbis,
> Te quoque nostra tuis promet bibliotheca libris
> Qua nova cum priscis condis donaria gazis.

Of this eulogy to St. Jerome, Bruce-Mitford translates the third line, "Our library will now also contain your works," and suggests that the reference is to Ceolfrith's addition of the pandect in the Vulgate to the library already containing the Old Latin pandect. It is, however, also possible that the verse was already included in the textual model for *Amiatinus* or that the verse, intended for the two pandects destined for the foundation libraries was accidentally copied into the gift volume as well. Given the scale of the volume, and the manufacture of three volumes where only two local foundations were to receive copies, it is likely that the *Amiatinus* was intended as a gift from the inception of the project. Ceolfrith himself attempted to deliver the codex to Rome, but died en route at Langres in 716. Some of his associates completed the journey, and a papal letter from Gregory II to Jarrow expresses gratitude for an unspecified gift, probably the codex.

70. *Anonymous Life of Ceolfrith* 37 (*Anglo-Saxon Saints and Heroes*, 269–70).

71. Bruce-Mitford, "*Codex Amiatinus*," 1.

72. Bede, *Lives of the Abbots*, 9 (*Anglo-Saxon Saints and Heroes*, 236), mentions that Biscop exchanged two silk cloaks for three hides of land.

73. D. H. Wright, "The Italian Stimulus on English Art around 700," *Stil und Überlieferung in der Kunst des Abendlandes*, Akten des 21. internationalen Kongres für Kunstgeschichte, Bonn,

1962, (Berlin: Mann, 1967) 1:84–86.

74. Alexander, *Insular Manuscripts,* 33.

75. Blum, "Über *Codex Amiatinus,*" 52–57.

76. Chapman, *Vulgate Gospels,* 16–23.

77. R. L. S. Bruce-Mitford, "The Reception by the Anglo-Saxons of Mediterranean Art following Their Conversion from Ireland and Rome," in *La conversione al cristianesimo nell'Europa dell'alto medioevo,* Settimane di Studio del Centro Italiano di Studi sull'Alto Medioevo Spoleto, 14 (1967): 797–825.

78. Alexander, *Insular Manuscripts,* pls. 23–27.

79. Bruce-Mitford, *"Codex Amiatinus"* 7–12; idem, "Reception by Anglo-Saxons," 816, suggests that the book on the floor may be the *Biblia Minutiore Manu Conscriptus,* the third of the Cassiodoran Squillace Bibles. Chapman, *Vulgate Gospels,* 23, believes that in the model the scribe was Cassiodorus and that the note identifying him as Ezra and the Jewish paraphernalia were later additions. However, such additions would have been nearly impossible in the insular milieu, where Jewish ritual equipment was virtually unknown.

80. T. J. Brown et al., *Codex Lindisfarnensis,* 2:143–44; Bede, *Lives of the Abbots* 11 (*Anglo-Saxon Saints and Heroes,* 238).

81. Bruce-Mitford, "*Codex Amiatinus,*" 12.

82. D. Robb, *The Art of the Illuminated Manuscript* (Philadelphia: Art Alliance Press, 1973), figs. 18, 19 (*Sermons of Gregory Nazianzus,* Paris, Bibl. Nat., MS Gr. 510).

83. P. J. Nordhagen, "An Italo-Byzantine Painter in the Scriptorium of Ceolfrith," in *Studia Romana in honorem Petri Krarup Septuagenarii* (Odense: University of Odense Press, 1976), 138–45; idem, *The "Codex Amiatinus" and the Byzantine Element in the Northumbrian Renaissance,* Jarrow Lecture (Jarrow: The Rectory, 1978), 1–11.

84. Bruce-Mitford, *"Codex Amiatinus,"* 145–46; Nordhagen, "Italo-Byzantine Painter," 139–45. Nordhagen points to similar "errors" in ninth- and tenth-century Mediterranean manuscripts, but these may be the result of a separate decline in Greek illumination in that period. There is little evidence of such "errors" in seventh-century Mediterranean illumination. Nordhagen's hypothetical Italo-Byzantine artist at Jarrow is also unconfirmed in Bede's *Lives of the Abbots,* where foreign visitors are usually given particular notice.

85. D. H. Wright, "Italian Stimulus," 84–86, also proposes Roman sources.

86. Bruce-Mitford, "*Codex Amiatinus,* 18.

87. K. Weitzmann, "Various Aspects of Byzantine Influence on the Latin Countries from the Sixth to the Twelfth Century," *Dumbarton Oaks Papers* 20 (1966):4–5; cf. Nordhagen, "Italo-Byzantine Painter," 139–45; idem, *Byzantine Element,*" 11; D. H. Wright, "Italian Stimulus," 84–86; Bruce-Mitford, *"Codex Amiatinus,"* 1–5. Nordhagen considers the artist of this page to be a native student of the Ezra Master, but the absence of Roman fresco influence here could be a question of the provenance of the model of this particular illumination, or of whether this artist had been to Rome, not necessarily of his nationality. Wright's tracing of seven different hands in the illumination of *Amiatinus* may well be, as Bruce-Mitford has suggested, the result of one or two Anglian artists working from widely differing models.

88. D. H. Wright, "Italian Stimulus," 84–86.

89. Eddius, *Life of Wilfrid* 1–68 (*Lives of the Saints,* 133–206).

90. Ibid., 14 (147).

91. Bede 4.19 (Colgrave and Mynors, 390–93).

92. Mayr-Harting, *Coming of Christianity,* 129.

93. E. S. Savage and C. C. Hodges, *A Record of All the Works connected with Hexham Abbey since January 1899 and Now in Progress* (Hexham: J. Cotterall, 1907); Taylor and Taylor, *Anglo-Saxon Architecture,* 1:299; is the first publication of Hodges's plan. See also. R. N. Bailey, "The Abbey Church of St. Andrew, Hexham. The Medieval Works," *Archaeological Journal* 133 (1976):197–201.

94. Bede 2.14 (Colgrave and Mynors, 186–87); cf. Gilbert, "Some Problems," 68–71, who sees Bede as implying a centriform square church on a square-within-a-square plan, similar to Etchmiadzin in Armenia.

95. Bede 2.20 (Colgrave and Mynors, 204–5).

96. Eddius, *Life of Wilfrid* 16 (*Lives of the Saints* 148–49).

97. Ibid., 17 (149).

98. G. Baldwin Brown, *The Arts in Early England* (London: J. Murray, 1925), 2:129–30.

99. Eddius, *Life of Wilfrid* 17 (*Lives of the Saints*, 149); B. Colgrave, ed., *The Life of Bishop Wilfrid by Eddius Stephanus* (Cambridge: Cambridge University Press, 1927), 36–37.

100. Taylor and Taylor *Anglo-Saxon Architecture*, 1:108–14.

101. Fletcher, "Early Kentish Churches," 16–18; Cherry, "Ecclesiastical Architecture," 170, 172.

102. Eddius, *Life of Wilfrid* 22 (*Lives of the Saints* 154–55).

103. G. B. Brown, *Arts in Early England*, 2:318; Cramp, "Monkwearmouth Church," 230–37.

104. Bede 5.20 (Colgrave and Mynors, 530–31).

105. R. N. Bailey and D. O'Sullivan, "Excavations over St. Wilfrid's Crypt at Hexham, 1978," *Archaeologia Aeliana*, 5th ser., 7 (1979):145–57.

106. E. Gilbert, "St. Wilfrid's Church at Hexham," in *St. Wilfrid at Hexham*, ed. D. P. Kirby (Newcastle upon Tyne: Oriel, 1974), 81–113, esp. 89–90, gives a survey of the early reconstructions.

107. Taylor and Taylor, *Anglo-Saxon Architecture*, 1: 297–312, fig.131; cf. Gilbert, "St. Wilfrid's Church," 89–113, suggesting a solid-wall nave church like St. Pierre at Vienne, with *g* and *j* as original nave walls, pierced with entrances to chamber porticus in the thickness of the wall itself, and *f* and *k* delineating extremely narrow access passageways around the outside of the church for the service of these porticus. This passage would, however, have been a meager eighteen inches in width, unlikely considering the luxurious proportions of the rest of the church (see also R. N. Bailey, "The Anglo-Saxon Church at Hexham," *Archaeologia Aeliana*, 5th ser., 4 [1976]: 54). Gilbert went on to suggest that Acca broadened the church by expanding the porticus outward to *g* and *i* and separating them with new party walls. This speculative reconstruction cannot be confirmed by early documents, by the Hodges plan, or by the observations of Savage and Hodges.

108. Bailey and O'Sullivan, "Excavations," 145–57.

109. E. Cambridge, "C. C. Hodges and the Nave of Hexham Abbey," *Archaeologia Aeliana*, 5th ser., 7 (1979): 159–68.

110. Gilbert, "St. Wilfrid's Church," 89ff., plans 6, 7, 12.

111. Cf. Taylor and Taylor, *Anglo-Saxon Architecture*, 1: 310–12, fig. 131, suggesting paired eastern porticus east of walls *m2* and *m3* functioning as pastophories, with the northern chamber accessible from the nave through a door in *m2* and the southern chamber bounded by *m3* and *o1*, accessible from the sanctuary alone. The crypt chapel would be accessible to clergy only via the southern prothesis, whereas the crypt vestibule would be open to the public via the northern diaconicon. The crypt passes under the eastward extension of wall *j* recently discovered by Bailey (Bailey and O'Sullivan, "Excavations," 145–57), which suggests that the crypt passage debouched in a chamber rather than a transept, but it is impossible to determine whether *j* was a riser (as Bailey suggests) or a sleeper bearing arcades for most of its length in the nave.

112. Taylor and Taylor, *Anglo-Saxon Architecture*, 1: 310–12; Gilbert, "St. Wilfrid's Church," 97; Bailey, "Anglo-Saxon Church," 54–55.

113. Bailey, "Anglo-Saxon Church," 56–57, considered wall *h* as the foundation of an eccentric solea based on eastern prototypes, but now believes that it may have supported an early schola cantorum.

114. Eddius, *Life of Wilfrid* 14, 65 (*Lives of the Saints*, 146–47, 202); Bede 5.20 (Colgrave and Mynors, 530–31).

115. T. F. Mathews, "An Early Roman Chancel Arrangement," *Rivista di archeologica cristiana* 38 (1962): 73–96.

116. Gilbert, "St. Wilfrid's Church," plans 6, 7.

117. Taylor and Taylor, *Anglo-Saxon Architecture*, 1:297–312, fig. 131; cf. Gilbert, "St. Wilfrid's Church," 97–98, who suggested that the apsidal oratory was attached to wall *g* by a passage running west from the corners of wall *r* and entering the main church by a doorway in *q*. He further suggests that the apsidal structure had its own crypt to the east of wall *r*, on the basis of Eddius's mention of "crypts," and of multiple-crypt structures on the Continent such as St. Servaas, Maastricht. However, this hypothesis is not borne out by Hodges's observations.

118. Bailey, "Anglo-Saxon Church," 66–67.

119. Taylor and Taylor, *Anglo-Saxon Architecture*, 1:298.

120. Mâle, *Fin du paganisme*, 130–35, contains also subsequent quotations of Apollinaris Sidonius.

121. Eddius, *Life of Wilfrid* 52 (*Lives of the Saints*, 185).

122. Clapham, *English Romanesque Architecture*, 44–45.

123. Mayr-Harting, *Coming of Christianity*, 159.

124. Edddius, *Life of Wilfrid* 17 (*Lives of the Saints*, 149–50).

125. Ibid., 150.

126. F. J. Haverfield and W. Greenwell, *A Catalogue of the Sculptured and Inscribed Stones in the Cathedral Library, Durham* (Durham: Thomas Caldcleugh, 1899), gives Durham stone numbers used here; R. Cramp, "Hexham Anglo-Saxon Sculpture (A Handlist)," in *St. Wilfrid at Hexham*, 172–79; hereafter refered to as Cramp, "Handlist."

127. Bede 5.20 (Colgrave and Mynors, 530–31).

128. W. G. Collingwood, *Northumbrian Crosses of the Pre-Norman Age* (London: Faber and Dwyer, 1927), 29; idem, "A Pedigree of Anglian Crosses," *Antiquity* 6 (1932): 35–54.

129. R. Cramp, "Early Northumbrian Sculpture at Hexham," in *St. Wilfrid at Hexham*, 115.

130. Ibid., 116; J. Raine, ed., *The Priory of Hexham: Its Chronicles, Endowments and Annals*, Surtees Society, vol. 44 (Durham: Andrews, and Company, 1864.), 1:12.

131. Cramp, "Sculpture at Hexham," 125–26; idem, "Handlist," 22a, b, c.

132. Cramp, "Handlist," 23, 10; Durham stone VI.

133. R. Cramp, "Mediterranean Elements in the Early Medieval Sculpture of England," in *Les relations entre l'Empire Romain tardif, l'Empire Franc, et ses voisins*, Ninth International Congress of Prehistoric and Protohistoric Sciences, Nice, 1976, Colloquium 30 (Paris: Centre National de la Recherche Scientifique, 1976), 266; idem, "Sculpture at Hexham," 4.

134. Henry, *IAECP*, 117–31.

135. Collingwood, *Northumbrian Crosses*, passim.

136. Cramp, "Mediterranean Elements," 263–76; idem, "Sculpture at Hexham," 4; Deanesley, *Pre-Conquest Church*, 173–75.

137. R. Cramp, "Schools of Mercian Sculpture," in *Mercian Studies*, ed. Ann Dornier (Leicester: Leicester University Press, 1977), 191–231.

138. Cramp, "Sculpture at Hexham," 127; Simeon of Durham, *Symeonis Monachi Opera Omnia*, ed. T. Arnold, Chronicles and Memorials of Great Britain and Ireland during the Middle Ages, vol. 75, pt. 1 (London: Longmans, 1882–85), 1:23.

139. Cramp, "Sculpture at Hexham," 127; idem, "Handlist," I; Haverfield and Greenwell, *Catalogue*, 57.

140. Ernst Kitzinger, "Anglo-Saxon Vinescroll Ornament," *Antiquity* 10 (1936): 133–35.

141. Cf. Cramp, "Mediterranean Elements," 226; idem, "Sculpture at Hexham," 129, postulates that the figure-eight vine motif arrived in Spain and England by separate routes from the Levant, possibly arriving in England via metalwork; cf. also Collingwood, "Pedigree," 35–36, suggesting a set of wooden panels as transmitter.

142. E. Coatsworth, "Two Examples of the Crucifixion at Hexham," *St. Wilfrid at Hexham*, 180–84; cf. M. J. Swanton, "Bishop Acca and the Cross at Hexham," *Archaeologia Aeliana*, 4th ser., 48 (1970): 157–68; see also H. M. Taylor, "Rediscovery of Important Anglo-Saxon Sculpture at Hexham," *Archaeologia Aeliana*, 4th ser., 44 (1966): 49–60.

143. Kendrick, *Anglo-Saxon Art*, 152; O. Demus, *Byzantine Art and the West*, Wrightsman Lectures, vol. 3 (New York: New York University Press, 1970), 49.

144. E. Panofsky, *Renaissance and Renascences in Western Art* (New York: Harper and Row, 1960), 43.

145. R. N. Bailey, "The Anglo-Saxon Metalwork from Hexham," in *St. Wilfrid at Hexham*, 155–58, pl. 27b, c.

Chapter 5. Northumbrian Synthesis

1. Eddius, *Life of Wilfrid* 17 (*Lives of the Saints*, 150).
2. Bede 4.4 (Colgrave and Mynors, 346–49).
3. Ibid., 3.26 (308–9).
4. Ibid., 3.15–17. 3.26, 4.3 (260–67, 308–11, 336–47).
5. Ibid., 3.26 (308–11).
6. Ibid., 3.3 (218–21).
7. *Anonymous Life of Cuthbert* (*Anglo-Saxons Saints and Heroes*, 31–84; Bede, *Life of Cuthbert* (*Lives of the Saints* 71–129).
8. E. G. Millar, *The Lindisfarne Gospels* (London: British Museum, 1923), 3–4.
9. Ibid., 5; T. J. Brown et al., *Codex Lindisfarnensis*, 2:11–12, 17–18; see also Bede, *Life of Cuthbert* 17 (*Lives of the Saints*, 104–5).
10. Anderson and Anderson, *Adomnan's Life of Columba*, 343–47, 451, 525.
11. G. Baldwin Brown, *The Ruthwell and Bewcastle Crosses and the Lindisfarne Gospels*, vol. 5 in *The Arts in Early England, 341:*

> Presbyter iste fuit Scottorum gente beatus
> Comtis qui potuit notis ornare libellos
> Hac arte hinc nullus potuit se acquare modernus scriptorum.

12. Millar, *Lindisfarne*, 5; T. J. Brown et al. *Codex Lindisfarnensis*, 2:84. The later history of the codex is known through Simeon of Durham, *Historia Dunelmensis Ecclesiae* 5–13, in *Symeonis Monachi Opera Omnia*, 50–71. In 875 the codex was taken from Lindisfarne along with the relics of St. Cuthbert because increasingly frequent Danish raids had made the island unsafe. After nine years of wandering, the Lindisfarne community settled temporarily at Chester-le-Street. Thence they were briefly removed by Bishop Aldhum to Ripon in 995 before they were permanently settled at Durham. The Durham priory was dissolved in 1539, and the codex passed through several hands before entering the collection of Robert Cotton. It appeared in the first Cotton inventory, survived the Ashburnham House fire of 1731 and was rebound in 1853. The jeweled cover was lost before or during the dissolution of the priory in 1539 (T. J. Brown et al., *Codex Lindisfarnensis*, 2:25).
13. T. J. Brown et al., *Codex Lindisfarnensis*, 2:89–96; Lowe, *Codices*, no. 258.
14. See Appendix, below.
15. *Treasures of Early Irish Art*, no. 32, with excellent plates by Lee Boltin.
16. The layout of the carpet-page is more tightly controlled here than in *Durrow*. However, this may be as much due to the development of the cross-carpet-page in insular manuscripts between *Durrow* and *Lindisfarne* as to the increasing influence of Mediterranean art or to some difference in ethnic temperament between the "wildly Celtic" Durrow and the "phlegmatically Anglo-Saxon" Lindisfarne. See T. J. Brown et al., *Codex Lindisfarnensis*, 2:194–96, on the "Italianate" spirit of the *Lindisfarne Gospels;* and Henry, *IAECP,* 194–95, on what she sees as the "monotony" and "frozen perfection" of *Lindisfarne*, which she considers to have been made outside the richly experimental context of Celtic illumination.
17. Alexander, *Insular Manuscripts*, no. 11, pls. 48, 51–56, 59. *The Gospels of St. Willibrord*, also known as the *Echternach Gospels* (Paris, Bib. Nat. MS Lat. 9389) has been traditionally associated with the mission of St. Willibrord to Frisia, and therefore are thought to antedate the beginning of that mission in 698. They have been attributed to Northumbria on paleographic grounds; T. J. Brown has argued that the *Echternach* scribe is identical with the writer of the *Durham Gospels* (Durham, Cathedral Library, A.II.17), and that the locus of manufacture was the scriptorium at Lindisfarne. If this is so, and if the *Gospels* was expressly made for the mission of Willibrord, then it is possible that the *Echternach* and *Lindisfarne* codices are simultaneous products of the same scriptorium. However, *Echternach* is decoratively consistently closer to *Durrow,* in the use of a grid layout for the canon tables and the Evangelist-symbol-page types found in *Durrow,* although new models have been introduced in the interval. Regardless of its date and

provenance, therefore, the *Echternach* codex may be construed as a product of the interval between *Durrow* and *Lindisfarne,* predating in actual manufacture or merely in artistic awareness the new wave of imported models influential in *Lindisfarne.* See also T. J. Brown, et al., *Codex Lindisfarnensis,* 2:89–90.

18. C. Nordenfalk, *Die spätantiken Kanontafeln* (Stockholm: O. Isacson, 1938), 208–11, 218 n. 2, 283.

19. Alexander, *Insular Manuscripts,* 37, fig. 15.

20. T. J. Brown et al., *Codex Lindisfarnensis,* 2:192, also notes birds on canon arcades in the *Rabbūlā Gospels* (Florence, Laurentian Library, Cod. Plut. I); and the *Etchmiadzin Gospels* (Etchmiadzin, Cathedral Treasury).

21. Ibid., 189–92.; Bruce-Mitford argues that the source of these canon arcades is the seventh volume of Cassiodorus's *Novem Codices,* despite Brown's argument (48) that the *Lindisfarne* canon tables themselves are not Cassiodoran. See also Appendix, below.

22. T. J. Brown et al., *Lindisfarne Gosples,* 192–203.; R. L. S. Bruce-Mitford argues that the animal friezes of the canon tables are an imported motif, not an example of the imposition of insular motifs on the Late Antique arcade formula. He believes that the frieze of birds in the great arches of two pages of the canon sequence in the *Maeseyck Gospels* (Maeseyck, Church of St. Catharine, Treasury, fols. 2r, 5v), an eighth-century codex with northern English associations, is sufficiently naturalistic to demand a generic imported prototype for this ornamental formulation (Alexander, *Insular Manuscripts,* nos. 22, 50–51, pls. 90, 92). However, the *Maeseyck Gospels* birds, on close examination, appear to be an uneasy later synthesis of the perched naturalistic peacocks of Late Antique canon tables and the tightly knotted birds of *Lindisfarne* and its followers, resulting in a claustrophobic line of plump peacocks, each about to trip over its predecessor. A classical frieze would certainly show more graceful spacing and less *horror vacui.* The canon arcades of the *Maeseyck Gospels* represent an eighth-century attempt to reconcile the established ornamental practices of an insular scriptorium with a new classical model possibly also responsible for the Evangelist portrait (fol. 10), the busts at the apexes of the canon table great arches (fols. 2–11), and the additional marginal birds perched outside these great arches (Alexander, *Insular Manuscripts,* pls. 87–101). The *Maeseyck* bird frieze therefore probably has no direct reference to models for the *Lindisfarne* animal friezes. Nonetheless, even if a Late Antique model did provide not only birds on the arcades but also birds in friezes within them, the insular transfiguration of the *Lindisfarne* birds is complete. The same is true of the *Lindisfarne* hound friezes, if, as David Wright has suggested, an eastern Mediterranean prototype, possibly a textile, is their point of origin (D. H. Wright, "Italian Stimulus," 1:87).

23. T. J. Brown et al., *Codex Lindisfarnensis,* 2:47; see also M. Esposito, "The Knowledge of Greek in Ireland during the Middle Ages," *Studies* 1 (1912): 665–83.

24. T. J. Brown et al., *Codex Lindisfarnensis,* 2:13–14, 147–49. Cf. E. H. Zimmerman, *Die Vorkarolingische Miniaturen* (Berlin: Deutsche Verein für Kunstwissenschaft, 1916), 113, typical of early scholars, suggesting that Ezra was the model for Matthew; and F. Saxl, "The Ruthwell Cross," *Journal of the Warburg and Courtauld Institutes* 6 (1943) 17–19, arguing that the two cannot derive from the same model because of differences in costume, but close observation indicates that Ezra's tunic is awkwardly derived from the longer pallium preserved in Matthew. The comparison of the two miniatures was first made by G. F. Browne in 1887 (Alexander, *Insular Manuscripts,* 37).

25. T. J. Brown et al., *Codex Lindisfarnensis,* 2:150–52; G. B. Brown, *Ruthwell and Bewcastle Crosses,* 350–51.

26. A. Baumstark, "Einer antike Bildkomposition in christlich-orientalischen Umdeutung," *Monatshefte für Kunstwissenschaft* 8 (1915): 118.

27. M. Backes and R. Dölling, *Art of the Dark Ages,* 95.

28. T. J. Brown et al., *Codex Lindisfarnensis,* 2:162.

29. Ibid., 154–55.

30. Ibid., 149–54; Alexander, *Insular Manuscripts,* 39; "De Illuminerede Haandschriften det store kongelige Bibliotek," *Aarberetninger og Meddelelser fra det store Kongelige Bibliotek* 3 (1874–1889): 34–37.

31. See Appendix, below.

32. T. J. Brown et al., *Codex Lindisfarnensis*, 2:156. For example, Brown hypothesizes that the Neapolitan codex used as a source for the liturgical apparatus of *Lindisfarne*, and possibly also as a text source, had a series of Evangelist portraits that provided a model for *Lindisfarne*. However, it is generally believed that the Neapolitan liturgical source lacked major illuminations.

33. C. A. Ralegh Radford, "The Portable Altar of St. Cuthbert," in *The Relics of St. Cuthbert*, ed. C. F. Battiscombe (Oxford: Oxford University Press, 1956), 326–35.

34. Alexander, *Insular Manuscripts*, 38; D. H. Wright, "Italian Stimulus," 89. Wright compares the *Lindisfarne* John to the Christ in Majesty from the Studion Basilica, Constantinople (Istanbul, Archaeological Museum). See also *Journal of the Walters Art Gallery* 10 (1947): 83.

35. See, for example, fourth-century Roman terra-cotta plaque (P. Brown, *The World of Late Antiquity from Marcus Aurelius to Mohammed* [London: Thames and Hudson, 1971], pl. 77); multiple diptych in ivory (Ravenna, Museo Nazionale), early sixth century, formerly in Murano (D. Talbot Rice, *Art of the Byzantine Era* [New York, Praeger, 1963], pl. 7).

36. Alexander, *Insular Manuscripts*, pls. 205, 211.

37. T. J. Brown et al., *Codex Lindisfarnensis*, 2:165.

38. The introductory verses to the colophon, in their entirety, read:

Littera me pandat sermonis fida ministra
Omnes alme meos fratres voce saluta:
Trinitus et unus Deus evangelium hoc ante saecula constituit
Mattheus ex ore Christi scripsit
Marcus ex ore Petri scripsit
Lucas de ore Pauli apostoli scripsit
Johannes in prochemio deinde extructuavit verbum deo donante et spiritu sancto scripsit.
(Millar, *Lindisfarne*, 3–4).

39. Bede, *Life of Cuthbert* 8 (*Lives of the Saints*, 82–83).

40. This codex, the Stonyhurst St. John (Lancaster, Stonyhurst College Library), was traditionally believed to be Boisil's own copy, but it is now considered on paleographic grounds to be a product of Jarrow/Monkswearmouth, dating after Boisil's death. See also D. Mynors and R. Powell, "The Stonyhurst Gospel," in *Relics of St. Cuthbert*, 356–74; T. J. Brown et al., *Codex Lindisfarnensis*, 2:57; *Anglo-Saxon Saints and Heroes*, 81–82.

41. Eddius, *Life of Wilfrid* 10 (*Lives of the Saints*, 141–43).

42. Alexander, *Insular Manuscripts*, 38–39. In the cases of Matthew's Man or Angel and John's Eagle, it is impossible to determine if the symbol is half- or full-length, as the former crouches and the latter flies from behind their respective Evangelists' halos.

43. D. H. Wright, "Italian Stimulus," 88–89; Bede; *Lives of the Abbots* 7 (*Anglo-Saxon Saints and Heroes*, 231–32). Also possibly derived from the Biscop Apocalypse model is the cycle of illumination in the *Valenciennes Apocalypse* (Valenciennes, Bibl. Munic. 99), with winged haloed Evanglist symbols carrying books and a trumpeting angel (fols. 10, 19) (Alexander, *Insular Manuscripts*, pls. 304, 306). Alexander, *Insular Manuscripts*, 39, suggests that the addition in *Lindisfarne* of trumpets to Evangelist symbols, particularly to Mark's Lion, may be a reference either to the Sedulius verse, "Marcus ut alta fremit," or to the *titulus* of Tours *Maiestas* pages, "Rex micat aethereus condigne/Hic evangelicae quattuor atque tubae." Alexander, however, gives no indication as to whether or how these verses were known in Northumbria.

44. Alexander, *Insular Manuscripts*, 39.

45. J. J. G. Alexander, "Some Aesthetic Principles in Colour Use in Anglo-Saxon Art," *Anglo-Saxon England* 4 (1975): 145–47.

46. C. Nordenfalk, "Eastern Style Elements in the *Lindisfarne Gospels*," *Acta Archaeologica* 13 (1942): 157–68. The ivories of the St. Mark group are:

St. Mark Preaching in Alexandria (Milan, Museo del Castello Sforzesco)
St. Mark Healing Animals (Milan, Museo del Castello Sforzesco
St. Mark Baptizing Ananias (Milan, Museo del Castello Sforzesco)

St. Mark Consecrating Ananias (Milan, Museo del Castello Sforzesco)
fragment, St. Mark with Codex (Milan, Museo del Castello Sforzesco
St. Peter Dictating the Gospel to St. Mark (London, Victoria and Albert Museum)

Some scholars also include the St. Mark Enthroned (Paris, Musée du Louvre). See also T. J. Brown et al., *Codex Lindisfarnensis,* 2:168–71, accepting a provenance in southern Italy for the ivories, but insisting on a manuscript source for the *Lindisfarne* Evangelists; and Mayr-Harting, *Coming of Christianity,* 159–61, tentatively accepting Nordenfalk's hypothesis of direct influence of ivories on the codex.

47. K. Weitzmann, "The Ivories of the So-Called Grado Chair," *Dumbarton Oaks Papers* 26 (1972): 43–91. Compare also the *Sacra Parallela* of John of Damascus (Paris, Bibl. Nat. Cod. Grec. 923), ca. 800–50 (D. Diringer, *The Illuminated Book: Its History and Production,* rev. ed. [New York: Praeger, 1967], pl. 2.21d); and the mosaics in the chapel of S. Zeno at S. Prassede, Rome, executed under Paschal I (817–24).

48. Saxl, "Ruthwell Cross," 18–19, argued that the anticlassical tradition had its roots in Palmyrene art, and that the immediate stylistic impulse for the *Lindisfarne* artist came from sub-Roman reliefs along Hadrian's Wall, where anticlassicism is already notable.

49. The unity of the *Lindisfarne Gospels* is also to some extent the result of the probable unity of the project under the direction of one scribe-artist, Eadfrith, and of the short period in which the codex was assembled.

50. Bede, *Life of Cuthbert* 42 (*Lives of the Saints,* 123–25).

51. E. Kitzinger, "The Coffin Reliquary," in *Relics of St. Cuthbert,* 202–304; cf. Henry, *IAECP,* 197, who debates the date of the incised ornament of the sarcophagus.

52. Alexander, *Insular Manuscripts,* 40–42, pls. 47, 202.

53. T. J. Brown et al., *Codex Lindisfarnensis,* 2:89ff.; G. Bonner, "Ireland and Rome: The Double Inheritance of Northumbria," in *Saints, Scholars and Heroes: Studies in Medieval Culture in Honour of Charles W. Jones,* ed. M. H. King and W. M. Stevens (Collegeville, Minn.: Hill Monastic Manuscript Library, 1979), 1:103–4. The last nine pages of the codex are written in a Jarrow uncial very similar to *Amiatinus.*

54. C. D. Verey, *A Collation of the Gospel Texts Contained in Durham Cathedral Manuscripts A.II.10, A.II.16, and A.II.17,* master's thesis, University of Durham, 1969. Part of the text of A.II.17 is in Cambridge (Magdelen College, Pepsyian MS 2981 [19]).

55. Alexander, *Insular Manuscripts,* 41.

56. The text of A.II.17 was considered part of a "mixed Irish" stemma (blending Vulgate and Old Latin readings) in the early literature, but Verey (*Collation,* 42) and Bonner ("Ireland and Rome," 105–6) agree that this stemma does not exist, since the use of Old Latin readings is inconsistent from text to text. The Vulgate text used in A.II.17 has its closest parallels in the OXZ group (Oxford, Bodleian MS Auct. D.II.14; Cambridge, Corpus Christi College MS 286; London, British Library Harley MS 1775). This group is associated with a southern Italian Gospels text possibly brought to Canterbury by Benedict Biscop during his 669–71 abbacy at SS. Peter and Paul. A copy of this text may have come north with Biscop to his foundations and traveled thence to Lindisfarne. The corrector of A.II.17 used a Vulgate very close to the *Lindisfarne Gospels,* possibly their exemplar.

57. Henry, *IAECP,* 184.

58. M. Richards, "The 'Lichfield' Gospels (Book of 'St. Chad')," *Journal of the National Library of Wales* 18 (1973): 135–46.

59. H. E. Savage, "The Story of the *St. Chad* Gospels," *Transactions of the Birmingham Archaeological Society* 41(1915): 5–21, esp. 8–21.

60. Ibid.; Alexander, *Insular Manuscripts,* 48–50.

61. Henry, *IAECP,* 185–88, suggested an Irish provenance for the *Book of St. Chad* on the basis of text associations and of the assumption that the assimilative tradition of the Celtic Church in the fusion of Mediterranean and indigenous elements would probably find equal if not preemptive fruit on Irish soil. However, there is no extant Irish illumination synchronous with *Lindisfarne* to prove Henry's hypothesis, unless *The Book of St. Chad* is Irish. Given the mobility of texts in the period

in question, the attribution of the *Book of St. Chad* to Ireland is difficult to establish.

62. Cramp, "Mercian Sculpture," 191–233.

63. H. E. Savage, *The St. Chad Gospels: An Address Given on the Festival of St. Chad* (Lichfield: Bull and Wiseman, 1931).

64. Alexander, *Insular Manuscripts,* pls. 203, 222, 223, 224.

65. Ibid., 46.

66. Ibid., pl. 302; C. Nordenfalk, *Celtic and Anglo-Saxon Painting* (New York: G. Braziller, 1977), 87.

67. Ibid.; Nordenfalk believes that the artist of the seated David was the teacher of the artist of the standing David, but that the student lacked his teacher's understanding of classical prototypes.

68. Panofsky, *Renaissance and Renascences,* 43.

69. Ibid.

70. G. B. Brown, *Ruthwell and Bewcastle Crosses,* 148–53. This cross might, however, have been inscribed on the wall rather than standing beside it.

71. Anderson and Anderson, *Adomnan's Life of Columba,* 307, 523. The use of plain crosses as commemorative markers was also borrowed by secular rulers, beginning with King Oswald of Northumbria at the Battle of Heavenfield in 634 (Bede 3.2 [Colgrave and Mynors, 214–15]). This cross was made of wood, and it is believed that many early crosses were of similarly perishable materials, some later replaced with stone monuments. However, documents reveal that some crosses were made of stone as early as the sixth century in Ireland. These were probably simple incised slabs like the Whithorn Cross. St. Patrick had a permanent staff of skilled stonecutters whose names are listed at the end of the *Tripartite Life,* and St. Coengen's stone hewer injured an eye with a flying chip, of which wound the saint miraculously cured him (G. B. Brown, *Ruthwell and Bewcastle Crosses,* 148–53). However, there is no evidence that these crosses had figural reliefs, and the earliest extant figural crosses in Ireland are dated to about 650.

72. Henry, *IAECP,* 133, on the use of crosses in the layout of the monastic plan in the *Book of Mulling* (Dublin, Trinity College MS 60). Henry argues that the Irish monastic crosses were both apotropaic signs protecting the monastery at the four cardinal points and personal nonfunerary monuments, bearing inscriptions requesting prayers for the builder. She additionally suggests that they served as gathering places for prayers and for offices.

73. Bede, *Life of Cuthbert* 37 (*Lives of the Saints,* 117).

74. The burial of Bishop Aldhelm of Malmesbury was also marked by standing crosses, according to William of Malmesbury's *Gesta Pontificarum.* William also mentions crosses set up within the monastic complex to honor particular individuals. He notes two stone "pyramids," probably cross shafts, at Glastonbury in his own day, one of which bore the names of Centwine (king of Wessex, 676–88), Alædde (bishop of Wessex, 677–705) and two late-seventh- and early-eighth-century abbots of Glastonbury (G. B. Brown, *Ruthwell and Bewcastle Crosses,* 148–53). Abbot Æthelwald of Lindisfarne also had a cross set up in his own name, around which cross it was customary to carry the relics of St. Cuthbert in procession (T. Allison, *English Religious Life in the Eighth Century* [New York: AMS, 1971], 101; A. S. Cook, *The Date of the Ruthwell and Bewcastle Crosses,* Transactions of the Connecticut Academy of Arts and Sciences, vol. 17 [New Haven: Yale University Press, 1912], 113).

75. Mayr-Harting, *Coming of Christianity,* 247–48; Theodore of Canterbury, *Penitential,* in McNeill, *Medieval Handbooks of Penance,* 204.

76. Paulinus of Nola, "The Decoration of His Churches," in C. D. Weyer, *Early Medieval Art, 300–1150,* Sources and Documents in the History of Art, ed. H. W. Janson (Englewood Cliffs, N.J.: Prentice-Hall, 1971), 17–19.

77. G. B. Brown, *Ruthwell and Bewcastle Crosses,* 109–10. Tradition held that a parishioner of Ruthwell was told in a dream to harness the oxen of a poor widow and drive his cart to Priestwoodside and remove the cross in the direction of Ruthwell, setting up the cross where the oxen first stopped and building a church around it. The legend follows a common medieval formula, but an ancient roadway still visible in the mid-eighteenth century connected Ruthwell to a site then called Priestside, a strip of arable land between the Morass and the Solway Firth. Priestside may be a derivation of Priestwoodside.

78. J. McFarlan, *Index of the Principal Acts of the Assembly of the Scottish Church*, St. Andrew's, 27 July 1642, sixth item, calls for the destruction of "idolatrous monuments at Ruthwell" (in Royal Commission, *Report [Dumfries]*, 220–22).

79. In 1697 William Nicholson, later bishop of Carlisle, noted in his diary, and in a letter of 22 April, the presence of "a most ravishing runic monument on a square [sectioned] cross stone in Revel Church," and recorded the local tradition of its origin, its contemporary state, and the dimensions of the extant fragments, giving also a transcription of the runic inscriptions of the cross (G. B. Brown, *Ruthwell and Bewcastle Crosses*, 106–7). At this time, some fragments were noted in the churchyard under throughstones, the typical local "table" tombstones. The remaining fragments were moved out into the churchyard in 1790 during work on the church. In 1792 Alexander Gordon published his *Itinerarium Septentrionale*, in which he noted the presence of a "capital with eagles," probably the upper cross arm (Cook, *Date of Crosses*, 5–6).

80. B. Dickins and A. S. C. Ross, *The Dream of the Rood* (London: Methuen, 1934), 8–13; A. Campbell, *Old English Grammar* (Oxford: Clarendon Press, 1959), 4; M. D. Forbes and B. Dickins, "The Inscriptions of the Ruthwell and Bewcastle Crosses and the Bridekirk Font," *Burlington Magazine* 25 (1914): 24–29; G. B. Brown, *Ruthwell and Bewcastle Crosses*, 203–44; Collingwood, *Northumbrian Crosses*, 117–19; F. Willet, "The Ruthwell and Bewcastle Crosses," *University of Manchester Museum Publications*, n.s., 7 (1957): 1–42. Willet suggests that the *Dream* was a later addition to the cross. This is difficult on the grounds that the runes and the Latin inscriptions, which are integral to the carved program, are generally considered to have been carved by the same hand.

81. W. S. Calverley, *Notes on the Early Sculptured Crosses, Shrines and Monuments in the Present Diocese of Carlisle*," Cumberland and Westmoreland Antiquarian and Archaeological Society, ex. ser., 11 (1899): 46–47; J. K. Hewison, *The Romance of the Bewcastle Cross, the Mystery of Alcfrith, and the Myths of Maughan* (Glasgow: J. Murray, 1923). See also H. Bütow, *Das altenglische Traumgeschichte vom Kreuz, Anglistische Forschungen* (Heidelberg: C. Winter, 1935), which gives a complete annotated early bibliography.

82. Page, "Bewcastle Cross," 36–57. This exhaustive study of the Bewcastle colophon indicated that only "lc[h]fri," of, presumably, "Alchfrith," and the name "Cyniburg" are legible. Page pointed out that Cyniburg is a fairly common early Anglian name, and the "lcfri" is part of a large number of Anglo-Saxon given names. Finally, he dated the form of the Bewcastle runes between 750 and 850.

83. G. B. Brown, *Ruthwell and Bewcastle Crosses*, 122–24.

84. Perhaps this Lamb was ignored by the same Reformation zealots who destroyed the cross transom above because they considerd that in this context the Lamb was emblematic of pastoral care and therefore not blasphemous. However, this Lamb, like the presumed Agnus Dei, above, wears a nimbus and is thus obviously also symbolic of Christ. Why it escaped the wrath of the destroyers of the cross is not completely resolved.

85. A. K. Porter, *The Crosses and Culture of Ireland* (New Haven: Yale University Press, 1931), 87.

86. D. J. Howlett, "Two Panels on the Ruthwell Cross," *Journal of the Warburg and Courtauld Institutes* 37(1974): 333–36, notes that Bede refers repeatedly to the "qui tollis" in his *In Lucam Evangelium Expositio* (709–15). P. Meyvaert, ("An Apocalypse Panel on the Ruthwell Cross," in *Medieval and Renaissance Studies; Proceedings of the Southeastern Institute of Medieval and Renaissance Studies; Summer, 1978*, ed. F. Tirro, vol. 9, (Durham: Duke University Press, 1982), 3–32), pointed out that if the inscription of this panel is read in the same sequence as those of the other panels of the cross, it should end rather than begin with the "Adoramus." For various well-argued reasons, Meyvaert identified the figure as an apocalyptic Christ rather than as the Baptist, despite the consequent lack of programmatic cohesion in the cross as a whole. Recently G. Henderson, ("The John the Baptist Panel on the Ruthwell Cross," *Gesta* 24 (1985): 3–12), has convincingly reestablished the identity of the figure as John the Baptist, also reinterpreting the figure of Christ below and the entire cross as programmatically eucharistic and liturgical. In this context, see also E. Ó Carragáin, "Liturgical Innovations Associated with Pope Sergius and the Iconography of the Ruthwell and Bewcastle Crosses," in *Bede and Anglo-Saxon England*, ed. R. T.

Farrell, British Archaeological Reports, vol. 46 (Oxford: British Archaeological Reports, 1978), 131–45. However, given the locus and probable function of the cross, in my view, so complex a program might well have been far too erudite to have meaning for the local laity and teaching clergy of Dumfries at the time.

87. Cf. a sarcophagus of the Pignatta family in S. Francesco, Ravenna; stuccos in the Orthodox Baptistry and a mosaic in the Archepiscopal Palace, both also in Ravenna; the *Palatine Sermons of St. Augustine* (Vat. Pal. 220, 1r); a sarcophagus in Gerona; and an early catacomb painting in Alexandria (G. B. Brown, *Arts in Early England*, 5:282–84); also a Merovingian stoup from Mianugy near Abbeville (O. M. Dalton, *Byzantine Art and Archaeology* [Oxford: Clarendon Press, 1911], 672).

88. M. Schapiro, "The Religious Meaning of the Ruthwell Cross," *Art Bulletin* 26 (1944): 232–45, esp. 232–35. The mainstream writers cited as using this passage in reference to the Temptation include Eusebius *(Commentaries on Matthew 4.4)*, Jerome *(Tractatus in Marcam 1.13)*, and Bede *(In Lucam Evangelium Expositio)*. John Cassian *(De incarnatione Christi, Contra Nestorium 7.2)* cites the Psalm as an argument against heretics who, like the Devil in the Temptation, leave out the passages that betray them. The messianic image is drawn from the prophecies of Isaiah 11:6–9, on the restoration of harmony with animals at the end of the tree of Jesse, and Habakkuk 3:2 in the Old Latin translation, "You shall know him between two animals," and builds on Pseudo-Matthew 35, in which Christ rebukes his listeners, "How much better than you are the beasts which know me and are tame, while men know me not," and on a poem prefaced to the Psalter in some texts, falsely attributed to both Jerome and Damasus, reading:

> Virtus regit omnia Christi
> Quia varias iunxit uno sub carmine linguas
> Ut pecudes volucresque Deum cognoscere possint.

89. Schapiro, "Religious Meaning," 239–40.

90. G. Baldwin Brown and W. R. Lethaby, "The Bewcastle and Ruthwell Crosses," *Burlington Magazine* 23(1913): 45.

91. The Irish crosses with this motif are: Castledermot (Kildare)—High Cross, west face, and North Cross, east face; Muirdach (Louth)—north face; Monasterboice (Louth)—West Cross; Kells (Meath)—Market Cross and Cross of SS Patrick and Columba; the Moone Abbey Cross (Kildare); and the Arboe Cross (Tyrone).

92. Schapiro, "Religious Meaning," 236. The basis for this association is Jerome, *Vita Pauli*, and *Epistolium ad Eustochium* 22; and John Cassian, *Collationes* 18.6 and 45.4, and *De Coenobiorum Institutis* 1.

93. Saxl, "Ruthwell Cross," 4.

94. G. B. Brown, *Ruthwell and Bewcastle Crosses*, 282.

95. Saxl, "Ruthwell Cross," 4; Schapiro, "Religious Meaning," 238.

96. W. R. Lethaby, "The Ruthwell Cross," *Burlington Magazine* 21(1912): 145–48.

97. Schapiro, "Religious Meaning," 238; G. B. Brown, *Ruthwell and Bewcastle Crosses*, 280–82; Cook, *Date*, 60–65; G. F. Browne, *The Ancient Cross Shafts at Bewcastle and Ruthwell* (Cambridge: Cambridge University Press, 1916), 33; M. Schapiro, "The Bowman and the Bird on the Ruthwell Cross and Other Works: The Interpretation of Secular Themes in Early Medieval Art," *Art Bulletin* 45(1963): 351–55.

98. Saxl, "Ruthwell Cross," 5–7.

99. Ibid.

100. E. H. Kantorowicz, "The Archer in the Ruthwell Cross," *Art Bulletin* 42(1960): 57–59. The identification of the archer as Ishmael has come under fire from M. Schapiro, ("The Bowman and the Bird," 351–5), who interprets the scene as a secular hunt, possibly apotropaic, and from R. T. Farrell, ("The Archer and Associated Figures on the Ruthwell Cross," in *Bede and Anglo-Saxon England*, ed. R. T. Farrell, British Archaeological Reports, vol. 46 (Oxford: British Archaeological Reports, 1978), 96–117), who prefers to identify the eagle as Christ protecting the faithful in the desert from evil, personified by the archer. Farrell refers to the scene of Christ on the Beasts on

the front of the cross and interprets the archer and the bird in light of Psalm 90, the Temptation of Christ and commentaries by Bede and by Church Fathers known in England in the period, notably Augustine, Jerome, and Arnobius Junior. This latter identification would not undermine the basic eremitic program of the Ruthwell Cross argued here.

101. Howlett, "Two Panels," 334–35.

102. Ibid., 335–36.

103. The scene has parallels in the *Rabbūlā Gospels* (Florence, Laurentian Library, Cod. Plut. I); the *Kludov Psalter* (Moscow, Historical Museum); and the tenth-century *Codex Egberti* (Trier, Staatsbibl. Cod. 24).

104. R. Hill, "Christianity and Geography in Early Northumbria," in *Studies in Church History*, ed. G. J. Cuming and D. Baker (Cambridge: Cambridge Univeristy Press, 1971), 7:133, suggests that the kneeling figure is incomplete—difficult to accept given the quantity of detail.

105. Schapiro, "Religious Meaning," 237–38, quotes John Cassian *(Collationes* 1.7); Jerome *(Epistolium in Eustochium);* Gregory *(Moralia in Job* 6.28); and Bede *(In Lucam Evangelium Expositio).*

106. G. Stuhlfauth, *Die Engel in der christliche Kunst,* Archäologische Schriften zur christlichen Kunst der Altertum und Mittelalter (Freiburg: J. C. B. Mohr, 1897), 3:71.

107. Schapiro, "Religious Meaning," 238.

108. Saxl, "Ruthwell Cross," 14.

109. Cook, *Date,* 18–19, saw the head of Christ turned to the right and the thieves' crosses to either side. W. R. Lethaby, "The Ruthwell Cross: An Anglo-Celtic Work," *Archaeological Journal* 70(1913): 148–49, refuted Cook on the basis of the extreme erosion of the panel.

110. The Crucifixion with sun and moon is rare before its popularization in Carolingian France, but thereafter appears regularly on ninth-century English crosses as at Hoddam (Dumf.) and Alnmouth (Nthld.), and in late Scottish crosses.

111. F. Henry, *Irish High Crosses,* Cultural Relations Committee of Ireland (Dublin: Three Candles, 1964), pls. 1, 6, 16.

112. Ernst Kitzinger, *Early Medieval Art in the British Museum* (London: British Museum, 1940), pl. 7.

113. Schapiro, "Religious Meaning," 238–40; Kantorowicz, "The Archer," 58–59.

114. Schapiro, "Religious Meaning," 244–45. Jocelin, *Life of Kentigern,* in *Pinkerton's The Scottish Saints,* rev. and enl. W. M. Metcalf (Paisley: Gardner, 1889), 2:1–116. Kentigern was an Egypto-Celtic recluse, compared in the biographies to Christ, Elijah, and John the Baptist. He habitually emerged from retreat on Maundy Thursday to wash the feet of paupers and lepers with his tears and dry them with his hair. He was also close to animals, in the eremitic tradition, and attempted to fulfill messianic prophecy by uniting the human and animal kingdoms: He brought a pet robin back to life, yoked wild bulls to a cart, and yoked a stag and a wolf to a plow, explaining that this combination would not have been unusual before the Fall of Man. He also restored the sight of a blind king. Schapiro points out that Germanus of Auxerre healed the blind daughter of a tribune (Bede 1.18 [Colgrave and Mynors, 58–59]), to convince the Britons of the error of the Pelagian heresy, that Kentigern's repetition of this miracle may consequently have been construed by the later Celtic Church as a sign of their divinely ordained superiority over the Roman mission, and that the inclusion of the scene on the Ruthwell Cross is therefore intensely political. However, this argument depends on a very early date for the legend of Kentigern's miracle, and on the unlikely universal recognition by Strathclyde viewers that the reference had a political reference to a relatively remote event in southern English ecclesiastical history.

115. D. Fyson, "Anglian Patterns: Some Sources and Developments," *Archaeologia Aeliana,* 4th ser., 35(1957): 64–71, esp. 69; O. E. Saunders, *History of English Art in the Middle Ages* (Oxford: Clarendon Press, 1932), 135; Bütow, *Traumgeschichte,* 135–38; Kitzinger, "Vinescroll Ornament," 61–71.

116. Browne, *Ancient Cross Shafts,* 22–23, believed the Ruthwell and Bewcastle craftsmen to be Syrian monastics fleeing the Islamic invasion of the Levant, or Lombards leaving a nation in turmoil. Porter, *Crosses and Culture,* 99–101, suggested that they might be Merovingian Franks, a branch workshop of the stone carvers at Biscop's foundations. M. Conway, "A Dangerous Archae-

ological Method, II," *Burlington Magazine* 24(1913–14): 86–89, believed they might be Ravennate, displaced by the Lombard invasion. However, none of these regions had stylistically comparable contemporary schools of stone carving. J. Strzygowski, *Der Norden in den bildenden Kunst Westeuropas* (Vienna: Krystall, 1926), 123, compared the English crosses to reliefs in churches in Armenia, and the House of Simon panel at Ruthwell is indeed close to a scene of Christ with a donor on the exterior wall of the south conch of the cruciform church at Mzchet. Moreover, Armenian artists would have had cause to be leaving their homeland in this period, under the impact of Islamic invasion. However, there is to my knowledge no documentary evidence of Armenian workshops or communities anywhere in northern Europe at this date, and the similarities of Ruthwell and Mzchet can be explained as parallel anticlassicism.

117. One center that has been suggested as the source of the Ruthwell workshop is Hoddam, a monastic foundation five miles from Ruthwell, of which the foundation has been traditionally attributed to St. Kentigern. Hoddam was in any case originally a Celtic foundation taken over by the Northumbrians in the reign of Oswy at the same time that the see of Whithorn was established under Northumbrian rule. It has been associated with Tigbrethingham, an important western complex included in a tenth-century listing of the ancient possessions of Lindisfarne. However, fragments of a cross from Hoddam (Edinburgh, National Museum of Scotland) show a totally different style, using half-length figures in very shallow relief. This may be a question of a generation's time lag, or of totally separate origin centers. C. A. Ralegh Radford, "Hoddam," *Transactions of the Dumfriesshire and Galloway Natural Historical and Antiquarian Society,* 3rd ser., 31 (1954): 174–97. R. Cramp, ("The Evangelist Symbols and Their Parallels in Anglo-Saxon Sculpture," in *Bede and Anglo-Saxon England,* ed. R. T. Farrell, British Archaeological Reports, vol. 46 (Oxford: British Archaeological Reports, 1978), 118–30, suggests a workshop provenance at Jarrow/Wearmouth, but if the present assessment of the program is correct, this association is unlikely, given the strongly Roman-biased viewpoint of Jarrow/Wearmouth.

118. J. Beckwith, "Reculver, Ruthwell and Bewcastle," *Kolloquium über spätantike und frühmittelalterliche Skulptur,* Heidelberg, 1970 (Mainz: P. von Zabern, 1972), 17–19.

119. The drapery in the Hoddam fragment is particularly reminiscent of the treatment of garments in the *St. Gall Gospels* (St. Gall, Stiftsbibliothek, Cod. 51, pp. 128, 267, etc.) (Alexander, *Insular Manuscripts,* pls. 203–8). Also, in Ruthwell, Christ has a mustache in this scene, whereas in Rothbury, the blind man sports luxurious whiskers of almost comic length and curliness.

120. Bede 4.26 (Colgrave and Mynors, 428–29).

121. E. Mercer, "The Ruthwell and Bewcastle Crosses," *Antiquity* 38 (1964): 268–76, esp. 270–74.

122. Levison, *England and the Continent,* 121–25; Cramp, "Mercian Sculpture," 191–233.

123. Compare the draperies of the Ascending Christ in the Rothbury font base to those of the angel to the right of Christ on the front cover of the *Lorsch Gospels* (Vatican Museo Sacro), and the Reculver draperies in general to the illuminations of the *Sacramentary of Archbishop Drogo of Metz* (825–55) (Paris, Bibl. Nat., MS Lat, 9428, fol. 71v, etc.).

124. Obviously, this summing up of the later history of the Anglian crosses is vastly simplified and generalized, and the circumstance of each particular cross deserves individual study. The reader is referred to the forthcoming corpus of the English crosses for a detailed analysis. See also R. Cramp, "The Position of the Otley Crosses in English Sculpture of the Eighth to Ninth Centuries," *Kolloquium über Skulptur,* 55–63; W. G. Collingwood, "Anglian and Anglo-Danish Sculpture in the North Riding of Yorkshire," *Yorkshire Archaeological Journal* pt. 75, 19 (1907): 267–413; B. Kurth, "Ecclesia and an Angel on the Andrew Auckland Cross," *Journal of the Warburg and Courtauld Institutes* 6 (1943): 213–14; M. Longhurst, "The Easby Cross," *Archaeologia* 81 (1931): 43–47; J. H. Nicholson, "The Sculptured Stones at Heysham," *Transactions of the Lancashire and Cheshire Antiquaries' Society* 9 (1891): 30–38; G. Tate, "Saxon Sculptured Stones at Norham," *History of the Berwickshire Naturalists' Club* 4 (1857–62): 218; H. M. Taylor, "The Chapel, Church, and Carved Stones at Heysham," *Archaeological Journal* 127 (1970): 185–87; J. Brøndsted, *Early English Ornament,* trans. A. F. Major (London: Hachette, 1924), passim, on development of vine scroll; Kendrick, *Anglo-Saxon Art,* 149–64; J. Calvert, "The Iconography of the St. Andrew Auckland Cross," *Art Bulletin* 66(1984): 543–55.

Chapter 6. Secular Traditions

1. Hope-Taylor, *Yeavering*, 276–324, esp. 312.

2. W. A. Chaney, *The Cult of Kingship in Anglo-Saxon England: Transitions from Paganism to Christianity* (Berkeley and Los Angeles: University of California Press, 1970), 35–42; J. G. H. Grattan and C. Singer, *Anglo-Saxon Magic and Medicine* (Oxford: Oxford University Press, 1952).

3. R. Cramp, "*Beowulf* and Archaeology," *Medieval Archaeology* 1 (1957): 57–77.

4. Bede 2.5 (Colgrave and Mynors, 150–51).

5. However, this may not have been so much an individual act of concupiscence as the fulfillment of legal obligation. Augustine's query to Gregory (Bede 1.27 [Colgrave and Mynors, 84–87]) as to the acceptability of a man's marriage with his stepmother suggests that this union was common and may have been part of pre-Christian Anglo-Saxon inheritance law or filial obligation.

6. Bede 2.5 (Colgrave and Mynors, 152–55).

7. Ibid., 2.6 (154–57).

8. Ibid., 4.27 (432–33).

9. Ibid., 1.30 (106–9).

10. B. Branston, *The Lost Gods of England* (New York: Oxford University Press, 1974), 41–42, quotes Bede, *De Ratione Tempore*.

11. R. I. Page, *Life in Anglo-Saxon England* (London: Batsford, 1970), 31; W. Bonser, "Survivals of Paganism in Anglo-Saxon England," *Transactions of the Birmingham Archaeological Society* 56 (1934): 55; McNeill, *Medieval Handbooks of Penance,* 198.

12. *Laws* of Wihtred of Kent, in M. Swanton, ed., *Anglo-Saxon Prose* (London: Dent, 1975), 1; Bonser, "Survivals of Paganism," 55; Mayr-Harting, *Coming of Christianity,* 239.

13. Mayr-Harting, *Coming of Christianity,* 223–28.

14. Bonser, "Survivals of Paganism," 55: Eighth- and ninth-century edicts prohibited dancing in churches on St. John's Eve, which falls on the summer solstice, a practice evidently carrying over from pagan custom. The Viking invaders brought their own pagan traditions and with their conversion a new round of prohibitions, some of which may, however, refer to practices with Anglo-Saxon rather than Scandinavian origins. The ninth-century *Canons of Edgar,* as recorded by Wulfstan, archbishop of York, prohibited priests from singing profane songs, even to themselves, and outlawed both *lic-wigelung,* or necromancy, the worship of trees, wells, stones, and groves, and changing one's shape to "go as a stag or as an old woman" on New Year's Eve. Page, *Life in Anglo-Saxon England,* 31: a ninth-century charter refers to an ash tree, "which the ignorant call holy." A deed between Æthelwald, bishop of Winchester, and Wulfstan Uccea (*Anglo-Saxon Prose,* 28–29) describes the drowning of a witch at London Bridge between 963 and 975. This marks the beginning of the long period in which individuals were prosecuted for practicing pagan rites. However, in the eleventh century, the Northumbrian Priest's Law still included the by-now-familiar prohibitions against the worship of trees, wells, and stones. See also Hill, "Christianity and Geography," 133–9.

15. Bede 2.15 (Colgrave and Mynors, 190–91).

16. See Chapter 1, 37.

17. C. W. Kennedy, ed. and trans., *Beowulf: The Oldest English Epic,* lines 30–52 (1940; reprint, Oxford: Oxford University Press, 1968), 4; Bruce-Mitford, *Sutton Hoo: Handbook,* 16, fig. 2. Note mounds 2, 3, 7, and 10. Mound 2 has been excavated and was found to contain a ransacked boat burial.

18. V. I. Evison, "Anglo-Saxon Whetstones," *Antiquaries Journal* 55 (1975): 70–85.

19. Bruce-Mitford, "Sutton Hoo Ship Burial," 8–9.

20. Page, *Life,* 46; Bruce-Mitford, *Sutton Hoo: Handbook,* 23.

21. Evison, "Whetstones" 70–85.

22. Bruce-Mitford, *Sutton Hoo: Handbook,* 23 and note 12; R. L. S. Bruce-Mitford, "The Sutton Hoo Ship Burial: Comments on General Interpretation," in *Aspects of Anglo-Saxon Archaeology: Sutton Hoo and Other Discoveries* (New York: Gollancz, 1972), pls. 7c and d.

23. MacCana, *Celtic Mythology,* 35.

24. Ibid., 35–36.

25. Stags are uncommon in Anglo-Saxon art. In Gallic Celtic mythology, they are associated with Cernunnos, the horned herdsman/hunter god, as on the Gundestrup Cauldron (Cophenhagen, National Museum) of the first century A.D. His primary attribute was mastery over animals, and his cult was known in Scotland and Ireland as well as on the Continent. See also MacCana, *Celtic,* 47. However, Heorot, Hrothgar's mead hall in *Beowulf,* translates as "the hall of the hart," which may indicate royal and/or mythological associations in the Anglo-Saxon cultural sphere as well.

26. The Anglo-Saxon hero/god Weland was also a smith, but his role is the classic anti-authoritarian trickster, and it would be difficult to link him to royalty.

27. Bede 2.5 (Colgrave and Mynors, 148–51).

28. Chaney, *Cult of Kingship,* 33. Only the East Saxon kings claimed descent from a divinity other than Woden. They began their genealogical listing with Seaxneat or Saxnot, "the need of the Saxons," possibly a tribal divinity, or equally possibly an honorific applying to Woden or another god. In later works, Saxnot is identified as Tyr or Balder, but this cannot be demonstrated to be an early reference.

29. M. Hunter, "Germanic and Roman Antiquity: The Sense of the Past in Anglo-Saxon England," *Anglo-Saxon England* (1974): 29–50. Such extension of ancestor lists into biblical history is the result either of postconversion paganophobia, or of a devaluation of Woden from god to historical hero in the same period, or of the Christian belief in the priority of biblical prehistory.

30. Branston, *Lost Gods,* 29, notes the Wansdyke running from Hampshire into Somerset passing spots once called Wodnes beorh (Woden's barrow), now Adam's Grave in Alton Priors, and Wodnes denu, (Woden's valley) in West Overton. Another center of worship near the headwaters of the Thames includes Wednesbury (Woden's fortress), and Wednesfield. One might also mention Wensleydale, (Yorks.), Wansfell (W. Mlds.), Wansford (Nthld.), and Wanswell (Glos.).

31. Bruce-Mitford, *Sutton Hoo: Handbook,* 24.

32. H. Shetelig and H. Falk, *Scandinavian Archaeology,* trans. E. V. Gordon (1937; reprint, New York: AMS Press, 1978), 257–59.

33. *Beowulf,* lines 1556, 1663 (Kennedy, 50, 54).

34. Bruce-Mitford, *Sutton Hoo: Handbook,* 30–31.

35. Ibid., 80–83; Bruce-Mitford, "Comments," 51. The archaeological resemblances are to finds north of Mälar Lake in the realm of the Svears, but the early names in the East Anglian regnal lists are closer to those of the Geats of central Sweden. Beowulf, too, was a Geat, and, if the Wulfingas, the royal house of East Anglia, were Geatish, East Anglia may have been the entry point in England for the oral tradition behind the epic. On the other hand, Northumbrian regnal lists of the ninth century also begin the mortal line with "Geat."

36. R. L. S. Bruce-Mitford and M. R. Luscombe, "The Benty Grange Helmet," in *Aspects of Anglos-Saxon Archaeology,* 223–42. Animal crest and brow ornaments also decorate the Coppergate helmet, although these cannot be conclusively identified as boars (see also P. V. Addyman, N. Pearson, and D. Tweddle, "The Coppergate Helmet," *Antiquity* 56 [1982]: 189–94). Boar helmets are also mentioned in the fragmentary *Lay of Finnsberg* in *Beowulf,* line 1086 (Kennedy, 36).

37. G. Speake, *Anglo-Saxon Animal Art and Its Germanic Background* (Oxford: Clarendon Press, 1980), 78–81.

38. Chaney, *Cult of Kingship,* 121–27.

39. Speake, *Anglo-Saxon Animal Art,* 79; Saxo Grammaticus, *The First Nine Books of the Danish History,* ed. and trans. O. Elton, and F. Y. Powell (London: D. Nutt, 1894), 49.

40. A. Meaney, *A Gazeteer of Early Anglo-Saxon Burial Sites* (London: G. Allen and Unwin, 1964), 13–21; A. Meaney and S. C. Hawkes, *Two Anglos-Saxon Cemeteries at Winall, Winchester, Hants.,* Society for Medieval Archaeology Monograph Series, vol. 4 (London, 1970), 50–55.

41. The transition at Garton from extramural to intramural cemeteries is dated by association with the date of death of Cuthbert of Canterbury, the first prelate buried in the Garton minster yard, between 740–41 and 756–60.

42. Deanesley, *The Pre-Conquest Church,* 65.

43. Inhumations in which a woman was sacrificially thrown into the grave of a man include burials at Finglesham, (Kent), and Farthingdown and Mitcham (Surrey). In all these cases the

female skeleton was found twisted and thrown across the male skeleton. Human sacrifice was otherwise unusual among the Anglo-Saxons, but this particular practice shows parallels to Viking practice and may be Scandinavian in origin (Meaney, *Gazeteer*, 18). See also Chaney, *Cult of Kingship*, 86–120, esp. 113, on the sacrifice of sacral kings in Anglo-Saxon England and Scandinavian parallels.

44. This may account for the relative distance between the Sutton Hoo burial precinct and the associated East Anglian court at Rendlesham.

45. T. C. Lethbridge, *Excavations in the Anglo-Saxon Cemeteries of Cambridge and Suffolk,* Cambridge Antiquaries' Society Quarto Publications, n.s. 3(1931): 53, pls. III 26–28; Bruce-Mitford, "Comments," p. 9a.

46. Mayr-Harting, *Coming of Christianity,* 223, believes the Burwell box lid shows Sigurd killing Fafnir, but the saga sources for that narrative are Norse and much later than the Burwell box.

47. Eddius, *Life of Wilfrid* 2 (*Lives of the Saints,* 134); *The Anonymous Life of Ceolfrith* 34 and Bede, *Lives of the Abbots,* 1 (*Anglo-Saxon Saints and Heroes,* 267–68, 225–26).

48. F. Ó. Briain, "Saga Themes in Irish Hagiography," in *Essays and Studies Presented to Professor Tadhg Ua Donnchadha (Torna),* ed. S. Pender (Cork: Cork University Press, 1947), 33–42. These include both folkloristic elements in the actions of saints (such as the triple-milking episode in Cogitosus's *Life of Brigid*) and references to particular mythological events and heroes (including Patick's audience with Ossian and Cailte in the *Aoallam na senorach,* the recovery of the Black Bull of Ulster through the fasting of St. Columba, and the narrative of his deeds by the hero Fergus mac Roich to the two Brendans when the latter visited his tomb).

49. Felix, *Life of Guthlac,* ed. B. Colgrave (Cambridge: Cambridge University Press, 1956), 3; Hunter, "Germanic and Roman Antiquity," 33; Felix, *Life of Guthlac,* in *Anglo-Saxon Saints and Heroes,* 171 n. 10., 174 n. 14, 176; Mayr-Harting, *Coming of Christianity,* 228. Felix traces Guthlac's descent from the Mercian royal house and hints that he may have had a claim to the throne. Guthlac ("battle-lay") is seen as a young warrior with a substantial *gesith.* Later, as a hermit, he fends off evil spirits who resemble Grendel as much as they do the persecutors of St. Anthony.

50. *Anonymous Life of Ceolfrith* 27 (*Anglo-Saxon Saints and Heroes,* 263). See also *Beowulf,* lines 3170–82 (Kennedy, 100–101).

51. Mayr-Harting, *Coming of Christianity,* 228; Hunter, "Germanic and Roman Antiquity," 46–48; Chaney, *Cult of Kingship,* 125. Ecclesiastical writers apply the terminology of Germanic heroic kingship equally to foreign worthies. In the *Elene,* an early Anglo-Saxon poem on the finding of the True Cross, Constantine appears as an Anglo-Saxon warrior leading his war band beneath a boar banner, and the Roman title *consul* in Bede's *Ecclesiastical History* is translated in the vernacular manuscripts into the local heroic idiom as *cyning* or "underking." See also C.E. Wright, *Cultivation of Saga,* 20–21; William of Malmesbury, in the *Gesta Pontificarum,* quotes the lost *Handbóc* of Alfred, in relating that Aldhelm, bishop of Sherbourne, found that by singing secular lays on the front steps of his church, he was able to entice the people back into the church for sermons given after Mass.

52. Bede, *Life of Cuthbert* 27 (*Lives of the Saints,*) 106).

53. Mayr-Harting, *Coming of Christianity,* 223–28; Hunter, "Germanic and Roman Antiquity," 31–32. Ingeld is also mentioned in *Beowulf,* line 2063 (Kennedy, 67).

54. Speake, *Anglo-Saxon Animal Art,* 85–92; H. Vierck, "Ein Relieffibelpaar aus Nordenorf," *Bayerische Vorgerichtsblätter* 32(1976): 104–43; A. Becker, *Franks Casket: Zu den Bildern und Inschriften des Runenkästchen von Auzon,* Regensburger Arbeiten zur Anglistik und Amerikanistik, vol. 5 (Regensburg: H. Carl, 1972), 123–24.

55. The ornamentation of later Norwegian stave churches demonstrates that such carving in wood was practiced by Germanic peoples.

56. Hunter, "Germanic and Roman Antiquity," 49–50.

57. Bede 2.16 (Colgrave and Mynors, 192–93).

58. Deanesley, *Pre-Conquest Church,* 71; Deanesley, "Roman Influence," 138–42.

59. *Beowulf,* line 1018 (Kennedy, 34).

60. Bruce-Mitford, "Comments," 7–17; c.f., B. Nerman, "The Standard of Sutton Hoo as a Torchholder," *Antiquaries' Journal* 50 (1970): 340–41.

61. Bede 2.5 (Colgrave and Mynors, 148–49).

62. Hope-Taylor, *Yeavering,* 46–69, 129–41, 246, 311.

63. Ibid., 363 n. 136; see also 200–203, 246, 270; M. Richards, *The Laws of Hywel Dda: The Book of Blegywrya* (Liverpool: Liverpool University Press, 1954), 39.

64. *Beowulf,* lines 331–63 (Kennedy 13–14).

65. Cf. Hope-Taylor, *Yeavering,* 202–3, who suggests the third alternative that the "staff" may be symbolic of a device for geometric calculation, akin to the Roman *groma,* used to lay out the hall and the site as a whole. Yeavering as a whole is sited on an upright wooden post set on an earlier grave and the grave with the device is set suggestively on the axis of the great hall. If so, the person buried here is more likely an architect than a door warden. However, given the ritual importance of geometry among the Anglo-Saxons, the device could still be a part of the paraphernalia of court protocol.

66. Ibid., 119–22, figs. 55, 56, 57.

67. Ibid., 241–44. The examples at Vindonissa and Carnuntum were founded in a series of discrete postholes rather than in continuous trenches as at Yeavering. On the other hand, the foundations of the stone amphitheater at Chester, excavated in 1960, cover a network of trenches that originally contained a grillage supporting a wooden amphitheater of the late first century A.D. Yeavering's construction is probably nonetheless derived independently from stone amphitheaters, since Chester is remote from Yeavering in date, location, and plan.

68. Ibid., 366 nn. 229–31.

69. Ibid., 161, 168–69.

70. Ibid., 279–80.

71. Wilson, *Archaeology of Anglo-Saxon England,* 7–8.

72. Bede, *Life of Cuthbert* 27 (*Lives of the Saints,* 105); *Anonymous Life of Cuthbert* 8 (*Anglo-Saxon Saints and Heroes,* 68–71).

73. Bede 4.19 (Colgrave and Mynors, 394–95).

74. Hunter, "Germanic and Roman Antiquity," 35–36.

75. Tower arch at Corbridge (Nthld.), chancel arch at Escomb (Durham), columns at St. Pancras, Canterbury, (Kent), among others.

76. Hunter, "Germanic and Roman Antiquity," 39–40; Deanesley, "Roman Influences," 130. Deanesley suggests that Edwin and other Anglo-Saxon kings arranged to be baptized in old Roman cities because baptism had become another route to self-identification with Rome and her legacy of authority.

77. Deanesley, "Roman Influences," 129; Hunter, "Germanic and Roman Antiquity," 39–40.

78. Hunter, "Germanic and Roman Antiquity," 39–40.

79. Ibid., 38–39; Deanesley, "Roman Influences," 145. The first English coin, the *thrymsa,* was copied from the *trientes,* the Roman coin worth a third of a *solidus aureus.* Other examples of emulative coinage include an Anglo-Saxon *solidus* from Markshall roughly reproducing the *Beata Tranquilitas* of 320–21, and the *sceatta* of Pada emulating a bronze of Crispus of ca. 319.

80. Esposito, "Knowledge of Greek," 665–83; W. B. Stanford, "Toward a History of Classical Influences in Ireland," *Proceedings of the Royal Irish Academy* 70(c) (1970): 23. Cf. Joyce, *Social History,* 1:411–12; W. Levison, "Die Iren und die Frankisch Kirche," *Historische Zeitschrift* 109 (1912): 1–22; K. Meyer, *Learning in Ireland in the Fifth Century and the Transmission of Letters,* School of Irish Learning (Dublin: Hodges, Figgis and Co., 1913); Louis Gougand, *Gaelic Pioneers of Christianity,* trans. V. Collins (Dublin, M. H. Gill and Son, 1923), 55–67.

81. Ludwig Bieler, "The Humanism of St. Columbanus," in *Mélanges Columbaniens: Actes du Congres International d'Etudes Columbaniennes,* Luxeuil, 1950 (Paris: Éditions Alsatia, 1951), 95–102; idem, "The Classics in Celtic Ireland," in *Classical Influences on European Culture, A.D. 500–1000,* ed. R. R. Bolgar (Cambridge: Cambridge University Press, 1971) 45–46; Masai and Bischoff, "Il monachesimo Irlandese nei suoi rapportical Continente," in *Il Monachesimo nell'alto Medioevo e la formazione della civiltà occidentale,* Settimane di Studio del Centro Italiano de Studi sull'Alto Medioevo 4 (1957): 123–24, 129–30. Columbanus's letter to Findolius, a tract on avarice and the evils of gold, cites Danae, Polydorus, the Golden Fleece, and other classical references. He composes the letter in adonic meter and gives his reader advice on its scansion, quoting Terentianus

Maurus on Sappho's uses of this meter. His fourth letter quotes Sallust (*Catilina* 20.4) on brotherly love and concord. Elsewhere he quotes Horace, Vergil, Ovid, Dracontius, and Fortunatus, showing in several cases by the depth of his commentary his awareness of the originals rather than the use of quotes from secondary sources. In his hymns, moreover, he frequently uses classical meter, particularly hexameter and adonics.

82. Stanford, "Toward a History," 21.

83. Bieler, "Classics," 46–48. Caesar was probably transmitted via Bobbio. See also Masai and Bischoff, "Il monachesimo," 130–32.

84. Stanford, "Toward a History," 21.

85. Ibid., 13, 21.

86. Blair, *Anglo-Saxon England*, 327.

87. Aldhelm, *Opera*, Monumenta Germaniae Historica: Auctores Antiquissimorum, vol. 15, ed. W. R. Ehwald (Berlin: Weidmans, 1913), 488; Hunter, "Germanic and Roman Antiquity," 41.

88. Hunter, "Germanic and Roman Antiquity," 41.

89. Bede 3.18 (Colgrave and Mynors, 266–69).

90. F. M. Stenton, *Anglo-Saxon England*, 3d ed. (Oxford: Clarendon Press, 1971), 189.

91. R. S. Lopez, "Le problème des relations anglo-byzantines du septième au dixième siècle," *Byzantion* 18 (1948): 149, suggests that Byzantine scholars fleeing the Arab invasion of the Levant may have come to Britain in this period to join the Canterbury school.

92. Bede 4.2 (Colgrave and Mynors, 332–35).

93. Blair, *Days of Bede*, 175.

94. Ibid.; Aldhelm, *Opera*, 492.

95. Bede, preface, 5.23 (Colgrave and Mynors, 2–5, 556–57).

96. Lopez, "Le problème," 148; J. M. Wallace-Hadrill, "Rome and the Early English Church," in *Le chiese nei regni del'Europa occidentale e i loro rapporti con Roma sino all'800*, vol. 2, Settimane de Studio del Centro Italiano di Studi sull'Alto Medioevo, 7 (Spoleto, 1960): 538–40.

97. Aldhelm, *Opera*, 494. Aldhelm was also the author of a treatise, *De Controversia Paschali*, directed against the still-schismatic Britons, and may have thought less of the Irish because of their past involvement in the Easter controversy, as suggested by the Ehfrid letter. His opinion of Irish scholarship could not have been improved by a letter he received from "a little Scot" requesting the loan of an unnamed text and also instruction, as the writer knew Latin and a little Greek but wanted access to a source of Greek less garbled than those available in Ireland. Aldhelm's reservations on Irish studies in the Wihtred letter may consequently have been founded on a concern over lack of clarity of instruction, and particularly the distinction between pagan and patristic sources.

98. J. H. Pitman, ed. and trans., *The Riddles of Aldhelm*, Yale Studies in English, vol. 67 (New Haven: Yale University Press, 1925), 9.

99. Ibid., 47.

100. Ibid., 68; Ogilvy, *Books Known*, 148–320 passim.

101. Hunter, "Germanic and Roman Antiquity," 41–42.

102. J. D. A. Ogilvy, *The Place of Wearmouth and Jarrow in Western Cultural History*, Jarrow Lecture (Jarrow: The Rectory, 1968) 1–6; M. L. W. Laistner, "The Library of the Venerable Bede," *Bede: His Life, Times and Writings*, ed. A. Hamilton Thompson (Oxford: Clarendon Press, 1935), 237–66.

103. Blair, *Days of Bede*, 52–53.

104. Bede 5.15 (Colgrave and Mynors, 508–9).

105. Blair, *Days of Bede*, 52–53.

106. Bede 3.1 (Colgrave and Mynors, 214–15).

107. P. H. Blair, "The Moore Memoranda on Northumbrian History," in *H. M. Chadwick Memorial Studies: Early Cultures of North-West Europe*, ed. C. F. Fox and B. Dickins (Cambridge: Cambridge University Press, 1950), 248–49. Blair suggests that the concept was taken from expunged legionary markers, but the reasons for the erasures on the stones were not inherently obvious and would have required additional explanation in literary sources.

108. The epic *Beowulf* is a candidate for attribution to Aldfrith's court. *Beowulf* contains substantial evidence of contact with classical literature, particularly Vergil's *Aeneid*, as well as

preserving a substantial body of epic material from the early Anglo-Saxon heroic tradition. The provenance of the epic in court or monastery is debated. The monastic life would have afforded the leisure for a man of letters to undertake a project on this scale, but is scarcely the most probable environment for so resolutely secular a work (cf. A. Campbell, "The Use in *Beowulf* of Earlier Heroic Verse," in *England before the Conquest: Studies in Primary Sources Presented to Dorothy Whitelock*, ed. P. A. M. Clemoes and K. Hughes [Cambridge: Cambridge University Press, 1971], 283–84, 191–92). Further, the level of literacy required for this project would not be inconsistent with Aldfrith's court. The Christian references, moreover, give Beowulf an approximate date in the eighth century (see also D. Whitelock, *The Audience of "Beowulf"* [Oxford: Clarendon Press, 1951], 103). The court of Aldfrith is thus a possible provenance for *Beowulf*, although the probably equally literate eighth-century court of Mercia cannot be excluded from consideration.

109. Becker, *Franks Casket*, 13–16; A. S. Napier, "Contributions to Old English Literature II: The Franks Casket," in *An English Miscellany: Presented to Dr. Furnivall in Honour of His Seventy-fifth Birthday*, ed. W. P. Ker, A. S. Napier, W. W. Skeat (Oxford: Clarendon Press, 1901), 362–65.

110. "News and Notes," *The Academy* 38 (1890) 90. Sven Söderberg's message from Copenhagen is acknowledged, that the right side of the Franks Casket is in the Bargello.

111. G. Baldwin Brown, *Completion of the Study of the Monuments of the Great Period of the Art of Anglian Northumbria*, vol. 6, pt. 1 of *The Arts in Early England*, 51.

112. The top of the back panel shows the marks of hinges, but these must have been a later addition as they obscured and damaged some of the carving, particularly the runic inscription. However, the front of the casket shows an original space for a fastening, which would only have functioned properly if the back and lid were mutually attached as well. The original form of this juncture is lost, however, obscured by the later hinge marks and the loss of the adjacent section of the lid.

113. E. Wadstein, "Zur Clermonter Runenkästchen," *Zeitschrift für deutsche Philologie* 34 (1902): 127, discusses the general *horror vacui* of the casket's reliefs, which may account for the crowding and confusion of contours. See also V. H. Elbern, review of Becker, *Franks Casket, Das Münster* 27 (1974): 343–44, comparing the Franks Casket Virgin and Child to the Byzantine *Nikopoia* and *Platyteria* types; P. W. Souers, "The Magi Scene on the Franks Casket," *Harvard Studies and Notes in Philology and Literature* 19 (1936): 249–54, comparing it to Syrian types; and J. Baum, *La sculpture figurale en Europe à d'époque mérovingienne* (Paris: L Éditions d'Art et d'Histoire, 1937), 95–96, comparing it to the Byzantine *Blachernitissa* type.

114. H. R. E. Davidson, "God and Heroes in Stone," in *H. M. Chadwick Memorial Lectures; Early Cultures of North-West Europe*, ed. C. F. Fox and Bruce Dickins (Cambridge: University Press, 1950), 123–39, gives an extensive overview of extant Weland sources.

115. Becker, *Franks Casket*, 79–80, 88–90; cf. Napier, "Contributions," 368; G. B. Brown, *Completion*, 30–31; P. W. Souers, "The Wayland Scene on the Franks Casket," *Speculum* 18 (1943): 104–11; S. Bugge, "The Norse Lay of Weland *(Volundarkviða)* and Its Relationship to the English Tradition," *Saga Book of the Viking Club* 2 (1898–1901): 271–312.

116. Becker, *Franks Casket*, 90.

117. Ibid., 19–20.

118. Ibid., 20–27; K. Schneider, "Zu den Inschriften und Bildern des Franks Casket und einer ae. Version des Mythos Balders Tod," in *Festschrift für Walther Fischer*, ed. E. Schuster and B. Fabian (Heidelberg: C. Winter, 1959), 7.

119. G. B. Brown, *Completion*, 31–32; H. R. E. Davidson, "The Smith and the Goddess," *Frühmittelalterliche Studien* 3 (1969):222–23.

120. Schneider, "Zu den Inschriften," 3–7, interprets the scene as Andromache's escape from Achilles. Wadstein, "Zur Clermonter Runenkästchen," 127, identifies it as English ballad material—the defense of his home by William of Cloudsley, possibly derivative of the earlier Egil material. H. Gering, "Zum Clermonter Runenkästchen," *Zeitschrift für Deutsche Philologie* 33 (1901): 140–41, sees it as Gunnar Hammundson's defense against Gissurr Huiti and Geirr Asgeirsson in *Njallsaga*. And A. C. Boumann, "The Franks Casket Right Side and Lid," *Neophilologus* 49 (1965): 247–49, reads it as Hengist and Horsa's attack on Aylesford in 455, as

documented in the *Anglo-Saxon Chronicle*.

121. P. W. Souers, "The Left Side of the Franks Casket," *Harvard Studies and Notes in Philology and Literature* 18 (1935): 199–209.

122. Becker, *Franks Casket*, 60–62.

123. Ibid., 62.

124. G. B. Brown, *Completion*, 34.

125. Becker, *Franks Casket*, 71.

126. Wadstein, "Zur Clermonter Runenkästchen," 127; G. B. Brown, *Completion*, 34–36; Cf. G. Stephens, *Handbook of the Old-Northern Runic Monuments of Scandinavia and England* (London: Williams and Norgate, 1884), 200–204; and F. C. Walker, "Fresh Light on the Franks Casket," *Washington University Studies,* 4th ser. 2 (1915): 171–73, who consider the scene to depict the Judgment of Pilate and the Torment of Christ, the justification, for later Christian historians, for Titus's sack of Jerusalem.

127. Becker, *Franks Casket*, 31–39.

128. However, most interpretations ignore the runes completely. T. Grienberger, "Zu den Inschriften des Klermonter Runenkästchens," *Anglia* 27 (1904): 436–49, considers the scene to be a distortion of Christian Scripture reinterpreted through northern mythology. K. Spiess, "Das Angelsächsischen Runenkästchen: Die Seite mit der *Hos*-Inschrift," in *Studien zur Kunst des Ostens: Josef Strzygowski zum sechzigsten geburtstag von seinen Freunden und Schülern* (Vienna: Avalun, 1932), 160–68, associates it with various individual elements in German folklore. Sven Söderberg, quoted in Becker, *Franks Casket*, 42; E. G. Clark, "The Right Side of the Franks Casket," *Publications of the Modern Language Association* 45. (1930): 339–53; and E. Wadstein, *The Clermont Runic Casket* (Uppsala: Almqvist and Wiksell, 1900), propose that the source is the death of Sigurd in *Volsungasaga.* Bouman, "The Franks Casket," 246–47; and S. R. T O. D'Ardenne, "Does the Right Side of the Franks Casket Represent the Burial of Sigurd?" *Etudes Germaniques* 21 (1966): 235–42, associate the scene with the Hengist and Horsa legend. R. C. Boer, quoted in Becker, *Franks Casket*, 45–46, proposes the *Ironssaga.* K. Hauck, "Vorbericht über das Kästchen von Auzon," *Frühmittelalterliche Studien* 2 (1968): 415–18, suggests that the scene might narrate the story of Slagfaðo, the brother of Weland and Egil, and his wife Hlaguðo. Schneider, "Zu den Inschriften," 7–15, links the relief to the death of Balder in the *Edda*.

129. Becker, *Franks Casket*, 48–55.

130. L. Stone, *Sculpture in Britain: The Middle Ages* (Harmondsworth: Penguin Books 1972), 14.

131. Becker, *Franks Casket*, 95–118.

132. Ibid., 125–34.

133. Hauck, "Vorbericht," 417, suggests that the selection of scenes for the Franks Casket was based on the genealogical claims of the owner to descent from Egil, Weland, Titus, Romulus or Remus, the Magi, and other heroic figures possibly depicted here. Such an association would enhance the effectiveness of Becker's program of sympathetic magic. However, none of these heroes occurs in the Northumbrian regnal lists or in other genealogies from the area, so Hauck's proposal cannot be substantiated.

134. Napier, "Contributions," 369.

135. A. Bauer and J. Strzygowski, *Eine Alexandrinische Weltchronik: Text und Miniaturen eines griechischen Papyrus der Sammlung W. Goleniščev,* Denkschriften der Kaiserlichen Akademie der Wissenschaften, Philosophische/Historische Klasse (Vienna: A. Hölder, 1906), vol. 2, 132.

136. Elbern, review, 343–44.

7. Parameters of the Northumbrian Renaissance

1. Kendrick, *Anglo-Saxon Art*, 152.

2. Bede 2.5 (Colgrave and Mynors, 148–51). The *Anglo-Saxon Chronicle* uses the term *bretwalda* for these high kings, but this may be a later interpolation. Cf. P. Wormald, "Bede," 104–17.

3. Panofsky, *Renaissance and Renascences*, 43.

Appendix: *Lindisfarne Gospels*

1. J. Chapman, *Vulgate Gospels*, 16–26.

2. P. Courcelle, *Les lettres grecques en Occident de Macrobe à Cassiodore*, 2d ed., Bibliothè-que des écoles françaises d'Athènes et de Rome, fasc. 159 (Paris: E.de Boccard, 1948), 356–62.

3. T. J. Brown, *Codex Lindisfarnensis*, 2 : 34–36, 49–50.

4. G. Morin, "La liturgie de Naples au temps de St.-Grégoire," *Revue Bénédictine* 8 (1891): 481–93.

5. T. J. Brown, *Codex Lindisfarnensis*, 2 : 49–50; Cassiodorus Flavius, *Institutiones* 1.23, ed. R .A. B. Mynors (Oxford: Oxford University Press, 1963).

6. J. Chapman, "Cassiodorus and the *Echternach Gospels*," *Revue Bénédictine* 27 (1911): 283–95.

7. J. M. Heer, *Evangelium Gratianum* (Freiburg: Herder, 1910), 54–56.

8. T. J. Brown, *Codex Lindisfarnensis*, 2 : 49–50.

Bibliography

Åberg, N. *The Anglo-Saxons in England during the Early Centuries after the Invasion.* Uppsala: Almqvist and Wiksells, 1926.

———. *The Occident and the Orient in the Art of the Seventh Century.* 3 vols. Stockholm: Wahlstrom and Widstrand, 1943–47.

Adams, W. Y. "Celtic Interlace and Coptic Interlace." *Antiquity* 49 (1975): 301–3.

Addyman, P. V. "The Anglo-Saxon House." In *The Anglo-Saxons: Studies in Some Aspects of Their History and Culture Presented to Bruce Dickins,* edited by P. A. M. Clemoes, 273–307. London: Bowes and Bowes, 1956.

———, N. Pearson, and D. Tweddle. "The Coppergate Helmet." *Antiquity* 56 (1982): 189–94.

Aird, R. "Seaham Church." *Proceedings of the Society of Antiquaries of Newcastle-upon-Tyne,* 3d ser., 6 (1913–23): 59–71.

Alcock, Leslie. *Arthur's Britain: History and Archaeology, A.D. 367–634.* Harmondsworth: Penguin Books, 1971.

———. *Dinas Powys: An Iron Age, Dark Age and Early Medieval Settlement in Glamorgan.* Cardiff: University of Wales Press, 1963.

Aldhelm. *Opera.* In Monumenta Germaniae Historica: Auctores Antiquissimorum, vol. 15, edited by W. R. Ehwald, 479–94. Berlin: Weidmans, 1918.

Alexander, J. J. G. *Insular Manuscripts: Sixth to the Ninth Century.* London: Harvey Miller, 1978.

———. "Some Aesthetic Principles in Colour Use in Anglo-Saxon Art." *Anglo-Saxon England* 4 (1975): 145–55.

Allen, J. Romilly. *Celtic Art in Pagan and Christian Times.* London: Philip Jacobs, [1904].

———, and J. Anderson. *Early Christian Monuments of Scotland: The Rhind Lectures in Archaeology for 1892.* Edinburgh: Neill, 1903.

———. *Early Christian Symbolism in Great Britain and Ireland: The Rhind Lectures in Archaeology for 1885.* London: Whiting, 1887.

———. "Pre-Norman Crosses at Halton and Heysham in Lancaster." *Journal of the*

British Archaeological Association 42 (1886): 328–44.

Allison, T. *English Religious Life in the Eighth Century.* New York: AMS Press, 1971.

Anderson, A. O., and M. O. Anderson. *Adomnan's Life of Colomba.* London: T. Nelson, 1961.

The Anglo-Saxon Chronicle. Edited and translated by G. N. Garmonsway. London: Dent; New York: Dutton, 1960.

The Anonymous Life of Ceolfrith. In *Anglo-Saxon Saints and Heroes,* edited and translated by C. Albertson, 247–71. New York: Fordham University Press, 1967.

The Anonymous Life of Cuthbert. In *Anglo-Saxon Saints and Heroes,* edited and translated by C. Albertson, 33–86. New York: Fordham University Press, 1967.

Armstrong, E. C. R., and R. A. S. MacAlister. "Wooden Box with Leaves Indented and Waxed Found near Springmount Bog, Co. Antrim." *Journal of the Royal Society of Antiquaries of Ireland,* 6th ser., 10 (1920): 160–66.

Avent, Richard. "An Anglo-Saxon Variant of a Merovingian Buckle." *Medieval Archaeology* 17 (1973): 126–28.

Backes, M., and R. Dölling. *Art of the Dark Ages.* New York: Harry N. Abrams, 1969.

Bailey, R. N. "The Abbey Church of St. Andrew, Hexham: The Medieval Works." *Archaeological Journal* 133 (1976): 197–201.

———. "The Anglo-Saxon Church at Hexham." *Archaeologia Aeliana,* 5th ser., 4 (1976): 47–67.

———. "The Anglo-Saxon Metalwork from Hexham." In *St. Wilfrid at Hexham,* edited by D. P. Kirby, 141–67. Newcastle Upon Tyne: Oriel Press, 1974.

———, and D. O'Sullivan. "Excavations over St. Wilfrid's Crypt at Hexham, 1978." *Archaeologia Aeliana,* 5th ser., 7 (1979): 145–57.

Bakka, E. "Some English Decorated Metal Objects Found in Norwegian Viking Graves: Contributions to the Art History of the Eighth Century A.D." *Aarbok for Universitet i Bergen: Humanistisk Serie,* 1963, 1–66.

Ball, C. J. E. "The Franks Casket, Right Side." *English Studies* 47 (1966): 119–26.

———. "The Franks Casket, Right Side, Again." *English Studies* 55 (1974): 512–13.

Bauer, A., and J. Strzygowski. *Eine Alexandrinische Weltchronik: Text und Miniaturen eines griechischen Papyrus der Sammlung W. Goleniščev.* 2 vols. Denkschriften der Kaiserlichen Akademie der Wissenschaften, Philosophische/Historische Klasse, vol. 51. Vienna: A. Hölder, 1906.

Baum, J. "Aufgaben der frühchristlichen Kunstforschung in Britannien und Irland." *Forschungen und Fortschritte: Nachrichtsblatt der deutschen Wissenschaft und Technik* 11 (1935): 222–23.

———. *La sculpture figurale en Europe à l'époque mérovingienne.* Paris: L'Editions d'Art et d'Histoire, 1937.

Baumstark, A. "Einer antike Bildkomposition im christlich-orientalischen Umdeutung." *Monatshefte für Kunstwissenschaft* 8 (1915): 118.

Becker, A. *Franks Casket: Zu den Bildern und Inschriften des Runenkästchen von Auzon.* Regensburger Arbeiten zur Anglistik und Amerikanistik, vol. 5. Regensburg: H. Carl, 1972.

Beckwith, J. "Reculver, Ruthwell, and Bewcastle." *Kolloquium über spätantike und frühmittelalterliche Skulptur,* Heidelberg, 1970, 17–19. Mainz: P. von Zabern, 1972.

Bede. *Ecclesiastical History of the English People.* Edited and translated by B. Colgrave and R. A. B. Mynors. Oxford Medieval Texts. Oxford: Oxford University Press, 1969.

————. *Life of Cuthbert*. In *Lives of the Saints*, translated by J. F. Webb, 69–129. Harmondsworth: Penguin Books, 1965.

————. *Lives of the Abbots*. In *Anglo-Saxon Saints and Heroes*, edited and translated by C. Albertson, 225–44. New York: Fordham University Press, 1967.

Betha Colaim Chille: The Life of Columcille, Compiled by Manus O'Donnell in 1532. Edited by A. O'Kelleher and G. Schoepperle. Urbana: University of Illinois Press, 1918.

Bieler, Ludwig. "The Classics in Celtic Ireland." In *Classical Influences on European Culture, A.D. 500–1500* edited by R. R. Bolgar, 45–50. Cambridge: Cambridge University Press, 1971.

————. "The Humanism of St. Columbanus." In *Mélanges Columbaniens: Actes du Congrès International d'Études Columbaniennes*, Luxeuil, 1950, 95–102. Paris: Editions Alsatia, 1951.

————, ed. *The Irish Penitentials*. Scriptores Latini Hiberniae, vol. 5. Dublin: Institute for Advanced Studies, 1963.

Birley, E. *Corbridge Roman Station: Department of the Environment Official Handbook*. London: HMSO, 1935.

Blair, Peter Hunter. *An Introduction to Anglo-Saxon England*. Cambridge: Cambridge University Press, 1956.

————. "The Moore Memoranda on Northumbrian History." In *H. M. Chadwick Memorial Studies: Early Cultures of North-West Europe*, edited by C. F. Fox and B. Dickins, 243–57. Cambridge: Cambridge University Press, 1950.

————. *Northumbria in the Days of Bede*. New York: St. Martin's Press, 1976.

————. *The Origins of Northumbria*. Gateshead: Northumbrian Press, 1948.

Blum, H. "Über den *Codex Amiatinus* und Cassiodors Bibliothek in Vivarium." *Zentralblatt für Bibliothekswesen* 64 (1950): 52–57.

Blunt, C. E., and R. H. M. Dolley. "The Anglo-Saxon Coins in the Vatican Library." *British Numismatic Journal*, 3d ser., 8 (1955–57): 449–58.

Bober, H. "On the Illumination of the *Glazier Codex*." In *Homage to a Bookman: Essays on Manuscripts, Books and Printing Written for Hans P. Kraus*, edited by H. Lehmann-Haupt, 31–49. Berlin: Mann, 1967.

Bonner, G. "Ireland and Rome: The Double Inheritance of Northumbria." In *Saints, Scholars, and Heroes: Studies in Medieval Culture in Honour of Charles W. Jones*, edited by M. H. King and W. M. Stevens, 101–16. Collegeville, Minn.: Hill Monastic Manuscript Library, 1976.

Bonser, W. *An Anglo-Saxon and Celtic Bibliography, 450–1087.* 2 vols. Oxford: Basil Blackwell, 1957.

————. "Survivals of Paganism in Anglo-Saxon England." *Transactions of the Birmingham Archaeological Society* 56 (1934): 37–70.

Boumann, A. C. "The Franks Casket, Right Side and Lid." *Neophilologus* 49 (1965): 242–48.

Bowen, E. G. *Saints, Seaways and Settlements*. Cardiff: University of Wales Press, 1969.

Brailsford, J. *Early Celtic Masterpieces from Britain in the British Museum*. London: British Museum, 1975.

Branston, B. *The Lost Gods of England*. Oxford: Oxford University Press, 1974.

Brøndsted, J. *Early English Ornament*. Translated by A. F. Major. London: Hachette, 1924.

Brown, G. Baldwin. *The Arts in Early England.* 6 vols. London: J. Murray, 1903–37.

——, and W. R. Lethaby. "The Bewcastle and Ruthwell Crosses." *Burlington Magazine* 23 (1913): 43–49.

Brown, P. *The World of Late Antiquity from Marcus Aurelius to Mohammed.* London: Thames and Hudson, 1971.

Brown, T. J. "Northumbria and the *Book of Kells.*" *Anglo-Saxon England* 1 (1972): 219–46.

——. *The Stonyhurst Gospel of St. John.* Oxford: Oxford University Press, 1969.

Brown, T. J., R. L. S. Bruce-Mitford, H. Roosen-Runge, A. S. C. Ross, E. G. Stanley, and A. E. A. Werner. *Evangeliorum Quattuor Codex Lindisfarnensis.* 2 vols. Edited by T. D. Kendrick. Olten: Urs Graf Verlag, 1956.

Browne, G. F. *The Ancient Cross Shafts at Bewcastle and Ruthwell.* Cambridge: Cambridge University Press, 1916.

——. *The Conversion of the Heptarchy: Seven Lectures Given at St. Paul's,* Rev. ed. London: Society for Promoting Christian Knowledge, 1906.

Bruce-Mitford, R. L. S. "The Art of the *Codex Amiatinus.*" *Journal of the British Archaeological Association,* 3d ser., 32 (1969): 1–25.

——. *Aspects of Anglo-Saxon Archaeology: Sutton Hoo and Other Discoveries.* New York: Gollancz, 1974.

——. "Late Saxon Disc Brooches." In *Dark Age Britain: Studies Presented to E. T. Leeds,* edited by D. B. Harden, 171–201. London: Methuen, 1956.

——. "The Pectoral Cross." In *The Relics of St. Cuthbert,* edited by C. F. Battiscombe, 308–25. Oxford: Oxford University Press, 1956.

——. "The Reception by the Anglo-Saxons of Mediterranean Art following Their Conversion from Ireland and Rome." In *La conversione al cristianesimo nell'Europa dell'alto medioevo.* Settimane di Studio del Centro Italiano di Studi sull'Alto Medioevo, Spoleto, 14 (1967): 797–825.

——. Review of M. de Paor and L. de Paor, *Early Christian Ireland. Medieval Archaeology* 2 (1958): 214–17.

——. "The Sutton Hoo Ship Burial." *Proceedings of the Suffolk Institute of Archaeology* 25 (1949–51): 1–78.

——. *The Sutton Hoo Ship Burial.* 3 vols. London: British Museum, 1975–83.

——. *The Sutton Hoo Ship Burial: A Handbook.* 2d ed. London: British Museum, 1972.

Bugge, S. "The Norse Lay of Wayland *(Volundarkviða)* and Its Relationship to the English Tradition." *Saga Book of the Viking Club* 2 (1898–1901): 271–312.

Burkitt, F. C. "*Kells, Durrow* and *Lindisfarne.*" *Antiquity* 9 (1935): 33–37.

Bütow, H. *Das altenglische Traumgeschichte vom Kreuz.* Heidelberg: C. Winter, 1935.

Calder, C. S. T. "Three Fragments of a Sculptured Cross of Anglian Type Now Preserved in Abercorn Church, West Lothian." *Proceedings of the Society of Antiquaries of Scotland* 72 (1937–38): 217.

Callander, J. G. "The Cross-Shaft from Morham, E. Lothian." *Proceedings of the Society of Antiquaries of Scotland* 67 (1932–33): 241–42.

Calverley, W. S. *Notes on the Early Sculptured Crosses, Shrines and Monuments in the Present Diocese of Carlisle.* Cumberland and Westmoreland Antiquarian and Archaeological Society, extra series, vol. 11. Kendal, 1899.

Calvert, J. "The Iconography of the St. Andrew Auckland Cross." *Art Bulletin* 66 (1984): 543–55.

Cambridge, E. "C. C. Hodges and the Nave of Hexham Abbey." *Archaeologia Aeliana,* 5th ser., 7 (1979): 159–68.

Campbell, A. *Old English Grammar.* Oxford: Clarendon Press, 1956.

————. "The Use in *Beowulf* of Earlier Heroic Verse." In *England before the Conquest: Studies in Primary Sources Presented to Dorothy Whitelock,* edited by P. A. M. Clemoes and K. Hughes, 283–92. Cambridge: Cambridge University Press, 1971.

Cassiodorus, Flavius. *Institutiones.* Edited by R. A. B. Mynors. Oxford: Clarendon Press, 1963.

Casson, S. "Byzantium and Anglo-Saxon Sculpture." *Burlington Magazine* 61 (1932): 265–74; 62 (1933): 26–36.

Cecchelli, C. "La pittura dei cimetarii cristiani dal V al VI secolo." *Corsi di Cultura sull'Arte Ravennate e Bizantine* 5 (1958): 45–56.

Chadwick, H. M. "Studies in Old English." *Transactions of the Cambridge Philological Society* 4 (1894–99): 87–265.

Chadwick, N. K. *The Age of the Saints in the Early Celtic Church.* University of Durham Riddell Memorial Lectures, 32d ser. Oxford: Oxford University Press, 1961.

————. *The Celts.* Harmondsworth: Penguin Books, 1970.

————. *Studies in the Early British Church.* 2 vols. Cambridge: Cambridge University Press, 1958.

Champneys, A. C. *Irish Ecclesiastical Architecture: With Some Notice of Similar or Related Works in England, Scotland and Elsewhere.* London: G. Bell and Sons, 1910.

Chaney, W. A. *The Cult of Kingship in Anglo-Saxon England: The Transition from Paganism to Christianity.* Berkeley and Los Angeles: University of California Press, 1970.

Chapman, J. "Cassiodorus and the *Echternach Gospels.*" *Revue Bénédictine* 28 (1911): 283.

————. "The *Codex Amiatinus* and Cassiodorus." *Revue Bénédictine* 38 (1926):139–50.

————. "The *Codex Amiatinus* Once More." *Revue Bénédictine* 40 (1928): 130–33.

————. *Notes on the Early History of the Vulgate Gospels.* Oxford: Clarendon Press, 1908.

Cherry, B. "Ecclesiastical Architecture." In *The Archaeology of Anglo-Saxon England,* edited by D. M. Wilson, 151–200. London: Methuen, 1976.

Clapham, A. W. "The Carved Stones at Breedon-on-the-Hill, Leics., and Their Position in English Art." *Archaeologia* 77 (1927): 219–40.

————. *English Romanesque Architecture before the Conquest.* Oxford: Clarendon Press, 1930.

————. "Notes on the Origins of Hiberno-Saxon Art." *Antiquity* 8 (1934): 43–57.

————. "Some Disputed Examples of Preconquest Sculpture." *Antiquity* 25 (1951): 191–95.

————. "Two Carved Stones at Monkwearmouth." *Archaeologia Aeliana,* 4th ser., 28 (1950): 1–6.

Clark, E. G. "The Right Side of the Franks Casket." *Publications of the Modern Language Association* 45 (1930): 339–53.

Coatsworth, E. "Two Examples of the Crucifixion at Hexham." *Saint Wilfrid at Hexham,* edited by D. P. Kirby, 180–84. Newcastle upon Tyne: Oriel Press, 1974.

Cockerton, R. W. P. "The Wirksworth Slab." *Derbyshire Archaeological Journal* 82 (1962): 1–20.

Colgrave, B., ed. *The Life of Bishop Wilfrid by Eddius Stephanus*. Cambridge: Cambridge University Press, 1927.

———. *Two Lives of St. Cuthbert*. Cambridge: Cambridge University Press, 1940.

Collingwood, W. G. "Anglian and Anglo-Danish Sculpture in the North Riding of Yorkshire." *Yorkshire Archaeological Journal*, pt. 75, 19 (1907): 267–413.

———. *Northumbrian Crosses of the Pre-Norman Age*. London: Faber and Dwyer, 1927.

———. "A Pedigree of Anglian Crosses." *Antiquity* 6 (1932): 35–54.

———. "The Ruthwell Cross in Its Relation to Other Monuments of the Early Christian Age." *Dumfriesshire and Galloway Natural Historical and Antiquarian Society: Transactions and Journal of Proceedings*, 3d ser., 5 (1916–18): 39–84.

Conway, M. "The Bewcastle and Ruthwell Crosses." *Burlington Magazine* 23 (1912): 193.

———. "A Dangerous Archaeological Method, II." *Burlington Magazine* 24 (1913–14): 86–89.

Cook, A. S. *The Date of the Ruthwell and Bewcastle Crosses*. Transactions of the Connecticut Academy of Arts and Sciences, vol. 17. New Haven: Yale University Press, 1912.

Courcelle, P. *Les lettres grecques en Occident de Macrobe à Cassiodore*, 2d. ed. Bibliothèque des écoles françaises d'Athènes et de Rome, fasc. 159. Paris: E. de Boccard, 1948.

Cramp, R. "Anglian Sculptured Crosses of Dumfriesshire." *Dumfriesshire and Galloway Natural Historical and Antiquarian Society: Transactions and Journal of Proceedings*, 4th ser., 38 (1961): 9–20.

———. "Anglo-Saxon Monasteries of the North." *Scottish Archaeological Forum* 5 (1973): 104–24.

———. "*Beowulf* and Archaeology." *Medieval Archaeology* 1 (1957): 57–77.

———. "Decorated Window Glass and Millefiori from Monkwearmouth." *Antiquaries' Journal* 1 (1970): 327–35.

———. *Early Northumbrian Sculpture*. Jarrow Lecture. Jarrow: The Rectory, 1966.

———. "Early Northumbrian Sculpture at Hexham." In *St. Wilfrid at Hexham*, edited by D. P. Kirby, 115–40. Newcastle upon Tyne: Oriel Press, 1974.

———. "The Evangelist Symbols and Their Parallels in Anglo-Saxon Sculpture." In *Bede and Anglo-Saxon England*, edited by R. T. Farrell, 118–30. British Archaeological Reports, vol. 46. Oxford: British Archaeological Reports, 1978.

———. "Excavations at the Saxon Monastic Sites of Wearmouth and Jarrow." *Medieval Archaeology* 13 (1969): 21–66.

———, "Hexham Anglo-Saxon Sculpture (A Handlist)." *Saint Wilfrid at Hexham*, edited by D. P. Kirby, 172–79. Newcastle upon Tyne: Oriel Press, 1974.

———. "Jarrow Church." *Archaeological Journal* 133 (1976): 220–26.

———. "Mediterranean Elements in the Early Medieval Sculpture of England." In *Les relations entre l'Empire Romain tardif, l'Empire Franc et ses voisins*. Ninth International Congress of Prehistoric and Protohistoric Sciences, Nice, 1976, Colloquium 30, 263–95. Paris: Centre National de la Recherche Scientifique, 1976.

———. *The Monastic Arts of Northumbria*. London: Arts Council of Britain, 1967.

———. "Monastic Sites." In *The Archaeology of Anglo-Saxon England*, edited by D. M. Wilson, 253–82. London: Methuen, 1976.

————. "Monkwearmouth Church." *Archaeological Journal* 133 (1976): 230–37.

————. "The Position of the Otley Crosses in English Sculpture of the Eighth to Ninth Centuries." In *Kolloquium über spätantike und frühmittelalterliche Skulptur,* Heidelberg, 1970, 55–63. Mainz: P. von Zabern, 1972.

————. "Schools of Mercian Sculpture." In *Mercian Studies,* edited by Ann Dornier, 191–231. Leicester: Leicester University Press, 1977.

Cramp, R., and J. T. Lang. *A Century of Anglo-Saxon Sculpture.* Newcastle upon Tyne: F. Graham, 1977.

Craster, E. "The Patrimony of St. Cuthbert." *English Historical Review* 69 (1954): 177–99.

Crawford, O. G. S. "The Vinescroll in Scotland." *Antiquity* 11 (1937): 467–73.

Crozet, R. "Les premières représentations anthropozoömorphiques des évangélistes." In *Études mérovingiennes,* edited by R. Crozet, 53–63. Paris: A. and J. Picard, 1953.

Cruden, S. *Early Christian and Pictish Monuments of Scotland: An Illustrated Introduction.* 2d ed. Edinburgh: HMSO, 1964.

Curle, A. O. *The Treasure of Traprain.* Glasgow: Maclehose and Jackson, 1923.

Curle, G. C. "The Chronology of the Early Christian Monuments of Scotland." *Proceedings of the Society of Antiquaries of Scotland* 74 (1939–40): 60–116.

Dalton, O. M. *Byzantine Art and Archaeology.* Oxford: Clarendon Press, 1911.

D'Ardenne, S. R. T. O. "Does the Right Side of the Franks Casket Represent the Burial of Sigurd?" *Études Germaniques* 21 (1966): 235–42.

Davidson, H. R. E. "Gods and Heroes in Stone." In *H. M. Chadwick Memorial Studies: Early Cultures of North-West Europe,* edited by C. F. Fox and Bruce Dickins, 129–39. Cambridge: Cambridge University Press, 1950.

————. "Sigurd in the Art of the Viking Age." *Antiquity* 16 (1942): 216–36.

————. "The Smith and the Goddess." *Frühmittelalterliche Studien* 3 (1969): 216–26.

Dawes, Elizabeth, and Norman H. Baynes. *Three Byzantine Saints.* Crestwood, N.Y.: St. Vladimir's Seminary Press, 1977.

Deanesley, M. *The Pre-Conquest Church in England.* Oxford: Oxford University Press, 1961.

————. "Roman Traditionalist Influences among the Anglo-Saxons." *English Historical Review* 58 (1943): 129–46.

Demus, O. *Byzantine Art and the West.* Wrightsman Lectures, vol. 3. New York: New York University, 1970.

de Paor, M. and L. de Paor. *Early Christian Ireland.* London: Thames and Hudson, 1964.

Dickins, B., and A. S. C. Ross. *The Dream of the Rood.* London: Methuen, 1934.

Dillon, M., and N. K. Chadwick. *The Celtic Realms.* New York: Weidenfeld and Nicholson, 1967.

Diringer, D. *The Illustrated Book: Its History and Production.* Rev. ed. New York: Praeger, 1967.

Dodd, E. C. *Byzantine Silver Stamps.* Washington, D.C.: Dumbarton Oaks, 1961.

Dold, A., and L. Eizenhöfer. "Das Irische Palimpsest-Sakramentar im Clm. 14429 der Staatsbibliothek München." With commentary by D. Wright. *Texte und Arbeiten* 53–54 (1964): 34–40.

Dornier, A., ed., *Mercian Studies.* Leicester: Leicester University Press, 1977.

Duft, J., and P. Meyer. *The Irish Miniatures in the Cathedral Library of St. Gall.* Olten: Urs Graf Verlag, 1954.

Dumville, D. "Nennius and the *Historia Brittonum.*" *Studia Celtica* 10–11 (1975–76): 78–95.

Dunning, G. C. "Trade Relations between England and the Continent in the Late Anglo-Saxon Period." In *Dark Age Britain: Studies Presented to E. T. Leeds,* edited by D. B. Harden, 202–17. London: Methuen, 1956.

Eddius Stephanus. *Life of Wilfrid.* In *Lives of the Saints,* translated by J. F. Webb, 131–206. Harmondsworth: Penguin Books, 1965.

Elbern, V. H. Review of A. Becker, *Franks Casket. Das Münster* 27 (1974): 343–44.

Ernulf, bishop of Rochester. *Textus Roffensis: Rochester Cathedral Library MS A.E.5.* Edited by Peter Sawyer. Copenhagen: Rosenkilde and Bagger, 1926.

Esposito, M. "The Knowledge of Greek in Ireland during the Middle Ages." *Studies* 1 (1912): 665–83.

———. "On the Earliest Latin Life of St. Brigid of Kildare." *Proceedings of the Royal Irish Academy* 30 (1912): 307–26.

Evison, V. I. "Anglo-Saxon Whetstones." *Antiquaries' Journal* 55 (1975): 70–85.

Farrell, R. T. "The Archer and Associated Figures on the Ruthwell Cross." In *Bede and Anglo-Saxon England,* edited by R. T. Farrell, 96–117. British Archaeological Reports, vol. 46. Oxford: British Archaeological Reports, 1978.

Felix. *Life of Guthlac.* Edited by B. Colgrave. Cambridge: Cambridge University Press, 1956.

———. *Life of Guthlac.* in *Anglo-Saxon Saints and Heroes,* edited and translated by C. Albertson, 167–222. New York: Fordham University Press, 1967.

Fleischmann, A. "References to Chant in Old Irish Manuscripts." In *Essays and Studies Presented to Professor Tadhg Ua Donnchada (Torna),* edited by S. Pender, 33–42. Cork: Cork University Press, 1947.

Fletcher, E. "Brixworth: Was There a Crypt?" *Journal of the British Archaeological Association,* 3d ser., 37 (1974): 88–96.

———. "Early Kentish Churches." *Medieval Archaeology* 9 (1965): 11–31.

Forbes, M. D., and B. Dickins. "The Inscriptions of the Ruthwell and Bewcastle Crosses and the Bridekirk Font." *Burlington Magazine* 25 (1914): 24–29.

Fowler, E. "Hanging Bowls." In *Studies in Ancient Europe: Essays Presented to Stuart Piggott,* edited by J. M. Coles and D. D. A. Simpson, 287–310. New York: Humanities Press, 1968.

Fyson, D. "Anglian Patterns: Some Sources and Developments." *Archaeologia Aeliana,* 4th ser., 35 (1957): 64–71.

Gering, H. "Zum Clermonter Runenkästchen." *Zeitschrift für Deutsche Philologie* 33 (1901): 140–41.

Gilbert, E. "The Anglian Remains at Jarrow Church." *Proceedings of the Society of Antiquaries of Newcastle-upon-Tyne,* 5th ser., 1 (1951–56): 311–33.

———. "St. Wilfrid's Church at Hexham." In *St. Wilfrid at Hexham,* edited by D. P. Kirby, 81–113. Newcastle upon Tyne: Oriel Press, 1974.

———. "Some Problems of Early Northumbrian Architecture." *Archaeologia Aeliana,* 4th ser., 42 (1964): 65–83.

Gildas. *De Excidio et Conquestu Britanniae.* In *Chronica Minora Saeculi IV, V, VI, VII,* edited by T. Mommsen, vol. 3, pt. 1. Monumenta Germaniae Historica: Auctores Antiquissimorum, vol. 13. Berlin: Weidmans, 1893.

Girvan, R. *Beowulf and the Seventh Century: Language and Content.* London: Methuen, 1935.

Gougaud, L. *Gaelic Pioneers of Christianity.* Translated by V. Collins. Dublin: M. H. Gill and Son, 1923.

Grabar, A., and C. Nordenfalk. *Early Medieval Painting, Fourth to Eleventh Centuries.* Geneva: Skira, 1957.

Grattan, J. G. H., and C. Singer. *Anglo-Saxon Medicine and Magic.* Oxford: Oxford University Press, 1952.

Graus, F. *Volk, Herrscher, und Heiliger im Reich der Merovinger.* Prague: Nakladatelstvi Československi Akademie věd, 1965.

Green, B. "An Anglo-Saxon Bone Plaque from Larling, Norfolk." *Antiquaries' Journal* 51 (1971): 321–23.

Green, Charles. *Sutton Hoo: The Excavation of a Royal Ship Burial.* 2d ed. London: Merlin Press, 1968.

Grienberger, T. "Zu den Inschriften des Klermonter Runenkästchens." *Anglia* 27 (1904): 436–49.

Grierson, P. "The Date of the Sutton Hoo Coins." *Antiquity* 26 (1952): 83–86.

Griffith, A. F. "An Anglo-Saxon Cemetery at Alfriston, Sussex." *Sussex Archaeological Collections* 57 (1905): 197–210.

Grosjean, P. "Sur quelques exégetes Irlandais du VIIe siècle." *Sacris Erudiri* 7 (1955): 67–98.

Haddan, A. W., and W. Stubbs. *Councils and Ecclesiastical Documents relating to Great Britain and Ireland.* 3 vols. Oxford: Clarendon Press, 1871.

Hadfield, A. M., J. S. Wacher, and D. J. Viner. *Cirencester: The Roman Corinium.* Gloucester: British Publishing Company, 1975.

Hardinge, L. *The Celtic Church in Britain.* London: Society for Promoting Christian Knowledge, 1972.

Haseloff, G. "Fragments of a Hanging Bowl from Bekesbourne, Kent, and Some Ornamental Problems." *Medieval Archaeology* 2 (1958): 72–103.

———. "Zum Ursprung der Germanischen Tierornamentik: Die spätromische Würzel." *Frühmittelalterliche Studien* 7 (1973): 406–42.

Hauck, K. "Vorbericht über das Kästchen von Auzon." *Frühmittelalterliche Studien* 2 (1968): 415–18.

Haverfield, F. J., and W. Greenwell. *A Catalogue of the Sculptured and Inscribed Stones in the Cathedral Library, Durham.* Durham: Thomas Caldcleugh, 1899.

Hawkes, S. C., J. M. Merrick, and D. M. Metcalf. "X-ray Fluorescent Analysis of Some Dark Age Coins and Jewellery." *Archaeometry* 9 (1966): 98–138.

Heer, J. M. *Evangelium Gratianum.* Freiburg: Herder, 1910.

Hempl, G. "Variant Runes on the Franks Casket." *Transactions of the American Philological Association* 32 (1902): 186–95.

Henderson, G. "The John the Baptist Panel on the Ruthwell Cross." *Gesta* 24 (1985): 3–12.

Henderson, I. M. "The Origin Centre of the Pictish Symbol Stones." *Proceedings of the Society of Antiquaries of Scotland* 91 (1957–58): 44–60.

———. *The Picts.* London: Thames and Hudson, 1967.

Henry, F. "Les débuts de la miniature irlandaise." *Gazette des Beaux Arts,* 6th ser., 37 (1950): 5–34.

———. "Hanging Bowls." *Journal of the Royal Society of Antiquaries of Ireland* 66 (1936): 209–46.

———. *Irish Art in the Early Christian Period (To A.D. 800).* Ithaca: Cornell University Press, 1965.

———. "Irish Enamels of the Dark Ages and Their Relation to the *Cloisonné* Techniques." In *Dark Age Britain: Studies Presented to E. T. Leeds,* edited by D. B. Harden, 71–88. London: Methuen, 1956.

———. *Irish High Crosses.* Cultural Relations Committee of Ireland. Dublin: Three Candles, 1964.

———. *La sculpture irlandaise pendant les douze premiers siècles de l'ére chrétienne.* 2 vols. Paris: E. Leroux, 1933.

Heusler, A. "Wieland." In *Reallexikon der germanischen Altertumskunde,* edited by J. Hoops, 4:528–29. Strassburg: K. J. Trübner, 1911–19.

Hewison, J. K. *The Romance of the Bewcastle Cross, the Mystery of Alcfrith, and the Myths of Maughan.* Glasgow: J. Murray, 1923.

Hill, R. "Christianity and Geography in Early Northumbria." In *Studies in Church History,* edited by G. J. Cuming and D. Baker, 7:126–39. Cambridge: Cambridge University Press, 1971.

———. *The Labourers in the Field.* Jarrow Lecture. Jarrow: The Rectory, 1974.

Hillgarth, J. N. "The East, Visigothic Spain and the Irish." *Studia Patristica* 4 (1961): 442–56.

———. "Visigothic Spain and Early Christian Ireland." *Proceedings of the Royal Irish Academy* 62 (1962): 167–94.

Hinton, D. A. *A Catalogue of the Anglo-Saxon Ornamental Metalwork, 700–1100, in the Department of Antiquities, Ashmolean Museum.* Oxford: Clarendon Press, 1974.

Hodgson, J. F. "The Churches of Escomb, Jarrow and Monkwearmouth." *Transactions of the Architectural and Archaeological Society of Durham and Northumberland* 6 (1906–11): 109–11.

Hope-Taylor, B. *Yeavering: An Anglo-British Centre of Early Northumbria.* Department of the Environment Archaeological Reports, vol. 7. London: HMSO, 1977.

Hopkin-James, L. J. *The Celtic Gospels: Their Story and Text.* London: Oxford University Press, 1934.

Horn, W., and E. Born. *The Plan of St. Gall.* Berkeley and Los Angeles: University of California Press, 1979.

Hovey, W. R. "Sources of the Irish Illumination." *Art Studies* 6 (1928): 105–20.

Howlett, D. J. "Two Panels on the Ruthwell Cross." *Journal of the Warburg and Courtauld Institutes* 37 (1974): 333–36.

Hubert, J. "Les Églises à rotonde orientale," In *Frühmittelalterliche Kunst in den Alpenlandern,* Akten zum III Internationalen Kongres für Frühmittelalterforschungen, 309–20. Olten: Urs Graf Verlag, 1954.

Hubert, J., J. Porscher, and W. Volbach. *Europe of the Invasions.* New York: G. Braziller, 1969.

Hughes, K. *The Church in Early Irish Society.* London: Methuen, 1966.

———. *Early Christian Ireland: An Introduction to the Sources.* Ithaca: Cornell University Press, 1972.

————. *Early Christianity in Pictland.* Jarrow Lecture. Jarrow: The Rectory, 1970.

————. "Evidence for Contact between the Churches of the Irish and the English from the Synod of Whitby to the Viking Age." In *England before the Conquest: Studies in Primary Sources Presented to Dorothy Whitelock,* edited by P. A. M. Clemoes and K. Hughes, 35–48. Cambridge: Cambridge University Press, 1971.

Hunter, M. "Germanic and Roman Antiquity: The Sense of the Past in Anglo-Saxon England." *Anglo-Saxon England* 3 (1974): 29–50.

Hurst, J. G. "The Pottery." In *The Archaeology of Anglo-Saxon England,* edited by David M. Wilson, 283–348. London: Methuen, 1976.

"De Illuminerede Haandskriften det store kongelige Bibliotek." *Aarberetninger og Meddelelser fra det Store Kongelige Bibliotek* 3 (1874–1889): 34–37.

Innocent, C. F. "Romano-British Precedents for Some English Romanesque Details." *Journal of the Royal Institute for British Archaeology,* 3d ser., 15 (1915): 649–50.

Jack. R. Ian. *Medieval Wales.* Ithaca: Cornell University Press, 1972.

Jackson, K. H. *The Gododdin.* Edinburgh: Edinburgh University Press, 1969.

Jacobus de Varagine. *The Golden Legend.* Translated by G. Ryan and H. Ripperger. London: Longmans, Green and Company, 1969.

Jessup, R. F. "Reculver." *Antiquity* 10 (1936): 179–94.

Joselin. *Life of Kentigern.* In *Pinkerton's The Scottish Saints,* revised and enlarged by W. M. Metcalf, 2:1–116. Paisley: Gardner, 1889.

John, E. "The Social and Political Problems of the Early English Church." In *Land, Church and People: Essays Presented to H. P. R. Finberg,* edited by D. Thirsk. Supplement to *Agricultural History Review* 18 (1970): 39–63.

Jones, C. W. *Bedae Opera de Temporibus.* Cambridge, Mass.: Medieval Academy of America, 1943.

Jones, L. W. "The Fate of Vivarium and Its Books." In *Introduction to Divine and Human Readings by Cassiodorus Senator,* edited and translated by L. W. Jones, 42–47. New York: Columbia University Press, 1946.

Joyce, P. W. *A Social History of Ancient Ireland.* 2 vols. London: Longmans, 1903.

Kantorowicz, E. H. "The Archer in the Ruthwell Cross." *Art Bulletin* 42 (1960): 57–59.

Kaske, R. E. "The Silver Spoons of Sutton Hoo. *Speculum* 52 (1967): 670–72.

Kendrick, T. D. *Anglo-Saxon Art to A.D. 900.* London: Methuen, 1938.

————. "British Hanging Bowls." *Antiquity* 6 (1932): 161–84.

Kennedy, C. W., ed. and trans. *Beowulf: The Oldest English Epic.* Oxford: Oxford University Press, 1968.

Kerlouégan, F. "Le Latin du *De Excidio Britanniae* de Gildas." In *Christianity in Britain, 300–700,* Conference on Christianity in Sub-Roman Britain, Nottingham, 17–20 April 1967, edited by M. W. Barley and R. P. C. Hanson, 151–76. Leicester: Leicester University Press, 1968.

Kirby, D. P. "Northumbria in the Time of Wilfrid." In *St. Wilfrid at Hexham,* edited by D. P. Kirby, 1–34. Newcastle upon Tyne: Oriel Press, 1974.

Kitzinger, Ernst. "Anglo-Saxon Vinescroll Ornament." *Antiquity* 10 (1936): 133–35.

————. "The Coffin Reliquary." In *The Relics of St. Cuthbert,* edited by C. F. Battiscombe, 202–304. Oxford: Oxford University Press, 1956.

————. *Early Medieval Art in the British Museum.* London: The British Museum, 1940.

————. "The Sutton Hoo Finds III: The Silver." *British Museum Quarterly* 13 (1938): 118–26.

Krautheimer, R. *Early Christian and Byzantine Architecture.* Pelican History of Art. Harmondsworth: Penguin Books, 1965.

Kurth, B. "Ecclesia and an Angel on the Andrew Auckland Cross." *Journal of the Warburg and Courtauld Institutes* 6 (1943): 213–14.

————. "The Iconography of the Wirksworth Slab." *Burlington Magazine* 86 (1945): 114–21.

Laing, L. *The Archaeology of Late Celtic Britain and Ireland, c. 400–1200.* London: Methuen, 1975.

————. "The Mote of Mark and the Origins of Celtic Interlace." *Antiquity* 49 (1975): 98–108.

Laistner, M. L. W. "The Library of the Venerable Bede." In *Bede: His Life, Times and Writings,* edited by A. Hamilton Thompson, 237–66. Oxford: Clarendon Press, 1935.

Lawlor, H. J. *Chapters on the Book of Mulling.* Edinburgh: D. Douglas, 1935.

Leeds, E. T. *Early Anglo-Saxon Art and Archaeology: Being the Rhind Lectures Delivered in Edinburgh in 1935.* Oxford: Clarendon Press, 1936.

Lethaby, W. R. "The Ruthwell Cross." *Burlington Magazine* 21 (1912): 145–48.

————. "The Ruthwell Cross: An Anglo-Celtic Work." *Archaeological Journal* 70 (1913): 145–61.

Lethbridge, T. C. *Excavations in the Anglo-Saxon Cemeteries of Cambridge and Suffolk.* Cambridge Antiquaries' Society Quarto Publications, n.s., vol. 3. Cambridge, 1913.

Levison, Wilhelm. *England and the Continent in the Eighth Century.* Oxford: Clarendon Press, 1943.

————. "Die Iren und die Frankische Kirche." *Historische Zeitschrift* 109 (1912): 1–22.

Lewis, A. R. "Le commerce maritime et les navires de la Gaule occidentale, 550–750." In *Études mérovingiennes,* edited by R. Crozet, 191–99. Paris: A. and J. Picard, 1953.

————. *The Northern Seas: Shipping and Commerce in Northern Europe, A.D. 300–1100.* Princeton: Princeton University Press, 1958.

Llewellyn, P. *Rome in the Dark Ages.* New York: Praeger, 1970.

Lohaus, Annethe. *Die Merovinger und England.* Münchener Beiträge zur Mediavistik und Renaissance-Forschung, vol. 19. Munich: Arbeo-Gesellschaft, 1974.

Longhurst, M. "The Easby Cross." *Archaeologia* 81 (1931): 43–47.

Longley, D. *Hanging Bowls, Penannular Brooches and the Anglo-Saxon Connection.* British Archaeological Reports, vol. 22. Oxford: British Archaeological Reports, 1975.

Lopez, R. S. "Le problème des relations anglo-byzantines du septième au dixième siècle." *Byzantion* 18 (1948): 139–62.

Lot, F. *Nennius et l'Historia Brittonum.* Bibliothèque de l'École des Hautes Études, Sciences Historiques et Philologiques, vol. 263. Paris: H. Champion, 1934.

Lowe, E. A. *Codices Latini Antiquiores.* Vols. 2 and 3. Oxford: Clarendon Press, 1935–38.

————. *English Uncial.* Oxford: Clarendon Press, 1960.

————. "The Uncial Gospel-Leaves Attached to the Utrecht Psalter." *Art Bulletin* 34 (1952): 237–38.

Luce, A. A., O. Simms, P. Meyer, and L. Bieler. *Evangeliorum Quattuor Codex Durmachensis.* 2 vols. Olten: Urs Graf Verlag, 1960.

MacAlister, R. A. S. "The Colophon of the *Lindisfarne Gospels*." *Essays and Studies in Honour of Sir William Ridgeway,* edited by E. C. Quiggan, 299–305. Cambridge: Cambridge University Press, 1913.

———. "The Inscription of the Slab at Fahan Mure, Co. Donegal." *Journal of the Royal Society of Antiquaries of Ireland* 59 (1929): 89–98.

MacCana, P. *Celtic Mythology.* Feltham: Hamlyn, 1970.

McGurk, P. M. J. "The Canon Tables in the *Book of Lindisfarne* and in the *Codex Fuldensis* of St. Victor of Capua." *Journal of Theological Studies,* n.s., 6 (1955): 192–98.

MacKinnon, J. *Ninian und sein Einfluss auf die Ausbreitung des Christenthums in Nord-Britannien.* Heidelberg: J. Hornung, 1891.

McNeill, J. T. *The Celtic Churches: A History, A.D. 200–1200.* Chicago: University of Chicago Press, 1974.

———. *Medieval Handbooks of Penance: A Translation of the Principal Libri Poenitentiales and Selections from Related Documents.* Records of Civilization, vol. 29. New York: Columbia University Press, 1965.

Mâle, E. *La fin du paganisme en Gaule et les plus anciennes basiliques chrétiennes.* Paris: Flammarion, 1950.

Masai, F. *Essai sur les origines de la miniature dite irlandese.* Brussels: Editions "Erasme," 1947.

———, and B. Bischoff. "Il monachesimo Irlandese nei suoi rapporti col Continente." In *Il monachesimo nell'alto medioevo e la forma della civiltà occidentale.* Settimane di Studio del Centro Italiano di Studi sull'Alto Medioevo, Spoleto, 4 (1957): 139–84.

Mathews, T. *The Early Churches of Constantinople: Architecture and Liturgy.* University Park: Pennsylvania University Press, 1971.

———. "An Early Roman Chancel Arrangement." *Rivista di Archeologica Christiana* 38 (1962): 73–96.

Mayr-Harting, H. *The Coming of Christianity to Britain.* New York: Schocken Books, 1972.

———. *The Venerable Bede, The Rule of St. Benedict, and Social Class.* Jarrow Lecture. Jarrow: The Rectory, 1976.

Meaney, A. *A Gazetteer of Early Anglo-Saxon Burial Sites.* London: G. Allen and Unwin, 1964.

———, and S. C. Hawkes. *Two Anglo-Saxon Cemeteries at Winall, Winchester, Hants.* Society for Medieval Archaeology Monograph Series, vol. 4. London, 1970.

Meissner, J. H. L. *The Celtic Church in England after the Synod of Whitby.* London: M. Hopkinson, 1929.

Mercer, E. "The Ruthwell and Bewcastle Crosses." *Antiquity* 38 (1964): 268–76.

Meyer, K. *Learning in Ireland in the Fifth Century and the Transmission of Letters.* School of Irish Learning. Dublin: Hodges, Figgis and Company, 1913.

Meyvaert, P. "An Apocalypse Panel on the Ruthwell Cross." In *Medieval and Renaissance Studies; Proceedings of the Southeastern Institute of Medieval and Renaissance Studies; Summer, 1978,* edited by F. Tirro, vol. 9, 3–32. Durham: Duke University Press, 1982.

Millar, E. G. *The Lindisfarne Gospels.* London: British Museum, 1923.

Minard, P. "L'évangélaire oncial de l'abbaye Ste.-Croix de Poitiers." *Revue Mabillion* 33 (1943): 1–17.

Moore, W. J. *The Saxon Pilgrims to Rome and the Schola Saxonum.* Fribourg: Society of St. Paul, 1937.

Morin, G. "La liturgie de Naples au temps de St.-Grégoire." *Revue Bénédictine* 8 (1891): 481–93.

Muller, S. O. *Dyreornamentiken i. Norden.* Copenhagen: Thieles, 1880.

Mynors, D., and R. Powell. "The *Stonyhurst Gospel.*" In *The Relics of St. Cuthbert,* edited by C. F. Battiscombe, 356–74. Oxford: Oxford University Press, 1956.

Mynors, R. A. B. *Durham Cathedral Manuscripts to the End of the Twelfth Century.* Oxford: Oxford University Press, 1939.

Napier, A. S. "Contributions to Old English Literature II: The Franks Casket." In *An English Miscellany: Presented to Dr. Furnivall in Honour of His Seventy-fifth Birthday,* edited by W. P. Ker, A. S. Napier, and W. W. Skeat, 362–81. Oxford: Clarendon Press, 1901.

Nees, L. "A Fifth-Century Bookcover and the Origin of the Four Evangelist Symbols Page in the *Book of Durrow.*" *Gesta* 17 (1978): 3–8.

Nerman, B. "The Standard of Sutton Hoo as a Torchholder." *Antiquaries' Journal* 50 (1970): 340–41.

Nicholson, J. H. "The Sculptured Stones at Heysham." *Transactions of the Lancashire and Cheshire Antiquaries' Society* 9 (1891): 30–38.

Nordenfalk, C. "Before the *Book of Durrow.*" *Acta Archaeologica* 18 (1947): 141–74.

———. *Celtic and Anglo-Saxon Painting.* New York: G. Braziller, 1977.

———. "The *Diatessaron* Miniatures Once More." *Art Bulletin* 55 (1973): 532–46.

———. "Eastern Style Elements in the *Lindisfarne Gospels.*" *Acta Archaeologica* 13 (1942): 157–68.

———. "An Illustrated *Diatessaron.*" *Art Bulletin* 50 (1968): 119–40.

———. "On the Age of the Earliest Echternach Manuscripts." *Acta Archaeologica* 3 (1932): 57–62.

———. *Die Spätantike Kanontafeln.* Stockholm: O. Isacson, 1938.

———. *Die Spätantike Zierbuchstaben.* Stockholm: Egnellska, 1970.

Nordhagen, P. J. "A Carved Marble Pilaster in the Vatican Grottoes: Some Remarks on the Sculptural Techniques of the Early Middle Ages." *Acta Institutum Romanum Norvegiae* 4 (1969): 113–20.

———. *The Codex Amiatinus and the Byzantine Element in the Northumbrian Renaissance.* Jarrow Lecture. Jarrow: The Rectory, 1977.

———. "An Italo-Byzantine Painter in the Scriptorium of Ceolfrith." In *Studia Romana in honorem Petri Krarup Septuagenarii,* 138–45. Odense: University of Odense Press, 1976.

Ó Briain, F. "Saga Themes in Irish Hagiography." In *Essays and Studies Presented to Professor Tadhg Ua Donnchadha (Torna),* edited by S. Pender, 33–42. Cork: Cork University Press, 1947.

Ó Carragáin, E. "Liturgical Innovations Associated with Pope Sergius and the Iconography of the Ruthwell and Bewcastle Crosses." In *Bede and Anglo-Saxon England,* edited by R. T. Farrell, 131–45. British Archaeological Reports, vol. 46. Oxford: British Archaeological Reports, 1978.

Ogilvy, J. D. A. *Books Known to the English, 597–1066.* Cambridge, Mass.: Medieval Academy of America, 1967.

———. *The Place of Wearmouth and Jarrow in Western Cultural History.* Jarrow Lecture. Jarrow: The Rectory, 1969.

O'Ríordáin, Sean P. "The Excavation of a Large Earthen Ringfort at Garranes, Co. Cork." *Proceedings of the Royal Irish Academy* 47 (1942): 77–150.

———. "Roman Material in Ireland." *Proceedings of the Royal Irish Academy* 51 (1947): 35–82.

Page, R. I. "The Bewcastle Cross." *Nottingham Medieval Studies* 4 (1960): 36–57.

———. *Introduction to English Runes.* London: Methuen, 1973.

———. *Life in Anglo-Saxon England.* London: Batsford, 1970.

Panofsky, E. *Renaissance and Renascences in Western Art.* New York: Harper and Row, 1960.

Peacock, David and Charles Thomas. "Class E Imported Pottery: A Suggested Origin." *Cornish Archaeology* 6 (1967): 35–46.

Peers, C. R. "English Ornament in the Seventh and Eighth Century: Annual Lecture on Aspects of Art, Henrietta Hertz Trust." *Proceedings of the British Academy* 12 (1926): 45–54.

———. "The Inscribed and Sculpted Stones of Lindisfarne." *Archaeologia* 74 (1923–24): 55–70.

———. "Monkwearmouth and Jarrow." In *Bede: His Life, Times and Writings,* edited by A. Hamilton Thompson, 60–101. Oxford: Clarendon Press, 1935.

———. "Reculver, Its Saxon Cross and Church." *Archaeologia* 77 (1927): 241–56.

Peers, C. R., and C. A. Ralegh Radford. "The Saxon Monastery at Whitby." *Archaeologia* 89 (1943): 27–88.

Pfeilstucker, S. *Spätantikes und germanisches Kunstgut in der frühangelsächsischer Kunst.* Berlin: Deutscher Kunstverlag, 1936.

Pitman, J. H., ed. and trans. *The Riddles of Aldhelm.* Yale Studies in English, vol. 67. New Haven: Yale University Press, 1925.

Pogatscher, A. "Angelsächsen und Romanen." *Englische Studien* 19 (1894): 329–52.

Porter, A. K. *The Crosses and Culture of Ireland.* New Haven: Yale University Press, 1931.

———. "An Egyptian Legend in Ireland." *Marburger Jahrbuch für Kunstwissenschaft* 5 (1929): 25–38.

Powell, R. "The *Book of Kells,* the *Book of Durrow.*" *Scriptorium* 10 (1956): 3–26.

Proudfoot, V. B. "The Economy of the Irish *Rath.*" *Medieval Archaeology* 5 (1961): 94–122.

Radford, C. A. Ralegh. "The Celtic Monastery in Britain." *Archaeologia Cambrensis* 3 (1962): 1–24.

———. "The Church in Celtic Britain." In *Atti: VI Congresso Internationale di Archaeologia Cristiana,* Ravenna, 1962. Rome: Pontificio Istituto di Archaeologia Cristiana, 1965.

———. "Hoddam." *Antiquity* 27 (1953): 153–60.

———. "Hoddam." *Transactions of the Dumfriesshire and Galloway Natural Historical and Antiquarian Society,* 3d ser., 31 (1954): 174–97.

———. "Imported Pottery in Tintagel, Cornwall: An Aspect of British Trade with the

Mediterranean in the Early Christian Period." In *Dark Age Britain: Studies Presented to E. T. Leeds*, edited by D. B. Harden, 59–70. London: Methuen, 1956.

———. "The Portable Altar of St. Cuthbert." In *The Relics of St. Cuthbert*, edited by C. F. Battiscombe, 326–35. Oxford: Oxford University Press, 1956.

———. "Roma e l'Arte dei Celti e degli Anglo-Sassoni dal V all'VIII secolo D.C." In vol. 3 of *Roma e le Province*, 3–15. Istituto di Studi Romani, vol. 17. Rome, 1938.

Raftery, J. "Ex Oriente." *Journal of the Royal Society of Antiquaries of Ireland* 95 (1965): 193–204.

Rahtz, P. "Buildings and Rural Settlement." In *The Archaeology of Anglo-Saxon England*, edited by D. M. Wilson, 49–98. London: Methuen, 1976.

———. "Monasteries as Settlements." *Scottish Archaeological Forum* 5 (1973): 125–35.

Raine, J., ed. *The Priory of Hexham: Its Chronicles, Endowments and Annals.* 2 vols. Surtees Society, vol. 44. Durham: Andrews and Company, 1864.

Reese, R. "Recent Work at Iona." *Scottish Archaeological Forum* 5 (1973): 36–46.

Renfrew, C. "Trade as Action at a Distance: Questions of Integration and Communication." In *Ancient Civilizations and Trade*, edited by J. A. Sabloff and C. C. Lamberg-Karlovsky, 3–59. Albuquerque: University of New Mexico Press, 1975.

Rice, D. T. *Art of the Byzantine Era.* New York: Praeger, 1963.

———. "Britain and the Byzantine World in the Middle Ages." In *Byzantine Art and European Art*, Lectures, Ninth Council of Europe Exhibition, 21–42. Athens: Zappeion, 1966.

Richards, M. *The Laws of Hywel Dda: The Book of Blegywrya.* Liverpool: Liverpool University Press, 1954.

———. "The 'Lichfield' Gospels (Book of 'St. Chad')." *Journal of the National Library of Wales* 18 (1973): 135–46.

Robb, D. *The Illuminated Manuscript.* Philadelphia: Art Alliance Press, 1973.

Ross, M. C. "A Suggested Interpretation of the Scene Depicted on the Right Side of the Franks Casket." *Medieval Archaeology* 14 (1970): 148–52.

Royal Commission on the Ancient and Historical Monuments and Constructions of Scotland. *Seventh Report, with Inventory of the Monuments and Constructions in the County of Dumfries.* Edinburgh: HMSO, 1920.

Rutherford, W. *The Druids and Their Heritage.* London: Gordon and Cremonesi, 1978.

Ruyschaert, José. "Essai d'interpretation synthétique de l'Arc de Constantin." *Atti della Pontificia Accademia Roma* 79 (1962–63): 79–100.

Ryan, A. M. *A Map of Old English Monasteries and Related Foundations, A.D. 400–1066.* Cornell Studies in English, vol. 28. Ithaca: Cornell University Press, 1939.

Ryan, J. "The Early Irish Church and the See of St. Peter." In *Le chiese nei regni dell'Europa occidentale e i loro rapporti con Roma sino all'800*, vol. 2. Settimane di Studio del Centro Italiana di Studi sull'Alto Medioevo, Spoleto, 7 (1960): 549–74.

Salin, B. *Die altgermanische Thierornamentik.* 2d ed. Translated by J. Mestorf. Stockholm: K. L. Beckmans, 1935.

Saunders, O. E. *History of English Art in the Middle Ages.* Oxford: Clarendon Press, 1932.

Savage, E. S. and C. C. Hodges. *A Record of All the Works connected with Hexham Abbey since January 1899 and Now in Progress.* Hexham: J. Cotterall, 1907.

Savage, H. E. *The St. Chad's Gospels: An Address Given on the Festival of St. Chad.* Lichfield: Bull and Wiseman, 1931.

————. "The Story of the *St. Chad Gospels.*" *Transactions of the Birmingham Archaeological Society* 41 (1915): 5–21.

Saxl, F. "The Ruthwell Cross." *Journal of the Warburg and Courtauld Institutes* 6 (1943): 1–19.

Saxl, F., and R. Wittkower. *British Art and the Mediterranean.* Oxford: Oxford University Press, 1948.

Saxo Grammaticus. *The First Nine Books of the Danish History.* Edited and translated by O. Elton and F. Y. Powell. London: D. Nutt, 1894.

Schapiro, M. "The Bowman and the Bird on the Ruthwell Cross and Other Works: The Interpretation of Secular Themes in Early Medieval Art." *Art Bulletin* 45 (1963): 351–55.

————. "The Religious Meaning of the Ruthwell Cross." *Art Bulletin* 26 (1944): 232–45.

Schapiro, M., et al. "The Miniatures in the Florence *Diatessaron* (Laur. MS Orient 81)." *Art Bulletin* 51 (1969): 494–531.

Schneider, K. "Zu den Inschriften und Bildern des Franks Casket und einer ae. Version des Mythos Balders Tod." In *Festschrift für Walther Fischer,* edited by E. Schuster and B. Fabian, 4–20. Heidelberg: C. Winter, 1959.

Schug-Wille, C. *Art of the Byzantine World.* New York: Harry N. Abrams, 1969.

Sexton, E. *Irish Figure Sculptures of the Early Christian Period.* Portland, Me.: Southworth-Anthoensen Press, 1946.

Sherlock, D. A. "Saul, Paul and the Silver Spoons from Sutton Hoo." *Speculum* 47 (1972): 91–95.

Shetelig, H., and H. Falk. *Scandinavian Archaeology.* Translated by E. V. Gordon. 1937. Reprint. New York: AMS Press, 1978.

Simeon of Durham. *Historia Dunelmensis Ecclesiae.* In *Symeonis Monachi Opera Omnia,* edited by T. Arnold, 50–71. Chronicles and Memorials of Great Britain and Ireland during the Middle Ages, vol. 75, pt. 1. London: Longmans, 1882–85.

Simpson, W. D. *The Celtic Church in Scotland.* Aberdeen: University of Aberdeen Press, 1975.

————."The Early Romanesque Tower at Restenneth Priory, Angus." *Antiquaries' Journal* 43 (1963): 269–83.

————.*St. Ninian and the Origins of Christianity in Scotland.* Edinburgh: Oliver and Boyd, 1940.

Sims-Williams, P. "Continental Influence at Bath in the Seventh Century." *Anglo-Saxon England* 4 (1975): 1–10.

Small, A., ed. *St. Ninian's Isle and Its Treasure.* Oxford: Oxford University Press, 1970.

Smith, C. R. Letter. *Archaeologia* 30 (1844): 133.

Smith, R. A. "Examples of Anglian Art." *Archaeologia* 74 (1925): 233–54.

————. *Guide to the Anglo-Saxon and Foreign Teutonic Antiquities in the British Museum.* London: British Museum, 1923.

Söderburg, Sven. "News and Notes." *Academy* 38 (1890): 90.

Souers, P. W. "The Left Side of the Franks Casket." *Harvard Studies and Notes in Philology and Literature* 18 (1935): 199–209.

————. "The Magi Scene on the Franks Casket." *Harvard Studies and Notes in Philology and Literature* 19 (1936): 249–54.

————. "The Top of the Franks Casket." *Harvard Studies and Notes in Philology and Literature* 17 (1934): 163–79.

————. "The Wayland Scene on the Franks Casket." *Speculum* 18 (1943): 104–11.

Speake, G. *Anglo-Saxon Animal Art and Its Germanic Background.* Oxford: Clarendon Press, 1980.

Spiess, K. "Das Angelsächsischen Runenkästchen: Die Seite mit der *Hos* Inschrift." In *Studien zur Kunst des Ostens: Josef Strzygowski zum sechzigsten Geburtstag von seinen Freunden und Schülern,* 160–68. Vienna: Avalun, 1932.

Stanford, W. B. "Toward a History of Classical Influences in Ireland." *Proceedings of the Royal Irish Academy* 70 (1970): 13–91.

Stenton, F. M. *Anglo-Saxon England.* 3d ed. Oxford: Clarendon Press, 1971.

Stephens, G. *Handbook of the Old-Northern Runic Monuments of Scandinavia and England.* London: Williams and Norgate, 1884.

Stevenson, R. B. K. "The Chronology and Relationships of Some Irish and Scottish Crosses." *Journal of the Royal Society of Antiquaries* 86 (1956): 84–89.

————. "The Penannular Brooches: Discussion." *Antiquity* 33 (1959): 255–56.

————. "Pictish Art." In *The Problem of the Picts,* edited by F. T. Wainwright, 106–12. Edinburgh: T. Nelson, 1955.

————. "Pictish Sculpture." *Scottish Archaeological Review* 4 (1952–53): 6–8.

————. "Sculpture in Scotland in the Sixth to Ninth Centuries A.D." In *Kolloquium über spätantike und frühmittelalterliche Skulptur,* Heidelberg, 1970, 68–74. Mainz: P. von Zabern, 1972.

Stokes, M. *Early Christian Art in Ireland.* 3d ed. Dublin: Stationery Office, 1928.

Stokes, W. *Lives of the Saints from the Book of Lismore.* Oxford: Clarendon Press, 1890.

Stone, L. *Sculpture in Britain: The Middle Ages.* Pelican History of Art. Harmondsworth: Penguin Books, 1972.

Strzygowski, J. *Die Baukunst der Armenier und Europa.* 2 vols. Arbeiten des Kunsthistorischen Instituts der Universität Wien, vols. 9–10. Vienna: A. Scholl and Company, 1918.

————. *Koptische Kunst.* Catalogue Générale des antiquités égyptiennes du Musée du Caire. Vienna: A. Holzhausen, 1904.

————. *Der Norden in der bildenden Kunst Westeuropas.* Vienna: Krystall, 1926.

Stuhlfauth, G. *Die Engel in der christliche Kunst.* Archäologische Schriften zur christliche Kunst der Altertum und Mittelalter, vol. 3. Freiburg: J. C. B. Mohr, 1897.

Sutherland, C. H. V. *Anglo-Saxon Gold Coinage and Currency in Light of the Crondall Hoard.* London: Oxford University Press, 1948.

Swanton, M. J., ed. *Anglo-Saxon Prose.* London: Dent, 1975.

————. "Bishop Acca and the Cross at Hexham." *Archaeologia Aeliana,* 4th ser., 48 (1970): 157–68.

Swenson, I. C. "The Symmetry Potentials of the Ornamental Pages of the *Lindisfarne Gospels.*" *Gesta* 17 (1978): 9–17.

Tate, G. "Saxon Sculptured Stones at Norham." *History of the Berwickshire Naturalists' Club* 4 (1857–62): 218.

Taylor, H. "The Architectural Interest of Æthelwulf's *De Abbatibus.*" *Anglo-Saxon England* 3 (1974): 163–73.

————. "The Chapel, Church and Carved Stones at Heysham." *Archaeological Journal* 127 (1970): 185–87.

———. "Corridor Crypts on the Continent and in England." *North Staffordshire Journal of Field Studies* 9 (1969): 17–32.

———. *English Architecture at the Time of Bede.* Jarrow Lecture. Jarrow: The Rectory, 1962.

———. "The Position of the Altar in Early Kentish Churches." *Antiquaries' Journal* 53 (1973): 52–58.

———. "Reculver Reconsidered." *Archaeological Journal* 125 (1968): 291–96.

———. "The Rediscovery of Important Anglo-Saxon Sculpture in Pre-Conquest Churches." In *The Anglo-Saxons: Studies in Some Aspects of Their History and Culture Presented to Bruce Dickins,* edited by P. A. M. Clemoes, 137–38. London: Bowes and Bowes, 1959.

Taylor, H. M., and J. Taylor. *Anglo-Saxon Architecture.* 3 vols. Cambridge: Cambridge University Press, 1965–78.

Thomas, Charles. *Bede, Archaeology and the Cult of Relics.* Jarrow Lecture. Jarrow: The Rectory, 1975.

———. *Britain and Ireland in Early Christian Times, A.D. 400–800.* London: McGraw-Hill, 1971.

———. *Early Christian Archaeology of North Britain: The Hunter Marshall Lectures Delivered at the University of Glasgow in January and February, 1968.* Oxford: Oxford University Press, 1971.

———. "Imported Pottery in Dark Age Britain." *Medieval Archaeology* 3 (1959): 89–111.

———. "The Interpretation of the Pictish Symbols." *Archaeological Journal* 120 (1963): 31–97.

Thompson, J. D. A. *Inventory of British Coin Hoards, A.D. 600–1500.* Royal Numismatic Society Special Publications, vol. 1. London, 1956.

Töbler, T., and A. Molinier. *Itinera Hierosolymitana et Descriptiones Terrae Sanctae.* 1879. Reprint. Osnabrück: Zeller, 1966.

Toynbee, J. M. C. "Christianity in Roman Britain." *Journal of the British Archaeological Association,* 3d ser., 16 (1953): 1–24.

Treasures of Early Irish Art, 1500 B.C. to 1500 A.D. Edited by P. Cone. New York: Metropolitan Museum of Art, 1977.

Turner, C. F. "Documents: Durham A.II.17." *Journal of Theological Studies* 10 (1909): 537–39.

Ussher, J. *Britannicarum ecclesiarum antiqvitates.* Dublin: Societas Bibliopolarum, 1639.

Vandersall, A. L. "The Date and Provenance of the Franks Casket." *Gesta* 11 (1972): 9–26.

Verey, C. D. *A Collation of the Gospel Texts Contained in Durham Cathedral Manuscripts A.II.10, A.II.16 and A.II.17.* Master's thesis, University of Durham, 1969.

Verzone, P. *The Art of Europe: The Dark Ages from Theodoric to Charlemagne.* Translated by P. Waley. New York: Crown, 1969.

Victoria History of the Counties of England: Buckinghamshire. Edited by William Page. 1905. Reprint. London: Dawson's, 1969.

Vierck, H. "*Cortina Tripodis:* Zu Aufhängung und Gebrauch südromischer Hängebecken aus Britannien und Irland." *Frühmittelalterliche Studien* 4 (1970): 8–52.

———. "Ein Relieffibelpaar aus Nordendorf." *Bayerische Vorgerichtsblätter* 32 (1967): 104–43.

Vita Eparchii reclusi Ecolismensis. In *Passione vitaque sanctorum aevi Merovingici,* edited by B. Krusch and W. Levison, 559. Monumenta Germaniae Historica: Scriptorum rerum Merovingicarum, vol. 3. Hanover: Hahn, 1896.

Vita Filiberti abbatis Gementicensis et Heriensis. In *Passione vitaque sanctorum aevi Merovingici,* edited by B. Krusch and W. Levison, 585. Monumenta Germaniae Historica: Scriptorum rerum Merovingicarum, vol. 3. Hanover: Hahn, 1896.

Wadstein, E. *The Clermont Runic Casket.* Uppsala: Almqvist and Wiksells, 1900.

———. "Zum Clermonter Runenkästchen." *Zeitschrift für deutsche Philologie* 34 (1902): 127.

Wailes, Bernard. *Some Imported Pottery in Western Britain, A.D. 400–800: Its Connections with Frankish and Visigothic Gaul.* 2 vols. Ph.D. diss. St. Catherine's College, Cambridge, 1963.

Wainwright, F. T. *The Problem of the Picts.* Edinburgh/London: Nelson, 1955.

Walker, F. C. "Fresh Light on the Franks Casket." *Washington University Studies,* 4th ser., 2 (1915): 165–76.

Wallace-Hadrill, J. M. "Rome and the Early English Church: Some Questions of Transmission." In *Le chiese nei regni dell'Europa occidentale e i loro rapporti con Roma sino all'800,* vol. 2. Settimane di Studio del Centro Italiano di Studi sull'Alto Medioevo, Spoleto, 7 (1960): 519–48.

Warren, F. E. *The Antiphonary of Bangor.* 2 vols. London: Harrison and Sons, 1893.

Weitzmann, K. "The Ivories of the So-Called Grado Chair." *Dumbarton Oaks Papers* 26 (1972): 43–91.

———. *Late Antique and Early Christian Book Illumination.* New York: G. Braziller, 1977.

———. "Various Aspects of Byzantine Influence on the Latin Countries from the Sixth to the Twelfth Century." *Dumbarton Oaks Papers* 20 (1966): 1–24.

Weitzmann-Fiedler, J. "Ein Evangelientyp mit Aposteln als Begleitsfiguren." In *Adolf Goldschmidt zu seinen siebenzigsten Geburtstag am 15. januar 1933, dargebracht von allen seinen Schülern . . . , 30–34. Berlin: Wurfel Verlag, 1935.*

Werckmeister, O. K. "Three Problems of Tradition in Pre-Carolingian Figure Style, From Visigothic to Insular Illumination." *Proceedings of the Royal Irish Academy* 63 (1963): 167–90.

Werner, M. "The *Durrow* Four Evangelist Symbols Page Once Again." *Gesta* 20 (1981): 23–33.

———. "The Four Evangelist Symbols Page in the *Book of Durrow.*" *Gesta* 8 (1969): 3–17.

Westwood, J. O. *Fac-Similes of the Miniatures and Ornaments of Anglo-Saxon and Irish Manuscripts.* London: B. Quaritch, 1868.

Weyer, C. D. *Early Medieval Art, 300–1150.* Sources and Documents in the History of Art, edited by H. W. Janson. Englewood Cliffs, N.J.: Prentice-Hall, 1971.

Whitelock, D. *The Audience of "Beowulf."* Oxford: Clarendon Press, 1951.

———. *The Beginnings of English Society.* Pelican History of England, vol. 2. Harmondsworth: Penguin Books, 1972.

Wilcock, P., trans. *The Lives of the Abbots of Wearmouth by the Venerable Bede.* Newcastle upon Tyne: Frank Graham, 1973.

Willet, F. "The Ruthwell and Bewcastle Crosses." *University of Manchester Museum Publications,* n.s., 7(1957): 1–42.

Williams ab Ithel, J., ed. *Annales Cambriae*. Rolls Series, Chronicles and Memorials of Great Britain and Ireland during the Middle Ages, vol. 20. London: Longman, Green, Longman and Roberts, 1860.

Wilson, D. M. "Introduction." In *The Archaeology of Anglo-Saxon England*, edited by D. M. Wilson, 1–22. London: Methuen, 1976.

———. *Reflections on the St. Ninian's Isle Treasure*. Jarrow Lecture. Jarrow: The Rectory, 1970.

Wolf, A. "Franks Casket in literaturhistorisches Sicht." *Frühmittelalterliche Studien* 3 (1969): 227–43.

Wormald. F. *The Miniatures of the Gospel of St. Augustine*. Cambridge: Cambridge University Press, 1954.

Wormald. Patrick. "Bede, the *Bretwaldas* and the Origins of the *Gens Anglorum*." In *Ideal and Reality in Frankish and Anglo-Saxon Society: Studies Presented to J. M. Wallace-Hadrill*, 99–129. Oxford: Basil Blackwell, 1983.

Wright, C. E. *The Cultivation of Saga in Anglo-Saxon England*. Edinburgh: Oliver and Boyd, 1939.

Wright, D. H. "The Italian Stimulus on English Art around 700." In *Stil und Überlieferung in der Kunst des Abendlandes*, Akten des 21. Internationalen Kongres für Kunstgeschichte, Bonn, 1964, 1:84–92. Berlin: Mann, 1967.

———. "Some Notes on English Uncial." *Traditio* 19 (1961): 441–56.

———. *The Vespasian Psalter*. Early English Manuscripts in Facsimile, vol. 14. Copenhagen: Rosenkilde and Bagger, 1967.

Young, B. *Merovingian Funeral Rites and the Evolution of Christianity: A Study in the Historical Interpretation of Archaeological Material*. Ph.D. diss., University of Pennsylvania, 1961.

Zimmerman, E. H. *Die Vorkarolingische Miniaturen*. Berlin: Deutsche Verein für Kunstwissenschaft, 1916.

Index

The Northumbrian Renaissance

A Study in the Transmission of Style

CAROL L. NEUMAN DE
VEGVAR

The Northumbrian Renaissance is the
term often given to the extraordinarily
rich period of art production between
about A.D. 650 and 750 in the early Anglian kingdom of Northumbria. In this
politically stable and prosperous environment the arts flourished under a variety of indigenous and imported influences. Among these, the greatest impact
was made by the influx of Mediterranean
models for art that followed the conversion of the Northumbrians to Christianity. The response to these models,
however, varied widely among the art-
producing centers of Northumbria. *The
Northumbrian Renaissance: A Study in
the Transmission of Style* is an investigation of the factors that stimulated these
variations and produced the resulting diversity in early Northumbrian art. Trade
patterns between the British Isles and
the Mediterranean in the preconversion
period and local ecclesiastical politics
after the conversion lay the groundwork
for the distinct differences of attitude toward Mediterranean art between the mission centers of the Celtic Church and the
foundations of the Roman Church.

Given the long history of trade between Celtic Britons and Irish and the
Mediterranean in everything from tin and
grain to wine and wolfhounds, the Celtic
Church was heir to a tradition of assimilation, wherein all imported motifs,
whether patterns stamped in the clay of a
wine jar or images carved in relief on
Roman legionary markers, were freely
borrowed and reworked by native crafts-